REINVENTING

Eden

REINVENTING

The Fate of Nature in Western Culture

CAROLYN MERCHANT

ROUTLEDGE   NEW YORK & LONDON

Published in 2003 by
Routledge
29 West 35th Street
New York, NY 10001
www.routledge-ny.com

Published in Great Britain by
Routledge
11 New Fetter Lane
London EC4P 4EE
www.routledge.co.uk

10 9 8 7 6 5 4 3 2 1

Library of Congress Cataloging-in-Publication Data

Merchant, Carolyn.
    Reinventing Eden : the fate of nature in Western culture / by Carolyn Merchant.
        p. cm.
    Includes bibliographical references (p.) and index.
    ISBN 0–415–93164–9 (alk. paper)
        1. Human ecology—Philosophy. 2. Human ecology—History. 3. Nature—Effect of human beings on. I. Title.

    GF21 .M473 2003
    304.2'8—dc21   2002036787

Portions of this book have appeared in somewhat different form in
Carolyn Merchant, *Radical Ecology: The Search for a Liveable World* (New York and London: Routledge, 1992), pp. 93–100.
Carolyn Merchant, *Earthcare: Women and the Environment* (New York: Routledge, 1996), pp. 216–223.
Carolyn Merchant, "Reinventing Eden: Western Culture as a Recovery Narrative," in William Cronon, ed., *Uncommon Ground: Toward Reinventing Nature* (New York: W. W. Norton, 1995), pp. 132–59.
Carolyn Merchant, "Partnership With Nature," *Landscape*, Special Issue (1998): 69–71.
Carolyn Merchant, "Partnership Ethics: Business and the Environment," in Patricia Werhane, ed. *Enviornmental Challenges to Business* (Bowling Green, OH: Society for Businesss Ethics, 2000), pp. 7–18.

FOR CHARLIE

CONTENTS

Illustrations ix

Acknowledgments xi

1. A Garden Planet 1

PART I. *Genesis of the Recovery Narrative*

2. The Fall from Eden 11

3. Recovering the Garden 39

4. From Wilderness to Civilization 65

PART II. *New World Edens*

5. Adam As Hero 93

6. Eve As Nature 117

7. Colonizing Eden 145

8. Eden Commodified 167

PART III. *New Stories*

9. Earth in Recovery 187

10. Order out of Chaos 205

11. Partnership 223

Epilogue 245

Notes 247

Bibliography 277

Index 293

ILLUSTRATIONS

Figure 2.1   Ludolphus de Saxonia, *Vita Christi* (1487)   15

Figure 2.2   J. J. du Pré, *Heures a l'usage de Rome* (1488)   17

Figure 2.3   G. B. Andreini, "Adamo," in *L'Adamo, Sacra*   19
             Rapresentatione (1617)

Figure 2.4   G. B. Andreini, "Eua, Adamo," *ibid.*, (1617)   19

Figure 2.5   Neolithic Figure, Tel Chagar Bazar, Mesopotamia   32

Figure 2.6   Isis, in Athanasius Kircher, *Oedipus Aegypticus* (1652)   34

Figure 3.1   "Dante's Conception of the Universe"   49

Figure 3.2   Ludolphus of Saxony (d. 1378), *Speculum*   51
             humanae salvationis, early 15th century

Figure 3.3   Lucas Cranach, *Adam and Eve* (1526)   52

Figure 3.4   *St. Genevieve Guarding her Flock*, French   55
             School, late 16th century

Figure 3.5   Sir Walter Raleigh, *The History of the World* (1614)   58

Figure 3.6   Salomon van Til, *Dissertationes philogico-theologicae*   60
             (1719)

Figure 3.7   "Chatsworth Garden," *Britannia illustrata* (1709)   62

Figure 4.1   Thomas Burnet, *The Sacred Theory of the Earth* (1684)   73

Figure 4.2   Francis Bacon, frontespiece, *Novum Organum* (Instauratio Magna) (1620)   74

Figure 5.1   Theodor de Bry, "Adam and Eve" (1590)   95

Figure 5.2   Thomas Cole, *Expulsion from the Garden of Eden* (1827–28)   107

Figure 5.3   Thomas Cole, *The Oxbow*, or *A View from Mount Holyoke* (1836)   108

Figure 6.1   Jan van der Straet, *America*, in *Nova Reperta* (Antwerp, 1579)   120

Figure 6.2   Abraham Ortelius, *Theatrum Orbus Terrarum* (Antwerp, 1579)   121

Figure 6.3   John Gast, *American Progress* (1872)   128

Figure 6.4   Emanuel Leutze, *Westward the Course of Empire Takes its Way* (1861)   129

Figure 6.5   Domenico Tojetti, *The Progress of America* (1875)   130

Figure 6.6   George Willoughby Maynard, *Civilization* (1893)   131

Figure 7.1   Pine Ridge Reservation, South Dakota (undated)   151

Figure 8.1   Bill Sanderson, "In the Beginning Was the Genome I" (1990)   176

Figure 8.2   Bill Sanderson, "In the Beginning Was the Genome II" (1990)   176

Figure 9.1   Alexander Hogue, *Erosion No. 2. Mother Earth Laid Bare* (1936)   188

Figure 11.1   Teresa Fasolino, *Adam and Eve* (1990)   243

Table

Table 2.1   Reinventing Eden: Narratives of Western Culture   21

Poem

"The Lesson," David Iltis   221

ACKNOWLEDGMENTS

Working on *Reinventing Eden* has afforded me the opportunity to synthesize formative ideas in my thinking over the past three decades. Many of the issues I explored as a historian of science that led to my 1980 book *The Death of Nature* have meshed with my more recent work as an environmental historian of North America and my explorations of the connections between gender and the environment.

It is a pleasure to acknowledge the many persons and institutions that have supported this work. The ideas behind this book were developed in lectures I gave on the topic "Women and Nature: A Declensionist Narrative?" at John Hopkins University in 1990, in Australia as an ecofeminist scholar in 1991 and at the Fifth Annual Conference on Narrative in Albany New York in 1993. In 1994, I was a member of a seminar, Reinventing Nature, led by William Cronon at the University of California-Irvine. Cronon had introduced the idea of environmental history as a narrative of decline from a prior pristine state of nature at a session of the American Society for Environmental History in 1987, and the idea became very influential in the field of environmental history and at the Irvine seminar. Some of the ideas that appear here were first developed in my article "Reinventing Eden" for the seminar's published volume, *Uncommon Ground: Rethinking the Human Place in Nature* (1995) that Cronon edited. I am grateful to Bill Cronon and all the members of that seminar for their inspiration, intellectual input, and stimulating conversations and to W. W. Norton for allowing me to include materials from the essay throughout the book.

I received additional support for developing my ideas as a 1995 John Simon Guggenheim Fellow, which allowed me to spend the 1996 year writing the book, and in 2001 as a John D. and Catherine T. MacArthur Fellow in the Ecological Humanities at the National Humanities Center in North Carolina, which allowed me to continue my research and writing. The fellows and staff at the Center were most helpful in contributing ideas and challenging my thinking in an extraordinarily congenial setting. In 2002, a fellowship from the Center for Theology and the Natural Sciences at the Graduate Theological Union in Berkeley allowed me to finalize the manuscript.

My colleagues and graduate students at the University of California-Berkeley have over the years helped me to fine-tune parts of my argument and challenged me to probe more deeply into particular ideas. Grants from the Committee on Research at the University of California-Berkeley have contributed to my research, acquisition of illustration permissions, and the preparation of the index. I am indebted to Mary Graham for editing the manuscript and contributing her keen insights to its argument and prose. My students Shana Cohen, Earth Trattner, and Ken Worthy read portions of the manuscript, encouraged my thinking, and helped me refine my ideas. Over the years students in my graduate courses have helped me to think through my arguments. I am especially grateful to Victor Rotenberg, Dean Bavington, Ron Feldman, Tim Hessel-Robinson, Carol Manahan, Ray Maria McNamara, Sarah Trainor, and Greg Zuschlag.

My editor at Routledge, Ilene Kalish, encouraged me to make my own perspective more visible throughout and to clarify the implications of my ideas. I am grateful to Celeste Newbrough, who prepared the index for this as well as several previous books and who has been an important inspiration in my thinking about women and nature. My son David Iltis has afforded me the pleasure of including his poem, "The Lesson," in the chapter on "Partnership." My partner and husband Charles Sellers has been my intellectual inspiration and rock of support through this process and to him I give my deepest thanks. This book is for him.

Berkeley, California
June 2002

ONE

A Garden Planet

A lush garden. Pathways wander invitingly among rolling lawns and fragrant flowers. Lilies, roses, and herbs send forth a sweet ambrosia. The air smells continuously fresh. Peacocks strut among the trees in the near distance and doves make their distinctive three-note coo. A cottontail, appearing unconcerned, nibbles at grass nearby, while lambs suckle at their mother's teat. Nearly hidden among the taller and more distant cedars, a doe and fawn munch at the undergrowth. A small grove of fig trees can be glimpsed down a side path. A couple strolls arm in arm toward a fig grove near the middle of the garden, where a waterfall gushes over rocks fed by a clear bubbling stream. At the garden's very center are two trees known simply as the tree of life and the tree of the knowledge of good and evil.

Where is this Eden? It is not in the Mesopotamian lands of the pre-Christian era. It is the new downtown square on the promenade in

Anytown, California. The square is replete with fountains, grassy knolls, meandering streams, and benches for passersby. Along each side of the river flowing through the square are the shops of the revived cityscape. Gracefully arched bridges connect the two sides of the street, and the shops face the greenbelt along the river. The stores are those found in hundreds of towns across the nation: Borders Books, Starbucks Coffee, Cost Plus World Market, Noah's Bagels, Banana Republic, The Gap, Crate and Barrel, and Jamba Juice. This is the new American Eden.[1]

The Garden of Eden story has shaped Western culture since earliest times and the American world since the 1600s. We have tried to reclaim the lost Eden by reinventing the entire earth as a garden. The shopping mall, the "new main street," the gated community, and the Internet are the latest visions of a reinvented Eden. From Christopher Columbus's voyages, to the search for the fountain of youth, to John Steinbeck's *East of Eden*, visions of finding a lost paradise have motivated global exploration, settlement, and hope for a better life.

The Recovery of Eden story is the mainstream narrative of Western culture. It is perhaps the most important mythology humans have developed to make sense of their relationship to the earth. Internalized by Europeans and Americans alike since the seventeenth century, this story has propelled countless efforts by humans to recover Eden by turning wilderness into garden, "female" nature into civilized society, and indigenous folkways into modern culture. Science, technology, and capitalism have provided the tools, male agency the power and impetus. Today's incarnations of Eden are the suburb, the mall, the clone, and the World Wide Web.

As with any mainstream story, however, a counternarrative challenges the plot. Recent postmodern and postcolonial stories reject the Enlightenment accounts of progress. Many environmentalists see the loss of wilderness as a decline from a pristine earth to a paved, scorched, endangered world. Many feminists see a nature once revered as mother now scarred, desecrated, and abused, and women as the victims of patriarchal culture. Similarly, many African Americans and Native Americans see their history as one of colonization by Europeans who "explored," "discovered," and took over their lands and viewed their bodies as animal-like and close to nature. But even as they call for new pathways to a just society, these counterstories of a slide downward (or declension) from Eden buy into the overarching, metanarrative of recovery. Both storylines, whether upward or downward, compel us to find a new story for the twenty-first century.

Narratives form our reality. We become their vessels. Stories find, capture, and hold us. Our lives are shaped by the stories we hear as children; some fade as we grow older, others are reinforced by our families, churches, and schools. From stories we absorb our goals in life, our morals, and our patterns of behavior. For many Americans, humanity's loss of the perfect Garden of Eden is among the most powerful of all stories. Consciously at times, unconsciously at others, we search for ways to reclaim our loss. We become actors in a storyline that has compelled allegiance for millennia.

But "mastering" nature to reclaim Eden has nearly destroyed the very nature people have tried to reclaim. The destruction of nature in America became clearly apparent in the late nineteenth century. The railroad, the steam engine, the factory, and the mine began to demolish forests, blemish landscapes, and muddy the air and water. Romantics reacted sharply. They began to tell a new story of what went wrong—a story of decline from pristine nature. Explorers, writers, poets, and painters proclaimed their love for untouched wilderness. The early conservation movement attempted to redeem both nature and humanity by saving places of pristine beauty.

Yet the new parks, the modern suburbs, and the garden cities reclaimed nature at a cost. These Edenic spaces ostracized those "others" of different classes and colors who did not fit into the story. The green veneer became a cover for the actual corruption of the earth and neglect of its poor; that green false consciousness threatened the hoped-for redemption of all people. The middle class appropriated wild nature at the expense of native peoples by carving national parks out of their homelands. The new suburbs existed at the cost of poor minorities who lived with polluted wells, blackened slums, and toxic dumps. Today, many people of color look back to an apparent Edenic past before slavery and colonization changed their lives forever.

The narrative of reinventing Eden, told by progressives as well as environmentalists, raises fundamental questions about the viability of the Recovery Narrative itself. Do not the earth and its people need a new story? What would a green justice for the earth and humanity really look like? Why do people tell stories, and whose ends do they serve? Both the modern progressive and declensionist stories, however compelling, are flawed.

They are products of the linear approach of modern scientific thinking and also reflect the oppositional polarities of *self* and *other*. New kinds of stories, new ways of thinking, and new ethics are required for the twenty-first century.

A narrative approach raises the question of the fit between stories and reality. There is a reality to the progressive story. Great strides have been made in many people's struggle for survival and ease of life. There is also a reality to the Decline from Eden narrative. The environmental crisis and its connections to overdevelopment, population, consumption, pollution, and scarcity are critical issues confronting all of humanity. Through these contrasting stories, we can see both progress and decline in different places at different times. Progressives want to continue the upward climb to recover the Garden of Eden by reinventing Eden on Earth, while environmentalists want to recover the original garden by restoring nature and creating sustainability.

The two stories seem locked in conflict. Played out to its logical conclusion, each narrative negates human life: the mainstream story leads to a totally artificial earth; the environmental story leads to a depopulated earth. Pushed to one extreme, the recovered Eden would be a completely reinvented, totally managed, artificially constructed planet in which shopping on the web would replace shopping at the mall, the gated community the urban jungle, and greenhouse farms the vicissitudes of nature's droughts and storms. Pushed to the opposite extreme, the recovery of wilderness implies a humanly depauperate earth. The tensions between the two plots create the need for a new story that entails a sustainable partnership with nature.

We interpret our hopes and fears through such powerful cultural stories. We act out our roles in the stories into which we were born. The American dream holds out a promise, dangling its rewards for those who work hard and are lucky enough to find its treasures. For those who fail, dire consequences may result. These larger stories propel those who act within them to reinvent the planet as a new world garden. Rich and poor alike buy into the mainstream recovery story and act it out over their lifetimes.

The environmental crisis of the 1960s showed that all was not well on the "garden planet." Rachel Carson's *Silent Spring* alerted the nation to the disruptive effects of pesticides on the food chain,[2] while the testing of nuclear weapons raised the specter of the widespread effects of radiation on biotic, especially human, life. In 1967, historian Lynn White Jr.'s classic article "The Historical Roots of our Ecologic Crisis" laid the blame for environmental disruption on an idea: Christian arrogance toward nature. "God . . . created Adam and, as an afterthought, Eve to keep man from being lonely," White wrote, "Man named all the animals, thus establishing his dominance over them. . . . Especially in its Western form, Christianity is the most anthropocentric religion the world has seen." White's assessment was, "We shall continue to have a worsening ecologic crisis until we reject the Christian axiom that nature has no reason for existence save to serve man," and the article brought forth cries of criticism over its assignment of the ecological crisis to a single cause. Critics such as Lewis Moncrief responded that a more complex scenario was needed that included capitalism, industrialization, the American frontier, manifest destiny, urbanization, population growth, and property ownership. Others argued that the rise of science and technology contributed to the ability of humanity to dominate nature and to the idea that mechanistic science promoted the separation of humans from nature.[3]

The complexity of causes leading to environmental degradation as well as efforts to conserve nature and its resources helped to spawn the field of environmental history. In the 1970s and 1980s, an array of books documented the loss of wilderness, the erosion of soils, increased urban pollution, and the decline of biotic diversity. The early successes of environmental history helped to create an overarching narrative of environmental decline as one of the dominant themes in the field. By the mid-1980s, Donald Worster, William Cronon, and others identified the plots of many environmental histories as "declensionist." Cronon compared two different narratives by two different authors about the 1930s Dust Bowl of the Great Plains, both with virtually the same title (*The Dust Bowl* and *Dust Bowl*), and both published in the same year (1979)—one a story of progress, the other a story of decline. Cronon wrote, "Although both narrate the same broad series of events with an essentially similar cast of characters, they tell two entirely different stories. In both texts, the story is inextricably bound to its conclusion, and the historical analysis derives much of its force from the upward or downward sweep of the plot." The question raised was one of the fit between stories and reality. How accurately did these or any histories fit the events in question? Who were the characters in the stories? Who was omitted? Was all environmental history declensionist history? And even if that were the case, did this insight in any way undercut the value of environmental history's insights into historical change?[4]

By the 1990s, chaos and complexity theory further challenged ecology and environmental history. The new approaches disrupted the idea of a balance of nature that humans could destroy but also restore. Humanity was not the only major disturber of an evolved prehuman ecosystem. Natural disturbances, such as tornadoes, hurricanes, fires, and earthquakes could in an instant wipe out an old-growth forest, demolish a meadow, or redirect the meander of a river. Humanity was less culprit and more victim; nature more violent and less passive. Environmental history moved away from assigning all destructive change to humans and toward chance and contingency in nature.[5]

My own view is that both progressive and declensionist stories reflect real world history, but from different perspectives. Both open windows onto the past, but they are only partial windows depending on the characters included and omitted. The linearity of the upward and downward plots also masks contingencies, meanderings, crises, and punctuations. Including nature and its climatic and biotic manifestations, however, adds complexity and contingencies to the unidirectional plots of progress and decline. Droughts, freezes, "little ice ages," domesticated animals and plants, invasive nonnative species, bacteria, viruses, and humans are all actors who are often unpredictable and unmanageable. They inject uncertainties into the trajectories of progress and decline. As environmental historian Theodore Steinberg argues, "it is quite simply wrong to view the natural world as an unchanging backdrop to the past. Nature can upset even the best-laid, most thoroughly orchestrated plans. . . . We must acknowledge the unpredictability involved in incorporating nature into human designs and, in so doing, bring natural forces to the fore of the historical process."[6]

My view is that the new sciences of chaos and complexity not only reinforce the role of natural forces in environmental history, they also challenge humanity to rethink its ethical relationship to nature. The new sciences suggest that we should consider ourselves as partners with the nonhuman world. We should think of ourselves not as dominant over nature (controlling and managing a passive, external nature) or of nature as dominant over us (casting humans as victims of an unpredictable, violent nature) but rather in dynamic relationship to nature as its partner. In the following pages I present a new perspective on the history of humanity's relationship to nature. I draw on the framework of progressive and declensionist plots, on the roles of men and women in transforming and appreciating the environment, on ideas of contingency and complexity in history, of nature as an actor, and of humanity as capable of achieving a new ethic of partnership with the nonhuman world.

In *Reinventing Eden*, I begin by naming the powerful, overarching story of modern history as a Recovery Narrative. I show how the new millennium presents a major turning point for both the progressive Enlightenment stories and the counternarratives told by women, minorities, and nature itself. I look at the origins of the Recovery Narrative as it arose through biblical, ancient, and medieval history and then set out its political and environmental codification during the Scientific Revolution and European Enlightenment. I focus on the role of Christianity in the formation of the Recovery Narrative and do not attempt to include the influence of Judaism or the Hebrew interpretation of the Genesis stories. Although I am aware that a very large and important literature on biblical interpretation exists, my goal is not to reinterpret biblical scholarship, to write a history of religion, or to examine the development of religious movements, denominations, and sects; nor do I attempt to review or assess the vast literature on Eden in Western culture or Edenic ideas in other cultures and throughout the world.[7]

I then examine the impact of the mainstream Recovery Narrative as it comprises European culture's development and transformation of the New World. American stories—from John Winthrop's Puritan garden to Thomas Hart Benton's manifest destiny—follow and re-create the progressive Recovery storyline. This powerful story of reclaiming and redeeming a fallen earth by human labor becomes the major justification for the westward movement and the effort to remake indigenous Americans in the image of European culture. Eastern wilderness and western deserts are turned into gardens for American settlers.

Throughout the ensuing chapters, I also examine the second story, or what went wrong—the story of Earth in decline. From Plato to Henry David Thoreau, writers have noted the destruction of nature and the problems of vanishing forests and fouled waters. I set out the nineteenth century origins of the romantic counternarrative, the conservation movement, and the late-twentieth-century narratives of environmental crisis. The effects of development on nature, women, and minorities are part of a larger counterstory of the loss of an evolved, earthly abundance and human equality. Despite nuances, hopeful advances, and upward trends, these counternarratives of decline and loss relate the all-too-real experiences of large numbers of people. The continued downward spiral leads to an impoverished earth where diversity is decreasing and environmental health is declining. This also is a story in which we live. It too affects our lives. Over time the Recovery Narrative with its two storylines—one of progress, the other of decline—has shaped the earth's landscape as well as human hopes, desires, and lives.

Within the broad arc of the Recovery Narrative, nature itself has played a major role in affecting outcomes. Despite the efforts of humans to control the natural world, contingencies and crises have occurred. Lurches, advances, and dips disrupt the apparent linearity of the narrative. Natural disturbances inject unpredictability and question the foundations of the narrative within the trajectory of modernity itself. From Noah's flood in Genesis 7 to the volcanic destruction of Pompei during the Roman Empire (C.E. 79), to the Lisbon earthquake of 1755 and Hurricane Gilbert in 1988, nature has shaped human actions and limited possibilities. Nature's actions along with new sciences that incorporate contingencies and complexities into their very assumptions suggest new ways for humanity to relate to the material world.[8]

Since the 1960s, I have witnessed enormous contention within the trajectories of progress and decline. Developers and wilderness advocates are in continual conflict. One group presses for ever greater profits at the earth's expense; the other struggles to save what remains of wilderness on the planet. In the final chapters of the book, I explore possibilities for new narratives about nature. I examine new ways of thinking about the human-nature relationship suggested by postmodern and postcolonial thinking, as well as the implications of recent theories of chaos and complexity. I offer some new ways to think about a multiplicity of stories and introduce ideas about nonlinear plots.

Throughout the book, I suggest possibilities for alternatives to domination based on a partnership between humanity and nature. Finally, I propose an environmental ethic based on a partnership between humans and the nonhuman world: rather than being either dominators or victims, people would cooperate with nature and each other in healthier, more just, and more environmentally sustainable ways. I show how complex interconnections can weave us into cyclical melodies and envelop us within new enigmatic, sacred tales.

PART I

Genesis of the Recovery Narrative

TWO

The Fall from Eden

SHE HAS TAKEN UP WITH A SNAKE NOW. THE OTHER ANIMALS
ARE GLAD, FOR SHE WAS ALWAYS EXPERIMENTING WITH THEM
AND BOTHERING THEM; AND I AM GLAD, BECAUSE THE SNAKE TALKS,
AND THIS ENABLES ME TO GET A REST. SHE SAYS THE SNAKE ADVISES
HER TO TRY THE FRUIT OF THAT TREE, AND SAYS THE RESULT WILL
BE A GREAT AND FINE AND NOBLE EDUCATION. . . . I ADVISED HER
TO KEEP AWAY FROM THE TREE. SHE SAID SHE WOULDN'T. I FORSEE
TROUBLE. WILL EMIGRATE.

—*Mark Twain, "Extracts from Adam's Diary"*

Two grand historical narratives explain how the human species arrived at
the present moment in history. Both are Recovery Narratives, but the two
stories have different plots, one upward, the other downward. The first
story is the traditional biblical narrative of the fall from the Garden of
Eden from which humanity can be redeemed through Christianity. But
the garden itself can also be recovered. By the time of the Scientific
Revolution of the seventeenth century, the Christian narrative had merged
with advances in science, technology, and capitalism to form the mainstream Recovery Narrative. The story begins with the precipitous fall from
Eden followed by a long, slow, upward attempt to recreate the Garden of
Eden on earth. The outcome is a better world for all people. This first

story—the mainstream Recovery Narrative—is a story of upward progress in which humanity gains the power to manage and control the earth.

The second story, also a Recovery Narrative, instead depicts a long, slow decline from a prehistoric past in which the world was ecologically more pristine and society was more equitable for all people and for both genders. The decline continues to the present, but the possibility and, indeed, the absolute necessity of a precipitous, rapid Recovery exists today and could be achieved through a sustainable ecology and an equitable society. This second story is one told by many environmentalists and feminists.

Both stories are enormously compelling, and both reflect the beliefs and hopes of many people for achieving a better world. They differ fundamentally, however, on who and what wins out. In the mainstream story, humanity regains its life of ease at the expense of the earth; in the environmental story, the earth is both the victim of exploitation and the beneficiary of restoration. Women play pivotal roles in the two stories, as cause and/or victims of decline and, along with men, as restorers of a reclaimed planet. But, I argue that a third story, one of a partnership between humanity and the earth and between women and men, that draws on many of the positive aspects of the two stories is also emerging. In this chapter I develop, compare, and critically assess the roots and broad outlines of these stories.

THE CHRISTIAN NARRATIVE

The Christian story of Fall and Recovery begins with the Garden of Eden as told in the Bible. The Christian story is marked by a precipitous fall from a pristine past. The initial lapsarian moment, or loss of innocence, is the decline from garden to desert as the first couple is cast from the light of an ordered paradise into a dark, disorderly wasteland to labor in the earth. Instead of giving fruit readily, the earth now extracts human labor. The blame for the Fall is placed on woman.

The biblical Garden of Eden story has three central chapters: Creation, temptation, and expulsion (later referred to as the Fall). A woman, Eve, is the central actress, and the story's plot is declensionist (a decline from Eden) and tragic. The end result is a poorer state of both nature and human nature. The valence of woman is bad; the end valence of nature is bad. Men become the agents of transformation. After the Fall, men must labor in the earth, to produce food. They become the earthly saviors who strive, through their own agricultural labor, to re-create the lost garden on earth, thereby turning the tragedy of the Fall into the comedy of Recovery. The New Testament adds the Resurrection—the time when the earth and all its creatures, especially humans, are reunited with God to recreate the original oneness in a heavenly paradise. The biblical Fall and Recovery story has become the mainstream narrative shaping and legitimating the course of Western culture.

The Bible offers two versions of the Christian origin story that preceded the Fall. In the Genesis 1 version, God created the land, sea, grass, herbs, and fruit; the stars, sun, and moon; and the birds, whales, cattle, and beasts, after which he made "man in his own image . . . male and female created he them." The couple was instructed "to be fruitful and multiply, replenish the earth, and subdue it," and was given "dominion over the fish of the sea, the fowl of the air, and over every living thing that moveth on the face of the earth." This version of creation is thought to have been contributed by the Priestly school of Hebrew scholars in the fifth century B.C.E. These scholars edited and codified earlier material into the first five books (or Pentateuch) of the Old Testament, adding the first chapter of Genesis.[1]

The alternative Garden of Eden story of creation, temptation, and expulsion (Genesis 2 and 3) derives from an earlier school. Writers in Judah in the ninth century B.C.E. produced a version of the Pentateuch known as the J source, *The Book of J*, or the Yahwist version (since Yahweh is the Hebrew deity). These writers recorded the oral traditions embodied in songs and folk stories handed down through previous centuries. In addition to the Garden of Eden story, these records include the heroic narratives of Abraham, Jacob, Joseph, and Moses; the escape from Egypt; and the settlement in the promised land of Canaan.[2]

In the Genesis 2 story, God first created "man" from the dust. The name Adam derives from the Hebrew word *adama*, meaning earth or arable land. *Adama* is a feminine noun, meaning an earth that gives birth to plants. God then created the Garden of Eden, the four rivers that flowed from it, and the trees for food (including the tree of life and the tree of the knowledge of good and evil in the center). He put "the man" in the garden "to dress and keep it," formed the birds and beasts from dust, and brought them to Adam to name. Only then did he create "the woman" from Adam's rib: "And Adam said, This is now bone of my bones, and flesh of my flesh: she shall be called Woman, because she was taken out of man."[3]

Biblical scholar Theodore Hiebert argues that the Yahwist's Eden narrative is told from the perspective of an audience outside the garden familiar with the post-Edenic landscape. The use of the word *before* in the phrases that described God making "every plant of the field before it was in the earth," and "every herb of the field before it grew" signify the pasturage and field crops of the post-Edenic cultivated land in which the listener is situated. Similarly, the phrases that note that "God had not caused it to rain upon the earth" and that "a mist from the earth" came that "watered the whole face of the ground" indicate a post-Edenic rain-based agriculture centered on cultivation of the adama, or arable land.[4]

The Garden of Eden described in Genesis 2, however, is a different landscape from that of the post-Edenic *adama*; it is filled with spring-fed water out of which the four rivers flow. It contains the "beasts of the field," "fowls of the air," cattle, snakes, and fruit trees, including the fig, as well as humans "to dress and keep it." The image of the garden in which animals, plants, man, and woman live together in peaceful abundance in a well-watered garden is a powerful image; it provides the starting and ending points for both plots of the overarching Recovery Narrative.

Hiebert compares the garden to a desert oasis irrigated by springs. "The term 'garden' (*gan*)," he notes, "is itself the common designation in biblical Hebrew for irrigation-supported agriculture." Irrigation agriculture was typified by the river valley civilizations of Mesopotamia and Egypt, in which rivers overflowed onto the land and water was channeled into ditches running to fields. Of the four rivers mentioned in Genesis 2, two are the Tigris (Hiddekel) and Euphrates of Mesopotamia, while the Pison and Gihon "are placed by the Yahwist south of Israel in the area of Arabia and Ethiopia (2:11–13), and have been identified by some as the headwaters of the Nile," notes Hiebert. The Edenic landscape is thus spring-fed, river-based, and irrigated, whereas the post-Edenic landscape initiated by the temptation is rain-based. Irrigation itself later becomes a technology of humanity's hoped-for return to the garden.[5]

Genesis 3 begins with "the woman's" temptation by the serpent and the consumption of the fruit from the tree of the knowledge of good and evil. (In the Renaissance this fruit became an apple, owing to a play on the Latin word bad, or *malum*, which also means apple). The story details the loss of innocence through the couple's discovery of nakedness followed by God's expulsion from the garden of Adam and his "wife," whom he now calls Eve, because she is to become "the mother of all the living." Adam is

Fig. 2.1. Adam and Eve enter the enclosed, circular Garden of Eden in lockstep. The Tree of Life and the Tree of the Knowledge of Good and Evil are at the center of the Garden, watered by a fountain, while the four rivers flow from the Garden. Ludolphus de Saxonia, *Vita Christi* (Antwerp, Gerard Leeu, 1487). Courtesy of the Huntington Library, San Marino, California

condemned to eat bread "in the sweat of thy face," and is "sent forth from the garden of Eden, to till the ground (the *adama* or arable land) from whence he was taken," the same *adama* to which he will return after death. But because Adam has listened to his wife, the *adama* was cursed. Thorns and thistles would henceforth grow in the ground where the "herb of the field" (field crops) must be grown for bread. After the couple's expulsion, God places "at the east of the garden of Eden" the cherubim and flaming sword to guard the tree of life.[6]

The landscape into which Adam and Eve are expelled is described by Evan Eisenberg in *The Ecology of Eden*. By 1100 B.C.E. the Israelites were farming the hills of Judea and Samaria in Canaan with ox-drawn scratch plows and planting wheat, barley, and legumes such as peas and lentils. They pastured sheep, goats, and cattle, and grew grapes in vineyards, olives on hillside groves, and figs, apricots, almonds, and pomegranates in orchards. "Where least disturbed," Eisenberg notes, "the landscape was [a] sort of open Mediterranean woodland . . . with evergreen oak, Aleppo pine, and pistachio. . . . Elsewhere this would dwindle to . . . a mix of shrubs and herbs such as rosemary, sage, summer savory, rock rose, and thorny burnet. The settlers cleared a good deal of this forest for pasture and cropland." They captured water in cisterns and terraced the land to retain the rich, but shallow red soil for planting, using the drier areas for pasturage. The arid hill country in which arable and pasturage lands was mingled was therefore the landscape that would be inhabited by the descendants of Adam and Eve.[7]

Genesis 4 recounts the fate of Adam and Eve's sons, Abel ("keeper of sheep"—a pastoralist) and Cain ("tiller of the ground"—a farmer). God accepts Abel's lamb as a first fruit, but rejects Cain's offering of the "fruit of the ground," grown on the *adama*. Although the seminomadic pastoralists and farmers of the Near East often existed in mutual support, they also engaged in conflict. Cain's killing of Abel may represent both that conflict and the historical ascendancy of settled farmers over nomadic pastoralists. A second explanation stems from the fact that Israelite farms in the hill country incorporated both farming and pastoralism into a subsistence way of life. According to Hiebert, the elder son was responsible for the tilling of the land, whereas the younger son was the keeper of the sheep. Hiebert argues that God's banishment of Cain after the killing of Abel represents a prohibition against settling disputes through the killing of kin.[8]

Fig. 2.2. In the background Eve, tempted by the serpent, holds the apple from the Tree of the Knowledge of Good and Evil as Adam looks on. In the foreground Adam and Eve, having tasted the fruit, are expelled from the Garden, no longer in lockstep, leaving the angel with the flaming sword to guard the Tree of Life. *Adam and Eve with a Serpent* from *Heures à l'usage de Rome*, 1488 by J. J. de Pré. Reproduced in *The Garden of Eden* by John M. Prest, 1982 and originally from *Medieval Gardens* by Sir Frank Crisp, 1924. Reference (shelfmark) 19183 d.26.

When human beings fell into a more labor-intensive way of life, their view of nature reflected this decline. Nature acting through God meted out floods, droughts, plagues, and disasters in response to humanity's sins or bountiful harvests in response to obedience. J. L. Russell notes that the Christian interpreter Paul "regarded the whole of nature as being in some way involved in the fall and redemption of man. He spoke of nature as "groaning and travailing" (Romans 8.22)—striving blindly towards the same goal of union with Christ to which the Church is tending, until finally it is re-established in that harmony with man and God which was disrupted by the Fall." While the term *fall* to characterize the expulsion or going forth from Eden is absent from the Bible, it becomes commonplace in the ensuing Christian tradition. Beginning with St. Augustine, the story is interpreted as a Fall that can be undone by a savior.[9]

Before the Fall, nature was an entirely positive presence. The garden, which is the beginning and end of the Recovery Narrative, is an idealized landscape. The beasts and herbs of Genesis 1 are described as "very good," as are the cattle, fowl, beasts, and trees in the Genesis 2 Garden of Eden. The dust of Genesis 2, from which "man" was formed and which was watered by "a mist from the earth," is positive in valence. The ground, from which the other creatures are made is positive as well. But after the couple disobeys God, the ground is cursed. Adam eats of it in sorrow, and it brings forth thorns and thistles. The serpent changes from being "more subtle" than the other beasts to being "cursed above all cattle and above every beast of the field." In the Christian tradition, the thorns, thistles, and serpent symbolize barren desert and infertile ground, a negative nature from which humanity must recover to regain the garden.[10]

With the Fall from Eden, humanity abandons an original, "untouched" nature and enters into history. Nature is now a fallen world and humans fallen beings. But this Fall through the lapsarian moment sets up the opposite—or Recovery—moment. The effort to recover Eden henceforth encompasses all of human history. Reattaining the lost garden, its life of ease from labor, and its innocent happiness (and, I would add, the potential for human partnership with the earth) become the primary human endeavor. The Eden narrative is, according to Henry Goldschmidt, "a story of originary presence which is subsequently usurped by difference; and then of a final presence, reinstituted, sweeping away the unfortunate misadventure."[11]

The Recovery story begins with the Fall from the garden into the desert (and the loss of an original partnership with the land), moves upward to the re-creation of Eden on earth (the earthly paradise), and culminates with the vision of attainment of a heavenly paradise, a recovered garden. Paradise is defined as heaven, a state of bliss, an enclosed garden or park—an Eden. Derived from a Sumerian word, *paradise* was once the name of a fertile place that had become dry and barren; the Persian word for park, or enclosure, evolves through Greek and Latin to take on the meaning of garden, so that by the medieval period Eden is depicted as an

Fig. 2.3. After the expulsion from Eden, Adam is forced to till the barren ground with plow and oxen. G. B. Andreini. "Adamo," *L'Adamo, Sacra Rapresentatione* (Milan, 1617), p. 110. Courtesy of the Huntington Library, San Marino, California

Fig. 2.4. After the Fall, nature becomes a disorderly wilderness in which animals, who once lived in harmony, devour each other, while Adam and Eve are forced to live in caves and clothe themselves in skins. G. B. Andreini. "Eua, Adamo," *L'Adamo, Sacra Rapresentatione* (Milan, 1617), p. 115. Courtesy of the Huntington Library, San Marino, California

enclosed garden. The religious path to a heavenly paradise, practiced throughout the early Christian and medieval periods, incorporated the promise of salvation to atone for the original sin of tasting the forbidden fruit. In the Christian story, time has two poles—beginning and end, creation and salvation.[12]

The resurrection or end drama, heralded in the New Testament, envisions an earth reunited with God when the redeemed earthly garden merges into a higher heavenly paradise. The second coming of Christ was to occur either at the outset of the thousand-year period of his reign of peace on earth, as foretold in Revelation 20 (the millennium), or at the last judgment, when the faithful were reunited with God at the resurrection. Since medieval times, millenarian sects have awaited the advent of Christ on earth.[13]

The Parousia is the idea of the end of the world, expressed as the hope set forth in the New Testament that "he shall come again to judge both the quick and the dead." It depicts a redeemed earth and redeemed humans. "The scene of the future consummation is a radically transformed earth," writes A. L. Moore. *Parousia* derives from the Latin *parere*, meaning to produce or bring forth. Hope for Parousia was a motivating force behind the Church's missionary work, both in its early development and in the New World; Christians prepared for this expected age of glory when God would enter history. Moore notes, "The coming of this Kingdom was conceptualized as a sudden catastrophic moment, or as preceded by the Messianic kingdom, during which it was anticipated that progressive work would take place."[14]

THE MODERN NARRATIVE

A secular version of the Recovery story became paramount during the Scientific Revolution of the seventeenth century, one in which the earth itself became a new Eden. This is the mainstream narrative of modern Western culture, one that continues to this day—it is *our* story, one so compelling we cannot escape its grasp. In the 1600s, Europeans and New World colonists began a massive effort to reinvent the whole earth in the image of the Garden of Eden. Aided by the Christian doctrine of redemption and the inventions of science, technology, and capitalism, the long-term goal of the Recovery project has been to turn the entire earth into a vast cultivated garden. The seventeenth-century concept of Recovery

TABLE 2.1.
REINVENTING EDEN:
NARRATIVES OF WESTERN CULTURE

Christian	Modern	Environmentalist	Feminist
Eden	Golden Age	Pristine Wilderness	Matriarchy or Equality
Fall	Dark Ages	Ecological Crisis	Patriarchy
Birth of Christ	Renaissance	Environmental Movement	Feminist Movement
Heaven	Capitalism	Restored Earth	Emancipation, Equality

came to mean more than Recovery from the Fall. It also entailed restoration of health, reclamation of land, and recovery of property. The strong interventionist version in Genesis 1 validates Recovery through domination, while the softer Genesis 2 version advocates dressing and keeping the garden through human management (stewardship). Human labor would redeem the souls of men and women, while the earthly wilderness would be redeemed through cultivation and domestication.[15]

The Garden of Eden origin story depicts a comic or happy state of human existence, while the Fall exemplifies a tragic state. Stories and descriptions about nature and human nature told by explorers, colonists, settlers, and developers present images of and movement between comic (positive) or tragic (negative) states. Northrop Frye describes the elements of these two states. In comic stories, he notes, the human world is a community and the animal world comprises domesticated flocks and birds of peace. The vegetable world is a garden or park with trees, while the mineral world is a city or temple with precious stones and starlit domes. And the unformed world is depicted as a river. In tragic stories, the human world is an anarchy of individuals and the animal world is filled with birds and beasts of prey (such as wolves, vultures, and serpents). The vegetable world is a wilderness, desert, or sinister forest, the mineral world is filled with rocks and ruins, and the unformed world is a sea or flood. All of these elements are present in the two versions of the Recovery Narrative.[16]

The plot of the tragedy moves from a better or comic state to a worse or tragic state (from the Garden of Eden to a desert wilderness). The comedy, on the other hand, moves from an initial tragic state to a comic outcome (from a desert to a recovered garden). Thus, the primary narrative of Western culture has been a precipitous, tragic Fall from the Garden of Eden, followed by a long, slow, upward Recovery to convert the fallen world of deserts and wilderness into a new earthly Eden. Tragedy is turned into comedy through human labor in the earth and the Christian faith in redemption. During the Scientific Revolution, the Christian and modern stories merged to become the mainstream Recovery Narrative of Western culture (see table 2.1).

THE ROLE OF GENDER

The way in which gender is encoded into the mainstream Recovery Narrative is crucial to the structure of the story. In the Christian tradition, God—the original oneness—is male, while in the garden the woman (Eve) is subordinate to the man (Adam). The fall from the garden is caused by the woman, Eve; Adam is the innocent bystander, forced to pay the consequences as his sons, Abel and Cain, are constrained to develop pastoralism and farming. While fallen Adam becomes the inventor of the tools and technologies that will restore the garden, fallen Eve becomes the nature that must be tamed into submission. In much of the imagery of Western culture, Eve is inherently connected to and associated symbolically with nature and the garden. In the European and American traditions, male science and technology mitigate the effects of fallen nature. The good state that keeps unruly nature in check is invented, engineered, and operated by men, and the good economy that organizes the labor needed to restore the garden historically has been male directed.

In Western culture, nature as Eve appears in three forms. As original Eve, nature is virgin, pure, and light—land that is pristine or barren but has the potential for development. As fallen Eve, nature is disorderly and chaotic; a wilderness, wasteland, or desert requiring improvement; dark and witchlike, the victim and mouthpiece of Satan as serpent. As mother Eve, nature is an improved garden; a nurturing earth bearing fruit; a ripened ovary; maturity. Original Adam is the image of God as creator, initial agent, activity. Fallen Adam appears as the agent of earthly transformation, the hero who redeems the fallen land. Father Adam is the image of God as patriarch, law, and rule, the model for kingdom and state.

These denotions of nature as female and agency as male are encoded
as symbols and myths into land that has the potential for development but
needs the male hero—Adam. But such symbols are not "essences" because
they do not represent characteristics necessary or essential to being female
or male. They are historically constructed meanings derived from the origin stories of European settlers and the cultural and economic practices
they transported to and developed in the New World. These gender symbols are not immutable; they can be changed by exposing their presence
and rethinking history.

The male/female hierarchy encoded into the Genesis texts both consciously and implicitly socializes the young into behavioral patterns. Eve,
after ingesting the fruit, is told she will be ruled by her husband, and the
conflation of animals with women as helpmates is also explicit. In all versions of the story, Eve became Adam's "wife" after the two became one
flesh, and she is to be "ruled over" or "dominated" by her husband after she
disobeys God.[17]

But there is another way to read the gendered message. In the feminist reading, Genesis 1's simultaneous creation of men and women indicates their potential equality ("male and female created He them").
Recovery, therefore, is an effort to reclaim an original gender equality or
partnership. Genesis 2, on the other hand, depicts the creation sequen-
tially, first, of a real, material male body from dust and, second, woman
from the body of the male. Hence Eve is second in the order of creation,
implying the subjection of woman to man.[18] But some feminists argue that
Eve is not derivative of Adam; he was not awake at her creation, nor was
he even consulted in advance. "Like man, woman owes her life solely to
God," states Phyllis Trible, "to claim that the rib means inferiority or subordination is to assign the man qualities over the woman which are not in
the narrative itself." Eve's role in initiating the Fall can also be debated.
Was she the weaker, more vulnerable sex and hence susceptible to the serpent's temptation? Or, was she actually the First Scientist—the more
independent and curious of the two—as in the Mark Twain epigraph
above. In this reading, Eve was the one who questioned the established
order of things and initiated change. As original biologist, Eve talks to the
snake and nature rather than to God as does Adam. As prototypic scientist, Eve could hold the key to recovering Eden through a new science.[19]

While the Bible does not employ the term *partner* for the male-
female relationship, today some people are rethinking the Genesis pas-

sages in terms of partnership. Theologian Ray Maria McNamara interprets the creation story in Genesis 1 in terms of a partnership between God and the earth. She notes that although God said "Let the earth bring forth grass and herb" it was actually the earth as an active partner that "brought forth grass and herb . . . and the tree yielding fruit." Another contribution to a partnership interpretation is made by the Reverend William M. Boyce Jr., who offers a free translation of several of the Genesis verses. He portrays Adam and Eve as helpers, partners, and colleagues to one another and a God who views the whole of creation as very, very good.[20]

STEWARDSHIP VERSUS DOMINION

While the role of gender is central to the story, equally critical is the question of human dominion versus stewardship of nature. If Genesis 1 is accepted as the ethical model, as it is in mainstream Western culture, then the domination of nature could be interpreted as the ideal pathway to Recovery. But if Genesis 2 represents the ethical ideal (humans as stewards over the animals), then Recovery could mean that humans are the caretakers and stewards of nature. The Bible and the Torah, in Christian and Judaic traditions, provide interesting variations on the language of the two creation stories leading to dominance or stewardship.

The terms *dominion, mastery, subduing, conquering,* and *ruling* predominate in different translations of the Genesis 1 story. In order to have dominion, men and women must "be fruitful," "be fertile," "become many," "increase," "multiply," "grow in number," "have many children," and then "replenish," "fill," "fill up," and "people" the "earth" or the "land."[21] If the fall from Eden entails the loss of immortality bestowed by the tree of life, humans can henceforth attain immortality only through sexual procreation. Thus, in the mainstream story of Western culture, to recover the Garden of Eden means that people must not only convert the earthly wilderness into a garden, but must also replenish the earth by expanding the human population over space and time. The Genesis 1 ethic, claims that humans must "replenish the earth and subdue it." Or, as historian Lynn White Jr. argued in 1967, it is "God's will that man exploit nature for his proper ends."[22]

Genesis 2 presents stewardship as an ethical alternative to the domination of nature. God puts "man" into the Garden of Eden and instructs him "to dress it and to keep it." The Genesis 2:15 ethic is often interpreted as the stewardship of nature, as opposed to the Genesis 1:28 ethic of dominion or mastery. In Genesis 2, the earth is a garden—a local plot of land rather than a vast area for spatial conquest—and the man is commanded to "dress," "keep," "tend," "guard," and "watch over" it. According to ecologist René Dubos, God "placed man in the Garden of Eden not as a master but rather in a spirit of stewardship." For many religious sects wishing to embrace an ecological ethic, stewardship is the most persuasive ethic that is also consistent with biblical traditions. Stewardship is a caretaker ethic, but it is still anthropocentric inasmuch as nature is created for human use.[23] Moreover, Nature is not an actor, but is rendered docile.

Throughout most of Western history, the biblical mandates of stewardship and dominion have sometimes been explicitly separated and at other times implicitly merged. For example, medieval enclosed gardens were often protected, carefully stewarded spaces, while eighteenth-century garden estates were vast displays of dominion and power. Early American farms ranged from small patches in the forest tended mainly for family provisions to large plantations and capitalist ranches that dominated the landscape. While the former exemplify potential partnerships between humanity and the land, the latter represent the potential for human mastery over the earth. Colonists, planters, and westward pioneers often explicitly cited the Genesis 1:28 mandate in order to justify expansion. In Western culture, the Genesis 1 and 2 accounts have usually been conflated. In the mainstream Recovery project, humanity has turned the entire earth into a vast garden by mastering nature. The Genesis 1:28 ethic of dominion has provided the rationale for the Recovery of the garden lost in Genesis 2 and 3, submerging the stewardship ethic of Genesis 2:15.

When Adam and Eve tasted the fruit of the tree of the knowledge of good and evil, humans acquired their potential omniscience of nature. Wanting to become more like God, humanity has craved knowledge of everything. Since the seventeenth century, mainstream Western culture has pursued the pathway to Eden's Recovery by using Christianity, science, technology, and capitalism in concert. That human dominion over nature, however, has costs in terms of the depletion of the planet's resources.[24]

The Genesis stories provide two ethical alternatives, dominion and stewardship—both of which are anthropocentric. They do not explicitly acknowledge nonanthropocentric ethics, such as ecocentrism in which humanity is only one of a number of equal parts—an ecocentric ethic; nor is biocentrism a possibility, in which value is grounded in life itself, rather than being centered on humanity. But another form of ethics is the partnership ethic I propose that posits nature and humanity as equal, interacting, mutually responsive partners (see chapter 11). This ethic combines human actions and nature's actions in a dynamic relationship with each other. Here nature is not created specifically for human use, nor are women and animals seen as helpmates for "man." Rather, human life and biotic life exist in mutual support, reciprocity, and partnership with each other. Gardens could exemplfy places in which the practice of gardening is a caretaking of the soil and the life it generates.[25]

ENVIRONMENTALIST AND FEMINIST NARRATIVES

An alternative to the mainstream story of Fall and Recovery is told by many environmentalists and feminists. This second narrative begins in a Stone-Age Garden of Eden and depicts a gradual, rather than precipitous, loss of a pristine condition. It uses archeological, anthropological, and ecological data, along with myth and art, to re-create a story of decline. Both environmental and feminist accounts idealize an Edenic prehistory in which both sexes lived in harmony with each other and nature, but they are nevertheless compelling in their critique of environmental disruption and the subjugation of both women and nature. When viewed critically, both can contribute to a new narrative of sustainable partnership between humanity and nature.

One version of the environmental narrative is exemplified by the work of philosopher Max Oelschlaeger. Paleolithic people, he notes, did not distinguish between nature and culture, but saw themselves "as one with plants and animals, rivers and forests, as part of a larger, encompassing whole. . . ." In that deep past, people in gathering/hunting bands lived sustainably and "comfortably in the wilderness," albeit within cycles of want and plenty. Contained within the sacred oneness of the *Magna Mater* (the Great Mother), hunters followed rituals that respected animals and obeyed rules for preparing food and disposing of remains. Cave paintings, for example, reveal human-animal hybrids that suggest identity with the *Magna Mater*, while the cave itself is her womb. Although myth rather than science explained life, Stone-Age peoples, argues Oelschlaeger, were just as intelligent as their "modern" counterparts.[26]

Oelschlaeger sees humankind's emergence from the original oneness with the *Magna Mater* as the beginning of a wrenching division, just as birth is a traumatic separation from the human mother. He writes, "No one knows for certain how long prehistoric people existed in an Edenlike condition of hunting-gathering, but 200,000 years or more is not an unreasonable estimate for the hegemony of the Great Hunt. Even while humankind lived the archaic life, clinging conceptually to the bosom of the *Magna Mater*, the course of cultural events contained the seeds of an agricultural revolution, since prehistoric peoples were practicing rudimentary farming and animal husbandry."[27]

Oelschlaeger's narrative is one of gradual decline from the Paleolithic era rather than a precipitous fall as depicted in the Genesis 3 story. Near the end of the last ice age, around 10000 B.C.E., changes in climate disrupted Paleolithic ecological relations. Animals and grains were gradually domesticated for herding and cultivation, heralding a change to pastoral and horticultural ways of life, particularly in the Near East. Once humans became agriculturists, Oelschlaeger observes, "the almost paradisiacal character of prehistory was irretrievably lost." Differences between humans and animals, male and female, people and nature became more distinct.[28] Humanity lost the intimacy it once had with the Magna Mater: "Western culture was now alienated from the Great Mother of the Paleolithic Mind."[29]

The first environmental problems stemming from large-scale agriculture occurred in Mesopotamia. Canals stretched from the Tigris to the Euphrates, bringing fertility to thousands of square miles of cropland; but as these irrigation waters evaporated, salts accumulated in the soils and reduced productivity. Oelschlager suggests that agriculture marks a decline from an Edenic past: "If the thesis that agriculture underlies humankind's turn upon the environment, even if out of climatological exigency, is cogent, then the ancient Mediterranean theater is where the 'fall from Paradise' was staged. . . ."[30]

In the Near East, the great town-based cultures emerged around 4000 B.C.E. By about 1000 B.C.E., the ancient tribes of Yahweh had become a single kingdom, ruled by David, that practiced rain-based agriculture. The God Yahweh above the earth represents a rupture with the Magna Mater of the Paleolithic era and a legitimization of the settled agriculture and pastoralism of the Neolithic era. The Hebrews rebelled against sacred animals as idols and placed Yahweh as the one god above and outside of nature. Time was no longer viewed as a cyclical return, but as a linear history with singular determinative events. As the "chosen people," Hebrew agriculturists and pastoralists became part of a broad-based transition from gathering/hunting to farming/herding.[31]

Ecologically, the fall from Eden, told in Genesis 2, may reflect the differences between gathering/hunting and farming/herding initiated thousands of years earlier. In the Garden of Eden's age of gathering, Adam and Eve pick the fruits of the trees without having to labor in the earth. The transition from foraging and hunting to settled agriculture took place some 9,000 to 10,000 years ago (7000–8000 B.C.E.) with the domestication of wheat and barley in the oak forests and steppes of the Near East. Around 5,000 years ago (3200–3100 B.C.E.), fruits such as the olive, grape, date, pomegranate, and fig were domesticated. By 600 B.C.E., when the biblical stories were codified, fruit trees were cultivated throughout the Near East. The Genesis 2 story may reflect the state of farming at the time and the labor required for tilling fields as opposed to tending and harvesting fruit trees.[32]

The tilling, planting, harvesting, and storing of wheat and barley represents a form of settled agriculture in which the earth was managed for grain production. "By the time the Genesis stories were composed," writes Oelschlaeger, "man had already embarked on the task of transforming nature. In the Genesis stories [he] justifies his actions."[33] In Genesis 1, the anthropocentric God of the Hebrews commands that the earth be subdued. This represents a rupture with the nature gods of the past that occurred during the transition from polytheism to monotheism and was codified during the years of Israelite exile in Babylon between 587 and 538 B.C.E.

During the Iron Age (1200–1000 B.C.E.), the cultures of Israel and Canaan had overlapped. Canaanite mythology included a pantheon of deities: the patriarch El; his consort and mother-goddess, Asherah; the storm-god Baal, and his sister/consort Anat. Although the worship of Yahweh predominated, Israelites also worshipped El, Baal, and Asherah. During the period of the monarchy (ca. 1000–587 B.C.E.), the figure of Yahweh assimilated characteristics of the other deities, and Israel then rejected Baal and Asherah as part of its religion. "By the end of the monarchy," states Mark S. Smith, "much of the spectrum of religious practice had largely disappeared; monolatrous Yahwism was the norm in Israel, setting the stage for the emergence of Israelite monotheism."[34]

Monotheism represented an irrevocable break with the natural world. Henri and H. A. Frankfort note that the emergence of monotheism represents the highest level of abstraction and constitutes the "emancipation of thought from myth." They write, "The dominant tenet of Hebrew

thought is the absolute transcendence of God. Yahweh is not in nature. . . .
The God of the Hebrews is pure being, unqualified, ineffable. . . . Hence
all concrete phenomena are devaluated." Although God had human characteristics, he was not human; although God had characteristics assimilated from other deities, he was the One God, not one among many gods.[35]

From an ecological perspective, the separation of God from nature constitutes a rupture with nature. God is not nature or of nature. God is
unchanging, nature is changing and inconstant. The human relationship to
nature was not one of *I* to *thou*, not one of subject to subject, nor of a human
being to a nature alive with gods and spirits. The intellectual construction of
a transcendent God is yet another point in a narrative of decline. The separation of God from nature legitimates humanity's separation from nature
and sets up the possibility of human domination and control over nature. In
the agricultural communities of the Old Testament, humanity is the link
between the soil and God. Humans are of the soil, but separate from and
above the soil: they till the land with plows and reap the harvest with
scythes; they clear the forests and pollute the rivers; their goats and sheep
devour the hillsides and erode the soil. Over time, the natural landscape is
irrevocably transformed. At the same time, however, nature is an unpre-
dictible actor in the story. Noah's flood, plagues of locusts, earthquakes,
droughts, and devastating diseases inject uncertainties into the outcome.
Efforts to control nature come up against chaotic events that upset the linearity of the storyline and create temporary or permanent setbacks.[36]

The environmentalist narrative of decline initiated by the transition to
agriculture continues to the present. Tools and technologies allow people
to spread over the entire globe and to subdue the earth. The colonizers
denude the earth for ores and build cities and highways across the land.
Despite this destruction, however, environmentalists hope for a Recovery
that reverses the decline by means of planetary restoration. The environmental Recovery begins with the conservation and preservation movements of the nineteenth century and continues with the environmental
movement of the late twentieth century.

FEMINIST NARRATIVES

Many feminists likewise see history as a downward spiral from a utopian
past in which women were held in equal or even higher esteem than men.
This storyline was developed in the nineteenth century by Marxist

philosopher Friedrich Engels, who saw the "worldwide defeat of the female sex" at the dawn of written history, and by anthropologists such as Johann Bachofen, August Bebel, and Robert Briffault. It was elaborated in a series of compelling studies by twentieth-century feminists such as Jane Harrison, Helen Diner, Esther Harding, Elizabeth Gould Davis, Merlin Stone, Adrienne Rich, Françoise d'Eaubonne, Marija Gimbutas, Pamela Berger, Gerda Lerner, Monica Sjöö, Barbara Mor, Riane Eisler, Elinor Gadon, Rosemary Radford Ruether, and a host of other feminists and ecofeminists. Like the environmental story, the feminist story captures the imagination by its symbolic force and its dramatic loss of female power. But like the environmental narrative, it must be critically evaluated for its overly utopian past from which women "fell" and its polarization of the sexes into positive female valences and negative male valences.[37]

In broad outlines the story of the decline of women, goddesses, and female symbolism woven by feminist writers is as follows. Elizabeth Gould Davis in *The First Sex*, sets out the storyline:

> When recorded history begins we behold the finale of the long pageant of pre-history. . . . On the stage, firmly entrenched on her ancient throne, appears woman, the heroine of the play. About her, her industrious subjects perform their age-old roles. Peace, Justice, Progress, Equality play their parts with a practiced perfection. . . . Off in the wings, however, we hear a faint rumbling—the . . . jealous complaints of the new men who are no longer satisfied with their secondary role in society. . . . [T]he rebellious males burst onstage, overturn the queen's throne, and take her captive. . . . The queen's subjects—Democracy, Peace, Justice, and the rest—flee the scene in disarray. And man, for the first time in history, stands triumphant, dominating the stage as the curtain falls.[38]

This story of decline from a past dominated by female cultural symbols and powerful female deities into one of female subordination is presented by many feminist writers. The plot is a downward trajectory throughout prehistory and written history in which female power is lost or obscured. Recovery, however, can occur with emancipation, social and economic equality, and the return of powerful cultural icons that validate women's power and promise. Merlin Stone conveys the argument when she writes that in the Neolithic era (ca. 7000 B.C.E.) people worshipped a female creator, a great goddess who was overthrown with the advent of newer religions. The loss of paradise, she holds, is the loss of a female deity. The beginnings of this narrative occur in the ancient Near East with the overthrow of goddess worshipping horticulturalists by warriors on horseback.[39]

Horticulturists who lived during the period from 7000 to 3500 B.C.E. in Old Europe—the area of present-day Greece and the former Yugoslavia—were, according to archeologist Marija Gimbutas, apparently peaceful groups who did not develop destructive weapons. Men and women were buried side by side, indicating equal status. Their lives revolved around fertility rituals based on the female principle. Birth, death, and regeneration were reflected in statues of female deities with large buttocks, pregnant bellies, and cylindrical necks. The concepts of male and female, animal and human, were fused. Nature was venerated. Artifacts show large eggs with snakes wound around them that symbolized the cosmos, while fish, water birds, butterflies, and bees captured the vibrancy of the natural world. Gimbutas's interpretation of grave sites as representing equality and her conjectures about the symbolic meanings of markers on vases and statues have been questioned, but her work is nonetheless compelling in part because the storyline she imposes on the past is one of great power especially for women.

Between 4400 and 2800 B.C.E., Gimbutas argues, the apparent oneness with nature and equality between genders was ruptured. She identifies three major waves of horse-mounted Kurgan invaders that conquered Old Europe and introduced hierarchical social relations and sun-god worship. Excavated graves from this period reveal male chiefs. They were buried with servants at their feet, and their graves contained weapons of human destruction and material possessions to indicate their high status. Sky gods rather than earth deities appear on pottery, suggesting a new worship of the heavens above rather than animate spirits within nature. This interpretation has likewise undergone scrutiny because it attributes all disruption to external forces and seems to give far less credence to internal social changes and adaptations to external events.[40]

The feminist narrative continues with the overthrow of goddesses in ancient Mesopotamia and Egypt and their replacement by male principles. Throughout the Mediterranean world, as a more settled way of life began, shifting settlements became towns, and civilizations with recorded histories arose. These cultures were rooted in the cyclical return of rains. Sumeria (Mesopotamia) blossomed in the fertile crescent between the Tigris and Euphrates Rivers. Sumerian gods were identified with nature:

Fig. 2.5. Stone-age female figure with large buttocks and breasts, interpreted by some arche-ologists and feminists as representing the fertility of the earth and women. Neolithic Figure, Tel Chagar Bazar, Mesopotamia. Copyright the British Museum, London

sky (An), earth (Ki), air (Enlil), and water (Enki). Domesticated animals, such as the bull and cow, symbolized fertility.[41]

A array of powerful female deities existed who were overthrown and replaced by male deities. In Mesopotamia, the Sumerian goddess Ishtar (Inanna) was portrayed with her much smaller son-lover, Tammuz. She renewed life each spring when she descended to the underworld to bring

Tammuz back from the dead. Over time, however, Ishtar faded in importance to Tammuz. Another female deity was the life-giving Tiamat, who symbolized the earth. She was slain by her great great grandson, Marduk, who went on to create the heavens and the earth, heralding the rise of patriarchal society. Similarly, the male hero Gilgamesh (second millennium B.C.E.), who slew the forest god Humbaba, symbolized agriculture's encroachment on the ancient forests.[42]

In Egypt, Isis represented the maternal principle. She produced vegetation when impregnated by Osiris, her brother-husband. Every spring her tears overflowed to flood the Nile, which made the soil fertile. In one hand she carried a sistrum, or rattle, to awaken the powers of nature. In the other she held a bucket of Nile water, and her gown was decorated with stars and flowers to symbolize nature.[43] Osiris was the god of the people and bestowed gifts on humankind. He was killed by his brother Seth and restored to life by Isis, his sister-wife. Osiris, however, was a deity who descended from Atum-Re, the Sun God, and was associated with the Egyptian Sun Kings, or pharaohs, who embodied male power and virility.[44]

Feminists argue that a similar transition in the worship of goddesses to that of gods and a decline in the relative importance of female to male principles also occurred in ancient Greece. The Mycenaeans, who worshipped the goddess on the island of Crete at the Palace of Knossos about 1400 B.C.E., founded cities on mainland Greece, bringing with them worship of the mother goddess, which thrived from 1450 to 1100 B.C.E. Artemis, goddess of the hunt, was worshipped, as were the fertility goddesses Demeter and Persephone. The Achaean invasions of the thirteenth century B.C.E. began to weaken matrilineal traditions and by the close of the second millennium B.C.E., with the advent of the Dorians, patrilineal succession became established. The goddess Athene was reconfigured as a motherless female, free of maternal desire and labor pains, springing from the head of the male god Zeus. Here the male gives birth to the female, reversing the natural birth process. While the common people continued to worship Artemis, Demeter and Persephone, the ruling elite set up Olympian Gods, such as Zeus and Apollo as a patriarchal, rational idealized pantheon.[45]

The feminist narrative also reverses the biblical story. It begins with powerful female creative principles. It was the goddess Anat (Eve), mother of all the living, who created Yahweh. And, following the tradition in which

Fig. 2.6. The Egyptian female deity, Isis, symbolized the fertility of nature as the Nile annually overflowed to produce crops. She rattles her sistrum to awaken the powers of nature and with her pail pours water onto the land. Isis, in Athanasius Kircher, *Oedipus Aegypticus* (1652). Courtesy of the Bancroft Library, University of California, Berkeley

goddesses gave birth to sons who then became their spouses, Eve created Adam, who then became her consort. Moreover, in the feminist story, Adam was born of Eve's rib, not vice versa. The very idea that Adam should give birth to Eve (as Zeus similarly gave birth to Athena) reverses the biological process in which women give birth to men. Notes Elizabeth Gould Davis, "[T]he whole intention of the distortion manifested in the Hebrew tale of Adam and Eve is twofold: first, to deny the tradition of a female creator; and second, to deny the original supremacy of the female sex."[46]

The feminist narrative likewise reveals important relationships between Eve and nature. Eve's mythological connections to the mother goddesses Tiamat, Inanna, Ishtar, Isis, and Demeter are reinforced by her associations with the garden, the serpent, and the tree, all of which were both nature and *of* nature. First, the Garden of Eden itself is nature. It was originally created by the mother goddess, and its loss represents the loss of intimacy between woman and nature. Second, the serpent, associated as divine counsel with the mother goddesses and female deities of Mesopotamia (Tiamat, Ishtar); Egypt (Hathor, Maat); Crete (the priestesses of Knossos); and Greece (Athena, Hera, Gaia) was the intimate link between Eve and a nature with which she communicated through speech. Third, the tree symbolized the fertility of nature and Eve's initial ingestion of its fruit initiated sexual consciousness. In the biblical expulsion story, Eve, the serpent, nature, and the body are all relegated, after the Fall, to the lowest levels of being. Merlin Stone sums up the consequences of these ancient associations between Eve and Nature: "[A] woman, listening to the advice of the serpent, eating the forbidden fruit, suggesting that men try it too and join her in sexual consciousness . . . caused the downfall and misery of all humankind."[47]

While many feminists have found evidence for a transition from matriarchy to patriarchy, other writers such as Riane Eisler see humanity as taking a five-thousand-year detour from a partnership society in prehistory to a dominator society that has existed throughout most of recorded history. She argues that today we have the possibility of reestablishing a partnership society in which men and women are linked as equals rather than ranked as dominant and submissive. Although feminist theologian Rosemary Radford Ruether does not employ the term *partnership*, in *Gaia and God* she calls for a healing process that will reconfigure the positive features of Western culture and Christianity. She advocates a reordering of social relations that will promote justice in relationships between women and men and among races, classes, and nations. And in "Gender and the Problem of Prehistory," Ruether suggests that "the only way we can, as human, integrate ourselves into a life-sustaining relationship to nature, is for both of us, males as much as females, to see ourselves as equally rooted in the cycles of life and death, and equally responsible for creating ways of living sustainably together in that relationship."[48]

COMPARING THE NARRATIVES

The mainstream, environmentalist, and feminist Recovery Narratives all have strengths and weaknesses. The mainstream story of the Recovery of Eden through modern science, technology, and capitalism is perhaps the most powerful narrative in Western culture. It has been absorbed consciously and unconsciously by millions of people over several centuries. This story writ large is one in which people participate as actors and which they incorporate into their daily lives. As a narrative it is both inspiring and realizable, providing a positive earthly goal and a promise of ultimate salvation. A vast treasury of first-rate scholarship exists on the origins and transmission of the Christian and modern stories and their impacts and implications for history and society.

Yet however comprehensive and positive as a narrative, the mainstream Recovery story is also an ideology of domination over nature and other people. In the following chapters, I will argue that, among other things, this narrative provides a justification for the takeover of New World lands and peoples and the management and transformation of forests, fields, and deserts. The Christian narrative is based on the belief and assumption that a monotheistic deity exists who has ordained a mode of behavior for humanity and designated roles for men and women. Such beliefs are based on acts of faith rather than credible evidence. Whatever positive ethics of care and stewardship arise from such beliefs, there exists an equal catalogue of war and violence against humanity and atrocities against the earth in the name of that deity. The deity can take on any attributes any group wishes to assign to it, and becomes a rationale for any actions a particular group wishes to take. As such, God (however defined and by whatever religion or sect) can be seen as a social construct that becomes a justification and an ideology for human behavior. The sacred texts that reveal such a deity can be viewed as humanly constructed stories arising out of specific social, historical, and environmental circumstances.

The environmentalist and feminist narratives likewise have strengths and weaknesses. They use climatological, archeological, anthropological, historical, and mythological evidence to support the storylines. The stories can be criticized, revised, or rejected on the basis of how they use, accept, and organize their evidence. To the extent that they deal with prehistory, their validity depends on how they interpret archeological, anthropological, and mythological evidence and the generalizability of that evidence.

Deciding how an early society behaved toward nature from surviving, nondecomposable artifacts is enormously difficult. Whether a Magna Mater or a variety of nature spirits or goddesses existed in prehistory is built on conjecture and extrapolation from later historical documents and anthropological observations. Whether mythologies recorded later in time actually reflect social realities or influence human behavior is problematical. Moreover, of the many statues and images that have survived, some are female, others are male, and still others are male/female or simply anthropomorphic. Some female images are buxom or pregnant with broad buttocks oriented toward the earth, while others are slender with outstretched arms reaching toward the sky, casting doubt on the universality of female fertility symbols. Other problems arise from the causes of transformation from a presumed egalitarian or matriarchal to a patriarchal society. External migrations such as warriors on horseback who infused sky gods into earth-centered egalitarian cultures or invasions of dominant outsiders places too much weight on external as opposed to internal processes, adaptations, and mutual influences. Such critiques undercut the power of the overarching storyline of the environmental and feminist narratives.

Additional problems exist with respect to the very concept of narrative itself. A narrative, whether Christian, environmentalist, or feminist, is an ideal form into which particular bits of content are poured. The form is the organizing principle; the content is the matter. Like Plato's pure forms that explain the changing world of appearances, a narrative is a variant of idealism. What is real is the idea itself. In this sense, a Recovery Narrative is an idealist philosophy. To the extent to which people believe in or absorb the story, it organizes their behavior and hence their perception of the material world. The narrative thus entails an ethic and the ethic gives permission to act in a particular way toward nature and other people.

Narratives however are not deterministic. Their plots and ethical implications can be embraced or challenged. Naming the narrative gives people the power to change it, to move outside it, and to reconstruct it.

People as material actors living in a real world can organize that world and their behaviors to bring about change and to break out of the confines a particular storyline.

My own view is that out of the global ecological crisis a new story or set of stories will emerge, but the new stories will arise out of new forms of production and reproduction as sustainable partnerships with nature are tested and become viable. Revisions of older spiritual traditions may help to create a new story, but spirituality alone cannot bring about a transformation. Nevertheless, probing the meanings of narrative, gender, and ethics embedded in the Bible and other historical narratives is critical for the planet's future. In chapter 11, I propose a partnership ethic that may help to guide decision making and the construction of sustainable livelihoods in the twenty-first century.

THREE

Recovering the Garden

Columbus,
Admiral of the Ocean Sea,
Cataloging, controlling, leading me
Out of the shadow of that netherworld,
Where all lies silent and unheard.
—*Carolyn Merchant, 1998*

The dreams of the Greeks, Romans, and early Christians were motivated by their longing for a better world beyond the shadows of their everyday lives. In between Old World biblical accounts of a lost Eden and Christopher Columbus's voyages to find Eden in the New World, Western history is filled with Greek and Roman images of a golden age and Christian visions of salvation. By 1300, Dante Alighieri's *Divine Comedy* had deftly entwined these two narratives. In this classic allegory, Virgil guides Dante out of a forested wilderness, through the Fall into the Inferno, and then upward to the earthly Eden of purgatory whence he enters the heavenly Eden of salvation.

In this chapter, I argue that these ancient and medieval narratives are integral steps toward the mainstream Recovery Narrative of reinventing the entire earth as Eden. By the seventeenth century, the medieval escape from Earth to a heavenly Eden would become the secular creation of an earthly Eden. The Greek and medieval stories are thus vital components that merge into Western civilization's transformation of nature into culture, darkness into light, and chaos into order. My own view is that while these progressive developments are positive for Western middle- and upper-class society, they are achieved at the cost of the earth's cultural and biotic diversity. The divergent stories of human progress and environmental decline do not lead to the possibility of partnership between humanity and nature, yet elements of the two stories suggest that a sustainable synthesis might be found in the future.

THE MEDITERRANEAN ENVIRONMENT

Integral to the mainstream Recovery Narrative is the development of domesticated animals and crops, along with literacy, art, and philosophy that culminated in the Mediterranean world. Classical Greece, during the period 600–200 B.C.E., was situated within mountainous, forested uplands with rocky, but fertile soils. An agricultural system that included cattle, sheep, pigs, and goats provided meat, leather, and dairy products; horses and donkeys supplied transportation and hauling; barley and wheat produced bread. Additionally there were now grapes, olives, and fig trees for fruits; chickens and geese for eggs; and bees for honey.

Greek and Roman civilizations were the beneficiaries of livestock and crop domestication that had occurred centuries earlier. Jared Diamond has argued that the "major five" Eurasian domesticated animals (the sheep, goat, cow, pig, and horse) gave the ancient world as well as modern Europeans a biological advantage as they expanded around the globe. The sheep and goat were domesticated around 8000 B.C.E., the cow, which is part of the larger group of cattle, including oxen, about 6000 B.C.E. in Asia, India, and north Africa. The pig was domesticated in China and southwest Asia around 8000 B.C.E. and the horse in the Ukraine around 4000 B.C.E. Diamond further argues that the grain crops that made settled agriculture possible were domesticated in the Fertile Crescent around 8000 B.C.E. These included the broadcast cereal crops: two types of wheat, Emmer and Einkorn (the first with two grains in each spikelet, the second with one) and barley; the pulses—lentils, peas, and chickpeas—and flax that yielded fibers for clothing. Additionally, nuts and fruits, in particular olives, figs, dates, and grapes appeared in the Fertile Crescent around 4000 B.C.E. Finally, fruits, such as apples, pears, plums, and cherries, were domesticated in the Fertile Crescent by around 500 B.C.E. (the period of the Garden of Eden story). Diamond's conclusion is that the major five domesticated animals, along with broadcast grains and fruits, provided the foundations for settled agriculture, which in turn spawned the development of culture: writing, mathematics, art, music, law, literature, and especially philosophy.[1]

GREEK AND ROMAN NARRATIVES

By the fifth century B.C.E., Greek philosophers had established a dichotomy between a changing natural world and an unchanging abstract world of ideas, creating the philosophical assumptions behind the Recovery Narrative's movement from inconstant fallen nature to the prediction and management of nature. Heraclitus of Ephesus (540–475 B.C.E.) boldly asserted that all is change: "You cannot step twice into the same river, for other waters are ever flowing onward." By contrast, Parmenides of Elea (504 B.C.E.) argued that no change is possible because of the tautology: Being *is*. Being is one, whole, indivisible, irreducible, and unchangeable. In short, it is existence itself and can be divided only by nonexistence. But *not* being, by definition, does not exist. These two contradictory philosophies formed the basis of Plato's (427–347 B.C.E.) distinction between the ever-changing world of appearances and the unchanging real world of pure forms, exemplified by mathematics and ideals such as *the good*. Plato argued that the natural world can never lead to truth. Truth is constituted only by the world of pure forms divorced from nature. The appearances therefore constitute the unpredictable, natural world, while mathematical ideals become the basis for the predictable, managed world. Greek philosophy's narrative movement from inconstancy to predictability is a major foundation of the progressive Recovery Narrative.

Western culture merged the Greek and Christian narratives to create a compelling vision of the Recovery of Eden. The Greek world of appearances is strikingly similar to the Christian world of fallen nature. Greek philosophy contributed the intellectual framework for the modern version of the Recovery Narrative. Parmenidean oneness represents the unchanging natural law that has lapsed into the appearances of the Platonic world. This phenomenal world, like the Christian world, is incomplete, corrupt, and inconstant. The fallen can partake of the original unity only by recollecting the pure unchanging forms. By the time of the Renaissance, Platonism had become sufficiently Christianized to provide paradigmatic ideals (such as the Garden of Eden) to convey the meaning of the earthly signs and signatures leading to the Recovery.

NARRATIVES OF DECLINE

Yet Greek narratives also depicted a slide downward from a prior golden age. Hesiod (eighth century B.C.E.) told of a time when immortal men lived "like gods" on Olympus, where all was "of gold," and were fed by the spontaneity of the earth's products. The "grain-giving soil bore its fruits of its own accord in unstinted plenty, while they at their leisure harvested their fields in contentment amid abundance." In subsequent periods—the Ages of Silver, Bronze, Heroes, and Iron, the last of which was the present age—the environment degenerated and people were subjected to unceasing agricultural work, trouble, and discord. The Golden Age and its life of leisure seemed forever lost.[2]

The degradation of the Greek environment bore out Hesiod's story. Domesticated animals covered most of the landscape, overgrazing the vegetation, devouring new shoots of grass and trees, and cutting the soils with their sharp hooves. Intensive cultivation on limited fertile soils promoted erosion and depleted nutrients, offset to some extent by contour plowing and terracing. Harvesting wood for dwellings, temples, carts, chariots, ships, furniture, weapons, and fuel wrought havoc on the higher mountain forests, reducing their extent from approximately one-half to a current one-tenth of the land cover, and resulting in erosion of soil and sand. Hunting of large animals and birds, fishing and shellfish gathering; quarrying of marble; and mining for gold, silver, and iron depleted biota and nonrenewable ores.[3]

Plato, in the *Critias*, described the environmental destruction. In ancient times—nine thousand years ago—the gods had tended humans as if they were sheep, guiding them not by force, but as a helmsman steers a boat. Society comprised artisans, farmers, and warriors and the land supported the people, as well as a vast army. Attica contained excellent fruits, pastures for animals, and brought forth an abundance of produce. Wood was plentiful, the hills and plains contained rich soils, and rainfall was captured in streams, rivers, and fountains. Trees were tall and of sufficient diameter to form strong roof timbers. Plato goes on to observe: "Such was the natural state of the country, which was cultivated . . . by true husband-men, who made husbandry their business. [It] had a soil the best in the world, and abundance of water, and in the heaven above an excellently attempered climate." Now, however, the remnant of land that still existed was "a mere skeleton," in which remained only "the bones of a wasted body." Only traces of timber were to be found in the mountains, and the woodlands sustained only bees. Rainfall was no longer absorbed by the soil, but poured down the barren hills to the sea, eroding the land.[4]

Roman writiers were likewise sensitive to environmental destruction. Ovid, in the *Metamorphoses* (c.e. 7) depicted the changes to nature and humanity after the decline from an initial golden age. The golden age, he held, was a time when a bountiful (unplowed) mother earth brought forth grains, fruits, honey, and nectar. People were happy, peaceful, "unaggressive, and unanxious." Spring lasted forever, people gathered berries on the mountains, and the wind blew gently across native flowers. But in the subsequent silver, bronze, and iron ages, swindling, strife, violence, and war became commonplace. People dug into the earth for gold and mother earth gave birth to monsters in the shape of men who were "contemptuous of gods, and murder-hungry and violent."[5]

This Greco-Roman framework of decline from a prior state of leisure, happiness, and plenty in a bountiful, diverse environment to one of labor and discord in a degraded environment is similar to the loss of a life of leisure in the Garden of Eden depicted in the biblical stories.

NARRATIVES OF PROGRESS

The Roman tradition, however, also generated a progressive narrative based on the cycles of nature and a positive view of human potential. During the Renaissance, this narrative would become incorporated into a story of human and natural development set out in stages. Virgil (70–19 B.C.E.) wrote of a progress from "savagery" to "civilization" imbedded within a metanarrative of cyclical return. Nature was a principle of development that derived from the Latin word *nascere*, "to be born." Each developmental stage was inherent in its predecessor—an actualization of a prior potential. The word *nation* also derived from *nascere*; hence the nation-state was born from the state of nature.[6]

Virgil's narrative of the development from nature to nation moves through four stages that mimic the human life cycle. The first stage is death and chaos—a world filled with presocial "wild" peoples (winter). This gives way to stage two: birth and the pastoral, in which people graze their sheep on pastured lands (spring). The third stage is symbolized by youth or farming, by plowing and planting gardens (summer). Stage four is maturity, represented by Rome as the city in the garden (fall). Virgil believed that these stages continually cycled, so that stage four was followed by a return to death and chaos. This contrasts with the Christian myth, where recovery leads to redemption and a return to the original Garden of Eden. Within each of Virgil's stages, however, lies the potential to lapse prematurely into the earlier chaotic or "savage" state.

The *Eclogues*, or pastoral poems, characterize Virgil's idyllic stage two. Human labor has domesticated animals, transformed forests into meadows, and dammed springs to form pools for watering livestock. But Virgil's shepherd is relatively passive, watching flocks while reclining in the shade of a tree. This pastoral stage is like the Christian Garden of Eden—its loss is mourned and its innocence yearned for—but in the Roman story, the pastoral passes "naturally" to the third, or agricultural, stage.

Virgil's *Georgics*, or agricultural poems, describe a period in which humans actively labor to cultivate not only the earth but themselves. In this stage, the potentials of both society and earth are actualized and perfected. When farmers till the ground and tend their crops, nature's bounty brings forth fruits: "Father Air with fruitful rains" descends on the "bosom of his smiling bride" to feed her "teeming womb." Agriculture is initiated by one of the most important gods, Jove, who earlier had "endowed that cursed thing the snake with venom and the wolf with thirst for blood." "Toil taught men the use and method of the plough." Agricultural instruments are forged for the first time, becoming "weapons hardy rustics need ere they can plow or sow the crop to come."[7]

The *Aeneid* reveals Virgil's view of the fourth stage. Here Rome emerges as a city of culture and civilization within a pastoral and agricultural landscape. This is *urbs in horto*—the city in the garden. The four developmental phases of nature and nation exist both temporally as stages and spatially as zones. The city actualizes the progression from a chaotic "wild" periphery, through a pastoral outer zone and a cultivated inner zone, to a central "civilized" place. Because nature is viewed as a cyclical development, the decline and fall of Rome is preordained in the final return to winter and chaos.

Yet a second golden age evolves from this chaos as "the great line of the ages is born anew." The "virgin" (justice) returns and a "newborn boy" appears "at whose coming the iron race shall first cease and a golden race will spring up in the whole world." The Roman idea of a newborn child and the Christian vision of the incarnation of Christ converge, offering future Europeans and Americans the possibility of a new birth into an Edenic golden age.[8]

Like Virgil, the Roman poet Lucretius (98–55 B.C.E.) saw nature as a movement from savagery to civilization, but unlike Virgil's optimistic story of continual rebirth, Lucretius's story is pessimistic and tragic. Nevertheless, it too points toward the possibility of a progressive outcome. In *De Rerum Natura* (*Of the Nature of Things*) the early state of human nature was disorderly, lawless, and chaotic. Before the discovery of plow agriculture, wild beasts consumed humans and starvation was rampant. But early civilization, nurtured by the taming of fire and the cooking of food, foundered on the discovery of gold, as violent wars were spawned by human greed. Lucretius lamented that "things down to the vilest lees of brawling mobs succumbed, whilst each man sought unto himself dominion and supremacy." But out of chaos came order and civilization. People out of their own free will submitted to laws and codes. The creation of civil law imposed order on disorderly humans.[9]

Lucretius's pessimistic view of nature and human nature presaged political theorist Thomas Hobbes's (1588–1679) "state of nature" and "war of all against all," out of which would emerge the seventeenth century social-contract theory of government, a political philosophy integral to the Recovery Narrative (see chapter 4). In Lucretius's poem, humans were competitive and warlike, contesting with each other on the commons and in the marketplace. The poem ended in death, as plague and pestilence overcame the city, breaking off on a note of extreme pessimism and utter terror as piles of dead bodies burned on funeral pyres and all hope was lost. Similarly, the earth went through cycles of life and death. At first, the earth "who deserves her name as mother" brought forth birds, beasts, and humans. "When the earth and air were younger, more and larger things came into being." The fields were like wombs, and the earth's pores gave forth milk like a mother's breasts. But when the earth aged, she became a worn-out woman. Nature died, returning to the chaos of winter.[10]

The Greco-Roman view of nature as a cyclical process of movement from savagery to civilization and back to conflagration and rebirth would be transformed to one of a linear escape from the earth to a heavenly Eden in the Middle Ages and to a recovery of Eden on earth during the Scientific Revolution of the seventeenth century.

ROMAN AND CHRISTIAN STORIES CONVERGE

During the final years of the Roman Empire, the Greco-Roman tradition of confidence in human reason, physical ability, and potential to transform the Earth was challenged by the Christian view of escape from the Earth into other-worldly salvation. Greeks and Romans had seen themselves as godlike men who were remarkably similar to manlike gods. Christians created a gulf between humanity and God. St. Augustine (C.E. 354–430) articulated the Christian belief that humans were sinful, fallible, and helpless. They were continually mortified by the sins of the flesh, and could seek redemption only in Christ. Their sole hope for betterment lay in the afterlife.

Between the fall of Rome (C.E. 476) and the Renaissance, Europe passed through the Dark Ages, feudalism, the Crusades, and the subsequent revival of classical learning. In the Dark Ages, communities were isolated from each other by stretches of thick forest, symbolically filled with darkness, danger, wolves, and witches. These dark forests constituted the wilderness out of which modern society would craft its narrative of emergence into enlightenment. The darkness-into-light story was consistent with a hierarchical cosmos with the dark interior of the earth at the bottom and the brilliant light of God's empyrean sphere at the top.

Over the five centuries from C.E. 1000 to 1500, forests were cut, swamps were drained, and pasture lands created. Feudal manors, including their villages and surrounding farms, and religious cloisters isolated their inhabitants from the dangers lurking in the darkness. These enclosed places constituted reclaimed, earthly gardens offering protective spaces against the wild. They reflected an effort to make the everyday realities of medieval Europe more secure. In the farmlands of England, gardens were fenced off from both hunted wild animals and herded domestic animals. Walls, hedges, and thorn fences surrounded secure, often circular, spaces. Villagers cooperatively plowed the open fields where grain was grown, while domestic animals grazed on the pastures of the commons. Forests, too, held common resources—deer, rabbits, berries, firewood, and water. Over the centuries, darkness receded into the light of open fields punctuated by church steeples reaching toward the heavens.

DANTE'S FALL AND SALVATION NARRATIVE

The primary narrative of medieval Christianized Europe was a rejection of a painful earthly wilderness and a fervid hope for a heavenly paradise in the afterlife. Although Virgil's story was a narrative of cyclical return rather than one of Fall and Salvation, the Roman poet Virgil was accepted as an early prophet of the new Christian religion. Dante Alighieri (1265–1321) chose Virgil to be his guide as he transformed the Greco-Roman cyclical plot into the medieval Fall and Salvation narrative.

Dante's *Divine Comedy* (1300) illustrates the comic, happy outcome of the search for redemption of both the fallen human soul and the fallen desecrated earth. The plot begins in a dark wilderness. Dante and Virgil move down through the levels of limbo and hell to the center of the earth. Then they progress upward to the earthly paradise on the mountain of purgatory, where the pagan Virgil leaves Dante and the Christian Beatrice takes over. Together Dante and Beatrice ascend through the highest levels of the celestial and Empyrean spheres to the heavenly paradise. Although Dante encounters the earthly Eden as part of his pilgrimage, he continues upward on his journey to salvation. The plot anticipates the redeemed earth, but does not yet embrace the modern story's possibility of reinventing the earth as Eden.[11]

In the classic comic plot, exemplified by the *Divine Comedy*, the tragic elements of decline are converted to the happy outcome of salvation. "In Christianity's vision of redemption," observes literary scholar Robert Pogue Harrison, "the entire earth and all of its nature become . . . a park, or artificial garden." In the Christian belief system, nature—including fallen human nature—is redeemed through Adam's mastery over the animals, just as Dante's own wilderness is redeemed during his epic journey. Through an individual's own will, the wilderness or animal within can be rehumanized and saved. Over historical time, the will of nature can also be tamed, sanctioned by God's own law and plan for salvation. "Whether we call it redemption or mastery," states Harrison, "this law guarantees the happy ending of the comedy as a whole."[12]

In the process of redeeming the earth, human salvation may also be found. "The comedy in this case," writes Harrison, "is 'salvation history.' Its law declares that the wildly diversified freedom of nature shall be overcome and that only the human will shall remain 'free,' in accordance with God's law." In the religious vision, nature and human nature are both integral components of the recovery process: "According to Christian doctrine, the process of redemption involves the redemption of the earth as a whole, not merely its transcendence. . . . Nature too must be drawn into the comedy."[13] The three books of the *Divine Comedy* structure the Fall and Salvation narrative.

The *Inferno* begins with Dante's own "bewilderment" in the wilderness of the "dark forest." Dante is lost, an outlaw from God's moral law. "In the middle of our life's path," he confesses, "I found myself in a dark forest, where the straight way was lost." The forest is deprived of the light of God, just as Dante's own soul is deprived of the light of salvation. The wilderness represents the animality of the fallen material world. When the landscape changes from forest to desert, it is still a wilderness, but it now leads to a mountain that reveals the light of transcendence. But beasts block Dante's way. The forest traps his will, preventing his ascent through reason to the light above. His guide, Virgil, then appears. Paradoxically, Virgil first leads him downward through the circles of Hell into the material center of the world.[14]

While lost in the forest, Dante describes nature in the wild and bleak symbols of tragedy. He finds himself in a "dark wood," a "wood of wilderness, savage and stubborn," "a bitter place." The beasts that spring across his path are the wild beasts of the forest and jungle—a leopard, a lion, and a she-wolf. The mountain that he must ascend seems to be a "barren slope," a "wasteland," an "evil place." Turning downward under Virgil's guidance, Dante descends into hell, crossing a "desert slope" in a "whirling storm" surrounded by "air of endless black." The travelers encounter the souls of the damned, tormented by hornets, wasps, and "disgusting maggots." Nature is portrayed as a fallen world caused by the sin of Adam and Eve. "As in autumn when the leaves begin to fall, one after the other. . . so did the evil seed of Adam's Fall drop from that shore. . . ."[15]

When Dante emerges from hell onto the opposite side of the world, he encounters the mountain of purgatory. During his climb up the mountain, he articulates a new vision of human possibility consistent with the classical learning represented by Virgil. On completing his ascent, Dante once again finds himself in a forest. But this time it is the prelapsarian forest of the earthly paradise—the Garden of Eden. In this divine forest all savagery has vanished; it is a forest redeemed as a park. This "heavenly forest" is "thick with living green," filled with "sweet air," the "joyful sounds" of birds, and the "clearest of all waters on our earth." It is an "ancient wood," the "cradle of mankind," a land "rich in every species." Its trees

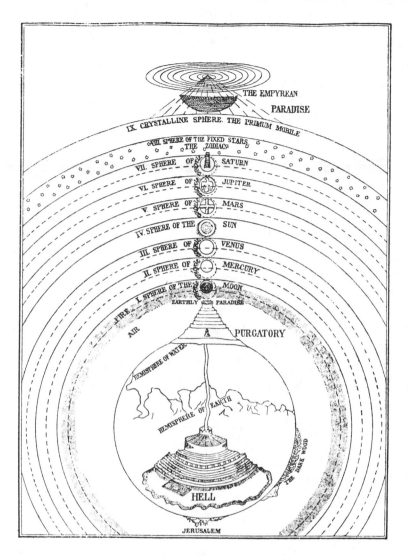

Fig. 3.1. Dante's concept of the cosmos was earth-centered, with Hell on the opposite side of the earth, Purgatory above the earth, and Paradise in the realm of the Empyrean, beyond the spheres of the planets and fixed stars. "Dante's Conception of the Universe," reproduced from F. J. C. Hearnshaw, *Medieval Contributions to Modern Civilisation* (New York Henry Holt, 1922)

bring forth "fruit that no man has ever plucked on earth."[16] This vision of the earthly Eden will constitute modernity's Recovery Narrative.

In this divine forest, Dante encounters the consequences of Eve's original sin. He is indignant: "The righteous zeal made me curse the presumptuousness of Eve: to think that, while all earth and Heaven obeyed His will, a single woman, newly made, would dare strip off the veil imposed by Him!" Eve should have been submissive rather than willful. But if Eve is responsible for the loss of the earthly paradise, Beatrice represents the possibility of attaining the heavenly one. She appears here for the first time as Dante's new guide.

Dante walks with Beatrice "through the high wood, empty now because of her who listened to the snake."[17] He encounters the "Tree of the Knowledge of Good and Evil" whose "every branch has been stripped of leaf and fruit." On their approach, however, the tree bursts into bloom as if springtime has just arrived. The blooming tree symbolizes the possibility of a redeemed earth. Dante falls asleep and awakens to see apples on the tree, symbolizing Christ and the promise of resurrection. He feels himself to be "a tree renewed, in bloom with newborn foliage, immaculate, eager to rise, now ready for the stars." Yet even this renewed promise does not tempt him to linger in this earthly Eden. He continues the upward journey toward the heavenly Eden and the possibility of salvation above the earth.[18]

With Beatrice guiding him, Dante ascends through the celestial spheres toward the heavenly paradise. This heavenly territory is portrayed in happy, comic symbols. A stream flows "between two banks painted by spring in miracles of color." Sparks of dew reflecting off fragrant flowers look "like rubies set in rings of gold." The Empyrean heaven is a "hillside rich in grass and flowers," and the souls of the redeemed are reflected in a serene lake. The petals of an eternal rose open perfectly before him. Here "God rules directly without agents" and the "laws of Nature in no way apply." The wilderness of the Inferno has given way to the garden park of purgatory, which in turn has been replaced by the rose of paradise. Darkness has been transcended, material nature vanquished, and wilderness mastered by law. God's law, says Harrison, is the "will of civilization to overcome nature and achieve unconditional human mastery over the earth."[19]

When he reaches the heavenly paradise, Dante first focuses on the Virgin Mary so he can gain the strength to see "the lovely garden flowering in the radiance of Christ." Sitting at Mary's left is Adam, "that father, the one through whose presumptuous appetite mankind still tastes the bitterness of shame." Saint Peter sits on her right. Adam represents belief in the Christ to come, while Saint Peter symbolizes the Christ already come.

Fig. 3.2. After the Fall from Eden, labor was divided between the sexes. Here Adam labors in the earth with his spade, while Eve rocks her child's cradle and spins. Ludolphus of Saxony (d. 1378). *Speculum humanae salvationis* (early 15th century). Courtesy of Corpus Christi College, Oxford University

Adam, who paid the penalty for his sin for over five thousand years, has been redeemed and is now in heaven.[20]

Eve, however, is nowhere to be found. She is absent from the comedy, berated for her sin, and only acknowledged as the mother of all mankind. It is another woman, Beatrice, who with Christ guides Dante toward resurrection. Beatrice is an intellectual pilot who answers his fumbling questions with clear logic and sets up scientific experiments with mirrors and light rays to demonstrate her points. She prefigures *scientia*—Enlightenment science as the road to the recovery of paradise.[21]

EVE AS THE FALL, MARY AS THE RECOVERY

Eve is blamed even more forcefully for the loss of paradise in subsequent versions of the Fall and Salvation narrative. The late fourteenth-century writer Ludolphus of Saxony's (d. 1378) *The Mirror of Man's Salvation*

Fig. 3.3. Eve offers Adam an apple from the Tree of the Knowledge of Good and Evil in the Garden of Eden. *Adam and Eve*, Lucas Cranach, 1526. Courtauld Institute Gallery, Somerset House, London, used by permission

(*Speculum humanae salvationis*), and artist Lucas Cranach's "Adam and Eve" (1526) made Eve responsible for the loss of Eden. Ludolphus's version begins with Lucifer's "fall" from God's grace. Lucifer descends from heaven into hell, and then returns as a serpent to tempt Eve. He selects the woman for his victim, believing her to be less wise and wary than the man. Eve was created not from Adam's foot to be despised, nor from his head to override him, but from his side to be his helpmate. But Eve violated her mandate causing the Fall from paradise.

Had she remained sweet and meek, Ludolphus asserted, paradise would never have been lost. In responding to Lucifer's temptation, Eve attempted to be like God. Adam, on the other hand, ate the fruit only out of love for Eve: "The woman therefore sinned more than the man because she thought herself capable of being made like God."[22]

Ludolphus warned his readers to be wary of wicked women and to admire the nobility of Adam. Eve's boldness had caused her husband's fall along with her own. If God's commandment had been kept, neither death, illness, adversity, nor natural disaster (in the form of fire, floods, or wild beasts) would ever have been cast on "man." A similar message is conveyed by Lucas Cranach. Here Eve is the bold instigator of the unfortunate experiment, while Adam is a reluctant participant.

The outcome of the medieval narratives is that through Christianity, the Fall can be reversed by the hope of Salvation, presaging the optimism of the modern Recovery Narrative. The Virgin Mary's womb becomes a metaphor for the garden into which the Holy Ghost cast his special blessing, producing Christ as mankind's savior. The enclosed garden symbolized the womb of the virgin. Mary was a garden of sweetness, blossoming with the fullness of life. She offered hope for recovering heaven.

Dante and Ludolphus play critical roles in setting up the modern Recovery Narrative. Their stories are compelling, blaming Eve for the Fall and crediting the possibility of Recovery to Beatrice and Mary. Eve represents fallen nature, which must be transformed and redeemed, while Beatrice and Mary symbolize the recovered garden that can be penetrated through science and faith. But while Eve's curiosity initiates the Fall, it also sets up a method of questioning nature that Beatrice's enlightened knowledge brings to fruition. While Mary's womb symbolizes the enclosed medieval garden, its penetration also sets up the possibility of the expansive, geometrically designed gardens of the eighteenth century Enlightenment.[23]

THE VIRGIN MARY AS GARDEN

Small enclosed gardens, symbols for the womb of the Virgin, were cultivated outside churches and monasteries in medieval Europe. Like the
ancient goddesses of Mesopotamia and Egypt who awakened the fertility
of the land, the Virgin Mary was associated with the fertility of the garden and the harvest of crops. Like the mother goddess Ishtar holding her
son Tammuz on her lap and Isis suckling her son Horus, the virgin Mary
cradles the infant Jesus. Art historian Pamela Berger, in *The Goddess
Obscured*, traces the transformation of the Greco-Roman grain protectress
Ceres (Demeter) into Mary, mother of the male Christ. Demeter is shown
holding stalks of wheat, with serpents around her arms. By the eleventh
century C.E., the grain protectress is shown nursing a serpent and cow. In
later paintings, she appears with Adam and Eve on her lap, with the snake
now depicted as the serpent of the Garden of Eden story. In the grain miracle stories of the medieval Christian church, the grain protectress was
transformed into a saint, protecting the harvest from evil and miraculously
causing grain to ripen as she passed. Over the course of time, Mary
replaced Demeter, obscuring the pagan origins of the grain goddess and
replacing her with a Christian symbol.[24]

The medieval enclosed gardens also symbolized the mysteries of
womanhood, the sexual purity of the Virgin, and the association of virginity with the Garden of Eden. Christ grew in the womb of the Virgin
Mary, just as the tree of life had grown in the Garden of Eden. A monk,
by symbolically penetrating the womb of the Virgin, gained access to the
mysteries of everlasting life once found in Eden. Sacred herbs facilitated
the path to redemption. Their emblematic qualities could be ingested
visually, psychically, or physically to simulate a resemblance between the
individual soul and God.[25]

The enclosed garden was infused with sexual imagery. This *hortus con-
clusus* derived from erotic passages in the biblical Song of Solomon: "A
Garden enclosed is my sister, my spouse; a spring shut up, a fountain
sealed." In Geoffrey Chaucer's *Merchant's Tale* (c. 1386), the lover,
Damyan, fabricates a key to unlock the circular garden and makes love to
a maiden sitting in a fruit-bearing tree. In gaining access to the garden, the
male lover simultaneously penetrates the female womb.

The enclosed garden not only symbolized sexual access to the inner
secrets of nature, it contrasted sharply with the wilderness outside its walls.
The sixteenth century French painting *St. Genevieve with her Flock* por-

Fig. 3.4. The medieval enclosed garden, shown here as a circle of stones protecting St. Genevieve and her flocks, symbolized an Edenic age in which humans and animals lived in harmony. *St. Genevieve Guarding her Flock* (Oil on canvas) by French School, 16th century, Musée de la Ville de Paris, Musée Carnavalet, Paris, France, archives Charmet/Bridgeman Art Library, used by permission

trays the consecrated virgin (Patron Saint of Paris) with a flock of sheep encircled by a protective stone wall set on a hillside with trees and flowers. The wilderness outside the garden contains the thorns, thistles, and serpents of the desert as well as the wolves, bears, and stags of the dark forest. These wild beasts reveal a fallen nature run amok, depicting the landscape of the Fall from Eden.[26]

The enclosed garden of the medieval world exhibits the potential for the practice of a partnership ethic between people and the earth, inasmuch as the garden is small and can be tended by a caring gardener who assists the earth in bringing forth life. The small-scale garden and the cooperative field system of the medieval period could fulfill both human needs and nature's needs for the reproduction of life. But the symbolic associations of the enclosed garden that posit domesticity against a negative wilderness and female against male undercut its potential for a sustainable partnership. The direction of mainstream culture was away from the small-scale garden and rotated fields and toward the estate garden as display of power and the plantation as large-scale agriculture.

During the seventeenth century, Francis Bacon would combine the idea of a fallen nature caused by Eve's disobedience with the idea of regaining the garden by penetrating the female womb. His Recovery project proposed wresting from nature "her" secrets in order to recover the dominion lost in the Fall (see chapter 4). This story, written by Bacon and the fathers of modern science from the "book of nature," presented the possibility of recreating the entire earth as a new Eden. It was propelled both by a new hope of restoring the perfection of Adam and by the millenarianism of the late Middle Ages.[27]

MILLENARIAN OPTIMISM

The redemption of fallen humanity and the fallen earth at the millennium is described in the biblical Book of Revelation. From this source, Joachim of Fiore (1135–1202) constructed a dramatic historical narrative that gave hope of restoring the earth and recovering the Garden of Eden. History's narrative structure now moved from the Creation (where Adam and Eve lived within God's garden) to the Fall (which severed man from God) to the Redemption, when humanity recovered the garden and the tree of life and returned to the original oneness with God. History had three ages, corresponding to the Father, the Son, and the Holy Spirit. The Old Testament began with the Creation and the Fall and covered the period through the Incarnation of Christ, while the New Testament spanned the Incarnation to the Last Judgment envisioned in Revelation. Joachim's narrative thus reversed the tragedy of the Fall to the comedy of creating a New Earth through the Second Coming of Christ.[28]

Millenarian sects anxiously awaited the Second Coming and the salvation and new life it promised. The year 1000 represented a rupture, or apocalyptic moment in history. The three nines of 999 and 1999 and the three zeros of 1000 and 2000 are numbers with cosmic import. The year 1000 was viewed as "an evening of the world," and as the year 999 progressed, cultural and artistic work in the monasteries of Europe came to a halt in anticipation of the millennium.[29]

The hope of creating the new earth through technology was suggested by John Scotus Erigena as early as the ninth century. Erigena called for the mechanical arts to assist humanity in its Recovery of the dominion lost by Adam in the Fall. Although Adam had full knowledge of the "useful arts," he had lost those insights through original sin. Like Plato, Erigena believed that humans once possessed full knowledge of truths that were now obscured in mankind's fallen state. Study of the arts, however, could assist humanity in regaining its initial state of perfection. The mechanical arts were humanity's link to God, and their pursuit was a means to redemption. Erigena suggested that recovery of the arts would restore fallen man to his state of original perfection and oneness with God.[30]

Influenced by Erigena, the twelfth-century canon, Hugh of St. Victor, concurred that developing the crafts in the present fallen world could contribute to the restoration of original perfection. Michael Scot (ca. 1175–1253) and Vincent de Beauvais (d. 1264) followed Hugh of St. Victor, proposing that "the primary purpose of the human sciences is to restore fallen man to his prelapsarian condition."[31]

The Franciscan scholar and scientist Roger Bacon (ca. 1210–1292) brought together Joachim of Fiore's narrative—that the end of history was the advent of a new earth—with the idea that humanity could restore its likeness to God through the mechanical arts. He advocated that these arts should be developed to prepare for the final battle against Satan (the Antichrist), and human knowledge lost in the Fall must be restored. The restoration story that took shape during the Renaissance coincided with the development of the mechanical arts—mills, pumps, gears, bridges, and presses—that processed nature's resources into items useful for the improvement of "man's estate." The great technological breakthroughs of the Renaissance—the printing press, the compass, and gunpowder—helped to propell the explorations of the New World and the trade of the emerging nation-states.[32]

EDEN MAPPED AND EXPLORED

The New World explorations were next steps toward first finding and then recreating Eden on earth. On his third voyage in 1498, Christopher Columbus believed he had discovered the Garden of Eden on the mainland of what is now known as South America. Here, "in the land I call Gracia, I found quite a mild climate where the land and the trees are as green and lovely as the orchard of Valencia in April." He associated the four rivers he found there with the four rivers flowing out of Eden. In a

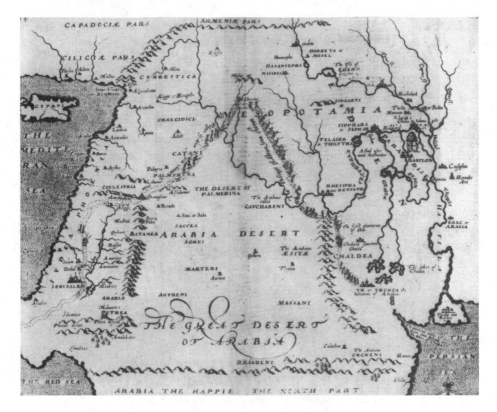

Fig. 3.5. Sir Walter Raleigh depicted the Garden of Eden, with its two trees and four
rivers (the Tigris, Euphrates, Pison, and Gihon) flowing from it, in Mesopotamia. Sir Walter Raleigh, *The History of the World* (1614). Courtesy of the Bancroft Library, University of California, Berkeley

letter he wrote, "Holy scripture testifies that Our Lord made the earthly paradise and in it placed the tree of life, and from it issues a fountain that produces the four great rivers of the world, the Ganges, the Tigris, the Euphrates, and the Nile. I do not find in any of the writings of the Romans or Greeks anything that establishes the location of this earthly paradise, nor have I seen it authoritatively placed on any map of the world. I do not believe that the earthly paradise in is the form of a rugged mountain as it has been described. Instead, I believe that it is at the summit of this pearlike protuberance, to which one can gradually ascend. . . . here I have found all the signs of this earthly paradise."[33]

Other explorers corroborated this Edenic description of the new lands of the Americas. In 1518 Alonxo da Zuarza called Hispaniola "an enchanted island where the fountains play, the streams are lined with gold, and where nature yields her fruits in marvellous abundance." The flowers of America reminded Amerigo Vespucci of Eden, while Simão di Vasconcelos located the earthly paradise in Brazil.[34]

Others located Eden in the Old World. Sir Walter Raleigh, in his 1614 *History of the World*, mapped Eden across the Arabian Desert in Mesopotamia. He depicted paradise and the four rivers flowing from it—the Tigris, Euphrates, Gihon, and Pison—beside an image of the tree of the knowledge of good and evil; Adam and Eve were shown below the tree. P. D. Huet's *De la situation du paradis terrestre* (1691) also set the terrestrial paradise in Mesopotamia near the Persian Gulf. Solomon van Til concurred. In 1719 he depicted Eden as a forest plantation of regularly planted trees located in Mesopotamia.[35]

A new attitude of mastery over nature accompanied the rise of mercantile capitalism made possible by both New and Old World explorations. As trade quickened in the northern countries of Europe, entrepreneurs mined the earth for metals, cut the forests for ships, and constructed roads, bridges, and mills. Nobles enclosed their fields for private use, producing grain and wool for local and international markets. Pasture sizes increased and an agricultural improvement movement stressed higher yields. Medieval symbols were traded for modern representations appropriate to the emerging capitalist economies.

RECREATING THE EARTHLY EDEN

Having discovered the apparent location and remnants of Eden, scientists took the next step in constructing the modern Recovery Narrative: they attempted to re-create the Garden of Eden physically. Seventeenth century botanical gardens and zoos were among the earliest efforts to reassemble the parts of the garden dispersed throughout the world after the Fall and the Flood. The scattered parts were collected and reassembled in one place to re-create the book of nature. Formal gardens were designed, planned, and superimposed on the "natural" landscape and meticulously maintained by the modern gardener. The gardens at Padua (1545), Leyden (1587), Oxford (1621), and Paris (1626) were laid out in squares with numbered beds and central fountains. They featured plants collected from the four quarters of the globe—Asia, Africa, Europe, and America. These ordered gardens symbolized both an improvement of nature through labor and an improvement of the human condition.[36]

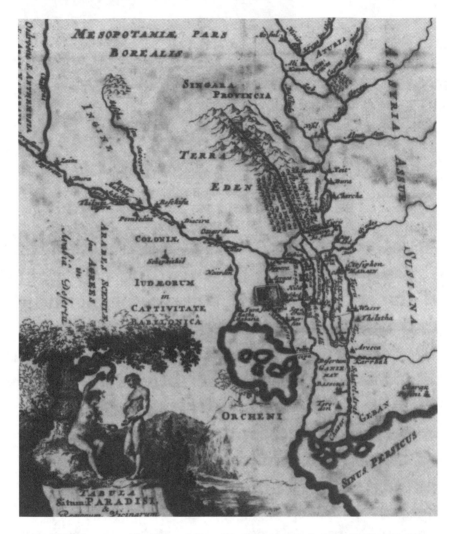

Fig. 3.6 Salomon van Til envisioned "Terra Eden" as a forest plantation in Mesopotamia, watered by mountain snows, out of which flowed the four Biblical rivers. Til, Salomon van. *Dissertationes philologico—theologicae*. Lugd. Batav., 1719, Tabula paradisi [map]. General Research Division, The New York Public Library, Astor, Lenox and Tilden Foundations.

During the seventeenth century, the "gamekeeper cultures" of the medieval period became the "garden cultures" of the modern world. According to sociologist Zygmunt Bauman, the premodern rulers or feudal lords were more like gamekeepers than monarchs. The gamekeeper-lord maintained his territory in a state of self-reproduction rather than molding and cultivating it in accordance with a preconceived plan as would a modern gardener. The "wild" plants and animals, including humans, lived off their own resources in response to time-evolved habits. The gamekeeper-ruler acted as a supervisor, or guardian, of this existing order. The earth continued to produce its own goods, while the gamekeeper guarded against "illegal" poaching by outsiders for the sake of his own subjects.[37]

The garden cultures of modernity, epitomized by the formal organization of Louis XIV's (1643–1715) palace and grounds at Versailles, represented a new form of social order. As opposed to a refuge against the wild, the modern garden was an active intervention in nature that remade the wild into the tame. The nobility's vast rectangular gardens displayed the power and wealth of the upper classes over both nature and the lower orders of society. The ornately walled gardens, with their carefully tended geometric beds of flowers, elaborate statuary, and elegant fountains that could be turned on and off to amaze visitors demonstrated the control of nature and society made possible through wealth.[38]

The stately garden of modernity had to be maintained against the encroachment of the social wilderness just outside its boundaries. In addition to the weeds, pests, and wild beasts that could undermine the garden's inherent order, there were social undesirables. Immigrants, minorities, misfits, and the dregs of society had to be kept beyond the garden gates. As opposed to feudal gamekeepers, modern gardeners required a higher level of self-conscious hubris to organize the land and society. They remade the entire territory around them in the image of a new social order. They developed and transmitted new techniques for ruling and maintaining an emerging political order through the power of the modern state.[39]

Yet the formal garden represented only the nascence of a much wider project to transform the entire earth into a garden. Elites came to believe that Eden could be re-created not only by assembling its pieces into gardens and zoos and by laying out geometrical patterns on the estates of nobles, they embraced the far grander vision that the whole earth could be reinvented as a second Eden.[40]

In settling the New World, a new earth could be reconstructed using the original garden as the paradigmatic ideal. The earth could be plowed, cultivated, and improved as people mixed their labor with the soil. Science and technology would be the means of transforming nature, while labor in the earth would be the means of saving human souls. Both the cultivated earth and cultivated humans could be prepared for the final moment of

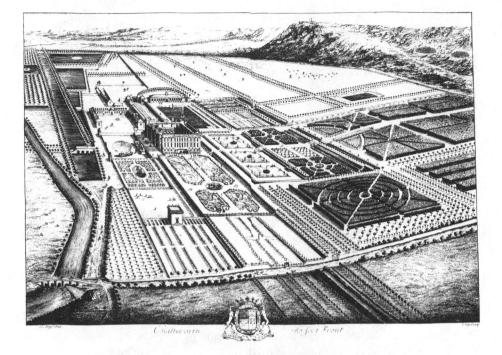

Fig. 3.7. The formal garden of the early modern world was a display of power that ordered the land in geometrical patterns, sharply demarcating the civilized world from the mountainous wilderness beyond. "Chatsworth Garden," reproduced from Johannes Kip, *Britannia illustrata* (London: H. Overton and J. Hoole, 1709), courtesy William Andrews Clark Memorial Library, University of California, Los Angeles

redemption, or parousia, when earth would merge with heaven to restore the original oneness.

The Recovery of Eden through its reinvention on earth is premised on the transformation of wilderness into garden. Nature must move from outlaw to law. This transformation of nature as active force to nature as law is reflected in the Renaissance distinction between *natura naturans* (nature naturing) and *natura naturata* (nature natured). As Eustace Tillyard explains in *The Elizabethan World Picture*, "This giving a soul to nature—nature, that is, in the sense of *natura naturans*, the creative force, not of *natura naturata*, the natural creation—was a mildly unorthodox addition to the [levels of] spiritual or intellectual beings. . . . [Richard] Hooker, orthodox as usual, is explicit on this matter. [Nature] cannot be allowed a will of her own. . . . She is not even an agent. . . [but] is the direct and involuntary tool of God himself."[41] Nature's chaos must be subdued.

CONCLUSION

Renaissance thinkers believed that both nature and human nature could be managed by natural law. To do so, the state of nature as an unruly and unpredictable form of "natural" society needed to become the predictable, manageable state of civil society. The unpredictability of nature's droughts, diseases, and disasters needed to be tamed. During the seventeenth century, the Genesis narrative of the Fall into wilderness and the medieval story of the Fall and Salvation would be converted to the modern Enlightenment story of the Recovery of Eden on earth. The declensionist narrative depicting a precipitous fall from Eden to desert, the slide downward from golden age to Iron Age, from original wisdom to ignorance, was reversed by hope of Recovery. Both nature and human nature were capable of redemption. The way upward could be found through science, technology, capitalist development, and a new vision of the modern state.

FOUR

From Wilderness to Civilization

WHEN I LOOK BACK, THE GARDEN IS A DREAM TO ME. IT WAS BEAUTI-
FUL, SURPASSINGLY BEAUTIFUL, ENCHANTINGLY BEAUTIFUL; AND NOW IT
IS LOST, AND I SHALL NOT SEE IT ANY MORE. . . . I HAVE LEARNED A
NUMBER OF THINGS, AND AM EDUCATED NOW, BUT I WASN'T AT FIRST. I
WAS IGNORANT AT FIRST. . . . IT IS BEST TO PROVE THINGS BY ACTUAL
EXPERIMENT; THEN YOU KNOW; WHEREAS IF YOU DEPEND ON GUESSING
AND SUPPOSING AND CONJECTURING, YOU WILL NEVER GET EDUCATED.
—*Mark Twain, "Eve's Diary"*

Recovering the lost Eden became Western culture's major project during the Scientific Revolution of the seventeenth century. Reason and experiment were the keys to reinventing Eden on earth. During this century-long transformation, the Fall and Salvation narrative of the Middle Ages was secularized. Rather than an escape from the earth to a heavenly Eden, the new narrative remade the planet in the image of the lost Eden. Explorations of the New World, expanding capitalism, and the rise of science and technology stimulated new visions for the mind and new possibilities for the land. In this chapter I argue that a secular Recovery Narrative took shape that offered a new story within which members of a rising middle-class could live their lives. Upward mobility, provided by expanding industries in Europe and property ownership in New World colonies, sparked the hopes of many for a better worldly life. In the Protestant countries of northern Europe, human labor was glorified as the means of improving nature. Nature could be reshaped to reclaim the lost Eden, while New World Edens could be settled and improved. A new scientific understanding of God as the laws of a rationally apprehended universe paved the way to the Enlightenment of the eighteenth century. God's glory in the world was celebrated through nature and nature's laws.

The new secular Recovery Narrative emerged from both a real and perceived decline of nature. Natural resources were exploited and depleted in the making of the modern world. Forests were cut, swamps drained, rivers dammed, common lands enclosed, wildlife decimated, and biotic diversity depleted. During the same period, elites lamented the "decay of nature," as order in both society and the cosmos seemed to be breaking down. Here I will show how an environmental narrative of declining resources and the "decay of nature" prepared the way for the mainstream, secular Recovery Narrative. My own view is that however beautiful and compelling the Scientific Revolution's analysis of nature as a mathematical order may be, its very success also implicates it in the domination of nature. The very linearity and determinism of its mathematical analysis, combined with its construction of nature as passive and manipulable, preclude the possibility of a sustainable partnership. Nevertheless, the beginnings of environmental conservation and wilderness appreciation that become elements of a sustainable partnership begin to emerge by the late seventeenth century.

TRANSFORMING THE EUROPEAN ENVIRONMENT

During the twelfth and thirteenth centuries, populations all over Europe gradually increased, rising from around thirty six million in 1000 to about eighty million in 1300, stimulating the reclamation of arable and pasture lands from surrounding forests and wetlands. In 1000, the peninsulas and islands of Europe (Italy, Spain, Portugal, Denmark, the Netherlands, and the British Isles) had been about 5–10 percent forested; in France, Germany, and Austria a quarter of the land was in forests; and in central Europe and Scandinavia one to two-thirds of the land was forested. As towns grew, food surpluses produced in the countryside to feed townspeople increased pressure on arable lands, stimulating additional forest clearing. The heavy plow, invented in the sixth century, and the three-field system of agriculture, introduced in France around 800, spread across Europe during the ensuing centuries. The three-field system left one-third of the arable land fallow each year, while wheat, rye, oats, barley, and peas were rotated on the remaining two-thirds. Nature's unpredictability in the form of droughts, freezes, cold winters, storms, and climate variations often meant food shortages and famines. In many regions, soils became eroded and exhausted of nutrients. Pasture and marginal soils were brought into production. By 1300, forest cover had dramatically declined over much of Europe.[1]

From the mid-fourteenth to the mid-fifteenth centuries, outbreaks of bubonic plague—another of nature's unpredictable actors—decimated populations. The "Black Death," so terrible in scope for the human populace, temporarily restored much of the land's fecundity. Forests grew back renewing timber supplies, marshes returned, and soils recovered fertility. Yet environmental recovery was short-lived as the European population again increased (from approximately ninety million in 1600 to around two hundred million in 1800). Population pressure was coupled with a new phenomenon—mercantile capitalism—that reshaped European land and life beginning in the sixteenth century.[2]

An inexorably expanding market economy, which arose in the city-states of Renaissance Italy and spread gradually to northern Europe, intensified medieval tendencies toward capitalism. Stimulated by the European discovery and exploitation of the Americas, the spreading use of money facilitated open-ended accumulation. Cities flourished as centers of trade and handicraft production, giving rise to a new class of bourgeois entrepreneurs. These new businessmen supplied ambitious monarchs with the funds and expertise to build strong nation-states, and their rise undercut the power of the landowning nobility. As commerce and trade expanded, forests were cut for lumber and charcoal, and cleared lands were turned into pastures. Between 1650 and 1750, large tracts of forested lands were cleared for agriculture and industry. Shipbuilding; tanning; glass, and soap making; and tin, lead, copper, and iron mining and smelting helped denude the forest cover. Swamps were drained, mine shafts sunk, and ore extracted from the "bowels of the earth." Streams were polluted, fish killed, and fields fouled with runoff. Everywhere, early capitalist development altered the landscape. In 1700, European land use comprised 230 million hectares of forests and woodlands, 190 million hectares of pasture lands, and 67 million hectares of croplands. By 1850, forests and woodlands had declined to 205 million hectares, while pasture had risen to 150 million hectares and croplands to 132 million hectares.[3]

FROM WILDERNESS TO CIVILIZATION

The emerging bourgeoisie adopted a new secular narrative that legitimated the changes wrought on the earth. Capitalism's origin story moves from desert wilderness to cultivated garden. In the new story, undeveloped nature is transformed into a state of civility, producing a reclaimed Garden of Eden.[4] The wild is tamed, wilderness subdued. The Recovery of Eden Narrative is the story into which most Westerners have been socialized and within which we live our lives today. This story is one of converting wilderness into ordered civil society—creating a reinvented Eden—through science, technology, and capitalism.

In the sixteenth century, the most palpable forms of undeveloped nature were forests and wastes. Wild places were synonymous with uncultivated, uninhabited forests, wastes, and deserts. While woodlots on the edges of towns and fields were known and used, deep forests were dark and unknown—places in which one might become bewildered and lost. Wastes were open, unused lands with little vegetation. "Wilde" and "wylde" pertained to untamed animals living in a state of nature and to uncultivated, undomesticated plants. "Wild" persons were viewed as savage, uncivilized, rude, uncultured, licentious, unruly, and unpredictable.[5]

The term *wilderness* derives from teutonic terms dating back to the eleventh century, such as *wildern* (wild savage land), *wilddeor* (wild deer), and *wilddren* (wild man). Wilderness was a place in which travelers might lose their way and wander aimlessly without destination. Fairy tales and folk tales portrayed forests as evil places in which a hero or heroine might be abducted and led into temptation. Satanic rituals and witches gatherings were presumed to occur in evil haunts in the deep forest. In religious terms, lost in the wilderness meant a lost soul wandering in the present world, as contrasted with a future life in heaven.[6]

But *wildrenes* and *wylderne* could also mean a retreat, a place to worship God in the desert wilderness as described in the Bible. The wilderness was thus a place in which one could gain insights into the meaning of its opposite—*civility*. The inhospitable arid desert of the Old Testament contrasted sharply with the bountiful, fruitful Garden of Eden and with the promised land of milk and honey. The expulsion from the

Garden into the wilderness equated the latter with the evil introduced when Eve submitted to the temptation of the serpent. The desert represented a land to be subdued and irrigated, a land whose fertility was tied to the scarcity of rainfall. Indeed, humanity had a mandate to "make the desert blossom as the rose (Isaiah 35:1)."[7]

The perception of nature as forested wilderness or desert became important in the modern era. For Protestants such as John Calvin, John Locke, the New England Puritans, and the pioneers who settled the American West, God had authorized human dominion over the earth. Therefore forests and deserts ought to be improved by converting them to productive farms and gardens.[8]

The idea of "civilized society" contrasts with wilderness and postdates it. The word *civic*, which appeared in English literature in the late fifteenth century, pertained to a group of people living together as a community within a well-governed social order. To be "civil" was to act in a polite, courteous, and orderly manner. To become "civilized" was to be brought out of a state of barbarism, to be instructed in the arts of living, and to be elevated in the scale of humanity. A civilized person was enlightened, refined, and polished. The term *civilization* itself appeared in the eighteenth century and pertained to a developed or advanced state of human society.[9]

THE STATE OF NATURE

At stake in defining "civil society" as an antidote to the Fall from Eden was the very meaning of nature itself. The "state of nature" was the polar opposite of "civilization." Emerging during the Renaissance was a perception that bestial characteristics and animal-like passions in the human body and soul must be suppressed in all civilized humans. The opposites of wildness and animality were civilization and humanity. During the sixteenth century the lines drawn between animality and humanity, wilderness and civilization, disorder and order, sharpened. The wild, chaotic animal-like dances and sexual encounters of witches with the devil-goat at the witches' Sabbath revealed to "civilized" Europeans the weaknesses of women for the unbridled sexual lust of animal-like copulation and of errant males for the sins of sodomy and bestiality.[10]

Tales of wilderness in European and Anglo-Saxon folklore were dramatized by fifteenth- and sixteenth-century explorations of the New World. The "savages" of the new lands became symbols of the wildness and animality that could gain the upper hand in "civilized" persons. As European elite culture set itself increasingly above nature as represented by its own medieval past and by New World "savagery," a code of manners was adopted that advocated the suppression of beastlike qualities in humans and the transformation of wildness into civility.[11]

Knowing the habits of the "savages" of North America enabled elite Europeans to characterize themselves as civilized and their own society as civil. The voyages of discovery and descriptions of America by New World colonists were used to define the meaning of wild and by extension the meaning of "civilized." Persons living in the "state of nature" were presumed to be lawless. Wild men, it was argued, had no laws, religion, property, or manners. In his *Natural and Moral History of the Indies* (1604), Joseph de Acosta asserted that the first men to inhabit the Indies were "savage men and hunters," who then "bred up" into "civill and well governed Common-weales." In 1609, Garcilaso de la Vega observed that New World natives "lived like wild beasts without religion, nor government, nor towns, nor houses, without tilling or sowing the soil, or clothing or covering their flesh. . . . Like wild beasts they ate the herbs of the field and roots of trees and fruits growing wild and also human flesh."[12]

The 1607 settlement of Jamestown in North America engendered mixed reactions concerning Indians. In 1609, a Virginia colonist found people who lived "like herds of deer in the forest." Indians were seen as being as "wilde" as "wilde beasts." While some accounts portrayed Indians as happy in the state of nature, "courteous, gentle of disposition" and "civil and merry," the Virginia Massacre of 1622 that killed many of the Jamestown colonists, reinforced European fears of Indians as wild, brutish, and savage.[13] Indians, like nature, could be chaotic and unpredictable.

Contributing to the perception of nature as an unruly and lawless place therefore were human experiences of the deep forest, biblical accounts of the desert as wilderness, the witch trials of the sixteenth and early seventeenth centuries, and perceptions of New World peoples as wild and savage. Such factors pointed to the need to restore order to society and nature.

THE DECAY OF NATURE

The idea of nature as a lawless place was reinforced by the apparent decay in the cosmos itself. By the late sixteenth century, the medieval worldview of a hierarchically ordered, immutable cosmos was breaking down. The hierarchy of the heavens, that moved upward from the earth to the moon, through the seven spheres of planets, to the fixed stars and empyrean heaven, was challenged by the work of Copernicus (1473–1543). His 1543 book *On the Revolutions of the Heavenly Spheres* placed the sun in the center of the cosmos and removed the earth to the third sphere. Tycho Brahe's (1546–1601) observations of a new star in the heavens in 1572 and of comets blazing across the sphere of the fixed stars introduced the idea of corruptibility and decay in the cosmos. In 1609, Johannes Kepler's (1571–1630) *New Astronomy* demonstrated that the planets moved in elliptical orbits, challenging the notion of perfectly circular paths. Galileo Galilei's (1564–1642) observations with the telescope in the *Sidereal Messenger* (1610) showed the moon to have craters, the sun to have spots, Jupiter to have moons, and Venus to have phases. To elite Europeans, these observations reinforced biblical notions that the decay of nature had been introduced into the world by the Fall of Man.[14]

Godfrey Goodman's *The Fall of Man*, published in 1616, carried the theme of death and decay a step further. In the Fall from Eden, humanity not only introduced death to itself, but to all of nature. The parts of man and of nature had all declined from a perfect state of youth to old age, decay, and ultimately death. The Fall introduced decay into the human body, or microcosm, which in turn produced corruption in the larger world, or macrocosm. The decay of nature was evidenced by the decline of fish in the seas, infertility in the soils, and corruption in the heavens themselves (such as spots on the moon and comets that marred the perfection of the heavenly spheres). That nature needed repair, Goodman held, was shown by the development of technology. While the ancients had not needed agriculture, living as they did in a state of abundance, the moderns, who were in a state of decline, needed it to restore the lost fertility of nature.[15]

Other writers concurred that the Fall of Man had introduced death and decay into nature itself. The seventeenth-century poet Henry Vaughan (1622–95) wrote that man "drew the Curse upon the world, and Cracked the whole frame with his fall."[16] Henceforth, he "sighed for Eden" and longed "for home." In *Paradise Lost* (1668), John Milton (1608–74) wrote that when Eve ate the apple, "Earth felt the wound, and Nature from her seat,/Sighing through all her works, gave signs of woe." The earth "trembled from her entrails," "Nature gave a second groan," and the sky "wept at completing of the mortal Sin Original."[17] But for some writers, the idea of nature's decay was set within a larger story of cyclical decay, followed by the rebirth of the earth.

THE SACRED THEORY OF THE EARTH

Thomas Burnet's *Sacred Theory of the Earth* (1684) presented an epic narrative of the decline of the earth. The story began with the Creation, and proceeded to the Fall, and then the decay, and conflagration of the entire world. The destruction, however, ended with the subsequent rebirth of the earth, thus holding out hope of regaining paradise. Like the Christian Edenic and Greek golden-age theories, Burnet's narrative began with a perfect earth in perpetual spring, lapsed into a fall and period of decay, out of which it entered a new period of rebirth and rejuvenation. The earth, Burnet believed, was formed out of chaos with the four elements all in their proper spheres, earth at the center, water on the surface, air above, and fire beyond. The original earth was "smooth, regular, and uniform; without Mountains, and without a Sea." The earth known by Adam and Eve was one of perfection, as befitted a paradise.[18]

After the fall from Eden came the Great Flood, initiating decay throughout the entire surface of the once perfect earth. In the flood, the "Earth was broken and swallowed up," and "Nature seem'd to be in a second Chaos." Storms raged on the seas; forests and cities were drowned. The irregular, malformed earth that resulted was the earth of the present era.[19]

The next stage of the earth, Burnet predicted, would be its conflagration. The fire would begin in Rome, seat of the Antichrist. After the burning ceased, paradise would be reproduced and the thousand-year reign of Christ on earth would begin. A second race of men would then arise on the new earth. This "new Order of Nature" would last until the new race rose in final conflict destroying Satan, at which time the Saints would rise to heaven, and the earth itself would become a fixed star. At that point the "whole Circle of Time and Providence" would be completed.[20]

Burnet's sacred story of the earth's decay and conflagration represented the acme of the millennial religious narratives that saw the history of the world in pessimistic terms as a Fall followed by Salvation. It appeared during the same decades that the optimistic story of upward progress was emerging. By the 1620s, the secular, mainstream Recovery Narrative was beginning to take shape under the pen of Francis Bacon.

Fig. 4.1. Thomas Burnet's cyclical theory of history represented the creation of the perfect earth, followed by the Flood of Noah whose receding waters produced the malformed earth of the present era. After the present Earth's conflagration, a New Earth would be formed and a new race would destroy Satan, at which time the Saints would rise to heaven and the Earth would become a fixed star. Thomas Burnet, *The Sacred Theory of the Earth* (1684), courtesy of the Bancroft Library, University of California, Berkeley

Fig. 4.2. The frontispiece of Francis Bacon's (Baron Verulam) *Novum Organum* (*New Organon*), 1620, showed a ship sailing between the Pillars of Hercules bearing knowledge of the world. In Greek mythology, Hercules undertook a voyage to set free Prometheus who had stolen fire from the gods for mankind's benefit. The book formed part of Bacon's *Instauratio Magna* (*The Great Instauration*), or reorganization of the sciences and restoration of man to that command over nature lost in the Fall from Eden. Francis Bacon. *Novum Organum* (1620; reprint London, 1856)

FRANCIS BACON'S RECOVERY NARRATIVE

Modernity's vision of the Recovery of Eden derives most immediately from philosopher Francis Bacon (1561–1626). Lord Chancellor to King James I, who had commissioned the King James version of the *Bible*, Bacon was a prolific and persuasive writer. In the 1620s, he energetically proclaimed a secular program for recovering paradise. Bacon believed that the human race had lost its "dominion over creation." Before the Fall, Adam and Eve were sovereign over all other creatures and "like unto God." Bacon saw science and technology as the means to control nature and thereby recover the right to the original garden: "Man by the Fall, fell at the same time from his state of innocency and from his dominion over creation. Both of these losses can in this life be in some part repaired; the former by religion and faith, the latter by arts and science." He boldly asserted that "man" can "*recover* that right over nature which belongs to it by divine bequest. . . ." Bacon's narrative plot reversed the decay of nature. It moved from the tragedy of the Fall upward to the comedy of survival and recovery.[21]

The principal villain in Bacon's secular Recovery Narrative was nature, cast in the female gender. Although Eve's inquisitiveness may have caused "man's" Fall from "his" God-given domain, for Bacon the relentless interrogation of nature (as fallen Eve) could regain it. Bacon used the inquisition and the courtroom as models for cross-examination of nature: "I mean (according to the practice in civil causes) in this great plea or suit granted by the divine favor and providence (whereby the human race seeks to *recover* its right over nature) to examine nature herself and the arts upon interrogatories."[22]

Salomon's House, in Bacon's *New Atlantis* (1624), carried the Recovery theme further. Rather than extolling the traditional erotic or contemplative entry into the virgin's womb described in the biblical Song of Solomon, Bacon advocated a forceful entry into nature's womb through the Song of Science. In the "new Atlantis," plants and animals were actively manipulated "for the relief of man's estate." Interrogating nature through experiment, the Baconian scientists of Salomon's House could recover the human dominion over nature lost by Eve. Since the Fall, nature had become chaotic and plants and animals wild and uncontrollable. But scientists could restore order to the garden by inventing docile, domesticated plants and animals, such as those in the original Garden of Eden.[23]

Other philosophers realized even more clearly than did Bacon the connections among mechanics, the trades, middle-class commercial interests, and the domination of nature. Increasingly, they spoke out in favor of "mastering" and "managing" the earth for the benefit of humankind.

THE MECHANICAL WORLDVIEW

During the seventeenth century, the Christian narrative of dominion over nature was combined with science, technology, and capitalist development to reinforce the possibility of remaking the earth as a controlled, managed Garden of Eden. Social values of order and control paved the way toward acceptance of a new narrative of dominion over nature. The mechanical worldview created by the "fathers of modern science" drew on philosophical assumptions consistent with the power of machine technologies to control the natural world. Early capitalist development was based on watermills, windmills, furnaces, forges, cranes, and pumps that transformed and multiplied the energy of sun, wind, wood, and coal to produce ships, guns, cannons, ammunition, cloth, paper, planks, flour, glass, and a myriad of iron implements and utensils. The large pumping, milling, and lifting machines found everywhere in daily life made plausible a model of nature as a machine. The cosmos was likened to a clock that regulated time in equal units. God was depicted as a clockmaker, mathematician, and engineer who constructed and directed the world from outside.

In the 1620s, French natural philosophers Marin Mersenne (1588–1648), Pierre Gassendi (1592–1655), and René Descartes (1596–1650) revived and placed in a Christian context the ancient atomic theories espoused by the Greek pagan philosophers Democritus (460 B.C.E.) and Epicurus (341–270 B.C.E.) and the Roman poet Lucretius (98–55 B.C.E.). For the mechanists, it was God who created the atoms and put them into the cosmos at the beginning of time. The world was composed of material particles in motion that combined and separated to form the external world.

For Descartes, motion was not inherent in the corpuscles themselves, but was put into the world by God at the beginning of the cosmic story and transferred from one particle to another. God sustained the created world from instant to instant throughout time. Owing to God's immutable intellect, the laws of nature were both unchanging and intelligible to the human mind. The external (extended) world of nature was described in terms of measurable quantities such as size, weight, and speed. The internal (unextended) world of the mind was the source of clear and distinct ideas—the basis for truth. The logic underlying the mathematical method was the key to valid knowledge of the external world. Mathematical descriptions of the material world were the ground of certainty and yielded the laws of nature. In his *Discourse on Method* (1637), Descartes argued that through knowing the forces of bodies we could "render ourselves the masters and possessors of nature."[24]

The assumption that nature was subject to law-like behavior meant that phenomena could be reduced to orderly predictable rules, regulations, and laws. Sir Isaac Newton's laws of mechanics and the principle of gravitation, put forward in his 1687 *Mathematical Principles of Natural Philosophy*, described the actions of the "world machine." His mechanical worldview, fully formulated by the end of the seventeenth century, restored "law and order" to a society in chaos from the wars of religion, the English civil war, and the collapse of Ptolemy's earth-centered cosmos.[25]

Modern science depends on a structural reality that allows for the possibility of control whenever phenomena are predictable, regular, and subject to natural laws. The assumption of the order of nature is fundamental to the concept of power over nature, and both are integral components of the modern scientific worldview. Such a worldview, grounded in the prediction, management, and control of nature, is completely consistent with a Christian narrative of remaking the world in the image of the Garden of Eden. By the late seventeenth century, Christianity's idea of dominion over nature had merged with science, technology, and capitalism to form the secular, mainstream Recovery Narrative.[26]

PARADISE AND PROPERTY

The mainstream Recovery Narrative entailed reshaping the earth and manipulating its resources. While science and technology made the material transformation of nature possible, capitalism gave the emerging bourgeoisie the economic tools to change the earth. Capitalist development involved a new view of property. The premodern European tradition had associated property with the principles of hierarchy and patriarchy. God had established social rules at the creation that were passed down from Adam to succeeding generations. Property maintained the social order of monarchs and feudal lords by transferring family lands through the male line. Women could hold moveble property and were themselves forms of movable property who could be controlled by men. Authority and inequality were accepted as both proper and natural. These principles, sanctioned by the biblical story of the order of creation, ruled every aspect of life from the family upwards to the community, society, and the cosmos.[27] But the emerging bourgeoisie substituted a new origin story for the evolution of private property out of the "state of nature."[28]

The acquisition of private property was the key to humanity's progress from the "state of nature" into ordered civil society. As early as 1625, Dutch statesman Hugo Grotius (1583–1645) maintained that private property had been created through stages of development when "common ownership, first of movable objects, later also of immovable property, was abandoned." In 1651 English Philosopher Thomas Hobbes's (1588–1679) *Leviathan* described the "state of nature" as a place in which there were no arts or letters and where civil society itself could not even exist.[29] By 1672, German jurist Samuel Pufendorf (1632–94) had combined Grotius' view of private property with Hobbes's concept of nature. "The race of man," Pufendorf said, "never did live . . . in a simple state of nature." When Adam gave his children permission to set up different establishments, he wrote, "those things [were] made property which [were] immediately and indivisibly of use . . . ." Private property therefore could be extracted from nature.[30]

Ownership of private property became an integral part of the emergence of civilization from the state of nature. To be civilized was to impose order on personal life; civilization represented the imposition of order on the land. Laying out an orderly grid on the landscape enclosed land within a boundary, creating the potential for its ownership as private property. The bounds of that "improved" property separated it from the wild. Outside the boundary was disorderly wilderness, inside ordered civilization. The civil was thus imprisoned within the wild—an enclosed garden that offered protection from external disorder in either nature or society.

JOHN LOCKE'S CIVIL SOCIETY

English philosopher John Locke's (1632–1704) *Two Treatises of Government* (1690) set out the ideals of the new "civil society" that viewed the entire earth as an ordered garden. Today most people read only the "Second Treatise," relegating the first to the dustbins of an arcane past. But the two treatises must be read together to grasp why Locke's version of history turned the received story of his day upside down. Locke used his expert storytelling skills to reconstruct the past. His new ordering of information was designed to convince members of both his own and opposing political persuasions. His narrative bolstered the case that government received its mandate from the order of nature in the form of parliament, not from the *Bible* in the form of monarchy.[31]

Locke's work fits squarely on the cusp between the premodern and modern traditions. His new story showed that property was essential to the possibility of a reclaimed earthly paradise. He convincingly asserted that those who owned property had received their authority to govern from nature, not as a divine right from God. His new story thus wrested power from monarchs and placed it squarely in the hands of the bourgeoisie.[32]

Locke challenged the King's ownership of property by calling on the Christian doctrine of human dominion over nature. Even before land became private, he argued, creatures in the state of nature could be owned by individuals. After the Fall, the human race retained its dominion over "every living thing that moveth on the Earth." In Locke's story, God did not intend that a king have dominion over other human beings, but "only the Dominion of the whole Species of Mankind over the inferior Species of Creatures," those created on the fifth and sixth days, namely cattle (tame animals), beasts (wild animals), and reptiles (creeping animals).[33]

God reaffirmed mankind's rule over nature after the Flood, when Noah and his sons were given dominion over the "Fowls of the Air, the Fishes of the Sea, and the Terrestrial Creatures." These creatures, Locke proclaimed, became the property of "Man" because they were essential to his self-preservation and survival. They were used to fulfill individual needs, even before the advent of private land ownership. Thus, "Man's *Property* in the Creatures was founded upon the right he had, to make use of those things, that were necessary or useful to his Being." Property, therefore, derived first and foremost from a person's "natural right" to use the "inferior Creatures" for subsistence and even to destroy them to fulfill basic needs. The state of nature, not the monarchy, therefore legitimated the existence of private property.[34]

Locke further challenged the old story of the divine right of kings by creating a new story in which civil society itself arose out of "the state of nature." In the tradition of the new science, Locke used a series of logical arguments, but it was his brilliant new story that became historically persuasive. To convince his audience, he first rewrote the story of the Fall of Adam and Eve from paradise and then showed how the human race could recover from the Fall.[35] His Recovery of Eden story is embedded in the text of his *Two Treatises of Government*. We can extract the underlying narrative logic in five "chapters:" the Creation; the Fall; the State of Nature; the Evolution of Private Property; and the State of Civil Society.

"Chapter 1," as extracted from Locke's *First Treatise*, begins with the creation of Adam and Eve. God made Adam a "perfect man, his body and mind in full possession of their strength and reason." He gave Adam the ability to act according to "the dictates of the law of reason," so he could provide for his own support immediately and completely. As man and wife, Adam and Eve constituted the first society. In Locke's new story, Eve is a modern woman. Although she was subjugated to her husband Adam, as women in Locke's day were considered to be, Locke gives her reason and includes her in the dominion over the other creatures. In a further innovative move, he significantly lets her have property in these creatures. Living in the original Eden, therefore, nature is experienced by the first couple as peaceful; human beings are by nature altruistic; and society, as constituted by the first couple, is potentially egalitarian.[36]

Locke's next "chapter," like the Bible's, details a radical disjunction: humanity falls out of Eden into "the state of nature." Here again Locke makes the story consistent with the modern world for which he is writing. In his version of the Fall, Adam and Eve have retained their God-given ability to reason. After the Fall, they became the first parents. Because the children were products of natural birth, rather than God's immediate action, they were born with undeveloped powers of reason. While subject to the "law of nature," they required maturity to fully understand and act according to the laws of reason. In Locke's narrative, reason and dominion over nature afforded the first couple and their successors the possibility of reversing the Fall. The state of nature retained its paradisiacal potential. But nature was worthless until they acted to transform it into a new paradise.[37]

In Locke's third "chapter," the progeny of Adam and Eve continue in the state of nature, where they are free to act according to their own con-science. They continue to live in this state until they voluntarily form a community and begin to act as a political body. When people agree on a common government and set of laws to live by—and where the possibil-ity for judicial appeal exists—they can move out of the state of nature to a new life in the state of civil society.[38]

PRIVATE PROPERTY AND THE RECOVERY OF EDEN

The fourth "chapter" of Locke's narrative makes the final bold leap that creates capitalism's origin story as arising out of the state of nature through the evolution of private property. Locke recasts the mandate of Genesis 1:28 ("Be fruitful and multiply, and replenish the earth, and subdue it"), incorporating what are now modern society's concepts of appropriation, property, cultivation, improvement, and money directly into his own biblical account of subduing the earth. "The law [that] man was under was for appropriating," he asserted. "God commanded, and [man's] wants forced him to labor." Locke thus sets out the conditions necessary for mercantile capitalism: the transformation of undeveloped nature through labor and private property into civilized society.[39]

In the course of the long climb out of "the state of nature" into the recovered Eden, private property emerges in three stages. It evolves from gathering, hunting, and fishing to farming, and from farming to marketing commodities. First the extracted product, then the land, and finally the fabricated commodities become an individual's property to be bartered or exchanged for money. An extracted product, such as an acorn, becomes an individual's property from the moment it is gathered and continues to be personal property through each ensuing stage: bringing it home, cooking it, and eating it. Similarly, property emerges at each stage of the hunt, from the point of spotting a deer, to pursuing and capturing the animal, and finally to eating it, when the ingested meat has become one's own bodily property. Even fish captured from the ocean, "the last great common," Locke asserts, become the property of the fisher.[40]

Locke's second stage of property development entails the activity of farming the land. Land and labor together create property. Extending Genesis 1:28, from merely subduing the earth to *enclosing* land from the commons and *owning* it as private property, Locke writes: "That was his property which could not be taken from him wherever he had fixed it. And hence subduing or cultivating the earth, and having dominion, we see are joined together. The one gave title to the other."[41]

The third stage of property development is commerce (or commercial capitalism). At this stage an individual produces commodities for exchange according to the "agreed-upon" standard of money. The seventeenth century growth in commercial enterprise generated increased production and exchange of food. But commerce also required the construction of stone quarries, coal mines, saw mills, iron works, fulling mills, cloth-dying vats, brick works, furnaces, and ships. Gold, silver, and diamonds provided the medium for exchange and the incentive to increase the number and value of the goods produced. Land could be accumulated and gold and silver could be "hoarded up," leading to an unequal distribution of wealth.

Locke argued that such accumulation was fair, because it was done by the "tacit and voluntary consent" of society as a whole.[42] The progressive accumulation of goods and improvement of land was morally justifiable because it did not deprive anyone of the possibility of individual ownership. Locke reasoned that there was still plenty of land in the world for every person to acquire their own plot, even if the population were to double! Hence, acquisition of private property held no moral onus. Moreover, governments could regulate the amount of land an individual could own, even though people could still accumulate private possessions.[43]

The fifth and final "chapter" of Locke's Recovery Narrative is the creation of civil, political society. When people move out of nature into civil society, they have vanquished the state of nature. Only war or the dissolution of government can cause a relapse—a new lapsarian moment. Locke presents civil society as a peaceful state in which people act as one political body. Any number of people can consent to give up their "natural liberty" and "put on the bonds of civil society," leaving the rest behind in the state of nature.[44] Property is the incentive that causes them to give up their natural liberty. People will give up the power of self-preservation and individual punishment of others in the "unsafe" and "uneasy" state of nature in exchange for legislative and judicial protection in the state of civil society. The gain is peace, civility, and protection of private property.[45]

Locke's new version of history made him the dominant storyteller of his age. His narrative of Fall and Recovery set up his story as the new natural story. No longer is Adam the father of kings, no longer are people mere subjects of a divinely derived monarchy. Locke presents the emergence of "civilized man" from the state of nature by domination, the appropriation of nature by ownership, and the transformation of gathered goods into items of trade and commerce as the "natural" upward course of events. Future writers would elaborate and expand this basic storyline, turning it into the idea of progress. Locke's first chapter of the Fall from Eden would quickly become a mere prologue to the assumed trajectory of civilization's rise from the state of nature into modernization. The state of nature was accepted as a fallen world that could be reshaped and reconstituted as an improved garden, an ordered landscape, a redeemed earth.[46]

ADAM SMITH'S CAPITALIST NARRATIVE

During the eighteenth century, Adam Smith and others elaborated on the Baconian-Lockean Recovery Narrative. In contrast to Locke, who had concentrated on the consequences of the Fall, Smith focused exclusively on progress. He described four phases of economic development: "The four stages of society are hunting, pasturage, farming, and commerce." While Locke's story had omitted the pastoral stage and only begun to include the implications of commercial capitalism, Smith's narrative set out a "Newtonian" system of capitalist economic laws. Smith argued that the two lower stages of hunting and pasturage should eventually be replaced by the two higher stages of agriculture and commerce in an inter-linked system. Both Locke and Smith agreed that the emergence of private property was central to the progression.[47]

Smith's system of the four stages of the development of civil society was worked out and delivered in his lectures at Glasgow University during the 1750s and '60s. It appeared in the posthumously published *Lectures on Jurisprudence* (compiled by a student in 1762–63) and in the *Wealth of Nations* in 1776. In his lectures, Smith connected each developmental stage to a mode of subsistence and a form of law and government. He cited Grotius, Hobbes, Pufendorf, and Locke as predecessors of his theory. Smith was critical of Jean-Jacques Rousseau's romantic version of "the savage life" which, he said, presented "only the indolent side" of "primitive" life. Smith's four-stage theory linked ideas of human social development with the Enlightenment concept of progress. Both ideas became very influential during the latter half of the eighteenth century.[48]

An interpretation of the state of nature as potentially good but worthless without improvement is integral to the Enlightenment's narrative of Recovery through progress, property, and polity. While nature has the potential to provide humans with the necessities of life, it is doomed to lie in waste unless transformed by human intellectual and physical labor (science and technology). But nature is also the source of the moral order that guides human development away from evil and toward good. Human society, through the administration of justice, can overcome those deficits that arise from a fallen nature and a fallen human nature.[49]

Smith argued that nature instills conscience in humans, helping them to carry out God's plan. But nature as actress can also be recalcitrant and mean, so that "she" herself must be kept in check by systems of science, technology, and justice. People must be prepared to override an unjust nature in favor of the divine plan originally imposed by God; thus, "man is by Nature directed to correct, in some measure, that distribution of things she herself would otherwise have made."[50]

Smith's reassessment of history constructed a "master narrative" in which males were the human heroes who raised society to ever higher economic levels, while women's labor was largely invisible. As Kathryn Sutherland points out, "The consumer economy which Smith celebrates declares at once the feminising properties of commodities and the strict masculine preserve of commercial activity. Establishing the ascendancy of the market place within a progressive society involved . . . its redescription as feminine space and its appropriation as the primary ground for the construction of male subjectivity in the person of the master-manufacturer. . . . Over two hundred years later, the question remains—where are the women in the wealth of nations?"[51]

The role that Smith and others assigned to men in the creation of property and polity fused premodern patriarchy with modern capitalism. It was men's role to keep unruly women, nature, and "uncivilized" peoples in check; it was civilization's role to keep wilderness in check. While private property was initially a sheltered enclosure within the wild, as capitalism became the dominant world system, property came to enclose the wild as an enclave within civilization. Order and rule surrounded the disorderly and unruly. Just as outlaws were incarcerated within the prison system, so the wild was incarcerated within the civilization system.[52]

THE ROOTS OF ENVIRONMENTAL CONSERVATION

Development of natural resources during the period of mercantile capitalism that spanned the late Renaissance to the Enlightenment produced an awareness of environmental decline and the need for its reversal through conservation. Here the possibility of environmental recovery begins to counter the downward trajectory of environmental decline. In England, a tremendous toll had been taken on the nation's forests as trees were cut for the shipbuilding and iron industries and for pasturing sheep for the clothing industry. Air and water pollution increased in urban areas due to iron manufacture, glassmaking, brewing, dying, lime burning, salt and soap boiling, and other small industries that depended on coal, wood, and charcoal. In 1661, diarist John Evelyn presented King Charles II with his book *Fumifugium*, a report on air pollution. In response to the problem of burning "sea-coal," a highly sulphurous coal that caused pneumatic distress among Londoners, Evelyn recommended that wood be substituted for coal by reforesting the woodlands surrounding the city. He also suggested that the substitution of coke for smelting be instituted, chimney heights increased, and flowers planted to offset the noxious odors of the sea-coal.[53]

In *Silva, A Discourse of Forest Trees and the Propagation of Timber in His Majesty's Dominions* (1662), Evelyn recommended that the decline of forests could be reversed by the replanting of trees. He noted that "prodigious havoc" had been wrought by the tendency to "extirpate, demolish, and raze . . . all those many goodly woods and forests, which our more prudent ancestors left standing." He recommended that England's forests be conserved, their trees replanted, and that laws be enacted to curtail cutting near navigable waterways. In France, Jean-Baptiste Colbert, minister to Louis XIV, reported to the king in 1661 that "France will perish for lack of woods." The French Forest Ordinance was passed in 1669 to reorganize the administration of the king's forests. The new method divided woods into equivalent sections to be harvested every 20 years while stands of large timber needed for shipbuilding were to be harvested every 120 years.[54]

The evolution of a conservation consciousness was supported by a new image of a designed universe with God as a wise conservator and humans as caretakers of nature. Theologian John Ray's *Wisdom of God Manifested in the Works of the Creation* (1691) argued that God expected humans to use nature's bounty to glorify their creator as they increased trade and prosperity throughout the globe. Gold and silver existed in the right abundance to use as money for commerce and trade. The abundance of life and resources on earth was evidence of the wisdom of God and his design of a "spacious and well furnished world." The present earth presented "natural advantages" to those willing to develop its vast variety of minerals, metals, animals, and plants. The "many pleasant and nourishing fruits, many liquors, drugs, and good medicines," were placed there by a wise creator whose products should be used for the improvement of human life.[55]

Similarly, William Derham's *Physico-Theology* (1713) accepted the idea of a designed earth in which humans were stewards over the creation. God made men in his own image as wise conservators whose mission was to glorify God and improve the human condition. Derham quoted Matthew 25:14: "That these things are the gifts of God, they are so many talents entrusted with us by the infinite Lord of the world, a stewardship, a trust reposed in us; for which we must give an account at the day when our Lord shall call." Like Ray, Derham called for the use and commercial development of the earth's resources, stating, "We can, if need be, ransack the whole globe, penetrate into the bowls of the earth, descend to the bottom of the deep, travel to the farthest regions of this world, to acquire wealth. . . ." Derham's language echoed that of Bacon and, like Bacon, his objective was the improvement of "man's estate," but by the late seventeenth century Derham could focus on the glory of God as manifested in the creation and humans as wise stewards of that creation. Just as God was the caretaker, steward, and wise manager of the natural world, so humans had a responsibility to imitate that mandate.[56]

In the conservation of John Evelyn and Jean-Baptise Colbert and the designed earth of John Ray and William Derham lie the roots of environmental recovery. Here an awareness of environmental decline wrought by improvident depletion of resources for commercial gain could be countered by conservation. Conservation was rooted in an ethic of human stewardship over creation while nevertheless supporting the growth of trade and commerce central to the mainstream Recovery Narrative.

THE EMERGENCE OF WILDERNESS APPRECIATION

The idea of a nature as a rational order that emerged during the Scientific Revolution led not only to conservation but to an aesthetic appreciation of nature. As civil society gained the upper hand over wild nature, an appreciation of the wild became possible. The disorder that remained outside the order of nature was divided into two states—the *negative wild* and the *positive wild*. The negative wild was exemplified by unruly passions aroused by the baseness of the body; the positive wild by the sublime passions of the soul. Poets and philosophers began to write about nature in terms of the emotions aroused by beautiful scenery and sublime vistas. God appeared as the creator of an awesome universe in which even chaos and disorder took on positive meaning.

Beyond the pure mathematical analysis of the world, which appealed to the power of reason, were the senses and the passions by which people perceived and felt the outer world of nature. Descartes's separation of mind and body raised questions about the emotions aroused by nature. As Marjorie Hope Nicolson puts it in *Mountain Gloom and Mountain Glory*, "The Cartesian shears that had separated 'the world out there' from 'the mind in here' had laid upon thoughtful men a burden of discovering how nature affected the mind and how [the] mind knew nature." In respond-

ing to nature, reason and emotion could become fused. "Under the stimu-
lus of 'extraordinary Ideas,'" states Nicolson, "Reason and Passion rise
together to new heights, one affecting the other, until the Soul reaches
that state of exaltation in which it both thinks more clearly and feels more
vehemently than before." This experience was the apprehension of the
sublime.[57]

In England, writers such as poet John Dennis (1657–1734), essayist
Anthony Ashley Cooper (the third Earl of Shaftesbury, 1621–83), and
playwright Joseph Addison (1672–1719) spoke of the "sublime" in their
literary work. For Dennis, God's works evoked feelings of "delightful
horror" and "terrible joy." Shaftsbury praised a diverse and abundant
nature whose "wildness pleases" and which was created by a God of
plenitude. In the *Pleasures of the Imagination* (1712), Addison distinguished between the "natural" and "rhetorical" sublime, with the former
evoking the "primary pleasure of the imagination" and the latter only
"secondary" pleasure.[58]

English philosopher Edmund Burke, in his *Philosophical Enquiry into
the Origins of Our Ideas of the Sublime and the Beautiful* (1757), viewed
forests, mountains, and waterfalls as sublime places. The sublime produced
emotions of awe, astonishment, and dread. Burke wrote: "The passion
caused by the great and sublime in nature, when those causes operate most
powerfully, is Astonishment; and astonishment is that state of the soul, in
which all its motions are suspended, with some degree of horror." In addition to the ability of nature to fill the viewer with awe, there were several
related dimensions of the sublime. "Astonishment," Burke continued, "is
the effect of the sublime in its highest degree; the inferior effects are admiration, reverence and respect." But the most noteworthy experience of the
sublime was terror. The notion of the sublime was akin to the experience
of terror and dread at the power of the Deity. "Indeed terror," Burke wrote,
"is in all cases whatsoever, either more openly or latently the ruling principle of the sublime."

Burke compared the sublime and the beautiful in terms of their power
to evoke feelings of awe and appreciation: "Sublime objects are vast in
their dimensions, beautiful ones comparatively small; beauty should be
smooth, and polished; the great, rugged and negligent . . . the great ought
to be dark and gloomy; beauty should be light and delicate; the great ought
to be solid, and even massive. They are indeed ideas of a very different
nature, one being founded on pain, the other on pleasure."[59]

In German philosopher Immanuel Kant's *Observations on the Feeling of the Beautiful and Sublime* (1761), wilderness took on new and positive meanings. Like Burke, Kant distinguished between feelings of beauty and sublimity aroused by views of nature: "Finer feeling, which we now wish to consider, is chiefly of two kinds: the feeling of the sublime and that of the beautiful," he wrote. "The stirring of each is pleasant, but in different ways. The sight of a mountain whose snow covered peak rises above the clouds, the description of a raging storm, or Milton's portrayal of the infernal kingdom, arouse enjoyment but with horror; on the other hand, the sight of flower-strewn meadows, valleys with winding brooks and covered with grazing flocks, the description of Elysium . . . also occasion a pleasant sensation but one that is joyous and smiling."

According to Kant, there were several types of sublime feelings all nuanced with respect to the emotions generated: "The sublime is in turn of different kinds. Its feeling is sometimes accompanied with a certain dread, or melancholy; in some cases merely with quiet wonder; and in still others with a beauty completely pervading a sublime plan. The first I shall call the terrifying sublime, the second the noble, and the third the splendid."[60]

Looking at mountains—seeing God's action in the land through thunderstorms and lightning—was now looked upon not as the work of the devil but as evidence of God's power and goodness. The sublime was manifested in waterfalls, mountains, and canyons, and in sunsets, rainbows, and oceans. The idea of the sublime as a religious experience became an important component of the European Enlightenment. Nature was now cathedral, temple, and Bible.

CONCLUSION

During the seventeenth and eighteenth centuries, a set of ideas emerged that became central to the possibility of reinventing Eden on earth. The construction of a secular narrative of Recovery through Enlightenment was based on a particular set of assumptions about nature and society. The "state of nature" was a fallen world (represented by the female gender) that could and should be improved by humans. The best state of nature was an ordered, improved garden rather than a forested wilderness or a barren desert. Human society could likewise develop from a fallen or "primitive" state to a higher or "civilized" state (through the agency of the male gender). Agriculture and commerce were higher and more desirable forms of human life than hunting or pastoralism, and both improved the state of nature. Private property became a necessary condition for the emergence of settled agriculture and commercial capitalism as stages of upward progress. Acting through reason and nature, God sanctioned the recovery process.

At the same time, ideas of the wild and of wilderness were split into positive and negative valences. The negative wild encompassed those outside of civilization: the lower classes, minorities, "savages," and wild animals who must be controlled so that civilization could exist and against which it could define itself. The positive wild exemplified God's awesome power to affect the natural world. While human reason allowed humanity to understand God's laws and to explain the natural order, human passions allowed the apprehension of his awesome power as manifested through the majesty of wilderness.

By the late-eighteenth century, the mainstream story of Western culture had become a secular Recovery Narrative—a story of reinventing the whole earth as a Garden of Eden. It was this narrative, first in its earlier Baconian-Lockean form, and later in Adam Smith's more fully articulated capitalist form, that subtly guided and legitimized the European settlement and development of the American continent. Simultaneously, however, a counternarrative of wilderness appreciation was emerging among elites that would be expressed through poetry, art, literature, and landscape architecture.

In their emphasis on the domination and control of nature, the philosophers of the Scientific Revolution moved away from the possibility of partnership ethics. Yet in John Locke's assignment of reason to Eve can be found a positive potential for full participation by women in the understanding of nature, a trajectory realized two centuries later in Mark Twain's characterization of Eve (in this chapter's epigraph) as experimental scientist. Moreover, Eve's emotions of the Garden of Eden as "surpassingly beautiful" are shared by the men of the Enlightenment who express awe over the sublimity of nature. A partnership ethic, which depends on the full participation of men and women in the care of nature and the acceptance of nature's wildness, as well as its predictability, can be seen as latent in the two narratives of progress and decline.

PART II

New World Edens

FIVE

Adam As Hero

SHE SAYS IT IS ORDERED THAT WE WORK FOR OUR LIVING
HEREAFTER. SHE WILL BE USEFUL. I WILL SUPERINTEND.
—*Mark Twain, "Extracts from Adam's Diary"*

Labor in the earth was the pathway to the recovery of Eden. The New World was the new garden. For over three hundred years, hope of Recovery helped to propel settlement and "improvement" of the American continent. Following the Lockean ideal, Europeans mixed their labor with the soil, claiming the product as private property. Euroamerican men acted to reverse the decline of nature initiated by Eve, turning it into an ascent back to the garden. Using science, technology, and biblical imagery, they first changed the eastern forests and then the western deserts into cultivated gardens. Sanctioned by the Genesis origin story, they subdued the "wilderness," replenished the earth, and appropriated Indian homelands as free lands for settlement. Mercantile capitalism cast America as the site of natural resources, Africa as the source of enslaved human resources, and Europe as the base of resource management. Timber, barrel staves, animal hides, herbal medicines, tobacco, sugar, and cotton were extracted from nature as part of the great project of "improving" the land. In this chapter I will show how American men, as fallen Adam, became the heroic agents who transformed and redeemed fallen nature and suggest some possibilities for partnerships between people and the land.

NEW WORLD EDENS

The Recovery Narrative in America is a story of two visions, one of an existing Eden, the other of an Eden to be improved. To many the New World was already an Eden overflowing with bounty. Arthur Barlowe reported, in 1584, that off the coast of the future state of North Carolina, his expedition had encountered "so sweet and so strong a smel, as if we had bene in the midst of some delicate garden." He described the soil on Roanoke Island as "the most plentifull, sweete, fruitful and wholesome of all the world." The following year, Ralph Lane wrote an account of a land that abounded in "sweete trees," "pleasant gummes," and "grapes of such greatness" as not found in all of Europe.[1]

In 1590, John White's drawings of Roanoke, engraved by Theodor de Bry, were published as an accompaniment to Thomas Harriot's *Brief and True Report of the Newfoundland of Virginia*. De Bry's lead illustration, introducing White's images of the New World, was of Adam and Eve shown with the tree of the knowledge of good and evil. Eve grasped an apple pointed out by Satan in the form of a snake, while Adam agonized over the act. In the foreground was a rabbit along with wild animals, including a lion and rodent, while in the background appeared a native woman and child in a thatched hut and a man hoeing the soil.

DeBry's "notice" began, "Although (friendly reader), man by his disobedience, weare deprived of those good Gifts wher with he was indued in his creation, yet he was not berefte of wit to provyde for him selfe, nor discretion to devise things necessire for his use, except suche as appartayne to his soules healthe, as may be gathered by this savag nations, of whome this present work intreateth. For although they have noe true knoledge of God nor of his holye worde and are destituted of all lerninge, Yet they passe us in many things, as in Sober feedinge and Dexteritye of witte in makinge without any instrument of mettall things so neate and so fine, as a man would scarsclye believe the same, Unless the Englishemen Had made proofe Thereof by their travailes into the contrye."[2]

Many of the voyagers saw the New World through the image of the Genesis 2 narrative. They expected to find an Eden in the New World and, equally clearly, natives existing in a state of "savagery" without letters

Fig. 5.1. Theodor de Bry's engraving of Adam and Eve in Thomas Hariot's *Briefe and True Report of the New Found Land of Virginia* (1590) depicting disobedience in paradise. (New York: Dover Publications, 1972)

or metal technologies consistent with earlier reports from explorers and with European images of wildness. Expectations both of Eden and of wilderness and savage peoples were thus lenses through which the new lands were interpreted. Such descriptions helped to lure colonists from a crowded, rapidly expanding Europe across the ocean to an Edenic land.

While to some settlers, the New World Eden was a bountiful land to be entered and enjoyed, to others it had the potential to become a new paradise, but required "improvement." A land of enormous "natural advantages," it would nevertheless require European refinement before it could be deemed "civilized." Forests, soils, and wildlife were not just nature's gifts to humanity, but resources to be extracted from nature. To fulfill the New World's potential, its products had to be turned into commodities that could be traded for profit. This second idea of an Eden to be recovered from nature was to became the dominant narrative of American culture.

Environmental historian Mark Stoll argues that Protestantism in America gave rise both to the capitalist impulse to transform nature into commodities for profit and to the preservationist impulse to glorify God in the creation. Thus, both the Genesis 1 account of dominion over nature and the Genesis 2 account of the stewardship of nature were enacted as Christianity became America's primary religion. Stoll notes, "Some [European settlers] filled their canvas with the wilderness of Sinai, where dangers and demons threatened Christian settlers. Others depicted a Canaan flowing with milk and honey, beckoning Europeans away from Egyptian slavery. Was America an Eden where fallen men struggled for redemption? Or were the colonists to follow God's plan and restore the howling wilderness to paradise?"[3] Christianity thus plays a dual role. It promotes the enjoyment and appreciation of nature as Eden (leading ultimately to the preservation of wilderness as parks and monuments), and the extraction of useful commodities by an acquisitive, get-ahead culture bent on subduing its environment.

In the project of transforming the New World lands into an Eden, first the Eastern forests were converted into garden farms and later the Western deserts were irrigated to form fertile fields and pastures. Forests once covered 54 percent of the present United States; today they have been reduced to 23 percent. Indians had burned the forest in order to plant corn, beans, and squash; for ease of passage; and to produce browse that attracted deer. European settlers along the eastern seaboard used Indian clearings for housesites, farms, and townsites, then expanded the sites and clearings by cutting or girdling the trees and later digging out the stumps. As the soils declined in fertility after several years of rotation, fields were abandoned, first to pasture and then to revert to forest. While the cleared land was used for settled agriculture, the timber itself was valuable for houses, fences, furniture, farm implements, fuel, barrels, potash, ships, masts, pitch, and turpentine. By 1650, an estimated six thousand square kilometers had been cleared along the eastern seaboard, eighty thousand by 1750 as the country expanded westward, an additional 380,000 by 1850, and a total of about 1.1 million by 1980.[4]

Clearing the forest produced ecological changes in the surrounding lands. Among these were increased winds, drier air, and exposed and eroded soils. Animals had been sharply reduced in numbers both for furs and hides and to remove pests and predators. Bear, foxes, beavers, otters, elk, and deer were decimated, to near extinction in particular areas; in their place cattle, sheep, pigs, goats, and horses roamed the hills and woods. Birds such as woodpeckers, crows, blue jays, blackbirds, and passenger pigeons were shot as pests. Native wildflowers were replaced by European weeds and crops. To those who would reinvent the New World Eden, the transformations were welcomed as "improvements." To others they would be seen as blemishes on an already existing Eden. How did the new American Adam act to bring these changes to the land, reversing the Fall from Eden? What alternatives existed to the Adamic hero's efforts to remake the landscape?

HEROIC AGENTS

James I of England died in 1625, and Francis Bacon followed a year later. But the two left undying legacies, the former in his King James version of the Bible and adamant opposition to Puritanism, the latter in his mandate to recover the dominion over nature lost in the Fall of Adam and Eve. When James's successor, Charles I, strengthened English opposition to Puritan religious dissent, it provoked a vast migration to the New World. In 1629 John Winthrop was elected governor of the Massachusetts Bay Company, a group that organized Puritan settlers to move to the New World. Winthrop quoted the King James Bible to help recruit the four hundred people who would sail with his company for the New World in April of 1630. He evoked the garden as the ideal habitat for humanity: "The whole earth is the Lord's garden and he has given it to the sons of man upon a condition (Genesis 1:28): Increase and multiply, replenish the earth and subdue it."[5]

When the Puritans reached Massachusetts Bay after a two-month voyage, they found the legacy of wilderness terror alive and well in the

New England forest. Pilgrim leader William Bradford, who had preceded John Winthrop by ten years, viewed the land as a "hideous and desolate wilderness full of wild beasts and wild men." "Our fathers were Englishmen which came over this great ocean and were ready to perish in this wilderness," he recalled in his account *Of Plimoth Plantation*. Bradford, Winthrop, and their followers set about transforming the eastern forest and its attendant evils into a New World garden.[6]

The heroic American Adam was born in New England. Here Pilgrim and Puritan settlers converted William Bradford's "hideous and desolate wilderness" into "a second England for fertileness" in the space of a few decades. The Pilgrim migration, as recorded in Bradford's text, conforms to the six elements of the mythic heroic narrative identified by Russian folklorist Vladimir Propp:

1. The hero's initial absence
2. His transference from one place to another
3. The combat between hero and villain
4. The hero's receipt of a gift
5. The victory
6. The final repair of the hero's initial absence

In this case the hero, Bradford, leads his people through trials and tests in the struggle to recreate the garden in the New World.[7]

In the preparatory or first phase of the New England recovery story, the land is absent of the hero. Shortly after contact with the settlers, Indian lands have become vacant, corn fields have been abandoned, and the Indians themselves have succumbed to disease. As Puritan minister John Cotton later explained it, "When the Lord chooses to transplant his people, he first makes a country . . . void in that place where they reside."[8]

In the second or transference phase, Bradford as hero is transported from Old England to New England by ship. Bradford moves between two kingdoms, one symbolically represented by the Antichrist (the "fleshpots" of Old England) and the other by New Canaan, the promised land of New England. In the third or combative phase, the hero is tested through combat with the villain. The mythic struggle is played out between Bradford and the devil, who is portrayed as the wilderness—the tempestuous ocean and the desolate forest, a land filled with "wild beasts and wild men." As storms wreak havoc with Bradford's small ship the *Mayflower* and his little band of settlers struggles to survive their first grim winter on the shores of an unforgiving land, Bradford is steadfast. He calls upon his faith in God as well as his leadership skills.

In the fourth phase, the hero receives a gift in the form of help from the Indian Squanto, "a special instrument sent [from] God." Squanto is able to speak the Pilgrims' language, and he shows Bradford's company how to "set their corn, where to take fish, and to procure other commodities." The fifth phase is the victory of the hero. The struggling Pilgrim band survives its first year. They reap a successful corn harvest and build sturdy cabins and a stockade for shelter. Nature, as wilderness, has been defeated.

In the sixth and climactic phase, the hero's initial absence is repaired, the misfortunes are reversed, and the Pilgrims are reborn. At their first harvest, they celebrate their triumph over wilderness, achieved through the miracle of the recreated garden. The story of how the Pilgrims' filled and replenished the land launches the recovery of the garden in the New World and creates the American Recovery Narrative.[9]

CARVING OUT A COASTAL EDEN

The New World wilderness tested the colonists' faith in God and their defiance of Satan. Their story was compared to the biblical *Exodus*, when Moses led the children of Israel out of Egypt, through the Red Sea, and into the wilderness of Sinai. After wandering for forty years, they reached the new Canaan, a land flowing with milk and honey. In his 1632 *New English Canaan*, Thomas Morton described that land in Edenic terms. He wrote of "goodly groues of trees," "sweet cristall fountaines," and cleare running streames." He described "fowles in abundance, fish in multitude, . . . millions of turtledoves, " and "ripe pleasant grapes," declaring that these natural riches "made the land to mee seeme paradice." But to Morton, the New World was not only an Eden to be settled and enjoyed, but a "glorious tombe" waiting be recovered for European use.[10]

Pilgrim victory was followed by Puritan victory as the Massachusetts Bay colony added thousands of additional settlers to the new land, repeating the heroic journey across the Atlantic to advance the Edenic Recovery. In 1635, Thomas Hooker led a group of adventurers from the Massachusetts Bay colony through the wild lands to Hartford, Connecticut. He likened the trials of New Englanders to those of the children of Israel. Puritans "must come into and go through a vast and roaring wilderness," before "they could possess that good land which abounded with all prosperity and flowed with milk and honey." Roger Williams, who founded the Rhode Island colony in 1636, sermonized about a "wild and howling" land, reminding his followers that they had fallen from grace and that their souls were spiritual wildernesses. In 1646, Peter Bulkeley, preached that "God hath dealt with us as his people Israel," for "we are brought out of a fat land into a wilderness." But "the hardships which Israel suffered for awhile in the wilderness were recompenced with a land flowing with milk and honey."[11] As the land itself became less threatening—and trade in furs, fish, and lumber flourished—the symbolic wilderness evoked by some of these early preachers persisted as a safeguard against spiritual decline.

A similar transformation took place in the forests of the Chesapeake Bay, where Jamestown (named after James I) had been founded in 1607. By the early eighteenth century, tobacco planters had converted the "unjustly neglected" and "abused" Chesapeake region of Virginia into a ravishing garden. Robert Beverley thought Virginia had the potential to be a "Garden of the World," akin to Canaan, Syria, and Persia. "Certainly it must be a happy Climate, since it is very near of the same latitude with the Land of Promise." But Beverley reproached his countrymen for "a Laziness that is unpardonable." "They sponge upon the blessings of a warm sun and a fruitful soil, and almost grutch [begrudge] the pains of gathering in the bounties of the earth." Tobacco became the means for participating in the European market, and its cultivation improved the land through labor. But the Recovery was ever in danger from new lapses into laziness if people allowed themselves to indulge in pleasure, narcotics, or alcohol to the exclusion of work.[12]

These coastal New England and tobacco colony gardens were invented spaces. While they conformed to the biblical ideals of Eden as abundance and of Adam as hero, they were integrally tied to the Atlantic mercantile economy. Instead of simply living within its presence, Puritans and planters acted on the land to reshape it and extract its resources. Coastal cities and southern plantations imitated European ideals of civility. Following the ideal progression of John Locke, these settlers transformed a "rude" nature occupied by "savages" into a civil society inhabited by plantation owners, lumberers, farmers, and commercial traders. This New World commercially minded society looked to Europe for both inspiration and profit.

POSSESSING THE INLAND EDEN

During the early years of the republic, market incentives shaped the political image of the "good state" and the "good economy." Benjamin Franklin's
get-ahead mentality, James Madison's strong central government, and
Alexander Hamilton's promotional state characterized the ideals of the
coastal commercial sector of American society. Fallen Adam, redeemed by
labor in the land, set up the state as Father Adam, exemplar of the law and
order needed for capitalist development. The good state as the image of
the coastal mercantile sector, however, had to coexist with the subsistence-
oriented vision of the inland farming sector. The ideals of these inland
farmers more closely matched the earlier image of nature as an Eden to be
possessed rather than transformed.[13]

Settlers cleared patches in the "almost universal" forest, carving farms
out of the dense woodlands. Much of this inland/upland farming country
had no easy access to the market. The incentives to grow and transport
bulky crops for Eastern cities and European markets were removed
because the roads were poor and the rivers either did not access coastal
ports or could not be navigated above the first line of waterfalls. While
some items such as potash made a long market journey worth the time and
effort, and while in some locations livestock could be driven to market on
hoof, for much of the inland/upland farm culture, trade was local and
community-oriented. Farmers exchanged labor for needed items such as
shoes and shovels and shared more expensive implements such as plows
and oxen. The storekeeper was the link to outside markets. Here farmers
could barter grain for salt, tea, ammunition, and glass.

The subsistence-oriented culture exemplified the possibility of partnership among community members and between people and nature.
Labor, tools, food, and crops were exchanged among neighbors. Within
households, men's and women's labor were both necessary to subsistence,
albeit within a patriarchal system of property ownership and social norms.
Farming itself necessarily entailed cooperation between people and the
land. Farmers used a long-fallow system of rotations, planting two to five
acres with enough corn, grain, and vegetables for family needs and a small
surplus for local barter. Fields were then abandoned to pasture and finally
reverted again to woods. The small fields were surrounded by rail fences
to keep out cattle and pigs grazing in the woods and the brush borders
harbored beneficial birds and insects that kept down pests. Water, light,
soil, crops, and climate combined to aid the farmer's subsistence, while

farmers themselves replensihed nutrients through the short-fallow crop rotation cycle and the long-fallow pasture to woodland cycle. Farmers used technologies such as plows and harrows to enhance crop yields, but accepted the hand that nature dealt in rainfall and temperature extremes.[14]

The political ideals of this subsistence-oriented culture contrasted in important ways with those of the profit-oriented coastal market culture. For the inland farming sector, the good economy was one that allowed each laboring Adam the independence to own and farm a plot of land, the liberty to worship as he pleased, and the freedom from oppressive government. The good state was one that interfered little, taxed less, and generally left people alone. J. Hector St. John de Crèvecoeur's "silken bands of mild government," Thomas Jefferson's independent Yeoman farmer, and Andrew Jackson's new democratic man characterized the political ideals of this subsistence-minded sector of American society.[15]

Because of the abundance of "free" land, for a time the American New World seemed to promise an exception to the reinvented garden. For those who settled its enormous interior, America was a garden to be possessed rather than remade. The land contained vast tracts of untouched forests, wild rivers, mountains, and fertile soils awaiting cultivation. "Free land" taken from the Indians reenacted the Edenic promise, and clearing that land created an illusion of innocence. To America's subsistence-minded culture, the New World garden seemed to be an unspoiled Eden, a romantic advance beyond the Puritans' "hideous and desolate wilderness."

To these settlers, America was akin to an "original" Eden. The garden was embodied in the seemingly unblemished, fertile nature of the land that stretched inland for hundreds of miles and teemed with unrefined bounty. As a place of moral purity, unblemished nature could restore humans who lived within its presence. This image of an untouched America contrasted sharply with that of a spoiled and corrupt Europe. The myth of America as an original, eternal Eden expressed the hope of returning to a past in which nature was pure and history unadulterated. Here the Edenic possibility of living within nature and outside of history thrived.[16]

THE AMERICAN ADAM

French nobleman Crèvecoeur popularized the agrarian ideal in America that exemplified the new Adam. In 1754, he traveled from France to

Canada where he fought in the French and Indian War. After the war, he toured Pennsylvania, New York, and the Atlantic coast, and then settled down to farm. He became an American citizen in 1765 and wrote *Letters from an American Farmer* between 1770 and 1775. Published in London in 1782, the *Letters* immediately became famous. Crèvecoeur's new American—"this new man"—carried forth an independent spirit as he settled the "virgin lands" of Pennsylvania and the Appalachian frontier. To Crèvecoeur, the men of the inland farms were "like plants," purified by the soil. Both the Jeffersonian subsistence farmer and the Jacksonian democratic man symbolized the reclamation of an original Adam who could be redeemed simply by living within the presence of nature. Outside the corrupting influence of the market, the yeoman farmer subsisted by simple means in a land of plenty.

As David W. Noble observes in *The Eternal Adam and the New World Garden*, "The soaring faith of the American romantic affirmed the ability of the average citizen to rise above his personal weaknesses and the traditions and institutions of his European ancestors because, in the United States, every individual was in close contact with nature [and] the West was a limitless national reservoir of spiritual strength."[17] Within the "purity" of the inland forests, the American Adam could be reborn through his engagement with nature. He could redeem himself through the very process of creating a garden home within it. Each forest clearing represented a New World Eden, where the fertile ground was a source of perpetual food and fruit. The garden in the wilderness, Noble notes, seemed to be a protective womb, a cradle in which simplicity could be regained and the human spirit reborn.

Each man, Noble argues, could become a new Adam, a romantic hero who could recreate the garden in the forest. This New World Adam would be the backbone of the fledgling democracy. American historian George Bancroft, writing in 1840, described Andrew Jackson as the "orphan hero" from whom democracy sprang. Jackson in his infancy "sported in the ancient forests, and his mind was nursed to freedom by their influence." Here was born "the unlettered man of the West, the nursling of the wilds . . . . What wisdom will he bring with him from the forest?" American democracy grew out of each new Adam's encounters with the wilderness and his insights about the forest garden.[18]

Moreover, each garden clearing was a "virgin" forest transformed by human engagement into a maternal encasement. The cabin was the space of patriarchal Adam and maternal Eve. Eve—symbolized as virgin and unproductive land—became fertile Eve, Mother Earth. In *The Lay of the Land*, Annette Kolodny points out that the gardens and cabins of forest clearings were gendered spaces. In the essays of John James Audubon, she argues, "each of the settlers' cabins [is] a . . . virtually archetypal balance of masculine and feminine components . . . . The feminine is always depicted as both wife and mother, and the planting or hunting activities of the male are experienced . . . as a means of protecting and providing for the feminine." Audubon in his visits to these forest cabins, according to Kolodny, was in many ways an intruder into an enclosed womb, where in order to paint the birds of America, he nonetheless violated "virgin" nature "as he kill[ed] or maim[ed] the 'beautiful birds' and small mammals that nature had provided for his admiration. . . ."[19]

THE REINVENTED EDEN

For a time the ideal of an inland Eden and reborn Adam coexisted with the humanly created "improved" gardens of coastal settlement. But the advance of commerce following the War of 1812 shattered the illusion that an original American Eden could be retained. In nineteenth-century America, a flurry of economic activity followed in the wake of the transportation and market revolutions of the 1820s–1850s. Americans began a frenzy of turnpike, canal, and railroad building. These commercial developments took an immediate toll on the forests. Trees were cut down to build railroads and canals, support mine shafts, and provide fuel for the steam-powered revolution. Landscapes were irrevocably altered by iron and coal strip mining in the East and by the gold and silver mining operations in the West.[20]

America's market culture embraced a "master narrative" of history that remade the American landscape. The heroic American Adam was not the reclaimed original Adam who existed within nature and outside of history; he had become a robust actor who created a new nature and a new history. The process of redemption did not consist of merely living within nature as innocent child; it was the act of laboring on the land to cultivate, tame, and subdue it. The way of Puritan and planter became that of the American entrepreneur. Instead of possessing the garden, the market culture reinvented it.

In 1844, Calvin Colton, political essayist and member of the Whig Party, characterized American resources as inexhaustible and males as "self-made men." He wrote, "Providence has given us a rich productive and glorious heritage. . . . The wealth of the country is inexhaustible and the enterprise of the people is unsubdued. . . . This is a country of self-made men than which nothing better could be said of any state of society."[21] Colton was a stalwart proponent of commercial development. The market elite, with whom Colton identified, supported the unrestrained use of natural resources that produced upwardly mobile, acquisitive men.

Ralph Waldo Emerson, also writing in 1844, enthusiastically embraced the recovered garden achieved through human dominion over nature: "This great savage country should be furrowed by the plough, and combed by the harrow; these rough Alleganies should know their master; these foaming torrents should be bestridden by proud arches of stone; these wild prairies should be loaded with wheat; the swamps with rice; the hill-tops should pasture innumerable sheep and cattle." "How much better," he exclaimed, "when the whole land is a garden, and the people have grown up in the bowers of a paradise."[22]

But the new reality of an American Adam who redeemed himself through transforming nature was not universally embraced. After experiencing intensive development along the eastern seaboard, a small number of nineteenth century urban artists, writers, scientists, and explorers began to question that reality and deplore the effects of the "machine in the garden." For them, an Adam redeemed by the garden became an Adam who corrupted it. Novelists, artists, nature writers, and conservationists began to rewrite the story as one of environmental decline. These critics embraced the pastoral ideal, even as they believed it was doomed. They acknowledged that ultimately, the greatest impact of nature on humans would become the greatest human impact on nature, turning an apparent Adamic Eden into a dammed Eden.[23]

Audubon found himself overwhelmed by the rapid transformation of the Mississippi River Valley—the very valley of democracy and home of the Adamic hero. He lamented the changes civilization had brought to the pastoral Edenic landscape:

> When I think of these times, and call back to my mind the grandeur
> and beauty of those almost uninhabited shores; when I picture to

myself the dense and lofty summits of the forest, that everywhere spread along the hills, and overhung the margins of the stream, unmolested by the axe of the settler. . . . When I see that no longer any Aborigines are to be found there, and that the vast herds of elks, deer and buffaloes which once pastured on these hills and in these valleys, making for themselves great roads to the several saltsprings, have ceased to exist; when I reflect that all this grand portion of our Union, instead of being in a state of nature, is now more or less covered with villages, farms, and towns, where the din of hammers and machinery is constantly heard; that the woods are fast disappearing under the axe by day, and the fire by night; that hundreds of steamboats are gliding to and fro, over the whole length of the majestic river, forcing commerce to take root and to prosper at every spot; when I see the surplus population of Europe coming to assist in the destruction of the forest, and transplanting civilization into its darkest recesses;—when I remember that these extraordinary changes have all taken place in the short period of twenty years, I pause, wonder, and although I know all to be fact, can scarcely believe its reality. . . .[24]

The reality of rapid economic transformation under the market revolution would leave a lasting imprint on American society and its landscape.

THE RECOVERY NARRATIVE IN ARTS AND LETTERS

James Fenimore Cooper's Leatherstocking tales depict the struggle between an idealized Edenic nature and an emerging acquisitive civilization. In *The Pioneers* (1823), Natty Bumppo represents the independent Adam who lives harmoniously within nature in a free and spontaneous innocence unencumbered by law. Judge Temple, spokesman for civilization, represents the American Adam of the Recovery Narrative. Clearing the land makes way for a civilization governed and protected by the laws of the good state. The pioneers of Judge Temple's town kill whole flocks of passenger pigeons for sport, but Natty refuses to shoot more than one bird at a time—just enough for a meal. He admonishes the judge, "Put an ind, Judge, to your clearings. Ain't the woods His work as well as the pigeons? Use, but don't waste. Wasn't the woods made for the beasts and birds to harbour in?" But Natty cannot escape the encroachment of civi-

Fig. 5.2. Thomas Cole's *Expulsion from the Garden of Eden* (1827–28) shows Adam and Eve being forcibly expelled from a luxurious garden into a barren wilderness. Copyright Museum of Fine Arts, Boston, 2002. Gift of Martha C. Karolik for the M. and M. Karolik Collection of American Paintings, 1815–1865

lization. In his final retreat to the prairies, he hears in the distance the sound of axes and the crash of falling trees. Before his death—the death of the possibility of a reclaimed original Adam—he admits his own inevitable complicity in the violation of nature and the impossibility of a redeemed innocence.[25]

Nineteenth century writers and painters gradually relinquished hope in an original American Eden that could redeem humanity by its very presence. This evolution can be traced through the work of Thomas Cole (1801–48), one of the most popular artists of the Hudson River school. His early *Expulsion from the Garden of Eden* (1827–28) contrasts the tranquil, original garden on the right of the canvas with the bleak, terrible desert on the left. At the center of the painting, God expels Adam and Eve through a gate. The garden is portrayed with luxuriant vegetation and a meandering stream, while the desert features barren rock, hot winds, a raging waterfall, an exploding volcano, and a wolf attacking a deer. Using

Fig. 5.3. In *View From Mt. Holyoke, Northhampton, Massachusetts, after a Thunderstorm (The Oxbow)*, Thomas Cole seems to suggest that over time much of America's forested wilderness may become a pastoral, cultivated landscape. Oil on canvas, courtesy of the Metropolitan Museum of Art, Gift of Mrs. Russell Sage, 1908

symbols of an American landscape unblemished by the machine, Cole's painting shows humanity being expelled from the original Eden.

Nearly ten years later, Cole's *The Oxbow* (1836) portrays the possibility of recovering Eden through recreating the garden on earth. This painting moves from dark wilderness on the left of the canvas to the light-filled tranquil and cultivated landscape on the right—a scene bordering a curve of the peaceful Connecticut River. The logging scars in the forest on the background hill appear to be the Hebrew letters for Noah. When viewed upside down from a God's eye view, these letters form the word *shaddai*, or "the Almighty." God's presence in the landscape underscores his covenant with Noah and anticipates the final reunion of God and the earth at the parousia. This painting suggests that humans can redeem the land itself as garden, even as they redeem themselves through laboring in the earth. They can reinvent the original Eden by transforming wilderness into a pastoral garden. But the scars on the hillside herald the decline of the garden and the smokey haze rising from the forest the end of unblemished wilderness.[26]

In a series of paintings produced in the 1830s, Cole depicted the movement from "savagery" to "civilization"—and the problem of lapsing back into the darkness of chaos. Of an 1831 painting, *A Wild Scene*, Cole wrote, "The first picture must be a savage wilderness . . . the figures must be savage—clothed in skins & occupied in the Chase— . . . as though nature was just waking from chaos." A subsequent allegorical series, *The Course of Empire*, echoed Virgil's cycle of emergence from "savagery to civilization and back to savagery." But Cole's the Savage State, the Pastoral State, Consummation of Empire, Destruction of Empire, and Desolation—warned of lapsarian dangers that thwart progress and end in the ruin of civilization. Cole's ideal landscape was the pastoral, but America seemed headed into an inevitable cycle of empire followed by decline.[27]

Herman Melville (1819–91) left his job as a bank clerk to voyage to the South Seas in search of adventure. His visit to the Galápagos Islands in 1841 caused him to view the earth as a fallen world instead of a redemptive garden. Boarding a whaling vessel in New Bedford, Melville was wrenched from a familiar pastoral New England landscape and eventually propelled into a land of barren rock, decaying shoreline refuse, and the raucous calls of seabirds. "In no world but a fallen one, could such lands exist," he exclaimed. He found that the South Seas natives were not the noble children of untouched nature, but fallen beings like those found in a sinful New England. In his subsequent disillusionment, he saw evidence of this "fallen world" not only in his native New England, but even in the "nature" of the eastern U.S. mountains. In *Moby-Dick* (1851), Melville shows that the sea—the last frontier of unblemished nature— fails to perfect humanity: "Nature absolutely paints like the harlot, whose allurements cover nothing but the charnel-house within." Yet Melville was equally skeptical of salvation through dominating nature. His character Ahab's efforts to escape death by conquering the white whale and the sea fail. Only Ishmael, who finally accepts that the sea is as mysterious as his own human imperfections, escapes.[28]

THE WESTWARD MOVEMENT

The competitive society fostered by the nineteenth-century market found its scientific justification in Darwinian evolution. Evolutionary theory, based on competition through survival of the fittest, was construed to mean that both nature and humanity could progress upward from a state of savagery to civilization. Nature, "red in tooth and claw," could be perfected and tamed, just as humanity could be perfected. And both would be remade in the process.

Thomas Huxley (1824–95), an ardent Darwinian, expressed the Victorian urge to re-create the earth in the image of the Garden of Eden. He envisioned a cultivated land "where every plant and every lower animal should be adapted to human wants." The spread of domesticated English crops and animals could create "an earthly paradise, a true garden of Eden, in which all things should work together towards the well-being of the gardeners."[29]

The principle that savagery could progress to civilization was embraced by many post–Civil War Americans to justify their taming of nature through domination. Dynamic action on the land to bring it closer to an Edenic state was more satisfying than living within an Eden already formed by nature. While perhaps not a conscious concept, the Baconian ideal of recovering humanity's right over nature through technology and industry seemed a realistic possibility. Actively reinventing Eden through the machine seemed superior to passively lamenting the loss of an original garden. Newtonian rationality, the hallmark of the Enlightenment, was coupled with the idea of an evolutionary, dynamic progress toward salvation. Both the earth and humanity could be prepared for the ultimate reunification of the earth with God at the Parousia.

During the westward movement, ambivalence about finding a redemptive natural Eden turned to faith in the Adamic hero's ability to reinvent Eden. In the second half of the nineteenth century, Euroamericans acted out the Recovery Narrative, transforming the American West. They were inspired by John Quincy Adams's 1846 call for expansion into Oregon, "to make the wilderness blossom as the rose, to establish laws, to increase, multiply, and subdue the earth, which we are commanded to do by the first behest of the God Almighty." That same year, Thomas Hart Benton rallied migrants to heed their manifest destiny. He argued that the white race had "alone received the divine command to subdue and replenish the earth: for it is the only race that . . . hunts out new and distant lands, and even a New World, to subdue and replenish. . . . The van of the Caucasian race now top the Rocky Mountains, and spread down on the shores of the Pacific. In a few years a great population will grow up there. . . ."[30]

In settling, ranching, and plowing the Great Plains and Far West, Euroamerican migrants reversed the biblical Fall by turning the "great

American desert" into yet another garden of the world. The reclamation of arid lands west of the 100th meridian through the technologies of irrigation fulfilled the biblical mandate of making "the desert blossom as the rose" (Isaiah 35:1), rendering the land productive for capitalist agriculture. Proud new Westerners commemorated the 1869 joining of the Central Pacific and Union Pacific railroads. In a highly publicized ceremony, the Reverend Dwinell used the Bible to sanction human alteration of the landscape. "Prepare ye the way of the Lord, make straight in the desert a highway before our God. Every valley shall be exalted, and every mountain and hill shall be made low and the crooked shall be made straight and the rough places plain" (Isaiah 40:3–4).[31]

The elements of the westward movement again conform to Vladimir Propp's heroic narrative. The land is absent of the heroes—the migrants themselves. They move across inhospitable desert lands; combat hostile Indians, diseases, and starvation; receive gifts from God in the form of gold and free land; emerge victorious over nature and Indians; and repair the initial absence of the hero by filling and replenishing the land.

Frederick Jackson Turner's 1893 essay on the closing of the frontier in American history is an updated version of the heroic recovery narrative introduced by William Bradford more than 250 years earlier. Propp's six phases of heroic victory are present in Turner's narrative, but he also warns of impending declension as the frontier closes. In the first phase, Turner defines the frontier by the absence of settlement and civilization: "Up to and including 1880, the country had a frontier of settlement, but at present the unsettled area has been . . . broken." In the second phase, Euroamericans are transferred across space as the succession of frontier lines moves west and they "adapt . . . to changes involved in crossing the continent." Stand at Cumberland Gap, Turner states, and watch the procession—the buffalo following the trail to the salt lick, the trapper, the miner, the rancher, and the farmer each follow in succession; stand at South Pass a century later and watch the same succession pass by again.

The third phase depicts the individual hero in combat with the villain. Here the villain is again portrayed as the wilderness, Indians, and wild beasts. "The wilderness masters the colonist"; it "strips off the garments" of European civilization and "puts him in the log cabin of the Cherokee and Iroquois." In the fourth phase, the heroes receive the gift of free land. But Turner is compelled to warn that "never again will such gifts of free land offer themselves."

The frontier encounter transforms hero into victor in the fifth phase. "Little by little he transforms the wilderness, but the outcome is not the old Europe . . . here is a new product that is American." The climactic and sixth phase embodies Democracy itself and American civilization "in a perennial rebirth" that fills the land, repairing the initial absence. "Democracy is born of free land," Turner pronounced. With frontier expansion, temporal recovery through science and capitalism merges with spatial recovery through acquisition of private property.[32]

THE RAPE OF NATURE

Although Puritans and political leaders of the new nation had used the Genesis 1:28 mandate to justify subduing the earth, the sexual conquest of nature became more explicit as the nineteenth century progressed. Advocates of commercial expansion, manifest destiny, and the domination of nature used aggressive masculine imagery to sanction exploiting the female earth in support of the new economic takeoff. Thomas Morton's marriage between "virgin" land and industry became the rape of nature.

Mining, railroad building, and logging represented the purest forms of male energy used to subdue nature. Rev. John Todd, for example, used the imagery of sexual assault to advocate mining the female earth for metals. Describing California mining camps in his *Sunset Land* (1870), he praised the men who "turn the coarse of the pit into the hairspring of the watch, or are able to take nature in her wild state and turn her wastes into gardens of beauty."[33] The gold, iron, lead, copper, quicksilver, coal and tin mines complemented "her deep rich soil" and made California a state unsurpassed in resources. Todd called it a state that would "cool the passions and moderate the spirits." Here few women existed to drain male energy.[34]

Railroad construction involved "unconquerable energy" in subduing and altering nature. Todd was enthusiastic about the effects of the masculine hand on nature, especially where machines had been used to reverse its processes. Built "against nature," the transcontinental railroad ran east to west instead of north to south, the direction that all the major rivers flowed. Echoing philosopher Francis Bacon, who had advocated that nature be "forced out of her natural state and molded" by "art and the hand of man," Todd wrote: "Skill hath laid his iron hand on the mane of the everlasting mountains, and grinding flinty rocks to powder beneath his heel, hath leaped over the barriers of nature."[35]

Completion of the railroad meant that the "virgin soil" of California could at last be brought into cultivation. Todd foresaw an agricultural paradise, where nature could be productively sown and cultivated by the farmer so that "every meadow [would be] reclaimed, every hill made fruitful and every conquest over Nature . . . a benefit to himself." "From the bosom of mother earth," Todd proclaimed, "all draw their nourishment. . . . Nature finds materials and it is for man to take and improve them."[36] Improvement of nature was the means of creating an Eden in the western United States.

IRRIGATED EDENS

The project of turning the American West into an Edenic landscape was radically different from that same goal in the eastern states, where forests could be cleared for farms and gardens. Westward of the 100th meridian, which ran roughly from eastern North Dakota through the southern tip of Texas, rainfall became unreliable, in most years falling below the 20 inches per year needed for successful farming. On the Great Plains, and in the Great Basin, the Southwest, and California's Central Valley and southern deserts, rainfall had to be supplemented by irrigation. Irrigation demanded new technologies of damming rivers and digging canals to lead water to fields and pastures, as well as new laws and regulations to distribute that water in times of drought.

Here nature became what historian Richard White, writing about the Columbia River dams, has called an "organic machine," a mixing of the natural and artificial in ways that blurred apparent boundaries between evolved nature and humanly-created nature. He notes, "Irrigation farmers not only take water from the Columbia, they commandeer waterways nature had once used and have built other artificial streams to contain water pumped from the river. . . . Similarly, the dams on the Columbia do not simply depend on the run of the river to turn the turbines. The creation of huge reservoirs allows some control over the flow of the river itself. . . . But the Columbia is not just a machine. It is an organic machine . . . . For no matter how much we have created many of its spaces and altered its behavior, it is still tied to larger organic cycles beyond our control."[37]

Throughout the West, small communities created on the land tapped into streams and led water in ditches to gardens and fields. When the Mormons arrived in their promised land of Utah, they brought with them a religious mandate to make the desert bloom and to re-create the Garden of Eden on earth. In 1856, Brigham Young wrote, "There is a great work for the Saints to do; . . . improve upon and make beautiful everything around you. Cultivate the earth and cultivate your minds. Build cities, adorn your habitations, make gardens, orchards and vineyards, and render the earth so pleasant that when you look upon your labors you may do so with pleasure, and that angels may delight to come and visit your beautiful locations." Likewise, George A. Smith told the settlers, "I feel anxious that you should begin to beautify Parowan, and make it like the garden of Eden."[38]

In the 1880s, Mormon pioneers moved into and settled the area of southern Idaho where the Teton and Snake Rivers flowed together. They built small dams of brush to divert water into ditches that watered their fields, rebuilding them each year after the spring floods demolished the temporary structures. Here humanity's hydraulic technology was joined with the nature's hydraulic cycle to remake the land. The settlers transformed an arid landscape into fertile fields, damming the Snake River and laying out a vast network of ditches on the landscape. In 1907, Jackson Dam was completed by the U.S. Bureau of Reclamation, forming a reservoir to store water and control spring flooding. Canals transported water between rivers and watersheds, and the land's natural arroyos and draws became humanly created creeks that flowed through meadows and pastures to water the fields of planted crops. Along the streams, irrigators planted cottonwoods, willows, and poplars to create parks and picnic places. "Irrigators," notes environmental historian Mark Fiege, "may not have overtly likened the sylvan glades to the biblical garden, but when they took their repose in the cool shade, they certainly acted out a pastoral idyll that harkened back to the lost Eden."[39]

Yet the new landscape was not one in which nature bent to the will of the machine in recreating a garden paradise. The fields and streams became a chaotic environment characterized by new humanly created "natural" habitats. New aquatic plants, seeds, birds, and fish entered the canals and transformed the "nature" that had once been a desert. Some species such as the carp became ubiquitous and uncontrollable. Algae, moss, waterweeds, and cattails filled the canals. Muskrats and beavers dug into the banks, destabilizing streams and wreaking havoc with headgates. "Farming involved a relentless struggle between what the irrigators sought to grow and what nature would allow." Fiege concludes, "As the irrigated landscape showed, nature often eluded ideals: a conquest myth did not produce a conquered land." Dramatic proof occurred a century later: in 1975, the Bureau of Reclamation filled the newest component of the irrigation project—the Teton Dam Reservoir in southeastern Idaho. On June 5, 1976, the dam's north end collapsed, killing eleven people, destroying 13,000 head of cattle, demolishing homes, and removing a billion tons of topsoil.[40]

Desert transformed into Edenic garden likewise epitomizes California's development. By the late nineteenth century, water had replaced gold as the state's premier resource. Access to vast resources of "white gold" (water) was the quintessential condition for reclaiming desert lands for the "green gold" produced by agriculture. In 1887, George Freeman assured potential settlers of Fresno, then a tiny community in the San Joaquin Valley, that the "conversion of a desert into a garden" would not be difficult, and he was right. A decade later, John Bennett declared the irrigated lands of the Central Valley to be among the most delightful and prosperous "garden spots" in the entire United States. By 1905, the *Los Angles Times* was promoting the conversion of southern California's San Fernando Valley into "a veritable Garden of Eden." Not a single acre should remain unproductive in the rush to create orchards and gardens. But in 1928, the St. Francis Dam, forty miles north of Los Angeles and engineered by William Mulholland as the apex of the Garden of Eden recovery project, collapsed, killing over four hundred people.[41]

California's initial forays into irrigated Edens led ultimately to a vast network of dams and canals running the entire length of the state, transporting water from the rain-rich north to the arid south. The Central Valley Project of the 1930s and the State Water Project of the 1960s formed two parallel systems that bought and sold water and electricty from each other and distributed both to farmers and urbanites. Concrete-lined canals paralleled north to south freeways, creating a transit system that intersected with agribusiness, large-scale corporations, and banking systems to form an empire of power over nature.

CONCLUSION

The Recovery Narrative that shaped America's development was fully articulated by the early twentieth century. The Fall and Recovery narrative of modernism had replaced the Fall and Salvation narrative of the Middle

Ages. The redemption of the Adamic hero through labor in the earth replaced the hope of redemption through mere presence in a "natural" Eden. A "civilized" world replaced the "savage" world; Turner's "American" superceded the Native American; the recovered garden of Eden transformed the "howling wilderness" and the "Great American Desert." Fallen nature could be redeemed through science, technology, and the market. The outcome is today's Garden Planet.

Yet just below the veneer of complete control over nature lay the cracks of potential collapse, not only of dams, but of the mainstream Recovery Narrative itself. Environmental historian Donald Worster warns, "Salinity, sedimentation, pesticide contamination, diminishing hopes of replenishment, the dangers of aging, collapsing dams: all these were the hydraulic society's worsening headaches. Yet there was another peril . . . even less manageable because it had to do with faith, not technique. A sense of irreparable loss began to settle about the water empire by the late twentieth century, a remembrance of things past. . . . Nostalgia for what has been lost might lead people to the discovery of new, radically disturbing moral principles, in this case the idea that pristine nature in the West has its own intrinsic value, one that humans ought to understand and learn to respect."[42]

Here, set starkly against the Recovery Narrative's ideal of a reinvented, irrigated Eden, is the environmentalist's narrative of decline. Nature captured and controlled in the grid lines of private property, electrical power, and concrete canals might break forth from its prison, in what Max Horkheimer called "the revolt of nature."[43] But as Worster and others suggest, there are other options to explore, options for a new ethic and a new kind of society. That society would be based not on Adamic heroes clear cutting the forests and harnessing the rivers with vast organic machines, but on sustainable livelihoods rooted in dynamic relationships of give and take between humanity and the land.

SIX

Eve As Nature

AFTER ALL THESE YEARS I SEE THAT I WAS MISTAKEN ABOUT
EVE IN THE BEGINNING. IT IS BETTER TO LIVE OUTSIDE THE GARDEN
WITH HER THAN INSIDE IT WITHOUT HER. AT FIRST I THOUGHT SHE
TALKED TOO MUCH, BUT NOW I SHOULD BE SORRY TO HAVE THAT VOICE
FALL SILENT AND PASS OUT OF MY LIFE. . . . WHERESOEVER SHE WAS,
THERE WAS EDEN.
—*Mark Twain, "Extracts from Adam's Diary"*

If Adam was the hero who transformed American lands, Eve was nature itself, gendered as female. The story of American settlement is filled with metaphors that cast nature as a female object to be improved by men. Images of Eve as virgin land to be exploited, as fallen nature to be redeemed through reclamation, and as fruitful garden to be harvested are deeply encoded in American history, art, and literature. These images acted as ethical imperatives and sustained settlement ideologies.

Associations of Eve with nature go back to the Genesis stories. Eve, more than Adam, is closely identified with nature in the form of the Garden of Eden itself and its trees, fruit, and serpent. As virgin Eve, she is untouched and unspoiled like the Garden and the two trees at its center. Eve, rather than Adam, communicates with nature in the form of the serpent. Eve, rather than Adam, is the first to ingest the fruit produced by nature on the tree of the knowledge of good and evil. In the process, she becomes one with nature and knows nature, gaining her knowledge from the tree's fruit. The tree symbolizes fertility, and Eve herself become fertile and bears fruit in the form of children after the Fall from the garden. As mother Eve ("mother of all the living"), she is a fruitful womb to be harvested and enjoyed or conversely to be exploited and made to pay in sorrow for her sin. After the Expulsion, initiated by Eve's tasting of the fruit, the ground is cursed and brings forth thorns and thistles and Adam is forced to "till the ground from which he was taken." Fallen Eve is a desert, a dark disorderly wasteland waiting to be reclaimed.

The image of Eve as nature played a vital role in the story of American culture. In the mainstream Recovery Narrative, nature is portrayed as undeveloped "virgin" land whose bountiful potential can be realized through human male ingenuity. Explorers and mapmakers cast the American continent as a naked or partly clothed female to be explored by men and seduced into service for settlers. Eve as "virgin" land submitted to the axe and plow in the east and the construction of dams and irrigation systems in the west, turning fertile soils into rich harvests. First by farms carved out as "wombs" within the "all-embracing" forest and later by large-scale agribusiness, men's plow agriculture triumphed over "virgin" nature. Driven by capitalist expansion, American men built toll roads, canals, and railroads to transport the fruits of the garden to market. In the mainstream Recovery Narrative, Eve becomes a fruitful land to be enjoyed; garden farms become the new Eden.

But nature as Eve is also central to the environmentalist counternarrative. Mid-nineteenth-century romantics and transcendentalists constructed an alternative to the mainstream story, personifying nature as a powerful female to be revered, rather than a virgin land to be plowed and improved. Writers such as Henry David Thoreau, Ralph Waldo Emerson, and John Muir rediscovered and drew upon images from the deep past that had portrayed nature as mother and teacher. They also began to incorporate images from their own personal experiences of nature as intimate companion. This image of nature harks back to the goddess imagery of the cultural feminist narrative. Both the environmentalist and feminist counternarratives view nature as originally positive and pristine, but as desecrated and downgraded by commercial and industrial development.

The environmentalist version of Recovery emerges fully with the conservation and preservation movements of the late nineteenth century. Here

Eve is seen as pristine nature to be conserved as forested resource and preserved for wilderness immersion. The environmentalist and feminist counternarratives converge in resurrecting, valorizing, and recovering nature as undesecrated forests and deserts to be appreciated for their beauty and experienced as antidotes to civilization. Here, wilderness becomes a retreat from capitalist production that preserves evolved landscapes. The two counternarratives diverge, however, in the conservation movement's validation of a male hero who could reenter the forest, confront and overcome wild nature, and reclaim a lost virility and the feminist critique of the "rape" of "virgin" nature through exploration and experiment.

My own view is that the deeply gendered character of the mainstream Recovery Narrative, as well as the environmentalist and feminist counternarratives, makes gender problematic as a basis for future narratives and ethics. While the use of the image of nature as fruitful female might be viewed as positive from the perspectives of either progress or decline, the negative associations of nature as virgin to be exploited need to be critically reassessed. My proposal for viewing nature as a partner retains the positive features of personal engagement with nature, as experienced by romantics and preservationists, but disengages from the negative sexual, acquisitive, and exploitative connotations of the image of nature as female.

"VIRGIN" NATURE TRANSFORMED

The mainstream Recovery Narrative begins with Eve as virgin land. Amerigo Vespucci's (1451–1512) voyages to the New World between 1497 and 1504 were illustrated by a German cartographer who feminized Vespucci's first name as America. He depicted America as a woman in a hammock, awakening in surprise and innocence from her slumber and seductively welcoming Vespucci, the explorer, who represents Europe. America is naked and sits on an open hammock with her legs slightly parted, gazing upward at a fully clothed Vespucci who stands dominant over her. Her awakening from slumber suggests that America is ripe for discovery and is ready to be seduced, even raped. She has the long flowing hair symbolic of maidenhood, her only clothing being a cap of leaves or feathers, a barely visible loin cloth, and an braided anklet, while her hammock is made of rope, the two features indicating "inferior" clothing and housing technologies.

Vespucci, by contrast, bears a sword representing European dominance and carries an astrolabe, symbolic of the science of astronomy useful in the

AMERICA.

Americen Americus retexit , &   *Semel vocauit inde femper excitam*

Fig. 6.1. In Jan van der Straet's *America*, Amerigo Vespucci startles a voluptuous maiden, America, who is seemingly ripe for discovery and seduction. *Nova Reperta* (Antwerp, 1579). Courtesy of the Burndy Library, Dibner Institute for the History of Science and Technology, Cambridge, Massachusetts

skilled arts of navigation and exploration. He plants a staff topped by the cross of Christianity and a banner bearing the stars of the southern cross firmly and authoritatively on the land. Behind Vespucci, his ship is shown in full sail, and a landing bark on the shore claim the sea and shoreline as that of Europe. A wooden war club leaning against a tree behind the maiden indicates the primitive weaponry of the natives, while in the distance naked men shown roasting body parts on a spit symbolize savagery and cannibalism. An anteater and other animals represent the wild nature of the New World. Here Vespucci is the European hero who dominates and seduces America, the virgin land. The illustration sets up a narrative of the transformation of undeveloped American nature into civilized European lands that will become the dominant story of American development.[1]

Another illustration of America as virgin land appeared as the title page of Abraham Ortelius's atlas *Theatrum Orbis Terrarum*, or *Picture of the World* (1579). Figures representing the four continents—Europe

Fig. 6.2. The title page of Abraham Ortelius's *Theatrum Orbus Terrarum* (Antwerp, 1579), published in English as *The Theatre of the Whole World* (London, 1661), shows the four known continents as female figures. America, representing the virgin land of the New World, reclines at the base of the pedestal. Courtesy of the Newberry Library, Chicago

(Europa), Asia, Africa, and America—all depicted as female are shown surrounding a pedestal framing the book's title. Europe, fully clothed (representing the known world), dominates the top of the pedestal, while partially clothed Asia and Africa (two partially known continents) stand in front of its two supporting pillars, and a naked America (the unknown New World), with legs slightly parted, reclines seductively at its base. America is placed in the foreground, eyes cast downward, bearing a wooden, feathered spear with two arrows under her leg and holding a decapitated, bearded head. She represents the wild, savage, uncivilized virgin land of the American continent, ready to be exploited and to receive the arts and letters of Europe. Again the image is consistent with the playing out of the mainstream Recovery Narrative of Western culture.[2]

Gerhard Mercator's *Atlas, or A Geographical Description of the World* (1636) likewise contained dualistic hierarchical meanings that associated the Old World and Europe with masculinity, knowledge, and power and the New World with femininity, subordination, and resources. Fully "civilized" Europe is depicted as female, while Asia is partly "civilized" and America and Africa are "uncivilized." Men—such as explorers, mapmakers, and colonizers—are the agents who convert uncivilized female nature (America and Africa) into civilized female society (Europe and Asia). Such oppositions confirm the hierarchies of culture over nature, civilized over savage, and nation over colony that would in turn drive and legitimate settlement of the New World by the Old World.[3]

On Mercator's map, the Earth—*Terra*—is portrayed as a fruitful mother, a female figure holding a cornucopia from which flow fruits from all over the world. Beside her sit animals from the several continents: an elephant, lion, camel, ox, and wildcat. Palm trees, mountains, and deciduous trees fill the background. Of the earth, Mercator wrote, "To her only, for her excellent worth, we have imposed the surname of *venerable mother*. Shee receiveth us from our first birth, and being borne nourisheth, and maintaines us thereafter without ceasing, and for the last office having received us into her bosome; abandoned of the rest of nature, covereth us as a good mother." The earth, however, could show her ferocity in the chaos of hail, floods, and tempests. Or, she could accommodate herself "as a handmayde, for the use of man," by nourishing and producing a diversity of colors, odors, saps, and juices of her own accord. Here nature as a mother, who is both nurturing and punishing, accommodating and witholding, sets up the dynamic of the Recovery of Eden narrative in the New World.[4]

Building on the mapmakers' images, colonial rhetoric characterized the continent as a virgin to be both enjoyed and exploited. While filled with potential, American lands required improvement. In 1616, John Smith extolled New England as a place in which "her treasures hauing yet neuer beene opened, nor her orginals wasted, consumed, nor abused" are available for European use and settlement. Thomas Morton, who in 1632 praised New England as a new Canaan, likened its potential for development by "art and industry" to a "faire virgin longing to be sped and meete her lover in a Nuptiall bed. "Her fruitfull wombe," he said, "not being enjoyed is like a glorious tombe."[5]

If New England's cold climate could engender images of paradise, encounters with Maryland and Virginia produced even more effusive prose. George Alsop's 1666 "Character of the Province of Maryland" publicized the land as a "natural womb [which] (by her plenty) maintains and preserves the several diversities of Animals" and "generously fructifie[s] this piece of Earth with almost all sorts of Vegetables." Robert Beverley, writing in 1705, described Virginia's fertile soils and pleasant climate as so seductive to Europeans that they might forget their mission of laboring on the land, returning in effect to that lost Eden of the past: "All their senses are entertained with an endless succession of Native Pleasures. Their Eyes are ravished with the Beauties of naked Nature. . . . Their Taste is regaled with the most delicious Fruits . . . and their smell is refreshed with an eternal fragrance of Flowers and Sweets, with which Nature perfumes and adorns the Woods almost the whole year round." In 1733, William Byrd set out to survey lands he had purchased along the North Carolina-Virginia border, an estate of 20,000 acres that he dubbed the "Land of Eden," where the waters were "as sweet as milk." These Edenic lands, however, could not be just enjoyed, they needed to be improved lest people fall into a slothful, lazy way of life. Plowing and planting were the ways to convert virgin nature into fields of plenty.[6]

VIRGIN LAND INTO FRUITFUL FIELD

In his book *Virgin Land*, Henry Nash Smith portrayed the West's "virgin land" as a region to be transformed from a great American desert into a garden of the world—a prototype of the Recovery Narrative in the American West. From Daniel Boone and Kit Carson as frontier heroes who explored the land to the Yeoman farmer who converted the desert into a garden, it was men who acted on the land to bring it to fruition. Annette Kolodny, however, in *The Lay of the Land*, removes Nash's gender-blind glasses and shows that his "virgin land" was in fact gendered as female—a land to be surveyed, laid waste, praised, and made to bear fruit in the process of creating an American paradise. Symbols, both argue, are powerful indicators of relationships between people and nature. They reflect, as Smith later put it, "a continuous dialectic interplay between the mind and its environment." From clearing womb-like places in the forest to plowing and planting "virgin soils" that bear fruit, male and female symbolism operate as ethical imperatives and as permissive ideologies. Thus what people believe and what they say permits them to act, and the way people act in turn indicates belief in stories and myths.[7]

Generations of American agriculturalists believed that plow technology would compel female nature to produce new bounty. In 1833, Henry Colman, the Massachusetts agricultural improver, promoted Francis Bacon's approach to recovering the garden through agriculture. "The effort to extend the dominion of man over nature," he wrote, "is the most healthy and most noble of all ambitions." He characterized the earth as a woman whose productivity could help to advance the progress of the human race. "Here man exercises dominion over nature; . . . commands the earth on which he treads to waken her mysterious energies . . . compels the inanimate earth to teem with life; and to impart sustenance and power, health and happiness to the countless multitudes who hang on her breast and are dependent on her bounty." Here the Recovery Narrative's progressive plot is revealed in its mandate to convert virgin land into fruitful field for the benefit of all Americans.[8]

Frank Norris provides a graphic example of female nature succumbing to the male plow in his 1901 novel *The Octopus*. In this story of the transformation of California by the railroad, the earth is portrayed as female, sexual, and alive. He writes, "The great brown earth turned a huge flank to [the sky], exhaling the moisture of the early dew. . . . One could not take a dozen steps upon the ranches without the brusque sensation that underfoot the land was alive, . . . palpitating with the desire of reproduction. Deep down there in the recesses of the soil, the great heart throbbed once more, thrilling with passion, vibrating with desire, offering itself to the caress of the plough, insistent, eager, imperious."[9]

Norris describes the female earth being seduced on a massive scale by thousands of men operating their plows in unison. "Everywhere through-

out the great San Joaquin, unseen and unheard, a thousand ploughs up-
stirred the land, tens of thousands of shears clutched deep into the warm,
moist soil." And he leaves no doubt that the seduction becomes violent
rape, as he writes, "It was the long stroking caress, vigorous, male, powerful, for which the Earth seemed panting. The heroic embrace of a multitude of iron hands, gripping deep into the brown, warm flesh of the land
that quivered responsive and passionate under this rude advance, so robust
as to be almost an assault, so violent as to be veritably brutal. There, under
the sun and under the speckless sheen of the sky, the wooing of the Titan
began, the vast primal passion, the two world-forces, the elemental Male
and Female, locked in a colossal embrace, at grapples in the throes of an
infinite desire, at once terrible and divine, knowing no law, untamed, savage, natural, sublime."[10]

The idea of an Edenic fruitful, female land—waiting to be seduced,
plowed, planted, and watered by male ingenuity—gripped the imaginations
of settlers and promoters of the American West. During the first quarter of
the twentieth century, California—the Golden State—sold itself through
richly colored brochures, flyers, five-color labels, and orange-crate art.
Images of "Eve" as the fertility of nature and of California as Edenic garden conveyed to the consumer a female nature as provider of fruit and food.
The Collins Fruit Company of Riverside, California displayed a young
woman holding orange blossoms and ripened fruit in her draped robe as if
pregnant, while a wreath of blossoms encircled her curly locks. Behind her
male workers picked ripened oranges from fully laden trees. Similar designs
by La Belle and Amethyst oranges showed voluptuous females, with
rounded bellies, wearing skirts filled with oranges.[11]

Other advertisements featured fruits, such as those found in the
Garden of Eden, waiting invitingly to be plucked by anyone strolling past.
Orchard Run of Riverside, California, displayed oranges pouring out of a
pathway between fruit-laden trees, while Rose-Garden of Redlands,
California, showed Sunkist oranges set against unending fields of green
orchards. The sexual temptations of the Garden of Eden were also used as
themes. Indian Belle seedless oranges featured an Indian warrior seducing
a voluptuous Indian maiden against a background of orchards, green hills,
and snow-capped mountains, while Yorba Linda Gem Valencias of
Orange County showed a young couple in an automobile driving under a
canopy of trees past ripened orange groves into an orange sun setting
against purple hills.[12]

Integral to the mainstream Recovery Narrative was the transformation of desert into garden. In the American West, water obtained from irrigation was a necessary component of turning the arid wastes into fertile fields. The "four rivers" that flowed out of the Garden of Eden were a persistent theme in attracting settlers to the West. An Idaho pamphlet in the early 1900s displayed a maiden in flowing robes pouring water from an urn onto a fertile land, while another brochure depicted a young couple under a fruitbearing tree looking out over well-watered planted fields.[13]

Once the land had been cultivated, the produce had to be distributed through the capitalist market system that permeated America from east to west by the last quarter of the nineteenth century. Railroads not only marketed the fruits of the garden, but also lured settlers to the irrigated Eden. The Southern Pacific Railroad published a series of promotional brochures entitled "California for the Settler." One cover depicted an arbor of oranges through which one could view a pastoral landscape filled with cows grazing on hillsides, a lake, and fields of neatly planted crops against a backdrop of sun-drenched mountains. Another brochure showed green pastures with hay mounds grazed by dairy cows in front of orchards and fields, while a third displayed fields of California poppies along ocean beaches with a train arriving under an enormous orange sun.[14]

The realities of living in the West belied the Edenic promotions. Women labored on the land and in the home with backbreaking work as intense as that of men. Digging irrigation ditches was expensive, time-consuming work frequently doomed to failure by disasters that ranged from financial and technological to frequent drought that ended in crop failures. The promises of yellow-gold ore, green-gold crops, and white-gold water under persistently sunny skies were often tarnished by the realities of settlement and the difficulties of creating family farms on arid lands. Yet the Recovery of Eden narrative in which anyone who worked hard enough could participate and from which anyone could profit continued to lure settlers and to create hope that a wild West could be turned into a Golden West.

FROM NATURE TO CIVILIZATION

The overarching mainstream Recovery Narrative is the movement from wild nature to civilized society. Presaged by John Locke and Adam Smith, the goal of Western culture has been to domesticate and improve the wild.

Wild lands and wild people are to be subdued in the quest for civilized society. Gathering, hunting, and pastoralism are to be superceded by agriculture and commerce. Civilization—land improved by male intervention—is the final end toward which "wild" nature is destined. The Recovery Narrative undoes the Fall. Here Eve is fallen nature—wild land, barren desert, impenetrable forest. Civilization is "the end of nature"; it is nature natured, *natura naturata*—the natural order—nature ordered and tamed. Nature is no longer inchoate matter endowed with a formative power (nature naturing, *natura naturans*—nature as creative force); it is the civilized natural order designed by God. The unruly energy of wild female nature is suppressed and pacified. The final happy state of nature natured is female and civilized—the restored garden of the world.[15]

John Gast depicts this ascensionist narrative in his 1872 painting *American Progress*. On the left—toward the west—is *natura naturans*, nature active, alive, wild, dark, and savage, filled, as William Bradford would have put it, with "wild beasts and wild men." Buffalo, wolves, and elk flee in dark disorder accompanied by Indians with horses and travois. On the right—advancing from east to west—is *natura naturata*, nature as ordered, civilized, and tamed. No longer to be feared or assaulted, she floats angelically through the air in flowing white robes, emblazoned with the star of empire. She carries telegraph wires in her left hand, symbols of the highest level of communication—language borne through the air, the word or logos from above. The domination of logic or pure form is repeated in the book she grasps in her right hand. It artfully touches the coiled telegraph wires. She represents the city, the civil, the civic order of government—the highest order of nature. She is pure Platonic form impressed on female matter, transforming and ordering all beneath her.[16]

It is American men who have prepared her way. They have dispelled the darkness, fought the Indian, killed the bear and buffalo. Pioneers in covered wagons, gold rush prospectors, and the pony express precede her. Farmers have settled and tamed the land, and now plow the soil near their fenced fields and crude cabins. Stagecoaches and trains follow, bringing waves of additional settlers. At the far right is the civilization of the Atlantic seaboard, where ships bearing the arts of the Old World arrive in the New. The painting's east to west progressive narrative presents a story of ascent and conquest.

A similar theme is portrayed in the mural Emanuel Leutze painted in the United States Capital in 1861. His famous *Westward the Course of*

Fig. 6.3. John Gast's *American Progress* (1872) shows the westward movement as the advancement of civilization represented by a female figure bearing the gifts of knowledge and communication. Courtesy of the Gene Autry Western Heritage Museum, Los Angeles

Empire Takes its Way illustrates a line from a poem by George Berkeley. A Madonna-like grouping of a pioneer with his wife and child are at the center of the mural. They stand on a rock outcrop and point west toward barren "virgin" lands. Below them pass armed and mounted men leading covered wagons that bear women, representing civilization. Men use axes and uproot trees to cut a path for the party. The mural's frame shows a view of San Francisco's Golden Gate flanked by portraits of explorers William Clark and Daniel Boone. Like Gast's "American Progress," this mural portrays a dynamic moment in the transformation of "virgin" nature into female civilized form through the agency of men.[17]

Domenico Tojetti's 1875 painting, *Progress of America*, is a third example. Personifying progress, a female Liberty figure drives a chariot pulled by two white horses. On the right, American Indians and buffalo flee into darkness and disorder before the advance of civilization. Behind the Liberty icon, female figures representing agriculture, medicine, mechanics, and the arts accompany her advance. Other women bear a tablet that sym-

Fig. 6.4. In *Westward the Course of Empire Takes its Way* (1861), Emanuel Leutze depicts pioneer families cutting forests enroute to "virgin" lands, while bearing the accoutrements of "civilization" in their covered wagons. Mural Study, United States Capitol, Smithsonian American Art Museum, Bequest of Sara Carr Upton

bolizes literacy, followed by a train bringing commerce and light to a barren "virgin" landscape.

Civilization, painted by George Willoughby Maynard in 1893, is a fourth representation. Here a white female figure is dressed in white robes and seated on a throne decorated with cornucopias. She holds the book of knowledge on her lap and points to its text as the epitome of enlightenment and education. The book represents the logos, the light or word from above. The woman's Anglo-Saxon whiteness excludes the blackness of matter, darkness, and dark-skinned peoples.

All four paintings portray movement from dark, virgin, undeveloped nature (*natura naturans*) to final platonic, civilized, ideal form (*natura naturata*). In the first two paintings, male agents effect the transformation from the undeveloped disorder of the wilderness to the ordered, idealized landscape. The final two paintings reveal the outcome, an enlightened world made safe for educated Euroamerican men and women.

Fig. 6.5. Domenico Tojetti's *The Progress of America* (1875) shows the flight of Indians and buffalo in the path of a chariot-driven Liberty figure followed by agriculture and the arts. Oakland Museum of California, The Oakland Museum of California Kahn Collection

The next stage of the Recovery Narrative is represented by the city, which developed in response to expanding capitalist markets. The city in the garden (Virgil's *urbs in horto*, discussed in chapter 3) epitomizes the transformation of female nature into female civilization through the mutually reinforcing powers of male energy and interest-earning capital. Frank Norris's second novel, *The Pit* (1903), captures these connections.[18]

Norris depicts the city as female in his story about the wheat pit at the Chicago Board of Trade.[19] The city is the locus of power that operates in the natural world, pulling everything toward its center. It functions as the bridge between the raw matter of the surrounding hinterlands and civilized female form. Norris describes Chicago drawing raw materials towards itself, transforming natural resources into capitalist commodities:

[T]he Great Grey City, brooking no rival, imposed its dominion upon a reach of country larger than many a kingdom of the Old World. For thousands of miles beyond its confines was its influence

Fig. 6.6. In *Civilization* (1893), by George Willoughby Maynard, knowledge and civilization are depicted as female, epitomizing the height of enlightenment and the arts. George Willoughby Maynard, Civilization, Oil on canvas, 54 $^1/_2$ x 36 $^5/_8$ National Academy of Design, New York (845–P)

felt. Out, far out, far away in the snow and shadow of Northern Wisconsin forests, axes and saws bit the bark of century old trees, stimulated by this city's energy. Just as far to the southward pick and drill leaped to the assault of veins of anthracite moved by her central power. Her force turned the wheels of harvester and seeder a thousand miles distant in Iowa and Kansas. Her force spun the screws and propellers of innumerable squadrons of lake steamers crowding the Sault Sainte Marie. For her and because of her all the Central States, all the Great Northwest roared with traffic and industry; sawmills screamed; factories, their smoke blackening the sky, slashed and flamed; wheels turned, pistons leaped in their cylinders; cog gripped cog; beltings clasped the drums of mammoth wheels; and converters of forges belched into the clouded air their tempest breath of molten steel.[20]

Like Plato's female soul of the world, turning herself within herself, the city provides the source of motion that permeates and energizes the world around it. It is the bridge between primal, changing matter and final, civilized form. In Norris's novel, men are subordinate agents to the city's higher force, facilitating the change from *natura naturans* into *natura naturata*, from natural resource into fabricated product. Men operate the steam engines, sawmills, factories, lumber barges, grain elevators, trains, and switches that make Chicago an industrial city. Business men travel to the city, bringing trade from the country. This process of "civilization in the making," says Norris, is like a "great tidal wave," an "elemental" and "primordial" force, "the first verses of Genesis." It "subdu[es] the wilderness in a single generation," through the "resistless subjugation of . . . the lakes and prairies."[21]

Yet behind the scenes, other men, the capitalist speculators of the Chicago Board of Trade, attempt to manipulate the very forces of nature by pushing the transformation faster and faster. Capitalism mystifies by converting living nature into dead matter and by changing inert metals into living money. To the speculators above the trading pit, nature is a doll-like puppet they can control by manipulating the strings of the wheat trade and changing money into interest-earning capital. Male minds calculate the motions that control the inert matter below.[22]

For Norris's capitalist trader, Curtis Jadwin, nature is dead. Only money is alive, multiplying through the daily trade of the wheat pit.

Because the bulls and bears of the marketplace comprise his only compelling encounters with living things, Jadwin utterly fails to account for the earth and the wheat as alive. But when Jadwin corners the market, the living wheat planted by hundreds of farmers throughout the heartland, rises from the soil as a gigantic irrepressible force, thwarting his apparent control. The capitalist's manipulation of apparently dead nature has widespread repercussions. Jadwin, Norris writes, had "laid his puny human grasp upon Creation and the very earth herself." The "great mother . . . had stirred at last in her sleep and sent her omnipotence moving through the grooves of the world, to find and crush the disturber of her appointed courses."[23] By the late nineteenth century, capitalism's domination of nature as female—of Eve as nature to be exploited for profit—was reaping the backlash of living nature's revolt.

ROMANTIC NATURE

During the nineteenth century, romanticism emerged as a powerful counternarrative to the mainstream Recovery Narrative. Based on the perception that America had declined from its Edenic natural state, the roots of romanticism lay in alternatives to dominant Western traditions. The romantics rediscovered a past in which nature had been positively personified as a mother, virgin, and teacher. The legacies of Plato and the philosophers of the Middle Ages, reflected in the writings of Renaissance neoplatonists and naturalists, were reminders of an idealized earlier time. The romantics deplored the mechanization of nature that had resulted in a cold, calculable order of Newtonian forces and a deforested, polluted landscape. As in the feminist narrative, nature was a revered female.[24]

For Thoreau, Walden Pond was like Eden before the Fall: "Perhaps on that spring morning when Adam and Eve were driven out of Eden," he wrote, "Walden Pond was already in existence . . . and covered with myriads of ducks, geese, which had not heard of the fall. . . ." He frequently quoted ancient writers as he articulated some cherished idea about the pristine beauty of nature. Emerson found that Neoplatonism validated his idea of nature as an emblem of universal truths. And preservationist Muir, writing effusive if less scholarly prose in the last quarter of the century, was also influenced by romantic ideas of an untouched pristine nature created by God.[25]

Thoreau and Muir drew on ancient traditions in their eulogies of nature, depicted in the female gender. Plato's *Timaeus* had described the world soul as female, the source of motion at the center of the cosmos. Over the centuries Neoplatonists had synthesized Christian principles and divided this female soul into two components. The higher *Endelechia* fashioned souls from divine ideas, while the lower *natura* created individuals as copies of these pure forms. By the twelfth century *natura* had been personified as a goddess, God's agent, whose creativity was greater than that of human artists.[26]

"Nature is a greater and more perfect art, the art of God," pronounced Thoreau, "though referred to herself she is genius." Muir agreed with the Renaissance humanists that nature as teacher and artist was superior to humans in ease of production: "It was delightful to witness here the infinite deliberation of Nature, and the simplicity of her methods in the production of such mighty results, such perfect repose combined with restless enthusiastic energy."[27]

A coherent interpretation of nature as a human being writ large—an individual with whom one develops an intimate personal relationship—is evident in the essays, letters, and books of the early founders of the preservationist philosophy in America. This vestige of personal animism—the I/thou relationship to nature so critical to the worldview of native, traditional societies—incorporates a restraining ethic. The prescriptive power of this environmental ethic is apparent in how these nineteenth century preservationists wrote about nature.[28]

Emerson, Thoreau, and Muir depicted nature as a female. Nature had physiological systems that were projections of human bodily functions onto nature. Thoreau pictured nature's perspiration in the form of "warm drizzling rain." But "after this long dripping and oozing from every pore, she began to respire again more healthily than ever." The late afternoon "haze over the woods was like the inaudible panting, or rather the gentle perspiration of resting nature rising from a myriad of pores into the attenuated atmosphere." Thoreau's poetics extended to nature's circulatory and nervous systems as well: "globule(s) from her veins steal . . . up into our own."[29]

It was a common nineteenth-century conceit to refer to nature as female—virgin, vixen, or mother. In contrast to many earlier American writers who had supported commercial enterprise and had described nature in exploitative terms, Thoreau and Muir depicted nature in deeply personal terms as mother and virgin that militated against aggressive postures.[30]

Thoreau and Muir gave nature the attributes of a nurturing mother. Thoreau once described a woodland lake in summer as "the earth's liquid eye, a mirror in the breast of nature." Tasting beer as "strong and stringent as the cedar sap" seemed "as if we had sucked at the very teats of Nature's pine-clad bosom." Muir celebrated nature with prose more purple: "fondly, too, with eternal love does Mother Nature clasp her small bee babies and suckle them, multitudes at once, on her warm Shasta breast."[31] These passages embody the idea of Eve as a mother whose archetypal purpose is realized through bearing and nurturing children.

Thoreau related to nature as a son to his mother. "Sometimes," he exclaimed, "a mortal feels in himself Nature—not his Father, but his Mother stirs within him, and he becomes immortal with her immortality." At other times he was aware of "a certain tender relation to Nature," one that for every man "must come very near to a personal one; he must be conscious of a friendliness in her." Similarly, Muir reveled in "tracing rivers to their sources, getting in touch with the nerves of Mother Earth."[32]

But these early preservationists also celebrated nature's virginity. Soils, forests, rocks, water—all the parts of nature that humanity had left undisturbed—were worthy of their admiration. This philosophy of valuing pristine nature contrasted with the idea of developing the potential of virgin nature so prevalent among the early entrepreneurs. As America's rich soils became exhausted or as forests were denuded in the rush for profits, the preservationists lamented the losses and championed restoration.

The prose of Thoreau and Muir personified virgin nature. Her face and mind were, like the Virgin Mary, the focus for adoration. Thoreau described a nature who "superior to all styles and ages, is now, with pensive face, composing her poem Autumn with which no work of man will bear to be compared." Her head was adorned "with a profusion of fringes and curls," although man was quite capable of "shearing off those woods, and making earth bald before her time." Muir, ever resourceful, found a sympathetic visage beneath Mount Gibbs which "enabled him to feel something of Nature's love even here, beneath the gaze of her coldest rocks."[33]

But Thoreau and Emerson also expressed a relationship to nature as a fallen virgin. Emerson found nature seductive and alluring, noting that "the solitude of wilderness is a sublime mistress, but an intolerable wife." Sometimes, Thoreau admonished, "as seductive as a mistress, by one bait or another, Nature allures inhabitants into all her recesses."[34]

The romantics found that nature could be schizophrenic—without notice "she" might become wild, savage, and vindictive. Here nature is akin to fallen Eve—dark, unknown, potentially savage, and chaotic. Thoreau sought to reverse the implications of nature's wilfulness when he wrote, "Man tames Nature only that he may at last make her more free even than he found her." Despite this unpredictable quality, associated culturally with witchcraft and defiled womanhood, Thoreau's faith in nature's capacity for forgiveness was unshaken. "Here is this vast, savage, howling mother of ours, Nature, lying all around, with such beauty, and such affection for her children as the leopard. . . ." Muir, wandering through sunny alpine meadows, was brought up short by a change in terrain when "suddenly we find ourselves in the shadowy canon, closeted with Nature in one of her wildest strongholds." His faith in nature was challenged during storms in the Sierras when he encountered the destructive power of hail, lightning, and avalanches. Yet "the manifest result of all this storm-culture is the glorious perfection we behold; then faith in Nature's forestry is established, and we cease to deplore the violence of her most destructive gales. . . ."[35]

The anxiety caused by the tension between nature's gentleness and destructive power demanded reassurance if one's faith in the goodness of universal nature were to be retained. For Muir, chaotic patterns were manifestations of the majestic power of nature despite their unpredictable and catastrophic potential for humanity. "By forces seemingly antagonistic and destructive," Muir marveled, "has Mother Nature accomplished her beneficent designs—now a flood of fire, now a flood of ice, now a flood of water; and at length an outburst of organic life, a milky way of snowy petals and wings, girdling the rugged mountain like a cloud. . . ."[36]

The romantics' construction of nature as a person writ large was a manifestation of a more widespread need to relate to nature in positive, but also deeply personal terms. Reacting to the mainstream Recovery Narrative's exploitation of nature for personal gain, the romantics looked to "her" for personal solace and wisdom. Through appreciation, preservation, and restoration, the decline of nature initiated by Eve could be reversed. The romantic conception of nature as a person writ large did not view nature as a partner, but rather drew on historical constructions of nature as a female—virgin, mother, or vixen—that placed nature above or below humanity rather than as equal partner. Nevertheless aspects of Thoreau's philosophy were compatible with a partnership ethic. His bean-field at Walden Pond was an example of working with the soil in ways that promoted the health of both the land and humanity. He wrote of his beans, "The earliest had grown considerably before the latest were in the ground; indeed they were not easily to be put off. What was the meaning of this so steady and self-respecting, this small Herculean labor, I knew not. I came to love my rows, my beans, though so many more than I wanted. They attached me to the earth, and so I got strength like Antaeus. . . .What shall I learn of beans or beans of me? I cherish them, I hoe them, early and late I have an eye to them; and this is my day's work."[37] Here the beans are autonomous actors and Thoreau is an assistant to their labors. His "auxiliaries are the dews and rains," his enemies are "worms, cool days, and most of all woodchucks." He used the soil and rains as helpers and did not make war on the woodchucks, but simply gave them their quarter acre's worth. On a small scale, Thoreau and his beanfield exemplified the potential for a partnership ethic.

NATURE CONSERVED, MANAGED, AND PRESERVED

During the late nineteenth century, the counternarrative of the romantics helped to forge the beginnings of the conservation and preservation movements in America. Conservationists and preservationists, like the romantics, viewed with alarm the decline of a pristine earth exploited for its natural resources. The goals of both the conservation and preservation movements were to recover the earth, but the two movements differed in approach. The conservation movement attempted to restrain shortsighted exploitation of natural resources, while supporting a utilitarian philosophy of wise use. The preservation movement, on the other hand, wished to preserve pristine nature in the form of parks and wilderness.

Early conservationists drew on a potpourri of rhetoric that warned of the consequences of exploiting the earth while acknowledging human dominion over it. No one could have predicted that *Man and Nature*, published in 1864 by Vermont statesman George Perkins Marsh, would become a best seller within a decade. Marsh chronicled the deterioration of the lands of Europe and America, beginning with the ancient civilizations of the Mediterranean and culminating in the environment of his native Vermont. He drew on the idea of nature as mother and provider, defiled by human carelessness and greed. After all, he claimed, human beings were not really nature's children, for they had powers surpassing those of other organisms. Marsh lamented, "man alone is to be regarded as essentially a destructive power." Humans derived from a power outside and above the earth, not from mother earth herself. "He is not of her, . . . he is of more exalted parentage, and belongs to a higher order of existences than those born of her womb and submissive to her dictates."

Marsh depicted nature in the female gender, strong and stable if left alone, but vulnerable to human technology and greed. Following in the tradition of Ovid's *Metamorphoses* (C.E. 7) and Edmund Spenser's *The Faerie Queen* (1595), Marsh's *Man and Nature* portrayed a set of creatures who have turned against the earth and destroyed "her." The ultimate result would be the ruin of the very nature upon which all humanity depended.[38]

Yet Marsh condoned human power over nature for human benefit, as long as it was contained within reasonable limits: "Man . . . cannot rise to the full development of his higher properties unless brute and unconscious nature be effectually combated, and in a great degree, vanquished by human art." He acknowledged that restraint was essential, given that ever since the colonization of the world by Europeans, "man" had sought "to subjugate the virgin earth." In Marsh's solution can be found the roots of a partnership ethic between humanity and nature. Marsh maintained that the proper ethical role was one of the restoration of nature through cooperation. "Man," Marsh said, "should become a co-worker with nature in the reconstruction of the damaged fabric." Humanity could cooperate with nature to repair the human damage and restore the lost harmonies.[39]

A broad-based movement for the conservation of the nation's waters, forests, and range lands had developed by the late nineteenth century. Embracing the rationale of progress through efficient technology, engineers built dams that would provide water and power, conserve watersheds, and distribute water throughout the year to dry farmlands. Foresters promoted selective harvesting and reforestation, while ranchers instituted forage, seeding, and fencing of range lands. The U.S. government created the Division of Forestry in 1886, headed by Bernhard Fernow. And the 1902 Reclamation Act provided for the construction of dams and irrigation works in the arid Western states.

Utilitarian conservationists such as Fernow challenged the idea of *laissez faire* capitalism, which allowed people to exploit resources for profit. The utilitarians substituted a *faire marcher* ("make it work") policy of government regulation. Unlike Thoreau and Muir, who felt a personal intimacy with "virgin" nature, Fernow was concerned that the virgin forests would soon disappear as commodities. He found the earth's bosom a source of production for human benefit, not a place to rest one's head in solitude. In his *Economics of Forestry* (1902), he quoted the French statesman Maximilien Sully: "'Tillage and pasturage are the two breasts of the state.' It is true the manufacturer increases the utility of things, but the farmer multiplies commodities. . . ." Fernow believed that frontier individualism was destroying "virgin" nature, and he argued that the state should restrict access on behalf of future generations. The "careless and extravagant use" of the "enormous resources in fields and forests and mines" had made "virgin supplies available more rapidly than the needs of a resident population," causing "rapacious exploitation and exportation." So as to guard the interests of the many, he advocated that American forests be managed to conserve water and prevent soil erosion.[40]

A new umbrella concept for natural resource conservation was introduced in Theodore Roosevelt's administration (1901–9). The ethic of the utilitarian conservation movement, as formulated by geologist WJ McGee and forester Gifford Pinchot, was "the use of natural resources for the greatest good of the greatest number for the longest time." Natural resource conservation brought together under one banner the previously separate efforts to deal with forests, mines, agriculture, soil erosion, fish, and game. Pinchot wrote that formulating the relationship among all these resources was like emerging from a dark tunnel and seeing, for the first time, the light of an entirely new landscape: "All these separate questions fitted into and made up the one great central problem of the use of the earth for the good of man."[41]

A major motif in the progressive conservation campaign was to decry the destructive nineteenth-century commercial assaults on nature—a nature cast in the female gender. President Roosevelt addressed the White House Conference of Governors in 1908: "Our position in the world has been attained by the extent and thoroughness of the control we have achieved over nature; but we are more, and not less, dependent upon what she furnishes than at any previous time of history since the days of primitive man."[42]

Roosevelt was a nature lover, writer, and a vigorous advocate of conservation; but he was also a champion of the manly virtues gained through encountering nature. His *Wilderness Writings* extolled the ruggedness of outdoor life, including colorful descriptions of hunters in the American West, the thrills of tracking African game, and the dangers of the Brazilian Amazon. His writing underscored the need to preserve both manly engagement with wild nature and to conserve dwindling natural resources.[43]

Acknowledging that nature could retaliate, conservationists advocated working with "her" through careful stewardship rather than conquering her with pickaxe and plow. Cardinal James Gibbons, in opening the second National Conservation Congress in 1910, called on the country to preserve its resources for future generations: "Mother Earth is not only a fruitful mother, she is also a grateful mother, and repays her children for every kindness and tenderness we exercise toward her. And there are also instances on record to show that she is relentless when she chastises." Here, nature as female is personified as both the giving and punishing mother of her human children.[44]

Careful stewardship meant educating people to appreciate nature deeply and to use "her" gifts in moderation. At the 1910 Conservation Congress, Mrs. Mathew Scott, president general of the Daughters of the American Revolution, spoke eloquently to this point: "It is well for youth to be at one with Nature and to learn of her; to know and feel the joy there is in bountiful, glorious nature; to be familiar with her song—the ripple of the river on its stones, the murmur of trees, the rhythm of the sap that rises in them. . . ." Educating all people, and particularly children, would teach them to honor and respect nature as a giving, fruitful mother.[45]

Here nature is engaged in deeply personal terms consistent with the romantic vision, but set within the early conservationists' concerns over dwindling resources and the decline of the earth. Women were active in setting aside the national parks and national forests, in saving California's redwood trees, and in founding Audubon Society chapters to prevent the desecration of birds for hat plumes.[46]

The women who helped to save parks, forests, and birds did so not only to preserve middle-class lifestyles, but also for reasons of deep personal engagement with nature. Women joined hiking clubs, such as the Appalachian Mountain Club and the Sierra Club, birdwatching clubs, and garden clubs. They entered the parks and wilderness in groups and alone. Some did so for aesthetic reasons, others for religious reasons, and still others for the sake of recreation, health, and healing. Among the latter was Isabella Bird, who hiked and rode her horse through the Colorado mountains, recording her reflections in a series of letters in 1878, later published as *A Lady's Life in the Rocky Mountains*. Among those who did so for aesthetic reasons was Mary Austin, whose books on the arid West, such as

The Land of Little Rain (1903), helped to create an appreciation for desert landscapes. Still others wrote on birds and the reasons to save them from the hunter's rifle. They included turn of the century writers Olive Thorne Miller, Mabel Osgood Wright, Florence Merriam Bailey, and Sarah Orne Jewett.[47]

The preservation movement built up during the same period as did conservation, but the two movements did not find separate definition until the proposal to dam Hetch Hetchy Valley came to public attention. Around this time, most women in the conservation movement began to remove their support from Pinchot's style of conservation and joined forces with Muir's preservationist movement.

The split between conservation and preservation took place during the controversy over the damming of Hetch Hetchy Valley in Yosemite National Park as a source of water and power for the city of San Francisco. Conservationists saw a greater public good in the use of water for the fulfillment of people's needs. Muir saw the greatest good in the preservation of the valley and its God-given waters and flowers for appreciation and reverence by humanity. Muir's theocentric ethic was rooted in the preservation of an earth created by a God whose power and majesty should revered by his earthly children.

Environmental historian Mark Stoll sees the conflict in terms of Christian religion and its role in humanity's attempt to recover the Garden of Eden in America:

> [T]he rhetoric of the Hetch Hetchy debates encapsulated the history of Christian attitudes toward and ethical impact on nature. Dam supporters marshaled a variety of age-old religious arguments. God had made the earth for man's benefit and put it under his dominion. . . . Defenders of the undammed valley also appealed to ancient religious doctrines. To dam opponents, the world was an emanation of God's glory and power; a place like Hetch Hetchy was a temple designed to worship in. Earthly beauty mirrored the beauty of God; the government must preserve the valley for the moral and spiritual uplift it invoked. . . . In America, the image of a renewed Eden, of humanity happy in abundant and harmonious nature, [had] created conflict between the ideals of capitalist plenty and nature preservation.[48]

The passage of the Raker Act in 1913 that authorized the damming of Hetch Hetchy Valley validated the conservationists' goals for the wise use of natural resources, while the passage of the National Park Service Act in 1916 reinforced the preservationists' objectives of setting aside natural areas to be appreciated for their beauty and managed for their recreational potential. Both movements fitted into the overarching narrative of the Recovery of Eden. Both started from the perception of an earth in decline, but conservation reclaimed a desecrated earth for human use within the capitalist system, while preservation saved and restored as yet unblemished landscapes for human appreciation and recreation within that same system.

NATURE AND MEN

As the frontier closed and civilization advanced, American men began to lament the loss of wild nature. There was an apparent need to retain the "virgin forest" as a wilderness for men to test their maleness, strength, and virility. While men were associated with nature, "civilized" women were symbolized as the moral model who suppressed internal sexual libido. Conservationists looked to mother earth to restore the vigor and strength sapped by the competitiveness of capitalist enterprise. J. Horace McFarland of the American Civic Association stressed in 1908 that "the noise and strain of the market place" caused people to flee to "the very bosom of nature . . . for that renewing spirit and strength which cannot be had elsewhere."[49]

In 1913, the nation was captivated by the saga of a naked man who had decamped into the Maine woods to live—"as Adam lived"—completely off the land. He fashioned clothing from a slain bear, gathered ripe berries, fished for trout, and hunted deer and ducks, which he cooked on a fire created by rubbing two sticks together. His "red blood" restored after two months in the wild, Joe Knowles, "primitive man," became a national hero. He turned his alleged encounter with the wild into a commercial success, writing a best-selling book, *Alone in the Wilderness*. This saga epitomizes the male encounter with female nature to restore the frontier ruggedness lost to the soft, civilized, city life also gendered as female.[50]

The wise-use ethic of utilitarian conservationists and the back-to-nature ethic of the preservationists were both responses to the rise of industrial capitalism. Nature was a resource for both economic well-being and spiritual growth, and each faction had a different strategy to recover the original Edenic oneness. The utilitarian conservationists advocated carefully using and improving a "virgin" nature, while the preservationists believed in protecting and merging with a pristine "virgin" nature.

The national parks and forests established at the turn of the century were a signal that preservationist values had been absorbed into mainstream American life. Wilderness preservation was no longer a mere counterpoint to capitalist development; it now acted as a safety valve for the new industrial order. Those who reaped the benefits of the urban industries that depended on nature as a resource were the same people who forcefully proclaimed the need for a rustic retreat from competition and the pressures of urban life.[51]

CONCLUSION

In the mainstream story of American progress, men continue to be the transforming agents between active female nature and civilized female form. Men are deemed to make the land safe for both women and men by suppressing unpredictable external nature and unruly internal nature. But nature as wilderness does not "become" male, nor does civilization "become" female. There is no reversal of male/female symbols in the closing chapters the frontier expansion story.

Symbols such as nature and culture or maleness and femaleness are not binary opposites with universal meanings encoded into the very "essence" of what it means to be a man or a woman. Nature, wilderness, and civilization are socially constructed concepts that change over time and function as stage settings in the progressive narrative. The roles that men and women act out on the stage of history are also social constructs. The authors of such powerful narratives as laissez-faire capitalism, mechanistic science, manifest destiny, and the frontier story were usually the privileged elites. Their words were read and interpreted by persons of power who added new chapters to the older biblical story. These books become the library of Western culture. This library functions as ideology when ordinary people read, listen to, internalize, and act out the stories told by their elders—parents, ministers, entrepreneurs, newspaper editors, and professors who teach and socialize the young.

The reinvention of Eden by a heroic Adam acting to improve a nature depicted variously as a virgin, fallen, or fruitful Eve is the mainstream story of most European Americans. But questions concerning non-Western and darker-skinned peoples are also a significant component of the Recovery Narrative. The ways that Native and African Americans were brought into the mainstream story—and how they resisted or accepted inclusion—are also integral to the plot.

SEVEN

Colonizing Eden

She knew things that nobody had ever told her. For instance, the words of the trees and the wind. She often spoke to falling seeds and said, "Ah hope you fall on soft ground," because she had heard seeds saying that to each other as they passed. She knew the world was a stallion rolling in the blue pasture of ether. She knew that God tore down the old world every evening and built a new one by sun-up. It was wonderful to see it take form with the sun and emerge from the gray dust of its making.

—*Zora Neale Hurston,* Their Eyes Were Watching God

Both American Indians and African Americans play central roles in the mainstream Recovery Narrative. Europeans took over and "improved" the Indians and their "natural" Edens by redeeming the eastern forests and western deserts. But blacks supplied much of the forced labor that enabled the Recovery project to proceed. The New World Eden became a colonized Eden with white Europeans at the center of the garden and Indians and blacks excluded or relegated to the periphery. In the process of reinventing the American Eden, the storyline itself expanded and stretched in order to justify unequal power relations among the three groups. The mainstream Recovery Narrative privileged and promoted European

Americans and legitimated their power over nonhuman nature and non-white peoples. As a consequence, minorities saw themselves as caught up in and resisting a narrative of decline. Looking more closely at Indian, black, and other immigrants' cultural practices, self-autonomy and resistance, and at each group's active use of sympathizers as allies makes history more complex. It also indicates possibilities for partnerships among ethnic groups and the potential for a partnership ethic.

INDIANS AND EDEN

A Penobscot Indian story from northern New England explains the origin of maize. A great famine had deprived people of food and water. A beautiful Indian maiden appeared and married one of the young men of the tribe, but soon succumbed to another lover, a snake. On being found out she promised to alleviate her husband's sorrow if he would plant a blade of green grass clinging to her ankle. First he must kill her with his axe, then drag her body through the forest clearing until all her flesh had been stripped, and finally bury her bones in the center of the clearing. She then appeared to him in a dream and taught him how to tend, harvest and cook corn, and smoke tobacco.[1]

This agricultural origin story taught the Indians not only how to plant their corn in forest clearings, but also that the earth would continue to regenerate the human body through the corn plant. It features a woman, the corn maiden, and a male lover as central actors. It begins with the state of nature as drought and famine. Nature is a desert, a poor place for human existence. The plot features a woman as savior. Through a willing sacrifice, she introduces agriculture to her husband and to the women who subsequently plant the corn, beans, and squash that provide the bulk of the food that sustains the life of the tribe. The result is an agroecological system based on the planting of interdependent polycultures in forest gardens. The story type is ascensionist and progressive. Women transform nature from a desert into a garden. From a tragic situation of despair and death, a comic, happy, and optimistic situation of continued life results. In this story, the valence of women as corn mothers is good; they bring bountiful gifts. The valence of nature ends as a good: the earth is an agent of regeneration. Death is transformed into life by the return of the corn mother's body to the earth. Even death therefore results in a higher good.[2]

Into this bountiful world of corn mothers enter the Puritan fathers, bringing with them their own agricultural origin story of Adam and Eve. The biblical myth begins where the Indian story ends, with an agroecological system of polycultures in the Garden of Eden. As in the Indian story, a woman, Eve, shows a man, Adam, how to harvest the fruits of the garden. But instead of obtaining valuable new knowledge of food gathering, the couple is cast out of the garden into a desert. Instead of moving from desert to garden, as in the Indian story, the European story moves from garden to desert. In both stories a woman is the central actress and both contain elements of violence toward women. In both men must labor in the earth. But the plot of the Indian story is progressive and comic, not declensionist and tragic as in the European story. The end result is a better state of nature than in the beginning. The valence of woman is good; the end valence of nature is good.[3]

According to Benjamin Franklin, Indians quickly perceived the difference between the two accounts. Franklin writes satirically that the Indians on being apprised of the "historical facts on which our [own] religion is founded; such as the fall of our first parents by eating an apple . . . an Indian orator stood up" to thank the Europeans. "What you have told us is all very good," he said. "It is, indeed, bad to eat apples. It is much better to make them all into cider. We are much obliged by your kindness in coming so far to tell us these things which you have heard from your mothers; in return I will tell you some of those which we have heard from ours."[4]

Historical events reversed the plots of the European and Indian origin stories. The Indians' comic happy ending changed to a story of decline and conquest, while Euroamericans were largely successful in creating a New World garden. Warfare, disease, and dependency on trade goods all undercut Indian power to resist European expansion. But even as Indians were succumbing to the notion of a "vanishing race," Europeans were importing another nonwhite population—this one from Africa—to work the American soils. As Indian populations declined, African-American populations increased, first from the slave trade and then, after its official demise in 1808, through smuggling and natural increase as tobacco dominance gave way to the cotton boom.

The heroic Recovery Narrative that guided settlement is notable for its treatment of Indians. Wilderness is the absence of civilization. Although most European Americans seem to have perceived Indians as the functional equivalent of "the wild," they nevertheless believed Indian survivors had the potential to be "civilized" and hence to participate in the recovery. American officials changed the Indians' own origin stories to make them descendants of Adam and Eve. Thomas L. McKenney, who formulated Indian policy in the 1840s said that the whole "family of man" came from "one original and common stock" of which the Indian was one branch. "Man . . . was put by his creator in the garden, which was eastward in Eden, whence flowed the river which parted, and became into four heads; and that from his fruitfulness his [the Indian] species were propagated." Because Eden was in the Old World and not the New, Indians were not indigenous to America, argued McKenny, but arrived via the Bering Strait. Since Indians were of the same ultimate parentage as whites and hence had the same "human nature," they could be educated and transformed into a "higher" stage of development.[5]

In 1868, the U.S. commissioner of Indian Affairs deemed them "capable of civilization and christianization." A successor in 1892 argued that since Indian children were "made in the image of God, being the likeness of their Creator," they had the "same possibilities of growth and development" as other children. An Indian baby could become "a cultivated refined Christian gentleman or lovely woman."[6]

INDIANS INTO FARMERS

Although eastern and southwestern Indians practiced horticulture and lived in settled communities, by the second half of the nineteenth century the primary concerns of Euroamericans were the "taming" and settling of the nomadic plains Indians on horseback. Euroamericans attempted to transform Indians into settled farmers first by removing eastern Indians to lands west of the Mississippi River, then by settling all Indians on reservations, and later by allotting them 160 acre plots of private property for farming. Indians, they believed, were capable of being "civilized," but were at a lower stage of economic development than whites. They fitted into Adam Smith's stages of hunters and pastoralists, but had not yet reached the agricultural and commercial levels. Thomas Jefferson saw them as capable of participating in the Recovery Narrative when he told a delegation in 1802 that he would be pleased to see them "cultivate the earth, to raise herds of useful animals and to spin and weave." Andrew Jackson recommended that they be relocated to an Indian territory especially set up for their habitation. In this way they would "share in the blessings of civilization and be saved from that degradation and destruction to which they were rapidly hastening. . . ."⁷

George Belden, who spent twelve years living with the Santee Sioux and thought they fit beautifully into an "Indian wilderness," nevertheless later made war on them, believing that they would develop greater respect for "civilization" if defeated and turned into farmers. As their lands were reduced they would turn "gradually from their wild habits of roving and living from day to day, to settle . . . and live as herders and farmers." It made no sense for fifteen to twenty thousand Indians, he believed, to occupy a territory four times the size of Illinois. There was no reason for white settlers to relinquish "a rich, fertile, and beautiful country to a few thousand savages, who can make no use of it but to chase the lessening herds of buffalo and deer."⁸

Some people, however, wanted to see Indians vanish from the United States. They believed that war would solve the "Indian problem," or in any case that Indians were doomed to extinction within a few years as whites advanced, game disappeared, and Indian resources became too scarce to support wandering and hunting. According to Samuel Bowles, the Indian's "game flies before the white man; we cannot restore it to him if we would; we would not if we could; it is his destiny to die. . . ." The Indian could not continue a "barbaric" way of life and would in all likelihood remain uncivilized. Bowles believed that "they are not our equals," and "we know that our right to the soil, as a race capable of its superior improvement is above theirs." He was also blatant about the necessity of attaining Indian lands. "Let us say to the Indian," he wrote, "we want your hunting grounds to dig gold from, to raise grain on, and you must 'move on.'"⁹

From an ecological point of view, as game diminished, diseases took their toll, and metal trade goods such as guns, traps, and kettles were introduced, Indians found it increasingly difficult to maintain their former way of life. The U.S. government first carried on numerous wars against the plains Indians and then, adopting a paternalistic stance, began to regard them as children for whom whites must provide and care. Treaties in the 1850s and 1860s removed them to reservations, allotted farming plots jointly to several families, and provided funds for education, cattle, farm equipment, and mills and blacksmith shops to bring them out of a state of wandering into one of settled agriculture. Indians, like whites, would advance to the next level of civilization, thereby incorporating them into the mainstream Recovery Narrative, even as they were colonized and marginalized on the periphery of the garden.

EDUCATING INDIANS

After the treaty system ended in 1871, the Board of Indian Commissioners drew up policies for Indian education and development. They proposed to treat Indians as wards of the state in order to "educate them in industry, the arts of civilization, and the principles of Christianity. . . ." Secretary of the Interior Carl Schurz advocated government protection during the "dangerous period of transition from savage to civilized life."[10]

In the late nineteenth century, reform groups pressed for a new approach. They advocated breaking up the reservations into property allotments based on the 160-acre homestead ideal and educating Indians in the ideals of reading, writing, arithmetic, and citizenship. In response, the 1887 Dawes Act was passed authorizing the breakup of communally held reservations into individual and family allotments, with the selling off of surplus lands for white settlement.[11]

These developments fit neatly into the metanarrative of Recovery. Indians would be Christianized and drawn into the biblical framework of salvation. They would be imbued with the Protestant work ethic needed to achieve that salvation and to cultivate the land. They would be raised to a more "civilized" state as farmers and commercial traders as they manufactured and sold surplus products and participated in the market economy. They would thus be educated and fully assimilated into the capitalist framework, realizing their potential "human nature" as competitors and becoming full American citizens.

The programs largely failed. Indians for the most part maintained a communal rather than individualistic ethos. They were accustomed to sharing, not accumulating. Although they were drawn into a system of trading for commodities that they could not produce for themselves, they did not readily adopt a get-ahead attitude or promote the rapid exploitation of natural resources to attain profits.[12]

Indeed, Indians for the most part rejected the new mainstream Recovery Narrative in which they were forced to become actors, seeing it as one of decline rather than progress. With some exceptions, they resisted the roles into which they were cast and the lines they were forced to speak. They rejected characterizations of their lands as wilderness or desert, calling them simply home. As Chief Luther Standing Bear put it, "We did not think of the great open plains, the beautiful rolling hills, and winding streams with tangled growth, as 'wild.' Only to the white man was

Fig. 7.1. In the late-nineteenth century the federal government removed many Indian tribes to reservations as exemplified by this undated photograph of Pine Ridge Reservation in South Dakota. Courtesy of the National Anthropological Archives, Smithsonian Institution

nature a wilderness and only to him was the land 'infested' with 'wild' animals and 'savage' people. To us it was tame. Earth was bountiful. . . ."[13]

While adopting the Christian religion, Indians often emphasized those aspects compatible with traditional beliefs and participated in the ceremonial and celebratory aspects with greater enthusiasm than the more austere, otherworldly practices. Although taught to read and "cipher," many rejected white society's science and technology as useless for living.[14]

Benjamin Franklin had satirized such efforts, noting that Indians refused participation in the story imposed on them. When offered the opportunity to attend the College of William and Mary in Virginia, the Indians politely considered the matter before refusing. Franklin noted, "Several of our young people were formerly brought up at the colleges of the northern provinces; they were instructed in all your sciences; but when they came back to us they were bad runners; ignorant of every means of living in the woods; unable to bear either cold or hunger; knew neither how to build a cabin, take a deer, or kill an enemy; spoke our language imperfectly, and were therefore neither fit for hunters, warriors, or counselors; they were totally good for nothing. We are however, none the less obliged by your kind offer, tho' we decline accepting it; and to show our grateful sense of it, if the gentlemen of Virginia will send us a dozen of their sons, we will take great care of their education, instruct them in all we know, and make men of them."[15]

INDIANS AND WILDERNESS

With Indians largely vanquished and moved to reservations by the 1890s, twentieth-century conservationists turned "recovered" Indian homelands into national parks and managed forests for maximum yield and efficiency.[16] By redefining wilderness as the polar opposite of civilization, wilderness in its ideal form could be viewed as free of people, while civilization by definition was full of people. This left Indians in limbo. For William Bradford, the New England forests had been filled with "wild beasts and wild men." For Henry David Thoreau, forests and parks were areas where native vegetation would be restored and where even the "red man" might walk again. National parks had initially been conceived by George Catlin as places where Indians would be free to roam and carry on their way of life. In the mid-nineteenth century, travelers going west expected to see Indians as part of the untamed wilderness.[17]

By the 1870s, however, with the creation of Yellowstone National Park in 1872, Indian removal became part of a program to provide tourists with access to wild animals and scenery, but without encounters with Indians. The parks were reconfigured as vast managed gardens in which the wild was contained for viewing. People could have a wilderness experience in a protected environment. Tourists by definition do not stay. They are visitors only.

Yet Yellowstone and other national parks had never before been wilderness in this new sense. Indians had in fact inhabited the area around Yellowstone for thousands of years. As mammoths, horses, and camels became extinct through a combination of climate change and predation, new forms of gathering plants and hunting smaller game shaped Indian life and land. Until the late nineteenth century, the Bannock, Shoshone, and Crow used the area for a variety of purposes, including gathering, bathing, cooking, and ritual, and transformed it with fire and hunting. Not until after the area was made into a national park were the several groups of Indians using the park lands removed, sometimes forcibly and sometimes through negotiation and treaty enforcement. By 1882 the park was ideologically reconfigured and marketed as a perfect, untouched Garden of Eden.[18]

Glacier National Park was created in 1910 following land cessions from the Blackfeet. Ancestral Blackfeet had used the land for thousands of years hunting bison, bighorn sheep, and deer, and gathering food, medicinal plants, firewood, and lodge poles. In 1891, George Bird Grinnell, admirer of the Blackfeet and founder of the National Audubon Society, engaged in efforts to set aside the "virgin ground" and to purchase the lands for a national park from Indians, whom he saw as just beginning the move from "primitive" to "civilized" peoples. Conversely, "overcivilized" Americans would be able to renew themselves through immersion in areas of pristine wilderness. In the "virgin" landscape of the park, men could reclaim their "vigorous manliness" and women could travel safely on their own expeditions. The Blackfeet ceded lands to the U.S. government in 1896, but retained usufruct rights, and in 1910 Glacier National Park was established. But while the Blackfeet were featured in park brochures and greeted tourists at the railroad station, their hunting and other usufruct rights in the park's backcountry remained in contention for decades. For tourists who came from around the world, the backcountry wilderness experience did not include Indians.[19]

In 1851, in the context of a military campaign to put down the California Indians, Lafayette Bunnell "discovered" Yosemite Valley. Inhabited by a group of Sierra-Miwok and Mono-Paiutes who commingled with Central Valley Yokuts, both the Indians and the park (set aside as a state park in 1864 and a national park in 1890) became known as the Yosemite. The campaign, which attempted to relocate the Indians under Chief Tenaya to the San Joaquin Valley, failed when Indians gradually returned and remained in Yosemite. John Muir, who traveled through the Sierras in 1868, denigrated an Indian woman as "sadly unlike Nature's neat well-dressed animals," and commented that "most Indians I have seen are not a whit more natural in their lives than we civilized whites. . . . The worst thing about them is their uncleanliness. Nothing truly wild is unclean." Yosemite park superintendent Captain Moses Harris argued in 1889 that unless these "marauding savages" stopped visiting their "wilderness haunts" they would never become properly "civilized." Despite disparaging opinions about the Indians over the years, their buckskins, baskets, and beadwork became part of the Yosemite experience until the few remaining Indians were relocated and their village burned down in the 1950s.[20]

The national parks were thus reconfigured as living Edens, in which the concept of Eden retained its original Persian meaning as a park or enclosure. Like Eden, the national parks were enclosed areas containing beautiful scenery, rivers, animals, flowering trees, and carpets of wildflowers. Like Eden, they were "virgin" places of rebirth in which people could be spiritually renewed. Most importantly, however, they were reinvented spaces. Redefined as positive, the new wilderness areas were managed places in which the wilderness encounter was predictable within given parameters. There were "wild beasts," but no "wild men." Unpredictable elements such as Indians were removed or carefully managed for tourists so that they became part of the total "wilderness experience." And here, as in Eden, in the words of the 1964 Wilderness Act, "man is a visitor who does not remain."

In 1903, Mary Austin published *The Land of Little Rain*. In contrast to Muir, Austin was an advocate for Native Americans and the deserts they inhabited. She began her book with an appreciation for those Indians whose lives blended with the limits of the West's arid lands in the "country of lost borders." "Ute, Paiute, Mojave, and Shoshone inhabit its frontiers" she wrote, and as far into the heart of it as man dare go. Not the law, but the land sets the limit. Desert is the name it wears upon the maps, but the Indian's is the better word. Desert is a loose term to indicate land that supports no man." Austin valued the desert landscape, not as a wilderness to be transformed into a garden, but as a place of awesome beauty, with sculpted vermillion hills and radiant flowers that bloomed in the rare rains. It was a land that "will not be lived in except in its own fashion," a land which the Shoshone Indians called their home. "Not the weathered hut is his home, but the land, the winds, the hill front, the stream." Here the Indians were not removed from the land or written out of the narrative as "visitors who did not remain," but integral to a sense of the land as home.[21]

BLACKS AND EDEN

If white people fit well into the green American Edens, and if red people could be Christianized or removed from them, black people presented more difficult problems to European colonizers. The Bible was clear that all humanity had been created at the same time and were a unity. English travelers to Africa in the seventeenth century even reported that black people knew of Adam and Eve, Noah's flood, and Moses. But to Europeans, Indians and blacks were not similar. Although both groups were regarded as savage, Africans and Indians were perceived differently and treated differently. While Indians were of a different color than whites, white/black differences were more pronounced. Whereas the English colonizers' "errand into the wilderness" of America was to live and Christianize the Indian, their business in Africa was to trade and enslave. Europeans associated blackness with witchcraft, Satan, beasts, and putrid, decaying matter. The concept of whiteness emerged as a contrast and "other" to blackness.[22]

It was difficult for Christian Europeans to explain how black Africans could have descended from an Adam and Eve who seemed clearly to be white and had been created in the image of a white God the Father. One explanation was that while Adam was white, Eve was actually black. As Hugh Brackenridge explained in his 1792 satire *Modern Chivalry*, "I am of the opinion that Adam was a tall, straight limbed, red haired man, with a fair complexion, blue eyes, and an aquiline nose; and that Eve was a negro woman." In fact, a door panel, cast in 1710 in Germany, reflected this theory. It showed the Garden of Eden with Adam as a white man and Eve a black woman. The most acceptable explanation, however, was environmental: the descendants of Adam and Eve were originally white, but had been scorched by living in the hot tropical sun of Africa. (If modern science's theory of an ancestral African "Adam" and "Eve" is considered—see chapter 8—both Adam and Eve were probably black.)[23]

In any case, black slavery in America was deemed essential to the re-creation of the American Eden. Environmental historian Donald Worster lampoons:

> America, we have believed, is literally the Garden of Eden restored. It is the paradise once lost, but now happily regained. In Judeo-Christian mythology the first humans, Adam and Eve, discovering evil after yielding to the Devil's temptation, had to be kicked out of the Garden. . . . But . . . a band of their [descendants] had made their way to the New World and there rediscovered it, with the gate standing wide open, undefended. . . . They brought along with them some Africans in chains to help enjoy the place, and by and by they let in a few others from Asia, but mainly

it was a fortunate band of white Europeans that destiny allowed to re-enter and repossess the long-lost paradise. No other people in the world has ever believed, as Americans have, that they are actually living in Eden . . . that the planet's last best place had been kept sequestered for us. . . .[24]

In America, the tobacco plantations of the south that flourished in the Chesapeake Bay area prior to the American Revolution were made successful by black slaves whose forced labor supplied the profits that created Edenic lifestyles for white planters. In the "Cotton South," between the invention of the Cotton Gin in 1793 and the Civil War, enormous profits from exports created a rural paradise for the 20 percent of southerners who owned slaves. The "big houses" of the planters were displays of wealth and power that contrasted with the slave houses relegated to the plantation outskirts beyond the garden. Black labor furnished much of the profit that fueled the American Revolution and later the industrial revolution in the north, but black people received no compensation for their contributions.[25]

Although "those who labor in the earth" were, in Thomas Jefferson's view, the "chosen people of God," Jefferson believed that labor in the form of slavery was wrong. In the Christian tradition, all people, like Adam, were cursed "in the sweat of thy face" to "till the ground," but Jefferson and the abolitionists opposed slavery on moral grounds. Nevertheless Jefferson, although one of the more enlightened southerners of his time, not only owned slaves, but believed that blacks were "inferior to the whites in the endowments of both body and mind." He wrote that "the real distinctions which nature has made" rendered blacks more suitable as laborers in southern soils than whites because they seemed to be more heat tolerant and need less sleep.[26]

On economic grounds, the slave system caused both the destruction of black bodies and contributed to the rapid degradation of southern soils as tobacco, rice, sugar, and cotton became cash crops in an expanding world market. Jefferson knew that tobacco production depleted soil fertility, while wheat and the application of fertilizers restored it. He also understood that as long as fresh land existed, it was cheaper to clear woodlands than to fertilize "worn out" soils. Unless slavery was abolished and tobacco replaced by wheat, Jefferson implied, slavery and tobacco would remain repressive to both blacks and soils.

RESISTING SLAVERY

The reinvented American Eden, as the declensionist narrative would maintain, was created at the expense of Indians, blacks, and the soil. Free soil may have provided white settlers with the freedom to recover Eden, but for Indians and African Americans that freedom was nonexistent or at best drastically circumscribed. Environmental justice advocate Robert Bullard put it blatently: "The nation was founded on the principles of "free land" (stolen from Native Americans and Mexicans), "free labor" (cruelly extracted from African slaves), and "free men" (white men with property)."[27]

Blacks, like Indians, resisted their roles in the mainstream Recovery project. Slave rebellions such as those of Denmark Vesey in 1822 and Nat Turner in 1831 were overt demonstrations against repression. But slaves also covertly appropriated food from their masters' gardens and kitchens, slacked off or ran away from field work, and even retaliated against their owners when the latter became too old or sick to enforce their superiority. In addition, blacks, like Indians, retained many of their own cultural traditions, foods, stories, religious practices, songs, clothing, and dance. Many believed that their owners would receive due punishment after death, while they themselves would end up in paradise.

One environmentalist protested slavery. Henry David Thoreau refused to pay poll taxes that supported the Mexican War and a government "which buys and sells men, women, and children like cattle at the door of its senate-house." While living at Walden Pond in July 1846, he was arrested and spent a night in jail as a consequence. He wrote "Civil Disobedience" (1849), "Slavery in Massachusetts" (1854) and "A Plea for Captain John Brown" (1859) in defiance of slavery. "I cannot for an instant recognize that political organization as my government which is the slave's government also," he wrote. More reprehensible even than southerners, Massachusetts farmers and merchants, Thoreau asserted, were far more interested in making money than they were "in humanity, and are not prepared to do justice to the slave and to Mexico, *cost what it may*." Thoreau argued vehemently against a citizen's utilitarian duty to submit to civil government and insisted instead that "this people must cease to hold slaves, and to make war on Mexico, though it cost them their existence as a people." Thoreau's concept of community not only included minorities, but, historian Roderick Nash points out; he "regarded sunfish, plants, skunks, and even stars as fellows and neighbors—members, in other words, of his community." His ethic was one of the individual self in partnership with the entire human community and the natural world. As Patricia Nelson Limerick argues, "Nature-loving and slavery-hating were compatible and matched projects in Thoreau's mind."[28]

During the 1850s, northern and southern abolitionists joined in the moral condemnation of slavery. Abraham Lincoln's Emancipation Proclamation of 1863 freed the slaves, and the Civil War (fought between 1861 and 1865) released slaves from bodily bondage and reconstituted the nation. But a new system of oppressive sharecropping and segregation of free blacks ensued, stimulating migrations to the north and west.

With increasing urbanization after the Civil War, many African Americans found themselves living in segregated areas within red-lined zones in America's cities. While the intermingling of races existed in the three decades following the war, by the 1890s, neighborhoods began to organize themselves along color lines. Separate black mainstreets and downtowns existed, and racial zoning arose as Jim Crow laws were enacted in southern cities. By the turn of the century, rigid separations arose with segregated black and white schools, train stations, parks, and streetcars. In northern cities, immigrants from southern Europe flooded through New York City's harbor to fuel the labor needed for the industrial takeoff. In the minds of many Americans, the valence of wilderness had been reversed. The city wilderness became a dark, negatively charged area, while mountains, forests, waterfalls, and canyons were viewed as sublime places of light. Robert Woods wrote *The City Wilderness* in 1898 to describe deteriorating urban neighborhoods that were morally and socially depraved, while Booth Tarkington in *The Turmoil* (1914) portrayed them as sooty, polluted, and diseased. Blackened, smoke-filled cities contrasted with the purity of mountain air and the clarity of whitewater rivers, waterfalls, and lakes. Sublime nature was now white and benign; the nature of cities black and malign.[29]

ENVIRONMENTALISM AND AFRICAN AMERICANS

The conservation movement at the turn of the nineteenth century emerged during the same period as the struggles of blacks for advancement in post–Civil War America. As Jeffrey Romm argues, the two movements existed in separate spheres, but were tightly bound together in ways that produced negative consequences for African Americans. The creation of the Forest Reserves (1891); the founding of the Sierra Club (1892), with John Muir as its first president (1892), the progressive conservation movement (1900–13), and passage of the Antiquities Act (1906) occurred during the same period as Booker T. Washington, Louis Hughes, George Washington Carver, and W. E. B. Du Bois were engaged in struggles to liberate blacks from the oppressions of post–Civil War sharecropping, soil degradation, and racial prejudice.

As Romm maintains, a "coincidental order of environmental injustice," evident in the late nineteenth century, hardened existing forms of institutional racism. "The Supreme Court's 'separate but equal' doctrine of its *Plessy v. Ferguson* [1896] decision legitimized racial segregation in the United States for the next seventy years. . . . While the forest reservations reduced people's access to land, racial segregation reserved ownership of the remaining private land for whites." In the South, freed slaves were expected to purchase land with wages at a time when lands in the West were promoted to whites as free lands. Boundaries created by natural resource regulations restrained opportunities for people of color, while protecting white power and privilege and promoting wilderness access.[30]

African-American environmentalist Carl Anthony argues that John Muir's encounters in the pristine wilderness of Canada and the Cotton South were actually made possible by the "occupied wilderness" of the Civil War and Native-American battles. Muir, Anthony states, had been a Civil War draft dodger who went to the Canadian wilds rather than fight. Environmental historian Roderick Nash concurs: "Muir's first encounter with the idea that nature had rights came as a consequence of draft-dodging. . . . Muir who was twenty-six and single, felt certain he would be called, and he apparently had no interest in the fight to save the Union or free the slaves." Biographer Stephen Fox portrays him instead as a pacifist who "was paralyzed by the threat of conscription" and who "had no strong feelings about the moral aspects of war." Nevertheless, John Muir fled to Canada after Lincoln signed an order to draft 500,000 men, and spent the war years as a fugitive, seeking peace in the "wilderness" north of Lake Huron, failing to communicate with family and friends for fear of being discovered. "Only once in my long Canada wanderings," Muir writes, "was the deep peace of the wilderness savagely broken . . . . I was awakened by the awfully dismal howling of the wolves."[31]

After the war, in 1867, Muir made his "Thousand Mile Walk to the Gulf" to study natural history through war-torn lands protected by soldiers of the U.S. government, but whose wilderness delights seemed to him Edenic. Here he encountered mountainous streams lined with "forest walls vine-draped and flowery as Eden," in the very place, he notes, where "General Scott had his headquarters when he removed the Cherokee Indians to a new home in the West."[32]

Muir was unsympathetic toward the "savages" and "Negroes" he encountered on his thousand-mile walk, although he described some as "well-trained," "extremely polite," and "very civil." Of his visit to Murphy, North Carolina, he wrote, "For the first time since leaving home I found a house decked with flowers and vines, clean within and without and stamped with the comforts of culture and refinement in all its arrangements. Striking contrast to the uncouth transitionist establishments from the wigwams of savages to the clumsy but clean log castle of the thrifty pioneer."[33]

Muir likewise reflected cultural prejudices against blacks when he wrote that "the Negroes are easy-going and merry, making a great deal of noise and doing little work. One energetic white man, working with a will, would easily pick as much cotton as half a dozen Sambos and Sallies." He described an evening campfire he attended as akin to deviltry: "In the center of this globe of light sat two Negroes. I could see their ivory gleaming from the great lips, and their smooth cheeks flashing off light as if made of glass. Seen anywhere but in the South, the glossy pair would have been taken for twin devils, but here it was only a Negro and his wife at their supper." Muir's environmental ethic included wilderness, but, unlike that of Thoreau, it was insensitive to much of humanity. He embraced all of nonhuman nature from bears to orchids to rattlesnakes as "fellow mortals," but his ethic, which was grounded in an individual self within nature, did not explicitly include the entire human community.[34]

In contrast to Muir's descriptions of blacks and nature in the south as disconnected opposites, African-American writer Zora Neale Hurston wrote of blacks as part of Florida's environment. In *Their Eyes Were Watching God* (1937), Hurston portrayed blacks who were planting and harvesting beans in the Florida Everglades as engaging with a wild, animate, spiritualized nature that produced "big beans, big cane, big weeds, big everything." The dirt was "so rich and black that a half mile of it would have fertilized a Kansas Wheat Field. Wild cane on either side of the road. . . . People wild too." While waiting for the beans to grow, blacks fished and hunted alligators as did the local Indians, who were "calmly winning their living in the trackless ways of the Everglades." Indians left the

'Glades in an impending hurricane; blacks stayed to combat and succumb to the fury of its winds.[35]

Hurston's unpredictable chaotic forces were male, not female: "The two hundred miles an hour wind had loosed his chains. He seized hold of his dikes and ran forward until he met the quarters; uprooted them like grass and rushed on after his supposed to be conquerors, rolling the dikes, rolling the houses, rolling the people in the houses along with other timbers. The sea was walking the earth with a heavy heel." Here nature and the human community were at odds, life hanging by a thread, a time of dying for all that lived. A time to face the desolation, a time to bury the dead, but then, "the time of dying was over." Here was an ethic at odds with Muir's ecstatic isolation in a lightning storm in a sublime sierra wilderness apart from civilization. It was an ethic of living on the land and of acceptance of nature as active and alive—"a bloom time, and a green time and an orange time, a potential for partnership with the land."[36]

Limerick argues that Aldo Leopold's 1949 "Land Ethic," which advocated enlarging the bounds of the community to include "soils, waters, plants, and animals," ignored communities of people of color. Leopold's ethical sequence moved from the self to the human community to the biotic community. The Mosaic Decalogue of the Old Testament imposed limits on the self, the Golden Rule of the New Testament imposed limits on the community, while the "Land Ethic" limited human actions with respect to the biotic community. Leopold began his essay with, "When god-like Odysseus returned from the wars in Troy, he hanged all on one rope a dozen slave-girls of his household whom he suspected of misbehavior during his absence. This hanging involved no question of propriety. The girls were property." To Leopold, both slavery and gender violence seemed to exist only in the deep past, rather than in twentieth century America in which segregation and patriarchy were both alive and well. "Not a word of the essay," Limerick writes, "suggested that the end of slavery left any unfinished business in the United States." Leopold's obliviousness to the legacy of slavery in Jim Crow America echoed the conservation movement's own obliviousness to a legacy that excluded people of color from equal access to natural and recreational resources.[37]

Yet in Leopold's writings, there is neither evidence of the exclusion of minorities from his ethic, as in the case of Muir, nor of inclusion, as in the case of Thoreau. He seems to have implicitly assumed the equality of all persons and biota in an era when slavery had officially been abolished. In his elaboration of the ethical sequence proposed by Leopold, environmental historian Roderick Nash argues that Leopold's ethic does in fact extend to African-American emancipation and American Indian citizenship. Nash explicates an environmental ethic that expanded rights to oppressed minorities first in Great Britain and then in the United States. The Magna Carta of 1215 and the Declaration of Independence in 1776 were followed by Abraham Lincoln's Emancipation Proclamation of 1863, the Nineteenth Amendment giving women the right to vote in 1920, the Indian Citizenship Act of 1924, the Fair Labor Standards Act of 1938, the Civil Rights Act of 1957, and the Endangered Species Act of 1973.

Nash made explicit the connections between the rights of minorities and the rights of nature implicit in Leopold's ethical sequence. "Assuming one regarded slaves as people," Nash wrote, "the new natural-rights philosophy made a strong case for including them in the ethical community. The abolitionists quickly seized on this idea as a powerful argument for terminating an institution that denied slaves something all people possessed by birth and which could never be alienated—namely their right to life and liberty." Those who extended the natural rights principles across the boundaries of species, he noted, "employed the same liberal faith that had served the antislavery partisans." My own view is that Leopold's "Land Ethic," which is based on "the tendency of interdependent individuals or groups to evolve modes of cooperation" might be viewed not as an extension of a Eurocentric rights-based ethic, but as one foundation for an ethic of partnership among humans and between human and nonhuman communities, an ethic that explicitly includes minorities (see chapter 11).[38]

Limerick points to two positive junctions between environmentalism and civil rights. In 1964, two acts were passed by the exact same Congress: The Wilderness Act and the Civil Rights Act. And thirty years later, in 1994, President William Jefferson Clinton created a federal mandate for environmental justice with the issuance of Executive Order 12898, directing all federal agencies to "make achieving environmental justice part of its mission by identifying and addressing as appropriate, disproportionately high and adverse human health or environmental effects of its programs, policies, and activities on minority populations and low-income populations."[39] Some progress seemed to have been made in reversing the decline of minorities and including them in the mainstream Recovery Narrative.

COLONIZED EDENS

Legislative and legal victories that linked human rights and nature's rights, however, were belied by the realities of life in late twentieth-century America. Segregation and poverty militated against equal access to resources and encouraged toxic waste "dumping in Dixie." Wilderness was redefined in ways that excluded Native Americans who had shaped it for millennia and discouraged access by minorities and disadvantaged peoples.[40]

With the taming of wilderness, the removal of "savages" and "wild men," and the repression of blacks, the American Eden had become a colonized Eden. People of privilege were inside the garden, colonized minorities outside it or on its margins. The control of the wild represented the kind of state that Western societies could export throughout the world to colonized "other" lands. That state was the "self" of Western European countries, in particular, those that exported their science, technologies, and methods of controlling resources to the "others." The others were the colonized indigenous people, immigrants, and people of color who were outside the controlled, managed garden. Throughout the world, as land was transformed into ordered gardens, what lay beyond the periphery were wastelands and deserts, the place of outcasts, of waste, of people of color, and of immigrants—in short, those colonized others not admitted into the enclosed space of the reinvented garden.[41]

From the perspective of the western European "subject," such wastelands were the locales of the "others." The garden and the desert were demarcated, both naturally and socially, in a moral narrative of progress capable of relapse if vigilance was not pursued. The sequence—first the forest, then the city, then the desert—intimates an impending decline if cities and civilizations are not managed properly. The idea of the desert encroaching on the city—of wastelands arriving at the city borders—is symptomatic of the global ecological crisis, exemplified by desertification, the failure of irrigation systems, and the salinization of soils.

Immigration policies preserve the enclosed garden, relegating undesirables to the presumed wastelands beyond. The crisis in Western-style progress is reflected in the reaction against multiculturalism and affirmative action. Other symptoms of a crisis in progress are policies directed against the environment—the property rights movement, erosion of the Endangered Species Act, efforts by ranchers to preserve "free" grazing on the Western range and the persistence of lumber companies in cutting old-growth forests.

The past failures of progress are returning as major environmental problems. Waste, pollution, landfills, and incinerators have been located in deserts, in inner cities, in ghettos, and on American Indian reservations and are often targeted for the neighborhoods of people of color. This became particularly apparent in 1987 when the United Church of Christ released its report "Toxic Waste and Race in the United States." That report revealed that "communities with the greatest number of commercial hazardous waste facilities have the highest composition of racial and ethnic residence." The statistics showed that 58 percent of the country's African Americans and 53 percent of its Hispanics live in communities where hazardous waste dumping is uncontrolled. Examples include Emelle, Alabama; Houston, Texas; Chicago's South Side; and Richmond and Oakland in California. On a more hopeful level, many grassroots organizations that arose in opposition to toxic dumping have become multiethnic and multiracial. Many local movements are woman-based and many are led by minority women. The mainstream environmental movement, however, remains largely white; and environmental organizations, with some exceptions, still work on issues most relevant to white communities.[42]

CONCLUSION

From a declensionist point of view, many people of color found themselves colonized or enslaved as European civilization spread throughout the globe over the past several centuries. As the Western narrative of progress has taken shape, they have been left out or victimized. Indians who lost their lands and blacks whose forced labor helped to create degraded soils find themselves again threatened by wastes dumped on their homelands and in their neighborhoods. For them the progressive story is a decline. They envision, instead, a new story—the possibility of a postcolonial world that could be a better place for indigenous peoples and people of color.[43]

The environmental justice movement includes justice for people of color, justice for women, and justice for nature. It reverses past environmental injustices disproportionately experienced by minorities. The struggles take place in various geographical and bodily locations. The bodies of women and men are sites of local contestation. When bodies are sick, polluted, or cancerous, people fight against the illness. The home, where many women and children spend much of their time, is polluted. Many communities—especially those of poor people, such as rural communities in Appalachia and Hispanic communities in California, Indian reservations, and urban inner cities—are polluted. They have become sites of local contestation and local movements for justice.

Environmental justice is the righting of the inequities of the past through laws, regulations, compensation, and removal of the causes of eco-injustice. Ecojustice entails the redistribution of wealth through the redistribution of environmental goods and services. For minorities, the Recovery story would be one of justice restored. Despite these hopeful signs, however, the progressive Recovery Narrative continues as the major story. Science, technology, and consumer capitalism remain the tools of mainstream culture's Recovery of the garden.

EIGHT

Eden Commodified

CORA HAD BEEN IN THE MALL SINCE EARLY MORNING. DONNING HER
PINK JOGGING SUIT, SHE JOINED TWELVE OTHER SENIORS WHO SET OUT
EACH DAY TO CIRCLE THE INNER MALL. AS SHE PASSED EACH SHOP SHE
GAZED LONGINGLY AT THE ORLON DRESSES, SILK PARISIAN SCARVES,
BLUE-STEEL TENNIS RACKETS, DVDs, TELEVISION SETS, CAFE LATTÉS,
AND ORANGE SMOOTHIES. HER LIMITED RETIREMENT BUDGET PRE-
VENTED HER FROM PURCHASING MORE THAN ONE LITTLE "LUXURY" A
MONTH, BUT SHE REVELED IN HER DAYDREAMS. AFTER HER AEROBIC
FITNESS EXERCISES ENDED, SHE FINISHED HER BAGEL AND COFFEE IN
THE GARDEN CAFÉ AND WANDERED THROUGH THE BIG DEPARTMENT
STORES CHECKING FOR NEW FALL STYLES AND JOTTING DOWN IDEAS FOR
CHRISTMAS. HOW LUCKY I AM, SHE THOUGHT. THIS BEAUTIFUL WORLD,
RIGHT ACROSS THE STREET FROM MY HOUSE, IS AN EDEN ON EARTH.
—*Carolyn Merchant, 1998*

The modern version of the Garden of Eden is the enclosed shopping mall.
Surrounded by a desert of parking lots, malls comprise gardens of shops
covered by glass domes, accessed by spiral staircases and escalators reaching upward toward heaven. Today's malls feature life-sized trees, trellises
decorated with flowers, stone grottoes, birds, animals, and even indoor
beaches that simulate nature as a cultivated, benign garden. The "river that

went out of the Eden to water the garden" is reclaimed in meandering tree-lined streams and ponds filled with bright orange goldfish. The commodified Eden is the Recovery Narrative's epitome in the modern world.

This garden in the city re-creates the pleasures and temptations of the original Eden, where people can peacefully harvest the fruits of earth with gold grown by the market. Within manicured spaces of trees, flowers, and fountains, we can shop for nature at the Nature Company, purchase "natural" clothing at Esprit, sample organic foods and "rainforest crunch" in kitchen gardens, buy twenty-first century products at The Sharper Image, and play virtual reality games in which SimEve is reinvented in cyberspace. The spaces and commodities of the shopping mall epitomize consumer capitalism's vision of Recovery from the Fall of Adam and Eve.[1]

CONSUMER'S NATURE

Canada's West Edmonton Mall, the first of a generation of megamalls, is eight city blocks long by four blocks wide and covers 5.2 million square feet. It sports an indoor surfing beach with adjustable wave heights, an amusement park, an ice-skating rink, a twenty-screen movie theater, and eight hundred stores. Cul de sacs within the mall replicate New Orleans's Bourbon Street and Paris's boulevards. It has a 360-room hotel, with theme rooms inspired by places such as Polynesia, Hollywood, and Victorian England, along with rooms based on transportation forms such as sports cars, pickup trucks, and horse-drawn carriages. People from around the world celebrate honeymoons, anniversaries, and birthdays in the hotel, while those with recreational vehicles may spend an entire summer camped in the parking lot to maximize shopping access.[2]

Malls are places of light, hope, and promise—transitions to new worlds. People are reinvented and redeemed by the mall. Said one ecstatic visitor, "I *am* the mall. . . . This place is heaven." In the film *Dawn of the Dead*, the apocalypse has come and the survivors have gathered in a shopping mall as the best place to make their last stand. Malls are designed to be morally uplifting places. Sanitized surroundings, central surveillance systems, noise restrictions, and strict behavioral rules regulate the undesirable, homeless, and criminal elements of society, while socializing both young and old into the acceptable consumer culture of the new 21st century. Like the enclosed gardens of the Middle Ages, they are redemptive places of ecstasy. Like the eighteenth-century gardens of the nobility, they are displays of power, surprise, and desire. Like the public parks of the nineteenth century, they uplift, temper, and socialize the masses.[3]

Malls have replaced orange groves, cornfields, and pine forests. Artificial nature has redeemed natural nature. Nature is captured in the West Edmonton Mall in a palm-lined beach, an artificial lagoon, an underwater seascape, performing dolphins, caged birds, and tame Siberian tigers. Sunlit gardens, tree-lined paths, meandering streams, and tropical flowers adorn courtyard restaurants. Nature in the mall is a dense text to be read by the visitors. It exemplifies not only human control over nonhuman nature, but the reinvention of nature itself as Edenic space. It portrays original innocence and delight in nature, calming the consumer as she contemplates elements for purchase and duplication in the home. Just as the mall keeps out the socially undesirable, it rejects the naturally undesirable—weeds, pests, and garbage.[4]

Outside of Minneapolis is the Mall of America, which aspires to the iconic and totemic status of the Grand Canyon, and in which four hundred trees are planted in interior gardens. At the mall's center is Knott's Camp Snoopy, a seven-acre theme park that "brings the outdoors indoors." "Inspired by Minnesota's natural habitat—forests, meadows, river banks, and marshes," it feels, smells, and sounds like a perpetual summer of 70-degree temperatures in the Minnesota woods. But those alien year-around temperatures forced Camp Snoopy to substitute 256 tons of non-Minnesota figs, azaleas, oleanders, jasmine, hibiscus, and olive trees from the tropics. Although marketers for Camp Snoopy assert that the park's mealy bugs, aphids, and spider mites are controlled through the use of integrated pest management methods (such as lady beetles), the staff actually spend nights spraying with pesticides to minimize insect damage.[5]

The Mall of America declares itself "the most environmentally conscious shopping center in the industry," and claims to recycle up to eighty percent of its refuse, as a "dedication to Mother Earth." Yet Rich Doering of Browning-Ferris Industries, the contractor responsible for dealing with the seven hundred tons of garbage produced at the mall each month, says that only about one-third of the stores' waste is actually recycled and very little of the shoppers' trash: "The venture is unprofitable to Browning-Ferris, which would find it far cheaper to recycle the mall's refuse somewhere other than in its basement."[6]

Mall culture has diversified to take advantage of changing economic times and consumer habits. The malling of America has become the malling of the world, reconstituting the Shakespearean dictum as, "All the world's a mall and all the men and women merely shoppers." Streets are blocked off to become pedestrian malls. Lifestyle malls target achievers, emulators, and belongers, while class-conscious malls focus on lower income and ethnic consumers. Specialty malls cater to New Age, new chic, and cool commodity shoppers. Boutiques, antiques, museum shops, art galleries, cultural centers, history theme parks, Renaissance fairs, piazzas, and discount malls are featured in a profusion of difference within unity. Even "hip teens" for whom malls are "totally uncool" reinvent the East Village streets of New York City, Goodwill and Salvation Army stores, and warehouse "labs" as "anti-mall Meccas." Malls, they claim, are all look-alikes, are not teen savvy, are designed for parents and kids, and have too many suffocating antinoise, antismoking, and antiskateboarding rules.[7]

As a way of life, consumer culture reclaims pleasure, innocence, tranquility, youth, and even nature itself as a garden. It replicates "the most enchanting dream which has ever consoled mankind, the myth of a Golden Age in which man lived on the fruits of the earth, peacefully, piously, and with primitive simplicity." As Joseph Addison put it in the eighteenth century, "I look upon the pleasure which we take in a Garden, as one of the most innocent Delights in Human . . . Life. A Garden was the Habitation of our first Parents before the Fall. . . . [The] satisfaction which a Man takes in these Works of Nature, [is] a laudable, if not a virtuous Habit of Mind."

BIOTECHNOLOGY

Just as the mall re-creates the Garden of Eden, biotechnology re-creates the tree of life at the center of the garden. While mechanistic science deciphered the book of nature, biotechnology decodes the book of life. It "improves" on nature's heritage, correcting "her" mistakes by removing genetic flaws, cloning genetically perfect organisms, and banking designer genes for future human brains and bodies. From genetically engineered apples to "Flavr-Savr" tomatoes, the fruits of the original, evolved garden are being redesigned so that the salinated, irrigated desert can continue to blossom as the rose. In the recovered Garden of Eden, fruits will ripen faster, have fewer seeds, need less water, require fewer pesticides, contain less saturated fat, and have longer shelf lives. The human temptation to engineer nature is reaching too close to the powers of God warn the Jeremiahs. Still, the progressive engineers who design the technologies that allow the Recovery of Eden to accelerate see only hope in the new fabrications.[8]

Biotechnology, the Recovery Narrative's newest chapter, illustrates the reading of nature's bible in sentences, books, and libraries comprising genetic sequences. Information encoded in the DNA of each species can be manipulated to create new books in the library of nature.[9] It assumes:

- DNA is composed of the four bases adenine, thymine, cytosine, and guanine that are the molecular "letters" that form the words needed to create the many hundred-word sentences that comprise the gene—the "universal building block of life."
- Genes are discrete bits of information assembled into "books" of chromosomal messages, "libraries" of bacterial clones, and data-banks to be edited, revised, and reorganized.
- Because the gene is the fundamental building block of life, a gene will maintain its identity through change when inserted into the matter of another species and yet continue to function as it did in the original.
- Individual genes can be studied and analyzed in models before being assembled into new combinations.
- Genetically engineered organisms can be introduced into new environmental contexts with little or no risk since the laboratory and the fields are one and continuous.

In the "garden of unearthly delights," genetically engineered food is created by taking genes from one life form and implanting them in another. The process ensures "summertime tastes" year around with "vine-ripened" flavors. Companies such as Calgene, Monsanto, Upjohn, Pioneer, and DeKalb are pioneering efforts to improve the genes of cantaloupes and squash to resist viruses, corn that requires fewer herbicides, potatoes with higher starch content, bell peppers that stay fresh longer, and rice with higher protein value. Calgene's tomatoes have a gene that reverses the action of the enzyme that causes decay, eliminating the need to pick green tomatoes for shipment followed by rapid ripening—degreening—with ethylene gas.[10]

Calgene's "MacGregor" tomato (so named for its warm Farmer MacGregor and Peter Rabbit feeling) was engineered by inserting a copy of the "rotting" gene backwards, allowing the tomato to stay in the field a few days longer and be picked pink, or vine-ripe, rather than green. The process of implanting this "antisense" gene was patented, so that in the future the company could collect royalties, not only on bioengineered tomatoes, but on any other crop altered by the same technique. The vertically integrated company controlled the entire process, from planting to processing and distributing the tomatoes. The bioengineered tomato, approved by the U.S. Food and Drug Administration (FDA) in early 1994, was the first step toward realizing huge profits on the new DNA technology. Unfortunately for investors, the Farmer MacGregor lacked the taste of a garden ripened tomato and Calgene lost value in the marketplace.[11]

Farmers prepare fields for engineered tomatoes by covering them with black plastic to prevent weed growth and soil erosion. Computer regulated, plastic drip-irrigation pipes ensure that correct amounts of water at proper times are released to the seedlings. The tomatoes are grown using techniques of sustainable agriculture. Correct amounts of nitrogen are applied to the fields and deep drainage ditches collect the runoff to prevent it from damaging the surrounding environment. Cover crops and fallowing improve soil quality and integrated pest management (IPM) techniques control pests through the use of beneficial insects and minimal pesticides. In the packing house the tomatoes are labeled with a brand-name sticker and boxed stem-side up so the customer will see the fruit in its prime, reminding her or him of its Edenic summer freshness and taste.[12]

Corn is another crop that biotechnology companies such as Monsanto are engineering as new marketplace commodities. Genetically modified varieties can be made resistant to pests, salinization, and drought. A problem arises, however, over the question of genetic pollution—a potential clash between genes versus ecosystems and genetics versus ecology. In some cases, engineered genes (transgenes) may cross over into other corn plants, via pollen from the modified plant that mixes with unmodified plants, thus "contaminating" them with engineered genes. In this way the evolutionary diversity of corn in its center of origin (Mexico) might become polluted with new genetically engineered varieties not heretofore found in nature. Such a situation apparently has occurred in Mexico and could be of concern for other crop cradles (such as rice, barley, wheat, potatoes, and so on) which have been sources of diversity for plant breeders responding to catastrophic diseases (such as the Irish potato blight). In the case of "polluted plants," the transgenes do not decline over time, but instead replicate their genetic information repeatedly.[13]

In the reinvented Eden, animals too would be modified for greater productivity, increasing their share in the commodities markets. Dairy cows produce more milk with less fat when cows are injected with a bovine growth hormone, such as Posilac, marketed by Monsanto Chemicals after FDA approval in November 1993. More milk per cow means more profit for the dairy farmer and for Monsanto. Monsanto's promotional video tells farmers that "Posilac is the single most tested product in history. . . . You'll want to inject Posilac in every eligible cow, as every cow not treated is a lost income opportunity." Observes critic Robin Mather, "There are dozens of cows in every [video] segment, but no one ever touches them— except to inject them. Cows are shown eating in long rows stretching to the camera's horizon; cows are shown in milking parlors. . . . There are cows in barns, but not cows in pastures. That's not how cows are 'managed' these days."[14]

Chickens are harder to engineer than cattle or fruit crops because the embryo is encased in the hard eggshell. Nevertheless bioengineers work toward genetically engineered chickens that will resist influenza and salmonella, while also attempting to breed docile chickens that will show less aggressiveness in the close quarters of today's vast poultry houses. Scientists aim to manipulate chicken DNA so that the birds produce more lean white meat, less dark meat, and less fat. If a poultry company could patent its new chicken, it could own it as well as the eggs it produces.[15]

While bioengineered domesticated animals may be controlled to some degree, transgenic wild animals are not so easily managed. Transgenic salmon are created by introducing genes from ocean pout fish that promote growth in the salmon. Such "Frankenfish" seem to biotechnologists to be the answer to feeding growing populations with healthy food, without depleting ocean supplies. Environmentalists, on the other hand, fear that transgenic fish might escape their ocean breeding pens, mate with wild fish and contaminate the wild salmon gene pool. In fact, one study showed that not only did wild salmon prefer to mate with transgenic fish, but that the offspring died young, raising fears that the wild fish would die out.[16]

Biotechnology contributes the science and technology needed for consumer capitalism's vision of Recovery from the Fall. Not only does bioengineering reinvent the products of fallen nature to make them more perfect, it redeems human labor by introducing new labor-saving technologies. Tomato planting is done by automatic drill and picking by the tomato harvester; dairy cows are milked by automatic carousel milkers; chickens are stunned by electric shock, killed by a spinning blade, plucked by "rubber fingers," and mechanically eviscerated. Now computer-driven robots are being designed to pick apples from the trees, saving Eve the task of reaching for the fruit, but not of tasting it.[17]

GENOMES

"In the beginning was the genome," reads molecular biology's new book of human origins. The Human Genome Project aims to map and sequence the human genetic blueprint—the nucleotide bases of the genes distributed on the twenty-two pairs of human chromosomes, plus the two sex-linked X and Y chromosomes. The long DNA molecule contained in each chromosome comprises four nucleotide bases in various combinations of order. The sequence of bases in the twenty-three pairs of chromosomes of the human genome reveals its genetic blueprint. Unraveling that order and the encoded information was estimated to cost about one dollar per base, or three billion dollars. Untold benefits for genetics and medicine are forecast. But the Jeremiahs who question the project instead depict the DNA spiral as the snake coiled around the tree of the knowledge of good and evil. Releasing that much knowledge for manipulation by humans is akin to biting the apple or releasing the snakes from Pandora's box.[18]

The Human Genome Project goes beyond humans to include the genomes of other key species, and the information gleaned will provide comparisons across species. The initial mapping and subsequent sequencing steps of the project are expected to reveal new options. New technologies for discovering the sequencing and new methods of handling the immense amount of resultant data are part of the project. The technologies devised will then be applied to the manipulation of nature on a wider scale.[19]

Environmental scientists, however, warn of unanticipated consequences from bioengineering and from introducing new organisms into nature:[20]

- Because of weblike interconnections, engineered organisms, such as frost-retarding ice-minus bacteria, might interact with the environment in unanticipated ways by spreading from crops to wild plants and trees. Wild plants might then grow longer, extending the growing season, depleting soil nutrients faster, slowing the rate of conversion of leaf litter by soil microbes, and eventually affecting the long term rates of photosynthesis and nitrogen fixation.

- Because the whole is greater than the sum of the parts, even if only one in 100 introductions became established a single species could disrupt the whole.
- Because nonhuman nature is a dynamic and responsive actor, introductions (such as DDT) whose effects are not initially apparent can trigger resistant mutants.
- Because of the primacy of ecological process, released organisms (such as new crops or pollutant-degrading bacteria) will have to be engineered for, rather than against, successful spreading within the ecosystem in accordance with the laws of ecology and plant succession.
- Because humans and nonhuman nature are a unity, genetic engineers, ecologists, and ordinary citizens should participate with nature as partners in survival (rather than masters of the planet), in considering obligations and in evaluating risks.

The cloning of "Dolly" the ewe in 1997 raised for humanity the question, "Will there be another you?" Such achievements seemed to herald a new step in commodifying animals and plants for life in the new Eden. Cloning—a breakthrough technology "of biblical proportions"—took an adult cell from the ewe's mammary gland and created an embryo, reversing the process of aging to one of birth. Dolly's cells later exhibited premature aging, representing a temporary setback to hopes for immortality. Nonetheless, Scottish scientist Ian Wilmut was compared to God. "Not since God took Adam's rib and fashioned a helpmate for him has anything so fantastic occurred," exalted *Time* magazine. An adult cell was now capable of reiterating dormant genetic instructions lost during the aging process and replicating anew a single individual. Dolly was a carbon copy of her mother. What was new was that mammals could now be cloned, not from undifferentiated embryonic cells, but from adult cells. Cloning from an adult cell ensures that the final product is already known.[21]

Is a Ewe an Eve? Are *you* Eve? Biologist Ursula Goodenough

Fig. 8.1. *In the Beginning Was the Genome* shows Adam and Eve grasping gentically-engineered apples plucked from a tree in the form of the DNA molecule. By Bill Sanderson in *The New Scientist* 21, July 1990, cover

Fig. 8.2. The temptations of genetic engineering are symbolized by a serpent emerging from the genome's double helix and evincing glee at the half-eaten apple. By Bill Sanderson in *The New Scientist* 21, July 1990, p. 34

observed that if the cloning technique were perfected "there'd be no need for men." The adult cell from Dolly's mother's udder was first deprived of nutrients for one week, then placed next to an empty egg cell from another Ewe (from which the nucleus had been removed). Then an electrical impulse triggered fusion between the two cells, and a second impulse triggered cell division, the start of new life. The new embryo was then implanted into the uterus of a surrogate ewe, from which Dolly the cloned sheep was born. From Eve, by God's impulse, another Eve is born; Adam is nowhere to be found. Or perhaps Adam, armed with electrical impulses, is a surrogate for a now unneeded primary creator.[22]

In the flurry of excitement, the media focused on the cloning of great American males: Albert Einstein, Thomas Jefferson, Martin Luther King Jr., Michael Jordan. Reporters hypothesized the replication of a corporate executive, a Nobel Prize–winning physicist, a great American president. Detractors feared the duplication of Adolf Hitler, Pol Pot, and a Frankenstein monster. Women, it seemed, would serve as surrogates, third world minorities as laborers for the brave new world. Illustrations showed men emerging fully clothed from cloning machines, bypassing the embarrassing fig-leaf phase of the biblical drama.[23]

Less easy to eliminate from the new Genesis story is the ethical question of the knowledge of good and evil. While the cloning of sheep and cows to produce better quality food might be condoned, the birth of a cloned "Eve," first claimed on December 26, 2002, is ethically problematical. Is it morally correct and medically acceptable to make carbon copies of human beings? Can the new technology be regulated or will it go underground in secret laboratories around the world? Who will want to or be able to pay for the costs of self-cloning? These difficult ethical questions are only the beginning of the implications of a new knowledge of good and evil resulting from biting the biotechnology apple.[24]

EVOLUTION

The reinvention of Eden as a shopping mall and bioengineered apples is the outcome of a story of human progress and ascent from ape to "man" that began in an African Eden. The story casts the upright ape as a male hero, an African Adam, who, thrust from his Edenic cradle, conquers space and overcomes adversity to attain the pinnacles of scientific achievement. The progressive narrative ends in the human ability to reinvent the entire planet as Eden. The upward progress of humankind from darkest wilderness to enlightened mind is a precondition for the new earthly garden:

> Once upon a time, there was an ape who lived in the middle of a dark forest. It spent most of its days in the trees, munching languidly on fruits and berries. But then one day the ape decided to leave the forest for the savanna nearby. . . . Life was harder on the savanna: there might be miles between one meal and another, there were seasons of drought to contend with, and large, fierce animals who didn't mind a little ape for lunch. But the ape did not run back into the forest. Instead it learned to adapt, walking from one place to another on two legs. And it learned to live by its wits. As the years passed, the ape grew smarter and smarter until it was too smart to be called an ape anymore. It lived anywhere it wanted and gradually made the whole world turn to its own purposes. Meanwhile, back in the forest, the other apes went on doing the same old thing, lazily munching on leaves and fruit. Which is why they are still just apes, even to this day.[25]

This wonderful story of human emergence from the dark jungle onto the bright savanna is a hero tale. First identified as such by Misia Landau, it conforms to the elements of the standard heroic narrative. The world—or vast grassy savanna—is absent of the hero, *Homo sapiens*. The ape or hero-to-be crosses space, emerging out of the deep forest. It undergoes trials and tests—drought, fierce animals, scarcity of food. Little by little, genetic gifts are selected for and enhanced—tendencies toward bipedalism, opposed thumbs, larger brains. The hero overcomes the harsh environment, adapting to it, claiming it as "his" own. The original absence is liquidated—humans have emerged from their ancient cradle to civilize and conquer space, filling the world.[26]

Why is this story so compelling? It is a tale of conquest and achievement. Modern humans, emerging from the dark forest, fanned northward out of the dark continent, where disease, humidity, and jungles held back progress, to develop and test their intellectual and inventive proclivities on the open plains. Instead of stooping to gather the fruits of the forest, they stood tall above the grasses, hunting the animals of the plains. All the elements and characters are strongly drawn, reinforcing underlying cultural and racial contrasts: light versus dark, plain versus forest, hunting versus gathering, enterprising human versus lazy ape, civilized European versus "primitive" African. Human evolution becomes an ascent out of darkest Africa into the light of the logos.[27]

Charles Darwin himself was of the opinion that humans had emerged from the forest: "Man is descended from a hairy, tailed quadruped . . . probably arboreal in its habits, and an inhabitant of the Old World," he surmised in his 1871 *Descent of Man*. He echoed the Lucretian-Hobbesian concept of the emergence of civilization out of barbarism. On arriving in Tierra del Fuego, he was revolted by the sight of the natives. "There can hardly be a doubt we are descended from barbarians," he wrote. "The astonishment which I felt on first seeing a party of Fuegians on a wild and broken shore will never be forgotten by me, for the reflection at once rushed into my mind—such were our ancestors. These men were absolutely naked and bedaubed with paint, their long hair was tangled, their mouths, frothed with excitement, and their expression was wild, startled, and distrustful. They possessed hardly any arts, and like wild animals lived on what they could catch; they had no government, and were merciless to every one not of their own small tribe."[28]

For Darwin and other nineteenth-century Europeans, humanity had left "savagism" and "barbarism" far behind as it walked northward out of the African savannah, ultimately settling and developing "civilized" characteristics in Europe. As compelling as it may sound, however, the savannah origin story is being questioned. The plains of early Africa were warmer and wetter than those of today, comprising varied mosaics of canopy forests, open bushlands, and extended grassy patches. New hominid fossils show bipedalism emerging in lakeside forests, grasslands with open forests, gallery forests with grassy patches, and forest/bushlands. In some fossils, erect postures coexist with tree-climbing capacities. No paradigm as compelling as adaptation to the savannah exists to explain the origins of walking. The simple, satisfying, darkness-into-light storyline fades into complication and complexity.[29]

The habitat dioramas in New York City's American Museum of Natural History portray the African Eden. As historian of science Donna Haraway interprets it, each diorama in the African hall, where big game mammals and primates are displayed, presents "an unspoiled garden in nature . . . a part of the story of salvation history . . . inviting the visitor to share in its revelation." The exhibits are set in lush grassland gardens with the animals peacefully grazing or watering.[30] Designed and executed by Carl Akeley at the turn of the century, the African Hall recreated the original presence of an uncontaminated habitat, the birthplace of humankind. Reacting against the loss of the hygienic world of preindustrial America and the perceived contamination of a fallen New York flooded with immigrants from southern Europe, the museum crews appropriated a pure, original nature unblemished by the new ills of civilization. It seemed to many that smokestack industries, polluted water, piles of garbage, and disease had created a wilderness in the city. In turn-of-the-century New York, manhood, health, and morality were all under siege.[31]

At the entrance to the museum is a statue of Theodore Roosevelt, African game hunter, potent symbol of the reclaimed manhood of America. The statue portrays Roosevelt as a patriarch on horseback, while an Indian male stands on one side and a black African male on the other, both representing earlier "childlike" states of human development. As Haraway describes it, "The Theodore Roosevelt Memorial presides [over] the central building of the American Museum of Natural History. . . . In the Garden, Western 'man' may begin again the first journey, the first birth from within the sanctuary of nature." Moving through the museum's atrium, murals about Roosevelt and epigraphs from his writings replay human moral development from the innocence of pure nature, through youth, manhood, and the civilized state.[32]

The museum is a monument to the growth of science, progress, and conservation. Nature's innocence, according to Haraway, is captured in pristine views unblemished by technology. The conservation of natural resources was meant to preserve the purity of first, or original, nature so that it could be transformed into second, or built nature through continued progress. The fear of lapsing back into a "darker," more "primitive" phase through the decadence of civilization was combated by the narrative of development built into the sequences of the exhibits. Human primate evolution revealed increasingly upright posture, loss of body hair, and vertical facial structure, and larger brains. Through progress and morality, the level of civilization achieved by human evolution and industrial capitalism could be maintained. Thus, the original Eden of grassland Africa would be reinvented and improved through the upward progress of American development.[33]

If the African savannah was hypothesized as the original Eden, was it also the home of the original Adam and Eve? New human origin stories rely not only on fossil records, but on molecular biology. Through genetic evidence, scientists claim to have identified an ancestral Adam and Eve. They have traced all modern humans to a single "African Eve," the "mother of us all," by analyzing the DNA of the mitochondria—cellular structures transmitted from mother to daughter through the cells of the placenta. All human mitochondrial DNA that currently exists seems to have derived from one ancestral molecule from one woman, a member of the *Homo erectus* lineage who lived in Africa approximately 200,000 years ago. Although many women lived at the time, the genes of only one in the small early population survived, while those of her contemporaries failed to be perpetuated in the procreation lottery. Somewhat similar studies of men on genetic material on the Y chromosome passed only from fathers to sons lead to an ancestral Adam who lived some 188,000 years ago. While many males lived at the time, only one individual left the genetic material in the Y chromosome that persists today.[34]

MALE GARDENERS AND FEMALE GARDENS

A striking example of reinventing the whole earth as a restored garden is provided by Michael Pollan in *Second Nature: A Gardener's Education* (1991). Here, consistent with biblical and Enlightenment imagery, the earth is cast as female garden and the gardener as male hero. Whether deliberate or accidental, Pollan's metaphors are set within Western culture's problematic notion of nature as female—virgin, mother, and fallen Eve— and with labor in the garden as male. Adam as the gardener is the father and patriarch whose labor will restore the earth. In his chapter "The Idea of a Garden," Pollan criticizes of the meaning of "wilderness" and instead proposes a "garden ethic," an idea filled with potential for a new relationship between humanity and nature, but flawed by problematic rhetoric.

When in 1989 a hurricane struck the old growth forest of white pines known as the Cathedral Pines in New England's Berkshire Mountains, a lively debate ensued as to how to restore the area and to what date in history to restore it. Villagers, New Yorkers, foresters, and the Nature Conservancy all weighed in on what the forest should look like. The Cathedral pines were not "virgin growth" dating back several millennia, but were actually new growth from the 1780s and even the 1840s. The Cathedral Pines area was not a wilderness, but regrown cut-over land. The "mess" that followed the hurricane's devastation was a common biological occurrence, said biologists, "just another link in the continuous chain of events that is responsible for shaping and changing this forest." According to the Nature Conservancy, it should be left in "the state of nature" to take its "natural course." To villagers, on the other hand, the trees represented an eyesore and a fire hazard and should be replanted at once. To developers, the land should be cleared, the lumber harvested, and the area turned into condominiums.[35]

Pollan proposes instead of a wilderness to be restored that we consider the land and the forest a garden. Instead of a wilderness ethic we should develop a garden ethic. But, in proposing his garden ethic, Pollan uses the rhetoric of the mainstream Recovery Narrative, representing nature as female—as virgin, mother, and fallen Eve. Nature has a mind of her own and she can and will do just as she pleases. She is uncontrollable by men. She is a fickle female who (like all stereotypical, essentialized females) doesn't know her own mind. Here are his words[36]:

- No one can say what will happen in Cathedral Pines . . . because *nature herself doesn't know what's going to happen here.* . . . [C]hance events can divert her course into an almost infinite number of different channels.
- Chance and contingency, it turns out, are everywhere in nature; she has no fixed goals, no unalterable pathways into the future, no inflexible rules that she herself can't bend or break at will. She is more like us (or we are more like her) than we ever imagined.
- But nature herself has no strong preference. That doesn't mean she will countenance any outcome; she's already ruled out many possible futures (tropical rain forest, desert, etc.) and, all things being equal, she'd probably lean toward oak. But all things aren't equal (her idea) and she is evidently happy to let the free play of numerous big and little contingencies settle the matter.
- It's a whole lot easier to assume that nature left to her own devices knows what's best for a place. . . .
- Once a landscape is no longer "virgin" it is typically written off as fallen, lost to nature, irredeemable.
- Nature may once again turn dangerous and capricious and unconquerable. When this happens, we will quickly lose our crush on her.

Not only is nature stereotypically female, but Pollan's gardener—the one who will manage the new landscape, plant the garden, and set up the new garden ethic—is male. Despite the long history of women as gardeners, only men (with one or two exceptions) are acknowledged as sources of gardening knowledge. The gardener is decisive, knowledgeable, and clear-headed. "He" doesn't waste time repeating what fickle female nature has already proven can't be done. The earth and all its plants and animals are his. They were placed here eons ago to be tended by him, reenacting the role of Adam before the Fall. The gardener is civilized and responsible, not changeable and erratic like nature "herself."[37]

- The gardener doesn't waste much time on metaphysics. . . . That's probably because he's noticed that most of the very long or wide perspectives we've recently been asked to adopt . . . are indifferent to our well-being and survival as a species.
- The gardener's conception of his self-interest is broad and enlightened. Anthropocentric as he may be, he recognizes that he is dependent for his health and survival on many other forms of life, so he is careful to take their interests into account in whatever he does. He is in fact a wilderness advocate of a certain kind. It is when he respects and nurtures the wilderness of his soil and his plants that his garden seems to flourish most. Wildness, he has found, resides not only out there, but right here: in his soils, in his plants, even in himself.
- The gardener feels he has a legitimate quarrel with nature—with her weeds and storms and plagues, her rot and death. What's more that quarrel has produced much of value, not only in his own time here (this garden, these fruits), but over the whole course of Western history.
- The gardener doesn't take it for granted that man's impact on nature will always be negative. Perhaps he's observed how his own garden has made this patch of land a better place, even by nature's own standards. His gardening has greatly increased the diversity and abundance of life in this place. . . . His soil supports a much richer community of microbes than it did before.
- The gardener in nature is that most artificial of creatures, a civilized human being: in control of his appetites, solicitous of nature, self-conscious, and responsible. . . .

Pollan's "garden ethic" is much like Francis Bacon's notion of a chaste marriage between man and nature, now updated and recast in modern terms. Pollan's goal is to restore the planet in the form of a garden. He wants to marry nature and learn how to live with her despite her fickleness and erratic uncontrollable behavior. "The old idea may have taught us how to worship nature," he writes, "but it didn't tell us how to live with her. It told us more than we needed to know about virginity and rape, and almost nothing about marriage." He uses the idea of restoration proposed by George Perkins Marsh and Aldo Leopold, but without their sophistication and without updating their gendered language. He states that "sometimes it is desirable, and possible, for man to intervene in nature in order to improve it. Specifically, man should intervene to re-create damaged ecosystems: polluted rivers, clear-cut forests, vanished prairies, dead lakes. . . . But the most important contribution of the restorationists has been to set forth a positive, active role for man in nature. . . ."[38]

Pollan's solution to the landscape at Cathedral Pines is to ask humanity to work with nature's ecological processes in landscape restoration. Not a bad idea, perhaps, and one with which many of the neighboring townspeople and environmentalists might agree, but Pollan casts the final goal in gendered terms: "A walk in a restored version of the precolonial forest might recall us to our culture's first, fateful impressions of America, to our thoughts on coming upon what Fitzgerald called the "fresh green breast of the new world."[39]

Pollan's image of nature's garden restored by humanity has the potential for a new partnership between humanity and nature. Restoration is one of the environmentalists' tools for healing the damage brought about by capitalist development. Absent its gendered language and stereotypic gender roles, the gardener's ethic could become an example of partnership ethics. But as proposed by Pollan, it falls into the overarching framework of the mainstream Recovery Narrative.

CONCLUSION

Stories of shopping malls, genetically engineered fruit, African Edens, and male gardeners restoring the female garden planet comprise the modern version of the story of the Fall of Adam and Eve and their Recovery of Eden. The mainstream Recovery Narrative is the outcome of two thousand years of human progress in overcoming wilderness, desert, and adversity by laboring in the earth and recreating the land as a Garden Planet. Eve's sin has been absolved. Humans have paid their debt to God. The planet has been reinvented as garden, awaiting the time when it will merge again into a higher heavenly paradise.

PART III

New Stories

NINE

Earth in Recovery

THERE WAS ONCE A TOWN IN THE HEART OF AMERICA WHERE ALL
LIFE SEEMED TO LIVE IN HARMONY WITH ITS SURROUNDINGS. THE
TOWN LAY IN THE MIDST OF A CHECKERBOARD OF PROSPEROUS FARMS,
WITH FIELDS OF GRAIN AND HILLSIDES OF ORCHARDS WHERE, IN SPRING,
WHITE CLOUDS OF BLOOM DRIFTED ABOVE THE GREEN FIELDS. . . .
THEN A STRANGE BLIGHT CREPT OVER THE AREA AND EVERYTHING
BEGAN TO CHANGE. . . . THERE WAS A STRANGE STILLNESS. . . . THE
FEW BIRDS SEEN ANYWHERE WERE MORIBUND. . . . IT WAS A SPRING
WITHOUT VOICES.
—*Rachel Carson,* Silent Spring

In 1962, Rachel Carson's *Silent Spring* energized Americans as has no
other work in recent decades. Enormously controversial at the time, the
book took on the chemical industries, pitting them against environmentalists and ordinary citizens. More fundamentally, Carson's book reversed
the mainstream progressive narrative. Biocides bludgeoned the landscape
and assaulted the environment with lethal weapons in "man's war against
nature," increasing alarm in a citizenry already mobilized over the hazards
of nuclear weapons and radioactive fallout. "How could intelligent
beings," she asked, "seek to control a few unwanted species by a method
that contaminated the entire environment and brought the threat of dis-

Fig. 9.1. Alexander Hogue's, *Erosion No. 2. Mother Earth Laid Bare* (1936) revealed the devastating effects on the earth wrought by the Dust Bowl of the Great Plains in the 1930s. The Philbrook Museum of Art, Tulsa, Oklahoma. Courtesy of Olivia Hogue Marino

ease and death even to their own kind?" Carson's book created a declensionist narrative that framed the insights of the environmental movement. Could the earth recover?[1]

Today many environmentalists see history as a decline, not a progressive movement that has made the desert blossom as the rose. To them, the Enlightenment Recovery Narrative is a false story. Instead of creating a new Eden on earth, the original, evolved garden has become a degraded desert. Pristine nature, not innocent man, has fallen. The decline from Eden was slow, rather than a precipitous lapsarian moment (or loss of innocence) as in the Adam and Eve origin story. Over the millennia from the Paleolithic era to the present, nature has been the victim of both human hubris and social changes that have overcome "the necessities of nature" through domestication, cultivation, and commodification of every aspect of an original, evolved, prehuman garden. So-called advances in science, technology, and economy actually accelerate the earth's decline. Yet environmentalists too argue for a Recovery Narrative—one focused on the

Recovery of the earth. In retelling history, they too frame their critiques within the larger plot of Recovery.

In this chapter, I will show how the plot of the mainstream Recovery Narrative has been reversed by environmentalists, feminists, and post-modern thinkers. Like environmentalists, many feminists see history as a slow decline from a prior Golden Age, not a progressive ascent to a new garden on earth. Postmodern thinkers contest Enlightenment assumptions that progress occurred through trickle-down economics and salvation through science and technology. The critics' plot moves not from the tragedy of the Fall upward to the comedy of an earthly or heavenly paradise, but descends from an original state of oneness with nature to the tragedy of nature's destruction.

Yet, the critics, too, hope for a Recovery, one that is rapid enough to save the earth and society by the mid-twenty-first century. The metanarrative of Recovery does not change, but the declensionist plot into which they have cast prior history must be radically reversed. My own view is that these narratives offer valuable deconstructions of Enlightenment thought as well as reconstructive proposals for a better future, but they do not go far enough. We also need new socioeconomic modes of engaging with the earth, new multicultural narratives, new approaches to science, and a new ethic of partnership between humanity and the Earth (see chapters 10 and 11).

ENVIRONMENTAL DECLINE

Today some 60 percent of Americans expect an end to the earth, whether at the millennium, in the next several decades, or at some point in the future. However doom is forecast—by ecological disaster, nuclear war, the Bible, political events, the AIDS crisis, or the "coming plague"—the end, they believe, will come long before the sun death predicted by science. Environmental apocalypse is one of a series of possible endings.[2]

Planet Earth is indeed in trouble. By the year 2000 there were 6 billion people on the planet with 8 billion projected by 2025 and somewhere between 9 and 11 billion by 2050. Global population was growing at about 1.4 percent per year. The United States had some 275 million people, with a growth rate of just under .8 percent per year, and a projection of 347 million by the year 2050. At the turn of the millennium, 77 percent of the U.S. population lived in cities; 47 percent did so in the world as a whole.

It is difficult to imagine the impact of such vast numbers of people on the environment.[3]

From the settlement of the United States until the present, forests have been cut and deserts irrigated in the process of reinventing the American Eden. Most of the country's fertile soils have been plowed for cropland. The land area of the United States is 915 million hectares. In the 1990s, there were 187 million hectares of land in cultivation, 11 percent of it under irrigation, and about 240 million hectares in pasture and rangelands. The original forest once covered 54 percent of the entire country. What remains today is only 23 percent of the original extent. Only 6.3 percent of forest cover is classified as untouched frontier forest and of that 85 percent is threatened. A mere 10 percent of temperate forests are protected, with another 9 percent in parklands. The mainstream Recovery Narrative of cutting down the Earth's forests and irrigating its deserts to reinvent the Garden of Eden has apparently been fulfilled.[4]

As the twenty-first century begins, the environmental decline approaches a crisis. The greenhouse effect, the population explosion, the destruction of the ozone layer, the extinction of species, toxic soils, polluted oceans, and the end of wilderness are all subplots in a grand narrative of environmental endism. Predictions of crisis, such as those of Paul Ehrlich in "Ecocatastrophe" (1969), the Club of Rome in *Limits to Growth* (1972) and of Bill McKibben in *The End of Nature* (1989), abound, as first (evolved, prehuman) nature is totally subsumed by humans and the human artifacts of second (commodified) nature.[5]

By the late 1990s, global energy use had risen by about 70 percent over that of 1970, with the highest use being in the developed world and the highest increases in the developing world. Environmentalists predicted that by 2025 a billion cars and trucks would be guzzling gasoline and emitting polluting gases. Tied to the increase in energy use is the predicted global warming, as greenhouse gases such as carbon dioxide affect the world's climate. Winters will start later and springs will come earlier. Plants will grow better in the higher latitudes, while droughts in lower latitudes will contribute to crop failures and species extinctions. A conference on global warming held in 1997 in Kyoto pushed developed countries to decrease greenhouse gases from industries and vehicles by 6–8 percent by 2005. Compounding the problem is the increase in acid rain caused by burning fossil fuels that are carried hundreds of miles in upper atmosphere winds and are then washed out by rain, snow, and fog. Forests and lakes are killed and soils permanently damaged from leaching. In the United States alone, some two billion tons of topsoil have been permanently lost through wind and water erosion. From the perspective of the environment, the agricultural revolution of ten thousand years ago and the industrial revolutions of the modern era are global disasters. For many environmentalists, these disasters stem from modern society's emphasis on progress at the expense of nature.[6]

The identification of modernism as a problem rather than as progress was sharply formulated by Frankfurt school philosophers Max Horkheimer and Theodor Adorno in the opening sentences of their 1944 *Dialectic of Enlightenment*: "The fully enlightened earth radiates disaster triumphant. The program of the enlightenment was the disenchantment of the world; the dissolution of myths and the substitution of knowledge for fancy." They criticized both Francis Bacon's concept of the domination of nature and Karl Marx and Friedrich Engels's optimism that the control of nature would lead to human progress. They faulted the reduction of nature to mere number by mechanistic science and capitalism: "Number becomes the canon of the Enlightenment. The same equations dominate bourgeois justice and commodity exchange. . . . Myth turns into enlightenment and nature into mere objectivity."[7] The Frankfurt's school's critique of modernism set the stage for postmodern narratives of environmental decline.

ENVIRONMENTAL NARRATIVES

Among the twentieth-century critics of modernism are many environmentalists and feminists who rewrite the story of history as a decline from an Edenic deep past. The postmodern critics of modernism condemn negative assessments of "primitive" peoples. Environmentalists such as Max Oelschlaeger and Paul Shepard, deep ecologists, social ecologists, and nature writers would reclaim the outlook of early cultures as the basis for Recovery. As Oelschlaeger puts it, "No longer can we dismiss the Paleolithic mind as a hopelessly retrograde form of consciousness held in the grip of magic and myth." He posits a Paleolithic intelligence that had no basis for distinguishing between what the "modern mind" would recognize as wilderness and that which it would call "home." For the "Paleolithic mind" both wilderness and home were one and the same thing, each inseparable from the other (see chapter 2).[8] Wilderness is Oelschlaeger's antidote to Western culture's manipulation of the natural world, a counter to the loss of spiritual oneness—an antidote to the Fall from Eden. Wilderness, not heaven, represents human salvation.[9]

Philosopher George Sessions likewise sees the history of nature as a decline from a prior Edenic state in which early peoples existed in close interrelationships with each other and the natural world. It was agriculture that ruptured these early person-planet bonds. Sessions argues that the philosophy of deep ecology, proposed by Norwegian philosopher Arne Naess in 1973, offers a new story, one that restores an ecocentric philosophy of egalitarian relationships between humanity and other entities of the ecosphere: "With the beginning of agriculture, most ecocentric cultures (and religions) were gradually replaced or driven off into remote corners of the earth by pastoral and eventually, 'civilized' cultures (Latin: *civitas*, cities). It seems likely that one of the functions of the Garden of Eden story, for instance, was to provide a moral justification for this process." For Sessions, anthropocentrism, or a philosophy of human dominance over nature, was a detour from the fundamentally egalitarian relationship between people and nature needed to sustain the earth in the twenty-first century.[10] Recovery of the earth is possible through deep ecology.

Social Ecologist Murray Bookchin's narrative differs from that of the deep ecologists in emphasizing people to people rather than people to nature relationships as the origin and goal of a sustainable ecological society. Bookchin interprets history as a decline from egalitarian "organic societies" that led first to the domination of human over human and then to the domination of humanity over nature. He writes, "I cannot emphasize too strongly that the concept [of the domination of nature] emerged very gradually from a broader social development: the increasing domination of human by human. The breakdown of primoridal equality into hierarchical systems of inequality, the disintegration of early kinship groups into social classes, the dissolution of tribal communities into the city, and finally the usurpation of social administration by the State—all profoundly altered not only social life but also the attitude of people toward each other, humanity's vision of itself, and ultimately its attitude toward the natural world." Bookchin uses the narrative of decline from social equality into hierarchy as a springboard to Recovery, i.e. a new "ecological society," in which freedom replaces domination and social equality replaces hierarchy.[11]

In addition to deep ecologists and social ecologists, environmental writers have also employed the narrative of Fall and Recovery to characterize the environmental crisis. Bill McKibben's *The End of Nature*, juxtaposes a narrative of environmental decline with the death of an idea—that pristine nature still exists on the planet. McKibben, like others concerned with ecocatastrophe, enumerates a litany of human effects on the environment from the greenhouse effect to ozone depletion, the loss of forests, species extinctions, and vanishing wildlife. In nineteenth-century America, he asserts, there were actually acres of fruitful, fragrant, beautiful lands to be explored by European settlers, and in the twentieth century, parts of Alaska and the Arctic still remained uninhabited and unpolluted. Today, even where wilderness has vanished or been degraded by the encroachments of civilization and the industrialized world, middle-class Americans still retain the idea that nature as pristine and pure exists somewhere on the planet. But now even that vision as a reality seems gone. "If the waves crash up against the beach, eroding dunes and destroying homes, it is not the awesome power of Mother Nature. It is the awesome power of Mother Nature as altered by the awesome power of man. . . ."[12]

The "end of nature" for McKibben is the end of an idea. It is the cessation of hope that a pristine world, majestic and beautiful, untouched and unaltered by humanity exists somewhere on earth. The death of that idea "begins with concrete changes in the reality around us—changes that scientists can measure and enumerate . . . until . . . our sense of nature as eternal and separate is washed away, and we will see all too clearly what we have done." Humanity's place in nature has been irrevocably transformed by its own ability, not only to change its own backyard, but even to alter the highest reaches of the atmosphere. There will still be sunshine and rain in the brave new world of the future, but they will fall on a much different landscape than when the earth was primary forest. For McKibben, what is needed is a new idea of humanity's place in the natural world. He, too, holds out hope for Recovery.[13]

Similarly, Daniel Quinn's *Ishmael* is an arresting story of a gorilla instructing a human disciple about the human propensity to destroy all life on the planet, while nevertheless proposing a Recovery—an alternative way of living within nature. According to Quinn, everyone contributes to the unrelenting daily destruction of the world. Humans have been unwittingly socialized into the wrong story, one that has been continually humming in the background for the past ten thousand years, a story from which we cannot extricate ourselves unless a new narrative emerges. "Anywhere you go in the world, you'll find the same story being enacted. . . . Mother Culture teaches you that this is as it should be. . . . This is the story man was born to enact. . . . To step out of this story is to fall off the edge of the world."[14]

Quinn interprets the story of Adam and Eve in terms of *leavers* and *takers*. For three million years, Adam and Eve lived in the Garden of Eden as leavers. When Eve picked the apple, humans became takers—they took into their own hands the power to decide who would live and who would die, including the life of the nonhuman world. Instead of living within the bounty of the gods, they now created their own agricultural bounty. The biblical story of Cain, the agriculturalist, killing his brother Abel, the pastoralist, is a story of the expansion of agricultural takers into the territory of pastoral leavers. "Don't fight us," said the takers, "join us. Join our revolution and help us turn the world into a paradise for man."[15]

Since the Fall, Quinn asserts, humanity has been divided into these two cultures. Takers have accepted the story that "the world was given to man to turn into a paradise." They have been living within a story of conquest and rule, whereas, for millennia, leavers had enacted a story of meaningful satisfaction with what they had been given. Ten thousand years ago, takers took control of the story and hence of power over life and death in the world. As agriculturalists, they determined that their way of life was superior to that of hunting and gathering. For the takers, "every last square yard of the planet had to be devoted to [agriculture]."[16]

Ishmael the gorilla, speaking for Quinn, argues that humanity needs to rethink itself as part of the leavers' story rather than the takers' story— we must change the story by which we live. This does not mean a return to hunting-gathering or pastoralism; rather, it means destroying the prison of taker culture that sees the world as belonging to humanity. It entails living, as do other forms of life, as "belonging to the world." It entails living in accordance with ecological laws. It means inventing a new narrative by which to live.[17]

Many environmentalists envision a new narrative, a restoration of an earth where people would live in a sustainable relationship with nature. To achieve sustainability, some argue, the current world population of six billion would have to decrease in some deliberate fashion that rules out genocide, starvation, or massive warfare over resources. Ecologists Paul and Anne Ehrlich submit that an optimal world population is 1.5 to 2 billion people, a number recently attained—and surpassed—in the 1930s.[18] Some envision even smaller human numbers: "A return to Eden would entail a slow depopulation of the planet until population fell to such a point that few pressures would exist on the environment to provide for a standard of living comparable to today's for everyone. I would estimate a world population of somewhere around one billion would suffice. Given that population level and the technology that currently exists, the abundance of resources could easily meet each person's needs."[19]

Each of the preceding environmental authors sets out their proposal for Recovery within the same narrative arc. In the distant past, humanity lived in a sustainable relationship with the environment. As society evolved, some event or process brought about a fall or decisive turning point that initiated a decline in environmental quality. Each author provides a complex analysis of that decline and proposes a visionary and often practical solution that will bring about a Recovery. Ideas such as reverence for wilderness, social equality, a sense of the human place in nature, of leaving rather than taking, of sustainable livelihoods, and optimum human populations are all elements in the environmentalists' metanarrative of Recovery. Each of these proposals has merit, and to the extent that it can be implemented will contribute to a sustainable planetary future. But each, despite its often complex and astute analysis of past problems, is set within by the linearity of the Fall and Recovery narrative. Nevertheless, each approach has the potential to become part of a new non-linear web of narratives and new partnerships between humanity and the natural world. What that new complex will look like over the next several decades is still emerging.

FEMINIST NARRATIVES

Like environmentalists, feminist and ecofeminist philosophers often cast history as a decline, while also posing viable alternatives that would heal the planet. In 1974, French feminist Françoise d'Eaubonne published a chapter entitled "The Time for Ecofeminism" in her book *Feminism or Death*. d'Eaubonne placed the problem of the death of the planet squarely on the shoulders of men. The goal of her Ecology-Feminism Center, founded in Paris in 1972, was "to tear the planet away from the male today in order to restore it for humanity of tomorrow. . . . If the male society persists there will be no tomorrow for humanity." For d'Eaubonne as well as other feminists and ecofeminsts, the real cause of the environmental crisis is patriarchal power. Like that of the preceding environmentalists, much of the feminist analysis is framed within the overarching narrative of Fall and Recovery.[20]

d'Eaubonne followed the analysis of nineteenth- and early-twentieth-century proponents of ancient "matriarchal" societies such as Johann Bachhofen, Friedrich Engels, Robert Briffault, and August Bebel, who saw "the great defeat of the feminine sex" some five thousand years ago as the beginning of an age of patriarchal power. Whether matriarchies ever existed has been questioned, but for d'Eaubonne, the turning point that brought about the Fall from a presumed matriarchy into patriarchy was the advent of plow agriculture introduced by men. It was the resulting male system, however—not capitalism or socialism—she argued, that gave men the power to sow both the earth (fertility) and women (fecundity). The iron age of the second sex began, women were caged, and the earth appropriated by males. The male society "built by males and for males" that took over running the planet did so in terms of competition, aggression, and sexual hierarchy, "allocated in such a way to be exercised by men over women." Patriarchal power led to agricultural overexploitation and industrial overexpansion, compounding the environmental crisis. "The earth, symbol and former preserve of the Great Mother," wrote d'Eaubonne, "has had a harder life and has resisted longer; today her conqueror has reduced her to agony. This is the price of phallocracy." Now husbands who control women's bodies and implant them with their seed, doctors who examine them, and male priests who call for large families are the bearers of phallocratic power over women's wombs.[21]

For d'Eaubonne, Recovery would be a feminist world. But a society cast in the feminine would not mean power in the hands of women, but rather a society in which no power existed at all. The human being would be treated as a person, not as male or female; women's *and* men's interests would be those of the entire human community. The preservation of the earth would be a question not just of change or improvement but of life or death. The problem, she said, paraphrasing Marx, is "to change the world . . . so that there can still be a world." But only the feminine, which is concerned with all levels of society and nature, could accomplish "the ecological revolution." She concluded her foundational essay with the telling words, "And the planet placed in the feminine will flourish for all."[22]

"My Name is Chellis and I'm in Recovery from Western Civilization." So Chellis Glendinning titles her book on the psychology of planetary trauma and "earthgrief." She details the psychosocial dynamics of overcivilized earthlings who have lost touch with their deepest roots. We are no longer "nature-based" peoples who directly depend on and participate in the cycles of nature by foraging for plants and perceiving the earth as sacred. Instead, most of us experience daily onslaughts of noise, traffic jams, smog, and all the stresses of mass technological society. Glendinning brings her own experiences with recovery from various forms of stress to bear on the history of Western culture.

For Glendinning, the major negative turning point was the Fall from foraging societies initiated by the domestication of animals. Humanity henceforth lost its connection with wild nature and transformed its gender roles: "Perhaps the saddest of all the effects caused by domestication concerns women and men: their identities, roles, and relationships became tragically distorted. This perversion unfolded in both farming and pastoral societies as men took over responsibility for all food production while women lost the ability to contribute directly to survival." The transformation affected both women and men. Women lost power and autonomy, while men resented the new burdens placed on them: "The tragedy is painfully clear: for over 99 percent of human existence, women's role had been absolutely vital for community survival. Now what women did was becoming 'women's work,' and in this lesser role, they were coming to be economically dependent, incapable of self-sufficiency—and vulnerable as the perfect targets for the mounting rage and terror men were feeling."[23]

After domestication and sedentary agriculture, Glendinning argues, a downward spiral of consequences set in that is felt to the present day: "For all the excitement that accompanied this new way of life, for all the grandiosity describing it as the greatest advance toward human achievement, for all the rationalizations hailing it as 'progress' and 'evolution'—the tame/wild dichotomy actually initiated a spiral of massive social, cultural, economic, and ecological disruption." Glendinning's answer to the rupture is to reconnect to the freedom of the wild. "[W]e each, alongside our families and friends, can initiate our recovery from western civilization with a simple but radical act; *praise Creation.*"[24]

In religion, a narrative of Fall and Recovery has likewise been compelling to many feminists. Some have argued that in early societies, goddesses, as bringers of life and fertility, have been worshipped as the dominant deities. With the rise of patriarchy, goddesses were replaced by male gods and ultimately by a single male deity (see chapter 2). In achieving the proposed Recovery, some feminists worship the goddess as symbol of female power over the creation. For others, religious history entails an inquiry into the gendered nature of the original oneness as being both male and female. Some go a step further to argue that the logos, or word, is itself gendered. As original purity, it is not male, but female—virgin, pristine, untouched. To such feminists, Recovery would entail a feminist or an egalitarian religious world.[25]

Some feminists have also reinterpreted science in the light of Fall and Recovery. With the rise of patriarchal society, women, despite their significant contributions to science and technology, have mainly been excluded from mainstream roles. It has largely been men who have held positions of power in the fields of science and technology and organized the market economies that made nature victim in the ascent of "man." Some feminists reenvision Eve as the first scientist and Sophia as ultimate wisdom. For others, feminist science would reinterpret the original mind as having no sex, and hence accessible to male and female minds alike. For such feminists, the Recovery Narrative would reclaim women's place in contemporary science and technology and their roles in history.[26]

Yet, some feminists argue, the principle of transcendent reason on which such theories are grounded is itself a product of Enlightenment thinking. According to Linda Nicholson, "The scholarship of modern Western culture has been marked by the attempt to reveal general, all-encompassing principles which can lay bare the basic features of natural and social reality. This attempt can be related to an earlier, more religiously based belief that the purpose of scholarship was to make evident the word of God as revealed in his creations." This objective, according to Nicholson, is specific to a particular period in Western history and culture, namely the Enlightenment and its focus is on the all encompassing role of reason. It ignores the inclusiveness of a multiplicity of views and cultures, particularly oral cultures, whether outside, or even within, the Western tradition. The "ideal of 'a God's eye view' must be situated within the context of modernity, a period whose organizing principles . . . are on the decline."[27]

The preceding feminist and ecofeminist narratives criticize the mainstream Enlightenment Recovery Narrative as patriarchal and rationalist. Patriarchy validates the authority of a male deity and a male society, while limiting women's full and equal participation in religion, science, and society. Enlightenment science and philosophy validate male reason, while limiting the value of women's reasoning and a multiplicity of non-Western voices and oral traditions. Like those of the environmentalists, the feminist critiques employ an overarching narrative of Fall and Recovery. The

Fall from a prior egalitarian (or for some, a matriarchal) society is triggered by animal domestication, plow agriculture, and the replacement of goddesses by a male God accessible to male minds who reveal "his" truths through science. For many feminists, the Recovery entails a more democratic society and mindset in which women and men are acknowledged to have equal reasoning capacities and equal opportunities to fulfill their human potentials. Such feminist critiques are complex and valuable contributions to the validation of women and their contributions to society. Yet, like the environmentalist narratives, when posited within a linear narrative of Fall and Recovery they may fall short of their potential. Possibilities for nonlinear narratives within weblike human and human/nature partnerships need to be explored and developed (see chapter 11).[28]

POSTMODERN CRITIQUES

From the perspective of postmodernism, these environmental and feminist narratives of decline, beginning in the Stone Age and proceeding to the present, not only reverse the Enlightenment plot, but question the primacy of the written word embedded in the biblical and patriarchal texts of Western culture. Stone Age culture, being oral, privileges the spoken word over the written word. Here truth lies, not in reason and law, but in being in the world of nature. For some critics, Stone Age culture is a living presence without hierarchical truth structures, transcendent causes, or patriarchal origins.

Christian religion and Greek philosophy, on the other hand, construct the transcendent word as the reality behind modernity's privileged texts. The logos as word, or truth, underlies all manifestations in the natural world. The "God word" is the ultimate cause or origin of the universe. God creates the rules by which the universe works—the unchanging laws of nature. The spoken word is present, the written word above and absent. The author is separated from the reader. But originally, as the Gospel of St. John states, "In the Beginning was the Word, and the Word was with God, and the Word was God." For some postmodernists, if God's word is the ultimate unending presence and if Stone Age culture is also an unending presence of spoken words, then the Paleolithic era is actually closer to the godliness of presence than Western culture's written texts. The marginalized "savage mind" (or Oelschlaeger's "Paleolithic mind") is privileged and Western culture's Enlightenment texts are marginalized. Nature as a living presence is outside of history, and the people who lived within it are "holy."

Privileging automatically creates a marginalized other. Privileging the central, progressive narrative of Western culture marginalizes other narratives. Privileging modernity's written tradition marginalizes its binary opposite—indigenous or oral cultures. Yet reversing the hierarchy by privileging the other (indigenous cultures), in its turn marginalizes the first (Western culture). Binary thinking itself sets up the dilemma: nature/culture, white/black, written/oral, male/female, speech/writing. One is central, the other excluded; one is higher, the other lower; one is true, the other false. The pairs can be reversed by raising the opposite. But in either case they are frozen in their new positions. There is no movement, process, or free play across differences.

Deconstruction, says Jacques Derrida, unfreezes the process, identifying the centrality of one term, then subverting that centrality to privilege the excluded term. But such moves are political. They represent possible ways to read history, literature, anthropology, and philosophy. No text is fixed by authority. By unfreezing the hierarchies and dualities, the terms become free to move across their differences.[29]

Similar problems of privileging and marginalization pertain to myth. Myth, Plato claims, is the passing down of stories orally, a mere repetition of words without knowledge. But if writing is just the reflection of the word, or logos, then writing too is an endless repetition of words without knowledge. Logos is not really a well-reasoned argument captured by the written text. It is just myth, repeated words without knowing. Christianity and Western philosophy that depend on the logos behind the well-reasoned argument are simply myths on the same level as the stories of non-Western peoples. The Bible is myth; Plato is myth; Immanuel Kant is myth; God is myth. But simultaneously, the Bible is logos; Plato is logos; Kant is logos; God is logos, and so are the stories of non-Western peoples. Neither is true; neither is false. Both myth and logos are endless plays of meaning; repetitions without knowing.

The story of history as a decline from the "Paleolithic mind"—as a decline from the spoken word—is the binary opposite of history as the rise of the "modern mind" through the written text. Both narratives are forms to which content has been added by historians, anthropologists, philosophers, and linguists. The story of decline or rise, economic progress or environmental crisis, is imposed by the narrative form on the material. Both story types are grand narratives told by master storytellers and internalized as truth or reality through socialization and acculturation. Yet there is truth in both stories, in both histories. For many people throughout the world, living conditions have improved over time and opportunities have led to upward mobility, freedom, and economic improvement (although for others these have worsened). At the same time, there is a reality to the environmental crisis. Wilderness areas, biodiversity, and air and water quality have all diminished over time while industrialization, population, resource depletion, and pollution have increased. Both stories have some degree of truth status. And both in turn can be deconstructed.

But deconstructive analysis is based on the assumption of binary opposites. It posits thinking itself in terms of opposites. Each idea, each concept has an other. Myth, reason, speech, writing, and dialogue, in fact, meaning itself, is based on the presumption that binary oppositions are the basis for spoken language and for written communication. But if everything is a mere play of differences across a tapestry of opposites, as Derrida asserts, then there are no fixed meanings, no truths, only the relativity of language. Deconstruction posits a nonmaterial world of differences as meaningful. All words have relative, changing meanings; the words, not the material things themselves, are real.

REALITY

Although deconstruction is an important analytical tool, I argue that realism, or the idea that the material world itself is real, is an important counter, or other, to deconstruction's focus on language. The material world is mentally constructed and interpreted in terms of language, but it exists as biophysical entities. Only biophysical beings, such as humans, have the tongues and brains to create and perform speech acts—to invent the logos, or word. The real physical world and the constructed mental world thus exist in dialectical relation to each other. Reality and narrative, I argue, interact with each other.

In *Postmodernism and the Environmental Crisis*, philosopher Arran Gare, acknowledges the postmodern critique of narratives, but calls for a new "postmodern grand narrative" that reconceptualizes humanity's place in nature through a new politics, economics, science, and ethics. The idea of a single grand narrative may be too absolute a viewpoint, but Gare's emphasis on a multitude of stories is an important contribution to a new perspective. Seeing ourselves as a part of a story in which we play a role guides our actions; the storyline often tells the actor what to do or conversely allows an individual to rebel and follow a different story. Gare argues that while "modern" stories had simple plots that were "monological," the new stories are "polyphonic." There are a multiplicity of perspectives imbedded in the new stories through which people define themselves, their place, and their active roles. The new stories have a diversity of cultural representations that reveal the many ways in which people have been socially and culturally formed.

All grand narratives, Gare believes, entail a cosmology that reveals people's places in the universe, how their cultures came to exist, and who within them hold positions of reverence or privilege. The problem with the narratives of Western culture for today is that they are too simplistic for living in the present global order. Gare's idea is that a new grand narrative will contain a multitude of stories told in many voices, integrated through alternative cosmologies and metaphysics. These stories will take into account the environmental crisis, needs for liberation and salvation, and the self-formation and self-determination of the participants.[30]

Although there may be no single new story or grand narrative, I agree with Gare that people can use stories to understand the histories through which they and others have been formed and by entering into these stories will appreciate their own places in the biophysical world of atoms, molecules, organisms, ecosystems, nations, planets, and galaxies. People will acknowledge their own location within nature and their own destructive and constructive roles in nature's continued existence. "Conceiving of narratives in this way," Gare concludes, "would avoid the tendency noted by poststructuralists of reducing people . . . to the 'Other.' . . . It would avoid the tendency of history to focus on the rise of Western civilization and to deny a story to societies subjugated by it. . . ."[31]

According to Gare, the new grand narrative must allow people, as active participants, to construct narratives for themselves, rather than submitting to a "master narrative" that has constructed them as passive, controllable entities. In the new stories, people will recreate themselves through culture and act out their own roles. "Each individual process or sub-process within the universe is like a melody singing itself within a symphony. . . . The whole duration of a symphony matters, and each melody within the symphony, each note within the melody, are significant in themselves as parts of this duration."[32]

This approach, I believe, offers possibilities for a new way of thinking about narratives. Rather than positing a linear narrative of Fall and Recovery, a synthesis or web of narratives may emerge. Those who construct and follow new synthesizing narratives will do so by allowing regional peoples to preserve and use their own bioregional environments in ways that counter the environmentally destructive modes of global capitalism. People will be able to redefine themselves such that justice within the region recognizes and serves all individuals, organisms, and ecosystems, and their potentialities and contributions to life, culture, and the sustainability of the world. New theories of science stemming from chaos and complexity theories and new ideas about ethics can contribute to new stories that will sustain the earth.[33]

CONCLUSION

Environmentalists, feminists, and philosophers all call for different pathways to sustaining the earth and for new Recovery Narratives. Many alternatives to modernism and capitalism would need to be explored to achieve sustainable livelihoods. Many narratives stemming from many groups of people worldwide may contend with each other or may at some point eventually come together. The new voices and stories that contribute to a sustainable world will have new visions of belonging to the earth.

Teacher Ron Zimmerman shared with me his own vision of how it would be to live in an ecologically restored Eden. If an earthly paradise or even a small homeplace on the larger garden planet were possible, it would retain wilderness within a rural setting and maintain natural and cultural diversity in all its forms: "The perfect human habitat would be a landscape that reflects nature's diversity in landforms, flora, and fauna. The image that comes to mind is in Northern California. Starting at the western seas, a cool moist wind moves east and waters the towering redwoods. As the air moves down the eastern slope it warms and brings the fertile valley below to life. In this valley small farms wake at the first light and start their busy day. To the east a rugged mountain range steals the last moisture from the wind. These mountains are called the Silver Mountains for their snow covered peaks. Once in a while a trout rises but is not taken; my creel is empty, but my mind is full. Heaven is on earth."[34]

TEN

Order out of Chaos

EVERYTHING LOOKS BETTER TO-DAY THAN IT DID YESTERDAY. IN THE
RUSH OF FINISHING UP YESTERDAY, THE MOUNTAINS WERE LEFT IN A
RAGGED CONDITION, AND SOME OF THE PLAINS WERE SO CLUTTERED
WITH RUBBISH AND REMNANTS THAT THE ASPECTS WERE QUITE DIS-
TRESSING. . . . THERE ARE TOO MANY STARS IN SOME PLACES AND NOT
ENOUGH IN OTHERS, BUT THAT CAN BE REMEDIED PRESENTLY, NO
DOUBT. THE MOON GOT LOOSE LAST NIGHT, AND SLID DOWN AND FELL
OUT OF THE SCHEME—A VERY GREAT LOSS; IT BREAKS MY HEART TO
THINK OF IT.
—*Mark Twain, "Eve's Diary"*

Central to the mainstream Recovery Narrative is the effort to create order
out of chaos. By contrast, newer narratives welcome and even valorize
chaos. The Scientific Revolution's success in formulating a mechanistic
approach to science allowed humanity to predict and therefore to control,
manage, and dominate nature. Mechanistic science coupled with technology and capitalism set up the possibility of reinventing Eden on earth. By
the late nineteenth century, the successes of mechanistic science included
not only mechanics and astronomy—which Newtonian physics had synthesized—but also optics, thermodynamics, electricity, and magnetism. By
the early twentieth century, however, mechanistic science had been chal-

lenged by relativity theory and quantum mechanics, and by the late twentieth century it was challenged by chaos and complexity theory. In this chapter, I will show how these new twentieth century sciences question the possibility of certainty and predictability and hence undermine mechanism's goal of controlling nature. My own view is that humanity must abandon the hubris of dominating nature—the central idea of the mainstream Recovery Narrative. Instead, the unpredictability of nature means that humans should use the new sciences as one basis for formulating a new relationship with nature—one based on partnership rather than domination (see chapter 11).

CHALLENGES TO CLASSICAL SCIENCE

Biologist Stuart Kauffman argues that science, not Eve, was the cause of our loss of Eden. Copernican, Newtonian, and Darwinian science removed humanity as God's chosen people from its Edenic home at the center of the cosmos. Copernicus's sun-centered universe displaced our terrestrial home and placed it in the third sphere from the central sun. Newton's clocklike universe removed the need for God's continuous action and presence. Seventeenth-century mechanics divided matter into parts whose motions, not God, accounted for change in the external world (a billiard ball model). As classical science progressed, God's role in creation seemed to diminish. By the eighteenth century, it seemed to many that God was a blind clockmaker. He merely created the universe, wound up the clock, and left it to tick away into eternity. By the nineteenth century, classical physics included mechanics, optics, astrophysics, thermodynamics, and electricity and magnetism. Science, it seemed, not God's action, accounted for events in the three-dimensional world. "How far we have come," Kauffman notes, "from the blessed children of God, at the center of the universe, walking among creatures created for our benefit, in a garden called Eden. Science, not sin, has indeed lost us our paradise."[1]

Furthermore, Kauffman points out, Darwinian evolution, operating by natural selection on chance mutations, makes humanity an accidental outcome of the emergence of life. If the drama were replayed, humans might not be around at all. Science has thus created a depressing story of decline from an original Eden in which God created humanity on an Earth at the center of the cosmos to one of chance evolution on the periphery of an ordinary galaxy. Kaufmann notes, "Somewhere along our path, paradise has been lost, lost to the Western mind, and in the spreading world civilization, lost to our collective mind. John Milton must have been the last superb poet of Western civilization who could have sought to justify the ways of God to man in those early years foreshadowing the modern era. Paradise has been lost, not to sin, but to science." In Kauffman's story, classical science is responsible for the decline from an original Eden.[2]

But classical science is likewise seen as a central component of the mainstream Recovery Narrative. Enlightenment science empowered humans with a godlike hubris capable of recreating Eden on earth. Mechanistic, deterministic science gave people the ability to predict the outcome of mathematically described events through algebra, calculus, and linear differential equations. It is prediction that leads to the possibility of control and hence to the domination of nature. The eighteenth-century Enlightenment brought hope of human progress through rational thought, science, and capitalist economic development. Mechanistic science became a powerful tool in the technological reclamation of the earth, turning forests into farms and deserts into irrigated gardens, reversing the fall from Eden by reinventing the earth in the image of the original garden.[3]

Classical science therefore has played two roles in the Recovery Narrative. In Kauffman's story, science is the cause of the decline from an original Eden. In the mainstream progressive story, science is part of the Recovery of that original Eden. Depending on which plot one choses, classical science is responsible either for the loss of the earth as humanity's original Edenic home at the center of the cosmos or for the recreation of the earth as an Eden. But new sciences emerging in the twentieth century help to create a new story. For Kauffman, the science of complex systems, along with other new sciences, offers possibilities. By seeing the emergence of life as a complex adaptive system that reflects an underlying cosmic order, humanity could once again be "at home in the universe."[4]

Like Kauffman, environmentalists want a new story. To many environmentalists, the very success of classical science has led to the widespread destruction of ancient forests, other species, entire ecosystems, and vital products of biological evolution. As environmental historian Steven Pyne sees it, "The real future of environmentalism is in rehabilitation and restoration. Environmentalists have told the story of the Garden of Eden and the fall from grace over and over again. But we haven't yet told the story of redemption. Now we need to tell that story." Many environmentalists thus opt for a new Recovery Narrative that could be put in place by the mid-twenty-first century. New approaches to the science of ecology are part of the new story.[5]

For environmentalists, "sustainability" offers a vision of a recovered garden, one in which humanity will live in a dynamically balanced relationship with the natural world. Environmentalists who press for sustainable development see Recovery as achievable through nondegrading forms of agriculture and industry. Preservationists and deep ecologists strive to save pristine nature as wilderness before it can be destroyed by development. Restoration ecologists wish to marshal human labor to restore an already degraded nature to an earlier pristine state. Social ecologists and green parties devise new economic and political structures that overcome the domination of human beings and nonhuman nature. The regeneration of nature and people will thus be achieved through social and environmental justice. The end drama envisions an ecologically sustainable, socially just ecotopia for the world of the twenty-first century.

But a new Recovery story or set of stories is tied not only to new approaches to science, but also to new possibilities for nonlinear plots. The progressive and declensionist plots that underlie the metanarrative of Recovery both gain power from their linearity. Linearity is not only conceptually easy to grasp, it is also a property of modernity itself. Mechanistic science, progress, and capitalism all draw power from the linear functions of mathematical equations—the upward and downward slopes of straight lines and curves. To the extent that these linear slopes intersect with a real material world, they refer to a limited domain only. But chaos and complexity theories suggest that only the unusual domain of mechanistic science can be described by linear differential equations. The usual, the domain of everyday occurrences—such as weather, turbulence, the shapes of coastlines, and the arrhythmic fibrillations of the human heart—cannot be so easily described. The world is more complex than we know or indeed can ever know. The comfortable predictability of the linear slips away into the uncertainty of the indeterminate—into discordant harmonies and disorderly order. New twentieth-century sciences can contribute to new stories with complex, nonlinear plots and less predictable outcomes.

NEW SCIENCES

New approaches to science in the twentieth century suggest new narratives that are influenced at least in part by skepticism about determinism, prediction, and control. While chaos theory disrupts hopes for complete prediction in certain domains of the everyday world, complexity theory operates in the realm between order and chaos to bring chance and necessity into new relationships. The Enlightenment hope of an orderly, upward trajectory is punctured by a recognition of the roles of unforeseen events, chance encounters, and branching histories to which communities and societies respond by adaptation, struggle, or disintegration. How did these changes come about and how do challenges to mechanistic science developing in the twentieth century suggest new stories about the universe, humanity, and the individual's place in the world?

Emerging over the past decade are a number of scientific proposals that challenge the Scientific Revolution's mechanistic view of nature. According to physicist David Bohm, a mechanistic science based on the assumption that matter is divisible into parts (such as atoms, electrons, or quarks) moved by external forces may be giving way to a new science based on the primacy of process. In the early twentieth century, he argues, relativity and quantum theory began to challenge mechanism. Relativity theory postulated that fields with varying strengths spread out in space. Strong, stable areas, much like whirlpools in a flowing stream, represented particles. They interacted with and modified each other, but were still considered external to and separate from each other. Quantum mechanics mounted a greater challenge. Motion was not continuous, as in mechanistic science, but occurred in leaps. Particles, such as electrons, behaved like waves, while waves, such as light waves, behaved like particles, depending on the experimental context. Context dependence, which was antithetical to mechanism and part of the organic worldview, was a fundamental characteristic of matter.

Bohm's process physics challenges mechanism still further. He argues that instead of starting with parts as primary and building up wholes as secondary phenomena, a physics is needed that starts with undivided, multidimensional wholeness (a flow of energy called the "holomovement") and derives the three-dimensional world of classical mechanics as a secondary phenomenon. The explicate order of the Newtonian world in which we live unfolds from the implicate order contained in the underlying flow of energy.

Bohm suggests that the holomovement contains the principle or seed of life that directs the environment as well as the energy that comes from the soil, water, air, and sunlight. Just as a forest contains trees that are con-

tinually being replaced by new ones, so a particle is in a stable but continual state of regular changes that manifest over and over again. Living and
inanimate things are similar in that they reproduce themselves over and
over by unfoldment and enfoldment. When inanimate matter is informed
by a seed containing information in its DNA, it produces a living plant
that in turn reproduces a seed. The plant exchanges matter and energy
with its environment; carbon dioxide and oxygen cross the cell boundaries.
At no point is there a sharp distinction between life and nonlife. "The
holomovement which is 'life-implicit,' says Bohm, "is the ground both of
'life-explicit' and of 'inanimate matter'. . . . Thus we do not fragment life
and inanimate matter, nor do we try to reduce the former completely to
nothing but an outcome of the latter."[6]

Another challenge to mechanism comes from the new thermodynamics of Ilya Prigogine. The clock-like machine model of nature and
society that dominated the past three centuries of Western thought may
be winding down. While Newtonian classical physics is still valid, it is
nonetheless limited to a clearly defined domain of the total world. It was
extended in the nineteenth century to include theories of thermodynamics that developed out of the needs of a steam-engine society, electricity
and magnetism that supplied the light and electricity that powered that
society, and hydrodynamics or the science associated with the dams and
water power that generated its electricity. The equilibrium and near-
equilibrium thermodynamics of nineteenth-century classical physics had
beautifully described closed, isolated systems such as steam engines and
refrigerators.

In dealing with the emergence of order out of chaos, Prigogine's
theory helped to clarify an apparent contradiction between two nineteenth century scientific developments. Classical thermodynamics,
which says that the universe is moving toward a greater state of chaos, is
based on two laws. The first law states that the total energy of the universe is constant and only changes its form as it is transferred from
mechanical, to chemical, to hydrodynamic, to metabolic, and so on. But
the second law states that the energy available for work—the useful
energy—is decreasing. The universe is running down, just as a clock
unwinds over time when no one is there to rewind it. The second law
implies that the world proceeds from order to disorder, that people grow
older, and that in billions of years the whole universe will reach a uniform temperature. The classical model of reality deals very adequately

with closed systems that are isolated from their environments—situations in which small inputs result in small outputs that can be described by linear mathematical relationships.

Yet the very concept of an unwinding clocklike universe is apparently contradicted by another startling nineteenth century theory—evolution, or the motion toward greater order. Darwinian evolution says that biological systems are evolving, not running down. They are moving from disorder to order; they are becoming more organized rather than disorganized. The direction of change over time is from simple to more complex life forms. The apparent contradiction lies in the domain in which the laws applied. Mechanical systems are closed systems isolated from the environment and their laws pertain to only a small part of the universe. In contrast, most biological and social systems are open, not closed. They exchange matter and energy with the environment.

Prigogine argued that classical thermodynamics holds in systems that are in equilibrium or near equilibrium, such as pendulum clocks, steam engines, and solar systems. These are stable systems in which small changes within the system lead to adjustments and adaptations. They are described mathematically by the great seventeenth- and eighteenth-century mathematical advances in calculus and linear differential equations. But what happens when the input is so large that a system cannot adjust? In these far-from-equilibrium systems, nonlinear relationships take over. In such cases small inputs can produce new and unexpected effects.

Prigogine's far-from-equilibrium thermodynamics allows for the possibility that higher levels of organization can spontaneously emerge out of disorder when a system breaks down. His approach applies to social and ecological systems, which are open rather than closed, and helps to account for biological and social evolution. In the biological realm, when old structures break down, small inputs can (but do not necessarily) lead to positive feedbacks that may produce new enzymes or new cellular structures. In the social sphere, revolutionary changes can take place. For example, a social or economic revolution can occur in which a society regroups around a different social or economic form, such as the change from gathering-hunting to horticulture, or from a feudal society to a preindustrial capitalist society. In the field of science, a revolutionary change could entail a paradigm shift toward new explanatory theories, such as the change from a geocentric Ptolemaic cosmos to a heliocentric Copernican universe.[7]

CHAOS THEORY

Quantum mechanics and relativity theory challenged the determinism of classical mechanics at the atomic and nuclear levels. W.K. Heisenberg's uncertainty principle emphasized the impossibility of simultaneously predicting both the momentum and position of a subatomic particle. But chaos theory went a step further, questioning the determinism of processes in the everyday world and suggesting that the human ability to predict the outcome of those processes, even when lawlike regularities are well described, is limited. It presented, instead, a world of disorderly order and uncertain outcomes.

Chaos theory suggests that deterministic, linear, predictive equations, which we learn in freshman calculus and which form the basis of mechanism, may apply to unusual rather than usual situations. Instead, chaos, in which a small effect may lead to a large effect, may be the norm. Thus, a butterfly flapping its wings in Brazil can result in a tornado in Texas. Chaos theory reveals patterns of complexity that lead to a greater understanding of global behaviors, but militate against overreliance on the simple predictions of linear differential equations.

The butterfly metaphor originated with Edward Lorenz, professor of meteorology at the Massachusetts Institute of Technology, who used it to describe the phenomenon of sensitive dependence on initial conditions. In an essay entitled "Predictability: Does the Flap of a Butterfly's Wings in Brazil Set Off a Tornado in Texas?" he wrote, "The question which really interests us is whether. . . for example, two particular weather situations differing by as little as the immediate influence of a single butterfly will generally after sufficient time evolve into two situations differing by as much as the presence of a tornado. In more technical language, is the behavior of the atmosphere unstable with respect to perturbations of small amplitude?"

Lorenz questioned the possibility of finding suitable linear prediction formulas for weather forecasting and proposed instead to develop models based on nonlinear equations. He argued that irregularity is a fundamental property of the atmosphere and that the rapid doubling of errors from the effects of physical features precludes great accuracy in real-world forecasting. Most environmental and biological systems, such as changing weather, population, noise, nonperiodic heart fibrillations, and ecological patterns, may in fact be governed by nonlinear chaotic relationships.[8]

What does chaos theory mean for the Recovery Narrative? It offers the possibility of new actors within nonlinear plots. The appearance of chaos as an actor in science and history fundamentally destabilizes the very concept of nature as a standard or referent. It disrupts the idea of nature as resilient actor or mother who will repair the errors of human actors and continue as fecund garden (Eve as mother). It questions the possibility that humans as agents can control and master nature through science and technology, undermining the myth of nature as virgin female to be developed (Eve as virgin). Chaos is the reemergence of nature as power over humans, nature as active, dark, wild, turbulent, and uncontrollable (fallen Eve). Ecologists characterize Mother Nature as a "strange attractor," while turbulence is seen to be encoded with gendered images of masculine channels and feminine flows. In the chaotic narrative, humans lose the hubris of fallen Adam that the garden can be recreated on earth. The world is not created by a patriarchal God *ex nihilo*, but emerges out of chaos. Thus the very possibility of the recovery of a stable original garden—the plot of the Recovery metanarrative—is itself challenged.[9]

While a certain domain of nature can be represented by linear, deterministic equations, and is therefore predictable (or can be subjected to probabilities, stochastic approximations, and systems analysis), a very large domain can be represented only through nonlinear equations that do not admit of solutions. The closed systems and determinism of classical physics described by Isaac Newton and Pierre Simon Laplace give way to a postclassical physics of open complex systems and chaos theory. These theories suggest that there are limits to the knowable world. This is not the same as saying there is an unknowable noumenal world behind the phenomena. Rather, there is a real, material, physical world, but a world that can never be fully known by means of mathematics. It is a world that is chaotic and unpredictable and therefore cannot be totally controlled by science and technology. Science can no longer perform the "God trick"— imposing the view of everything from nowhere. It cannot offer the totalizing viewpoint associated with modernism, the Enlightenment, and mechanistic science. The real world is both orderly and disorderly, predictable and unpredictable, controllable and uncontrollable, depending on context and situation.[10]

COMPLEXITY THEORY

Complexity theory is a new science that deals with the realm between chaos and order. It not only reconstructs the relationship between humans and nature, but also suggests the possibility of a nonlinear narrative that is more complicated than that of the Enlightenment Recovery story. The emerging science of complex systems bridges the gap between order and chaos and suggests a narrative of lawlike regularities, branching histories, "frozen accidents," and adaptive reorganizations—or failures to adapt. A range of entities and possibilities exists that moves from simplicity, to complexity, to complex adaptive systems—from the quark to the ecosystem to the nation state.

The term quark was invented by Nobel Award–winning physicist Murray Gell-Mann, to signify a fundamental building block of matter. In *The Quark and the Jaguar* he argues that the quark exemplifies a simple entity, the jaguar a complex organism, while human societies are complex adaptive systems. "A complex adaptive system is a system that learns or evolves by utilizing acquired information. . . . It compresses regularities into concise packages that are often called schemata. . . . In biological evolution, the genome of an organism is a schema. In the scientific enterprise, a theory is a schema. In the evolution of a society, such things as laws, traditions, kinship rules, and myths constitute schemata." The environment, societies, and the economy are all complex adaptive systems. The emergence of life, biological and cultural evolution, and computers are examples of the ways in which one complex system gives rise to another.[11]

According to Gell-Mann, we live in a quasi-classical world governed by quantum mechanical laws that, because of the limitations of our senses and instruments, can only be experienced as coarse grained—like the graininess of a blown-up photograph. Deviations from classically determined events can nevertheless be described by probabilities. But just as Heisenberg's uncertainty principle injects indeterminacy at the micro (or atomic level), so chaotic processes, or sensitive dependence on initial conditions (as in weather phenomena—Lorenz's "butterfly effect") inject indeterminacy at the macro (or everyday world) level. Alternative, and often unpredictable, pathways of development result. These branching histories, or "gardens of forking paths" (a metaphor created by writer Jorge Luis Borges) are mutually exclusive pathways that result in the evolution of complex adaptive systems. From the beginning of the universe, through all of time, the initial expansion branches into alternatives for which there are well-defined probabilities. But these alternative branches are mutually exclusive. In one branch a planet may ultimately result from a quantum accident billions of years ago, but in another no planet can occur.[12]

Chance operates in the realm between order and chaos to create complexity. Fundamental laws combine with chance to generate "frozen accidents"—events that could have been different, but because of the way they turn out produce a multitude of specific results, as when a vice-president becomes president after an assassination. "Complex adaptive systems," says Gell-Mann, "function best in a regime intermediate between order and disorder. They exploit the regularities provided by the approximate determinism of the quasiclassical domain, and at the same time they profit from . . . indeterminacies (describable as noise, fluctuations, heat, uncertainty, and so on). . . ."[13]

Complex biological and social systems are not controlled by central mechanisms and do not change in a linear manner. Their internal dynamics, operating in response to external conditions, can result in rapid change from a small input (the introduction of a disease or a natural disaster, for example). In biology, a genome responding favorably to selection pressure will survive and reproduce. In science, a theory or schema that explains empirical data and predicts verifiable results will be selected over those that fail in some major respect. In cultural development, societies that respond creatively to changing environmental and social conditions by successfully applying existing rules (moving to a new location when drought occurs) or developing new schemata (religious rituals or new agricultural techniques) will survive; those that fail will die out.[14]

Throughout the history of the earth, complex adaptive biological and social systems have developed that exhibit regularities in efficient organization and distribution of resources that allow them to persist over time, accumulate and exchange information, and continue to evolve. They interact with each other and with other parts of nonhuman nature, persisting in transition zones between order and disorder. Today many of these diverse biological systems and human cultures are threatened with decline or extinction. We need to try to imagine what an ecologically sustainable planet, in which both biological and cultural diversity are preserved, would look like. Gell-Mann urges, "It is worthwhile to try to construct models of the future—not as blueprints but as aids to the imagination—and see if paths can be sketched out that may lead to such a sustainable and desirable world late in the next century, a world in which humanity as a whole and the rest of nature operate as a complex adaptive system to a much greater degree than they do now." Complexity theory, like chaos theory, therefore opens possibilities for new narratives with nonlinear plots.[15]

ECOLOGY

Unlike mechanistic science, ecology is based on open rather than closed systems and emphasizes nature as continuous change and process. But chaos and complexity theories challenge two basic assumptions of ecology as it developed in the 1950s and '60s that formed the basis of environmental management—the ideas of the balance of nature and the diversity-stability hypothesis. These theories question the idea of the constancy and stability of nature, the idea that every organism has a place in the harmonious workings of nature, and that nature itself is fixed in time and space—like the environment in a petri dish in a modern scientific laboratory. Many ecologists also argue that diversity does not necessarily lead to stability, as in tropical rainforests that, while extremely diverse, can easily be destroyed by natural and human intervention.

The idea of a balance of nature that humans could disrupt implied that people could repair damaged ecosystems with better practices. The idea that biodiversity led to ecosystem stability meant that species conservation and ecological restoration could improve ecosystem health. But chaos theory suggests that natural disturbances and mosaic patches that do not exhibit regular or predictable patterns are the norm rather than the aberration. Moreover, the seemingly stable world that is the object of socially constructed representations can be destabilized by human social practices (as when pesticides produce mutant insects or antibiotics produce resistant bacteria). Such theories undercut assumptions of a stable, harmonious nature and question holism as a foundation for ecology. They reinforce the idea that predictability, while still useful, is more limited than previously assumed and that nature, while in part a human construct and a representation, is also a real, material, autonomous agent. A postclassical, postmodern science is a science of limited knowledge, of the primacy of process over parts, and of imbedded contexts within complex, open, ecological systems.[16]

Ecologist Daniel Botkin proposes the idea of discordant harmonies as an alternative to the concept of the balance of nature. Botkin argues that we must move to a deeper level of thought and "confront the very assumptions that have dominated perceptions of nature for a very long time. This will allow us to find the true idea of a harmony of nature, which as Plotinus wrote so long ago, is by its very essence discordant, created from the simultaneous movements of many tones, the combination of many processes flowing at the same time along various scales, leading not to a simple melody, but to a symphony sometimes harsh and sometimes pleasing." Discordant harmonies are part of a set of new narratives with non-linear plots and a new human relationship to nature.[17]

The concept of discordant harmonies, theories of the chaotic and complex behavior of nature, and the idea that natural disturbances (fires, tornadoes, and hurricanes) can be more rapid and drastic than disturbances by human beings (forest harvesting, real estate development, and dam construction) raise questions about earlier ethical approaches to environmental management. Self-interested, or egocentric ethics (what is good for the individual is good for society); social-interest, or homocentric ethics (the greatest good for the greatest number); and even earth-centered or ecocentric ethics (all living and nonliving things are morally considerable and have rights) all have problematical implications for a sustainable world. The growth-oriented capitalistic economy from which the egocentric ethic arises and the anthropocentric focus of the utilitarian cost-benefit approach from which the homocentric ethic arises both have negative implications for the environment. On the other hand, the idea that all nonhuman organisms have moral consideration equal to human beings—the ecocentric approach—undercuts the real struggles of the poor and of disadvantaged minorities for a better life. What is called for is a new ethic that arises out of both the needs of nature and the needs of humanity. Both must be considered as active agents. A new ethic of human partnership with nature—is needed, one in which nature is an active subject, not a passive object.

GAIA

The Gaia hypothesis of atmospheric chemist James Lovelock views nature as an actor in history. Named after the Greek earth goddess, Gaia, the hypothesis states that "the physical and chemical condition of the surface of the earth, of the atmosphere, and of the oceans has been and is actively made fit and comfortable by the presence of life itself." The biosphere is a self-regulating (cybernetic) system. The hypothesis challenges mechanism, by offering the idea that Gaia as a living earth is more than the mere sum of its parts. Life itself plays an active role in maintaining the conditions necessary for its own continuation. The hypothesis was proposed by Lovelock in 1972 in "Gaia As Seen through the Atmosphere," and elaborated with Lynn Margulis in 1973 and 1974 in essays on the "Gaia

Hypothesis." Lovelock's 1979 book *Gaia: A New Look at Life on Earth* set out additional details of the theory and its implications for the human relationship to nature.[18] Here nature is an active subject.

Lovelock's central idea is that "the living matter, air, oceans, and land surface form a complex system which can be seen as a single organism and which has the capacity to keep our planet a fit place for life." The atmosphere is not merely a collection of gases in more or less definite proportions, but a biological construction that is an extension of a living system, much like the hair on the back of a cat or the shell of a snail. If even small deviations from the present proportions of gases occurred, it would be a disaster for life itself. Oxygen, for example, which is 21 percent of the atmosphere, is in the safe upper limit in which life can exist; even small increases would lead to an increase in terrestrial fires. At 25 percent the planet would be a raging conflagration extinguishing even the possibility of life.

Other atmospheric gases are maintained by life processes. Methane, produced in the muds of wetlands by anaerobic bacteria, bubbles to the surface where it combines with oxygen to produce water and carbon dioxide, thus preventing the slow build up of atmospheric oxygen concentrations. Nitrous oxide is produced by microorganisms in the soils and seas. It provides a counterbalance to methane and also regulates the amount of oxygen. Nitrogen, which is 79 percent of the atmosphere, is produced by denitrifying bacteria, which return it to the air. Without life, nitrogen and oxygen would both return to the sea. Nitrogen dilutes oxygen, regulates combustion, and stabilizes climate. Ammonia is also of biological origin, producing rain with a pH of 8. Water, an essential, chemically neutral substance, returns oxygen to the atmosphere and hydrogen to outer space. The entire interconnected global system of living and nonliving things contains internal feedbacks that keep the chemical percentages within the ranges suitable for life's continuance. Later Lovelock, working with Margulis, extended his hypothesis to include oceans and soil.[19]

The Gaia hypothesis, however, has been criticized as being both teleological and tautological. In 1988, the American Geophysical Union held a conference in San Diego on the Gaia hypothesis that included well-known scientists (skeptics who questioned the extreme purposefulness built into the hypothesis), and supporters (who explored possible connections with hot springs, the human brain, and the extinction of dinosaurs).

James Kirchner of the University of California sees it as a nest of hypotheses ranging from the self-evident to the highly speculative. At the straightforward end of the scale, it simply reiterates the well-documented linkages between biogeochemical and biological processes, while emphasizing the importance of feedback loops between them. At the speculative end is the more questionable concept that biological processes regulate the physical environment maintaining favorable conditions for life. The latter, Kirchner asserts, is untestable, unprovable, and unfalsifiable. Gaia is perhaps nothing but a tautology.[20]

Gaia as a metaphor caught on rapidly as a powerful image for uniting the combined destinies of people, other organisms, and inorganic substances. In *Lost Goddesses of Early Greece* (1978), ecofeminist writer Charlene Spretnak wrote about Gaia as the ancient mother who gave birth to the world and the human race out of the gaping void. Environmental historian J. Donald Hughes looked at Greek ideas of the earth as a goddess and the cosmos as an organism in his 1982 article, "Gaia: An Ancient View of Our Planet." The National Audubon Society Expedition Institute sponsored a 1985 public symposium—"Is the Earth a Living Organism?"—that featured papers by scientists, anthropologists, historians, poets, Native Americans, and spiritualists. Feminists took up the theory as support for the ancient goddess Gaia and opened Gaia bookstores to market goddess statues, books, and records. Musician Paul Winter composed *Missa Gaia, A Mass in Celebration of Mother Earth*, which has been recorded live at the Cathedral of St. John the Divine in New York and in the Grand Canyon.[21]

The Gaia hypothesis also sparked an array of books that pictured threats to the global Gaian ecosystem, explored scientists' and economists' thoughts on its political implications, and extended the idea to the field of environmental ethics. Despite its potential to be a forceful image of nature as a person writ large, the hypothesis raised concerns that if Gaia is a self-regulating homeostatic system, then Gaia "herself" can correct problems caused by humans or perhaps even find humanity expendable. Feminists also raised doubts as to whether the notion of Gaia as a mother who cleans up after her messy children is an appropriate image for humanity to embrace. Despite these criticisms, however, the idea of the Earth as a subject and partner (as opposed to a mother or a goddess) has potential for a new story and a new environmental ethic (see chapter 11).[22]

CONCLUSION

The disorderly, ordered world of nonhuman nature must be acknowledged as a free autonomous actor, just as humans are free autonomous agents. Nature limits human freedom to totally dominate and control it, just as human power limits nature's and other humans' freedom. Science and technology can tell us that an event such as a hurricane, earthquake, flood, or fire is likely to happen in a certain locale, but not when it will happen. Because nature is fundamentally chaotic, it must be respected and related to as an active partner.

These new approaches to science are consistent with new narratives about the natural world and humanity's place within it. The new sciences are based on a different set of assumptions about the nature of reality than mechanism: wholeness rather than atomistic units, process rather than the rearrangement of parts, internal rather than external relations, the nonlinearity and unpredictability of fundamental change, and pluralism rather than reductionism. But could a postclassical science embodying such a vision be accepted by mainstream society? If so, it might be consistent with new ethical guidelines for humanity's relationship with the environment—an ethic of partnership among humans and between humanity and nature.

The Lesson

By David Iltis

Saturday Afternoon
and I have driven out to Farmington Bay
to watch the birds
hoping they will teach me
what they know about life.
So much more than I know
or less
For two hours I have been
here
Five People have come and gone
while the birds stay
patient teachers
Only five people and me
so close to the city
and the quiet solitude
is only broken by a howling
in the distance of tires on
concrete.

So close to the city
where is everyone?
stuck in ignorance?
asleep at the wheel?
There are patient teachers
here
but no patient students
save one
but I am in a hurry
so little time to learn
Am I missing the lesson completely?
or has school just begun?

Earlier, a snowy egret
appeared to me from afar
rippled by heatwaves

he stood there wisely waiting
perhaps talking
but too quietly for me to hear.

To move slowly at the edge of
the Great Salt Lake
is to move, hear
at the speed of life
to drink in the heat and the sun
to watch time unfold
and hear the song of the red winged blackbird
and see the ripples on the quiet water
from the grebe
to sit and see the butterflies
the city has no room for
to watch the work of the bees
in service of their queen
to ponder the weeds and the
native flora
to share this moment with a
damsel fly
to see in the distance the Wasatch
and the remnants of winter, fading
carpet of snow
to revel in the fruits of evolution
and get laughed at by the California
gulls
to stare uncomprehendingly at the
skeletons of trees, roosts for the
bald eagle and the great blue heron
to glimpse a spider's thread
sewing together two plants an eternity apart
to dream with eyes open
to awake from my lesson
sobbing at the beauty of it all
and my teachers sing back
"You are learning."

ELEVEN

Partnership

For the twenty-first century, I propose a new environmental ethic—a partnership ethic. It is an ethic based on the idea that people are helpers, partners, and colleagues and that people and nature are equally important to each other. If both people and nature are acknowledged as actors, we have the possibility of a mutually beneficial situation.

A partnership ethic holds that the greatest good for the human and nonhuman communities is in their mutual living interdependence.[1]

Like the Native-American idea of a sacred bundle of relationships and obligations, a partnership ethic is grounded in the ideas of relation and of mutual obligation.[2] Like the lessons to be learned from birds, a partnership ethic is drawn from the voice of nature. Like human partners, the earth and humanity communicate with each other.

ENVIRONMENTAL PARTNERSHIPS

Partnership is a word that is experiencing a renaissance in the discourse of environmental communities. Successful environmental partnerships, focused on resolving policy conflicts surrounding local issues, are forming among local communities, government agencies, corporations, and environmental organizations. Trees, rivers, endangered species, tribal groups, minority coalitions, and citizen activists all find representation along with business at the negotiating table. The partnership process offers a new approach to collaboration.[3]

Equally innovative is the idea that the term *partners* refers not only to societal entities and institutions, but to individuals and even natural entities. Domestic partners with legal status may include not only married couples but stable relationships between men and women, women and women, or men and men. A partnership ethic may offer guidelines for moving beyond the rhetoric of environmental conflict and toward a discourse of cooperation. But the term *partner* can also be used to represent gnatcatchers, coho salmon, grizzly bears, and checkerspot butterflies. Indeed, nonhuman nature itself can be our partner.

I propose five precepts for a human community in a sustainable partnership with a nonhuman community:

1. Equity between the human and nonhuman communities.
2. Moral consideration for both humans and other species.
3. Respect for both cultural diversity and biodiversity.
4. Inclusion of women, minorities, and nonhuman nature in the code of ethical accountability.
5. An ecologically sound management that is consistent with the continued health of both the human and the nonhuman communities.

A partnership ethic entails a viable relationship between a human community and a nonhuman community in a particular place, a place in which connections to the larger world are recognized through economic and ecological exchanges. It is an ethic in which humans act to fulfill both humanity's vital needs and nature's needs by restraining human hubris. It draws on the Earth Summit's 1992 "Rio Declaration on Environment and Development" and its call for a "global partnership to conserve, protect, and restore the health of the earth's ecosystems." It incorporates the 1991 Global Assembly of Women and the Environment's concept of "partners in life" and it reinforces the principle of the 1991 National People of Color Environmental Leadership Summit that "environmental justice demands the right to participate as equal partners at every level of decision-making." The concept of "ranges of new partnership activities" was reinforced by the World Summit on Sustainable Development head in Johannesburg, South Africa in 2002. Guided by a partnership ethic, people will select technologies that sustain the natural environment by becoming co-workers and partners with nonhuman nature, not dominators over it.[4]

For most of human history, nature had the upper hand over human beings, and humans fatalistically accepted the hand that nature dealt. People lived at the mercy of Nature's storms, droughts, frosts, and famines. They accepted fate while propitiating nature with gifts, sacrifices, and prayer (often within hierarchical human relationships). Harvests, famines, and droughts were considered God's, or the Great Spirit's, way of blaming human beings for acting in an unethical way. Only in the last few centuries have technologies and attitudes of domination stemming from the Scientific Revolution turned the tables, enabling humans to threaten nature with deforestation and desertification, chemical pollution, destruction of habitats and species, nuclear fallout, and ozone depletion. Since the seventeenth century, Western culture has developed the idea that humans are more powerful than nature and that Euroamericans have the tools to dominate, control, and manage it. Some groups of people have gained great power over nature and other human groups using the interlinked forces of science, politics, and religion.

Through mechanistic science, technology, capitalism, and the Baconian hubris that the human race should have dominion over the entire universe, humanity has gained an increasing ability to destroy nature *as we know it*. In the mechanistic framework of classical physics, nature was rendered passive and inert, subject to prediction and control through linear differential equations. Within that framework, suspension bridges, tunnels, and skyscrapers became engineering triumphs because mechanical systems were considered to be closed, spatially defined, and subject to the classical laws of statics and equilibrium dynamics.

In the late twentieth century, the environmental crisis and developments in postmodern science and philosophy have called into question the efficacy of the mechanistic worldview, the idea of Enlightenment progress, and the ethics of unrestrained development as a means of dominating nature. Both ecological and mechanical systems are vulnerable to chaotic forces created by unusual weather patterns or geological events generated from outside the system.

If we, as humans, place ourselves above nature, we convince ourselves that we can control farm, forest, and fishery harvests through such ideas as logistic curves and maximum or optimum sustained yields. We need to bring the pendulum back into balance so that there is greater equality between the human and nonhuman communities.[5]

PARTNERSHIP ETHICS

A partnership ethic is a synthesis between an ecological approach based on moral consideration for all living and nonliving things and a human-centered (or homocentric) approach based on the social good and the fulfillment of basic human needs. All humans have needs for food, clothing, shelter, and energy, but nature also has an equal need to survive. The new ethic questions the notion of the unregulated market, sharply criticizing egocentric ethics—what is good for the individual is good for society—and instead proposes a partnership between nonhuman nature and the human community.

A partnership ethic would bring humans and nonhuman nature into a dynamically balanced, more nearly equal relationship with each other. Humans, as the bearers of ethics, would acknowledge nonhuman nature as an autonomous actor which cannot be predicted or controlled except in very limited domains. We would also acknowledge that we have the potential to destroy life as we currently know it through nuclear power, pesticides, toxic chemicals, and unrestrained economic development and act to exercise specific restraints on that ability. We would cease to create profit for the few at the expense of the many. We would instead organize our economic and political forces to fulfill people's vital needs for food, clothing, shelter, and energy, and to provide security for health, jobs, education, children, and old age. Such forms of security would rapidly reduce population growth rates since a major means of providing security would not depend on having large numbers of children or on economies in which boys are favored over girls as is the case in many countries today.

If we know that a major earthquake in Los Angeles is likely in the next seventy-five years, a utilitarian, homocentric ethic would state that the government ought not to license the construction of a nuclear reactor on the faultline. But a partnership ethic would say that, we, the human community, ought to respect nature's autonomy as an actor by limiting building and leaving open space. If we know there is a possibility of a one-hundred-year flood on the Mississippi River, we respect human needs for navigation and power, but we also respect nature's autonomy by limiting our capacity to dam every tributary that feeds the river and build homes on every flood plain. We leave some rivers wild and free and leave some flood plains as wetlands, while using others to fulfill human needs. If we know that forest fires are likely in the Rockies, we do not build cities along forest edges. We limit the extent of development, leave open spaces, plant fire resistant vegetation, and use tile rather than shake roofs. If cutting tropical and temperate old-growth forests creates problems for both the global environment and local communities, but we cannot adequately predict the outcome or effects of those changes, we need to conduct partnership negotiations in which nonhuman nature and the people involved are equally represented.

HEARING NATURE'S VOICE

As humans, we need to cultivate a new ability to hear nature's voice. As philosopher Max Horkheimer put it in 1947, when he called for the revolt of nature, "Once it was the endeavor of art, literature, and philosophy to express the meaning of things and of life, to be the voice of all that is dumb, to endow nature with an organ for making known her sufferings. . . . Today nature's tongue is taken away." The voice with which nature speaks is tactile, sensual, auditory, odoriferous, and visual—a visceral understanding communicated through our hearts into our minds.[6]

Philosopher David Abram invites us into a more-than-human world through the semipermeable membranes of our bodies that allow us to communicate with nature through sensuous experience. Oral cultures maintain that contact better than those influenced by the written word, but such consciousness can be reclaimed by listening to the voice of nature: "The rustling of leaves in an oak tree or an aspen grove is itself a kind of voice." With the use of the alphabet, a barrier develops between the human as self and nature as other. Nevertheless, the writer's task is to release "the budded, earthly intelligence of our words, freeing them to respond to the speech of the things themselves—to the green uttering-forth of leaves from the spring branches." As we use narrative to re-create the human place in the more-than-human world, we can learn to reconnect with nature as an equal partner. For Abram that reconnection occurs through "the practice of spinning stories that have the rhythm and lilt of the local soundscape, tales for the tongue, tales that want to be told, again and again." The nature writer, philosopher, and poet can help us hear nature's voice by "finding phrases that place us in contact with the trembling neck-muscles of a deer holding its antlers high as it swims toward the mainland, or with the ant dragging a scavenged rice-grain through the grasses. . . letting language take root, once again, in the earthen silence of shadow and bone and leaf."[7]

Partnership ethics makes visible the connections between people and the environment in an effort to find new cultural and economic forms that fulfill vital needs, provide security, and enhance the quality of life without degrading the local or global environment. It creates both a structure and a set of goals that can enable decision making, consensus, and mediation to be achieved without contentious litigation. It relates work in the sciences of ecology, chaos, and complexity theory to new possibilities for nondominating relationships between humans and nonhuman nature.

Unlike the closed systems of classical mechanics, ecology deals with open systems that incorporate the flow of matter, energy, and information across boundaries. In ecological systems, nature's movements are not as readily controllable as classical mechanics assumes. While some phenomena can be predicted and managed, many occurrences are chaotic and can be represented only through nonlinear equations to which solutions are impossible or at best approximate. In such situations, nature is a dynamic actor, a force encountered on terms not as comfortable to the Enlightenment ideal of the control of nature. Nevertheless, nonhuman nature can become a partner with humanity by listening to the voice of nature and interacting with it through new forms of design and planning.

A new relationship with nature is necessary for the future welfare of both people and the earth on which we live. Environmental history reveals periods throughout time that are fraught with the exploitation of natural resources with little regard to long-term consequences. History teaches that many past interventions have been ecologically shortsighted. Today, we are beginning to consider nature as our partner in bringing the pendulum back into balance. To achieve a new relationship with nature, the past must be understood in terms of its ecological and human histories, as negative outcomes are reassessed.

NATURE AS A PARTNER AT THE TABLE

In a partnership ethic, both humans and nature are active agents. Both the needs of nature to continue to exist and the basic needs of human beings must be considered. How can a partnership ethic be enacted? In each linked human and nonhuman biotic community, all the parties and their representatives must sit as partners at the same table. This includes individuals, corporate and tribal representatives, foresters, dam builders, conservation trusts, scientists, community representatives, and spokespersons for wetlands, mountain lions, and gnatcatchers. The needs of other species and the needs of humans should both be discussed. Full recognition of both the environment and the particular human community as complex systems that can and need to adapt by devising new rules and schema will be acknowledged. Examples of efforts at such partnerships include resource advisory committees, watershed councils, self-governing democratic councils, collaborative processes, and cooperative management plans.

Consensus and negotiation should be attempted as partners speak together about the short and long-term interests of the interrelated human and nonhuman communities. The meetings will be lengthy and may continue over many weeks or months. As in any partnership relationship, there will be give and take as the needs of each party are expressed, heard, and acknowledged. If the partners identify their own ethical assumptions and agree to start anew from a partnership ethic of mutual obligation and respect, there is hope for consensus. Indeed, there is no other choice, for failure means a regression from consensus, into contention, and thence into litigation. A partnership ethic will not always work, but it is a beginning, and with it there is hope.

A partnership ethic recognizes both continuities and differences between humans and nonhuman nature. It admits that humans are part of and dependent on nature and that nonhuman nature has preceded and will postdate human nature. But also it recognizes that humans now have the power, knowledge, and technology to destroy life as we know it today. A partnership ethic therefore goes beyond egocentric and homocentric ethics in which the good of the human community wins out over the good of the biotic community to a new ethic which entails the good of both the human and the more-than-human communities. In some cases the needs of the more-than-human community will take precedence, as in preservation of wild areas, while in others, the needs of the human community will be paramount, as in sustainable agriculture and sustainable cities.

A new ethic entails a new consciousness and a new discourse about nature. Living with and communicating with nature opens the possibility of nondominating, nonhierarchical modes of interaction between humanity and nature. Rather than speaking about nature as a machine to be manipulated, a resource to be exploited, or an object to be studied and transformed, nature becomes a subject. Both nature and humans will have voices, and both voices will be heard.

Nature as actor appears everywhere on earth from "pristine" wilderness to parks, wetlands, farmlands, and city landscapes. Environmental philosopher Val Plumwood argues that the wild is present everywhere not just in wilderness areas. We must recognize the presence of the wild in places close to home as well as in wilderness areas. Preserving wild places in which nature is left free and unmanaged is also a vital part of partnership. We can choose to develop wild nature, to enclose it within parks, or to simply let it be. As conservationist Roger L. DiSilvestro puts it, "We are the first living things, as far as we know, to make a choice about the extent to which we will apply our abilities to influence the environment. We not only *can* do, but we can choose *not to do*. Thus, what is unique about the boundaries we place around parks and other sanctuaries is that these boundaries are created to protect a region from our own actions. . . . No longer can we think of ourselves as masters of the natural world. Rather, we are partners with it."[8]

Beyond the idea of the park as a sanctuary is unmanaged wilderness. Setting aside areas in which nature is off limits to humans is part of a partnership with the natural world. As wilderness, nature is active, alive, and often unpredictable. Environmentalist Dave Foreman writes, "The root for "wilderness" in Old English is wil-deor-ness: self-willed land. Self-willed land has fires, storms, and ecosystem changes. It has wild beasts who don't cotton to being pushed around by puny hominids."[9] Acceptance of unpredictability means acceptance of the idea of nature as subject in and for itself.

The new postmodern sciences of ecology, chaos, and complexity theory are consistent with the idea of nature as actor. Postmodern science reconstructs the relationship between humans and nature. While mechanistic science assumes that nature is divided into parts and that change comes from external forces (a billiard-ball model), ecology emphasizes nature as continuous change and process. Chaos theory goes a step further, suggesting that the human ability to predict the outcome of those processes is limited. Disorderly order, the world represented by chaos theory, becomes a component of the partnership ethic.[10]

Each of the time-consuming ethical and policy decisions involved in planning will be negotiated by a human community in a particular place, but the outcome will depend on the history of people and nature in the area, the narratives they tell themselves about the land, vital human needs, past and present land-use patterns, the larger global context, and the ability or lack of it to predict nature's events. Each human community is in a changing, evolving relationship with a nonhuman community that is local, but also connected to global environmental and human patterns. Each ethical instance is historical, contextual, and situational, but located within a larger environmental and economic system.

HISTORICAL ROOTS OF A PARTNERSHIP ETHIC

The antecedents of a partnership ethic come from environmentalists, philosophers, and feminists. One component is that of human cooperation with nature. As environmental writer George Perkins Marsh put it in 1864, humanity should "become a co-worker with nature in the reconstruction of the damaged fabric," by restoring the waters, forests, and bogs "laid waste by human improvidence or malice." While thunderstorms, tornadoes, volcanoes, and earthquakes represented nature's power over humanity to rearrange elementary matter, humans had the power "irreparably to derange the combinations of inorganic matter and of organic life, which through the night of aeons she had been proportioning and balancing. . . ."[11]

In the 1970s, philosopher Herbert Marcuse conceptualized nature as an opposing partner, emphasizing the differences as well as the continuities that people share with nature. Nature is an "ally," he held, not "mere organic and inorganic matter." It is a "life force in its own right," appearing as "subject-object." But Nature as subject "may well be hostile to man, in which case the relation would be one of struggle; but the struggle may also subside and make room for peace, tranquility, fulfillment." A nonexploitative relation would therefore be a "surrender, 'letting-be,' acceptance."[12]

One of the oldest ways in which humanity has interacted in partnership with nature is through agriculture. Farmers wooed the land and cajoled the earth with rituals and offerings to the earth mother. In the 1930s, ecologist Aldo Leopold formulated a conservation ethic in which farmland could be thought of in terms of partnership. "When land does well for its owner, and the owner does well by his land; when both end up better by reason of their partnership, we have conservation." Leopold advocated a range of human partnerships with the land that could result in protection of wild areas, farmland restoration, and sustainable agricultural practices.[13]

Feminists have also contributed to the concept of a partnership ethic, not only in the use of the word *partner* to embrace female/male and same-sex relationships, but also in formulating new ways to engage in politics and discourse. In *The Chalice and the Blade* (1988) Riane Eisler argues that an original partnership society in prehistory took a five-thousand-year detour into a dominator society. In the dominator model, symbolized by the blade, one sex is ranked higher than the other. The partnership model, symbolized by the chalice, is based on male-female linking, rather than ranking, and its recovery offers hope for an egalitarian political and economic society in the future. In *Sacred Pleasure* (1996) Eisler proposes a new "politics of partnership" based on nurturing and caring forms of socialization for both sexes and a grassroots politics of social equity. "Much in Western prehistory seems to prefigure the more partnership-oriented world view [that is] today struggling to emerge. . . . New beliefs, images, and stories more congruent with a partnership than dominator social organization [are] beginning to enter our consciousness. . . ." The future would thus be the product of new Eves and new Adams who would work together, making the "realities and myths of our future . . . very different from what they are now."[14]

A partnership ethic is grounded in the concept of relation rather than in the ego, society, or the cosmos. The idea of relation also offers possibilities for a new narrative about the human place in nature. In *Feminism and the Mastery of Nature* (1993) philosopher Val Plumwood argues that relation must be the basis for a new story, one that is rooted in continuity and difference, rather than mastery and colonization. "The relational self delineates the general structure of a relationship of respect, friendship, or care for the other." Plumwood draws on feminist ideals for nondominating interactions among persons and the natural world, such as care, benevolence, and solidarity, that would allow the earth community to flourish. Such qualities avoid the intense separation of self from world characteristic of the mechanistic, instrumental approach that masters nature as a slave. She argues: "The reason/nature story has been the master story of western culture. It is a story which has spoken mainly of conquest and control, of capture and use, of destruction and incorporation. . . . Much inspiration for new, less destructive stories can be drawn from sources other than the master, from subordinated and ignored parts of western culture, such as women's stories of care."[15]

Feminist philosopher Alison Jaggar has examined new forms of discourse that draw on both feminist ethics and multicultural democracies. These approaches have applicability to a partnership ethic among humans and between humanity and nature that recognize both inclusiveness and difference. She notes that "a feminist conception of discourse, with its emphasis on listening, personal friendship, and responsiveness to emotion, and its concern to address power inequalities is especially well suited to facilitate such an immersed evaluation." We should not idealize dialogue within small communities, however, as the best way to achieve democratic consensus as such groups may have histories that preclude productive discourse. Nevertheless, we need to examine commitments and perspectives heretofore excluded. "We should pursue critical engagement with those members of Nonwestern communities who share some of our own commitments but who may have disagreements or different perspectives on particular issues." Such approaches and caveats may be extended to include discourse with those who may speak for and ask us to listen to the voice of nature as a partner at the table.[16]

IMPLEMENTING PARTNERSHIPS

A partnership ethic offers a new approach to relationships between communities and the environment that can transcend the egocentric ethic's emphasis on the domination of nature and the get-ahead, individualistic mentality. Environmental partnerships are "voluntary collaborations among organizations working toward a common objective." They are formed, often among formerly contesting parties, to solve a specific problem and to avoid the acrimony and costs of litigation. Furthermore, the cooperative agreement that emerges from the process is one to which all parties have agreed and in which all have a stake. Hence the outcome may have the prospect of lasting longer than one settled through a series of courtroom battles.[17]

The potential for consensus building can be illustrated through a fictitious example. A manufacturing company in the Midwest is approached by a wildlife conservation organization about creating a wildlife reserve on 3,200 acres of company-owned grounds. The company has decided not to use the area for a formerly planned expansion. Employees are enthusiastic about developing the land for jogging, wildlife viewing, photography, and perhaps limited seasonal fishing and hunting. Schools and local Audubon Society chapters are eager to have an educational wildlife area. The com-

pany and the conservation organization agree to form a voluntary partnership and begin to hold regular meetings with the specific goal of "protecting, restoring, and enhancing the 3,200 acres as a wildlife conservation
area with recreational facilities."[18]

Seated at the table (situated off of each of the partners' home grounds)
are not only company representatives, wildlife biologists, planners, and
employees who wish to hunt and fish, but also people who speak on behalf
of deer and trout. The discourse begins by asking questions:

1. Will the partnership project solve or significantly impact a
   problem?
2. Are the goals consistent with the company's mission and objectives?
3. Are cooperation and collaboration needed to do the project?
4. Do the partners all have a reason to participate in the partnership?
5. Has the partnership identified all groups needed for the project
   to succeed?
6. Will the partnership be voluntary and equitable?[19]

After much discussion, the parties decide that a wildlife area will be
established on the 3,200-acre plot for a minimum of twenty years. The
company's image will be enhanced within the community; employees will
have an area for jogging and hiking; wildlife viewing areas will be set aside.
The interests of deer and fish have been heard and, after an intensely passionate discussion, their needs for survival are made compatible with limited hunting and fishing through a well-defined management plan. The
conservation group has acquired an addition to a migratory bird flyway, an
educational site for school children, a refuge for birdwatchers, and a recreational area for the surrounding community. While it has not set aside the
area in perpetuity, it has achieved a green zone in place of potential concrete and pollution and time to become involved in and respond to a
longer-term company and community planning process.[20]

What are some examples of actual, successful environmental partnerships and how has business participated in them?

- On the Cooper River, near Charleston, South Carolina, the
  Wildlife Habitat Enhancement Council worked with the
  Amoco and DuPont chemical companies to develop wildlife

management programs on company lands. Landholders in the vicinity then developed a "wildlife corridor" running ten miles between the two companies.[21]

- In 1989, a group of leading corporations that use chlorofluoro-carbons (CFCs) as solvents collaborated with each other and the U.S. Environmental Protection Agency in order to become CFC-free in advance of the deadlines established by regulation. Several companies have used the new technologies to replace CFC use in plants in developing countries.[22]

- In the Columbia River Basin, where salmon runs have declined from sixteen million per year in the 1800s to less than two million in the early 1990s, the Northwest Power Planning Council initiated a partnership negotiating group comprising American Indian tribes, environmental groups, corporations, and agencies to plan and implement harvesting reductions, habitat restoration, hatchery projects, water flow changes, and other means of enhancing the salmon's survival.[23]

- The East Bay Conservation Corps of the San Francisco Bay Area formed a partnership with public agencies that resulted in funds for developing an environmental ethic in minority and lower income youth through a summer program employing young people to assist with public land maintenance work.[24]

In these examples, the partnership process focused mainly on human-human interactions, but it opened the way for the inclusion of persons representing nonhuman entities and the chaotic patterns of nature. Partnerships are a new form of cooperative discourse aimed at reaching consensus rather than creating winners and losers.

The negotiating process draws on many of the skills and goals long advocated and practiced by women's groups. While not essentialist—that is, the position that cooperation is an essential trait of being female—partnership discourse is nevertheless rooted in many women's social experiences and attitudes toward problem solving. But this cooperative discourse does not claim that women have a special knowledge of nature or a special ability to care for nature. Nor is it a case where "some" women are speaking for "all" women or for "other" women who are capable of speaking for themselves. Here women and minorities participate in the process. But nature, which often speaks in a different voice, is also heard at the table.

DESIGN WITH NATURE

Ian McHarg's *Design with Nature* (1969) created a new paradigm that explored the potential for an ecological partnership between humanity and nature. His book moves from tidal zones, sand dunes, and the hydrology of river systems through urban greenbelts and city parks to elegant architectural wonders. His landscape architectural projects, such as *The Woodlands* in Texas, and *Village Homes* in Davis, California, combined innovative designs with ecological principles and economic efficiency, while preserving surrounding forests, watersheds, and natural habitats.

McHarg writes, "This book is a personal testament to the power and importance of sun, moon, and stars . . . clouds, rain, and rivers, the oceans and the forests, the creatures and the herbs. They are with us now, co-tenants of the phenomenal universe . . . vivid expressions of time past, essential partners in survival. . . ." Lewis Mumford, in his introduction to *Design with Nature*, notes the importance of cooperation with the natural world: "McHarg's emphasis is not on either design or nature by itself, but upon the preposition with, which implies human cooperation and biological partnership." McHarg's work therefore is an auspicious herald for what I have termed partnership with nature.[25]

In working with nature, landscape planners work cooperatively, not only with nature and local communities, but also with each other to achieve their goals. Men and women are both well-represented. Behind the partnership ethic lies an implicit assumption. Teams of men and women, women and women, men and men are equals. Moreover, nature, traditionally represented as mother, virgin, or witch, is not gendered as female to be managed, controlled, or exploited, but instead is accepted as a partner with humanity. Such cooperation, revealed in the resultant landscape designs, presents exciting new opportunities for working with nature. How have the precepts of partnership ethics (see p. 224) helped to shape landscape design?[26]

A partnership ethic is based on equity between human and nonhuman nature. In a Maplewood, Minnesota neighborhood, past problems with storm-water runoff offered an opportunity to rethink human needs together with nature's needs. Landscape architect Joan Iverson Nassauer worked with residents and city engineers to redesign yards, vacant lots, and curbside strips with native wetland and prairie plants that would use water runoff and at the same time enhance traditional neighborhood tidiness by adding a touch of wildness. Although neighbors dreaded the disruption of torn-up streets, they also saw opportunity in the new ecology as a way to improve runoff and create aesthetically pleasing gardens on their own property. Here the partnership process involved people talking with each other in community meetings to reach mutually acceptable.solutions. They reintroduced native plant communities along with new drains to resolve water problems. Interlinked water and plant community processes were made visible; human needs and nature's needs were considered and resolved together.

In Bladensburg, Maryland, the Anacostia River had been confined to a concrete channel built many years ago by the U.S. Army Corps of Engineers, the flow managed by pumps and flood gates on the premise that nature was controllable through engineering. Joseph Kevin Eades redesigned the landscape, allowing nature's older meander to be revealed by allowing the river to assume its former course through the center of town. The new channels were lined with native riparian vegetation and wetlands were reestablished to aid in removing pollutants. Restoring the river's ecological integrity allowed nature to become a partner with the town residents. By permitting the river to act freely, it removed storm-water runoff, provided habitat for riparian bird and animal life, and offered possibilities for river walkways that linked people to nature.

Nature's chaotic unpredictability exemplifies ways in which nature as an actor offers possibilities for human partnership with the land. To landscape architect Edward Blake Jr., nature becomes conscious of itself through design. "Nature," he states, "is a highly organized and complex pattern of phenomena often viewed as chaotic." So conceptualized, its successional changes needed to be revealed and enhanced rather than controlled and channeled. Blake designed a convention center in Hattiesburg, Mississippi, that re-created the original floodplain woodland on which the city was built, but which had been obliterated by construction dumping and debris-filled storm drains. The new convention center overlooked a restored sedge meadow, cypress swamp, woodland, and lake. People's use of the land for entertainment and education was integrated with nature's hydrological processes in the newly revealed floodplain where vistas and walkways coexisted with ancient magnolias and beech, waterlilies and egrets, turtles and dragonflies. Here people and nature could thrive together as actors.

While hydrological forces and turbulent water flows exemplify one type of chaos, fire represents another. Fire can strike suddenly, roar into violent action, and in minutes completely envelop a natural area that has emerged slowly over time through ecological processes. How can humans be partners with a phenomenon so deadly and potentially destructive as wildfire? One way is to practice wise restraint by not building structures with fire-prone materials such as shake roofs or allowing dry vegetation to accumulate near residences. This is especially important in urban areas and in suburbs near arid grasslands and chaparral. Another way to work with fire is to learn from the history of past fire policies such as the hundred-year fire-suppression regime adhered to in Yellowstone National Park between its creation in 1872 and its reassessment in 1972. David Kovacic constructed animations of fires in Yellowstone. His simulation models were useful tools in understanding how local ecologies respond to fire. Frequent, cool, ground fires enhance ecological diversity by opening up understories to forage, increasing varieties of plants and wildlife, and reju-venating old growth. Wisely used, fire can become a tool in a new human partnership with nature.

A partnership ethic respects both cultural diversity and biodiversity. In the hills above Oakland, California, a culturally diverse middle-class neighborhood consisting of a majority of African Americans along with many European, Asian, and Latin Americans worked in partnership with each other and with landscape architect Louise Mozingo of the University of California, Berkeley. The goal was to restore biodiversity to the oak groves from which the city derived its name and ecological heritage. Together they devised a plan to develop the neighborhood's Glenn W. Daniel King Estate Park to benefit from the diversity of perennial grasses, oak savannahs, and brushy chaparral indigenous to the area. At the same time, they revamped hiking trails, added a recreation center, and increased security. The resulting master plan provided "a template for how commu-nities can become active partners in the fulfillment of their own environ-mental visions."

In a partnership ethic, ecologically sound management is consistent with the continued health of both the human and nonhuman communi-ties. In southwestern Pennsylvania, a century-old coal mining town had closed its doors and moved out of the region. A human environmental his-tory that exploited the labor of eastern European immigrants who mined underground veins and stoked coke ovens remained in the outlines of cab-ins, mine buildings, washeries, machine shops, and railroad tracks. A min-ing economy founded on the extraction of coal as a resource for steel pro-

duction left unhealthy, dangerous acids and slag that drained into the surrounding watershed. Bright-orange iron oxides blemished the land,
threatening human health and poisoning the surrounding watershed and
forest food chains.

Here Julie Bargmann and Stacy Levy showed how humans could
become partners with nature by restoring healthy water and wildlife to the
previously lethal area. An ecochemical process cleansed the acid runoff
through a series of settling ponds and limestone channels, that gradually
raised the pH, creating clean water. The surrounding landscape was
redesigned to include trees and vegetation whose colors echoed the orange
to green to bluegreen colors of the treatment ponds that restored health to
the mined landscape, while preserving its past environmental history.
Inorganic chemistry and ecology thereby worked in partnership with
human design to preserve both history and nature.

Ecological and human health can also be restored to abandoned urban
industrial sites through a "windows of opportunity" program such as that
devised by Achva Benzinberg Stein and Norman Millar in Los Angeles.
Here, former industrial areas, asphalt parking lots, freeway residual areas,
and vacant urban lots are turned into opportunities for growing nonfood
crops with treated gray water, recreation sites for underprivileged children,
community gardens, and solar farms atop parking structures. In this case,
ethnically and culturally diverse communities entered into partnerships with
each other and with sunshine, rainwater, fragile soils, and native plants to
reclaim green open spaces that benefit both human and nonhuman health.

These examples show that humanity can indeed learn to listen to
nature's voice as revealed through ecological principles, ethics, poetry, and a
reverence for our nonhuman partner. Although, as partner, nature's language
differs from our own, we still have the possibility of working cooperatively
with it. The result is a healthier, more aesthetically pleasing environment for
our own and future generations. As Ian McHarg put it in 1969, humanity's
most vital problem is "the necessity of sustaining nature as source of life,
milieu, teacher, sanctum, challenge, and most of all of rediscovering nature's
corollary of the unknown in the self, the source of meaning."[27]

PROBLEMS WITH PARTNERSHIP

Many difficulties exist in implementing a partnership ethic. The free-market
economy's growth-oriented ethic, which uses both natural and human

resources inequitably to create profits, presents the greatest challenge. The power of the global capitalist system to remove resources—especially those in third world countries—without regard to restoration, reuse, or recycling is a major roadblock to reorganizing relations between production and ecology. Even as capitalism continues to undercut the grounds of its own perpetuation by using renewable resources, such as redwoods and fish, faster than the species or stock's own recruitment, so green capitalism attempts to bandaid the decline by submitting to some types of regulation and recycling. Ultimately new economic forms will need to found that are compatible with sustainablilty, intergenerational equity, and a partnership ethic.

Another source of resistance to a partnership ethic is the property rights movement, which in many ways is a backlash against both environmentalism and ecology. The protection of private property is integral to the growth and profit-maximization approaches of capitalism and egocentrism and to their preservation by government institutions and laws. While individual, community, or common ownership of "appropriate" amounts of property is not inconsistent with a partnership ethic, determining what is sustainable and hence appropriate to the continuation of human and nonhuman nature is both challenging and important.

A third problem is deep, long-standing, cultural differences among environmental advocates, corporate interests, and community governments. Problems may be intractable because of historically bitter debates or the continuing presence of uncompromising personalities. As is often the case with deep-seated differences among proponents of scientific and cultural paradigms, resolution of local problems may sometimes hinge on the introduction of new generations, new personalities, and new belief systems into the consensus-building, mediation process. Willingness to rethink the meanings inherent in the collective memory is often critical to resolving problems.

PARTNERSHIP AND NARRATIVE

Enacting a partnership ethic entails creating a new narrative or set of narratives about the human place in history and nature. Rethinking mainstream history as a metanarrative for the recovery of the Garden of Eden raises the question of the relativity of the histories through which we are educated and of our own lives as participants in the stories they tell. Like our counterparts in previous centuries, we live our lives as characters in the grand narrative into which we were socialized as children and conform as adults. That narrative is often the story told to itself by the dominant society of which we are a part. We internalize narrative as ideology, a story told by people in power. Once we identify ideology as a story—powerful and compelling, but still only a story—we realize that by rewriting the story, we can begin to challenge the structures of power. We recognize that all stories can and should be challenged.

But can we actually step outside the story into which we have been cast as characters and enter into a story with a different plot? More important, can we change the plot of the grand master narrative of modernism? Where do I, as author of this text, stand in relationship to it? As a product of modernism, mechanism, and capitalism, I have internalized the values of the Recovery Narrative I have sought to identify. I participate in the progressive Recovery Narrative in my daily work, my wages for intellectual labor, my aspirations for a better material life, and my enjoyment of the profits my individual achievements have wrought. Yet I also believe, despite the relativism of environmental endism, that the environmental crisis is real—that the vanishing frogs, fish, and songbirds are telling us a truth. I am also a product of linear thinking and have set up this Recovery Narrative to reflect the very linearity of progressive history. This is history seen from a particular point of view, the view I have identified as the dominant ideology of modernism. Nevertheless, I believe that the idea of a Recovery Narrative reflects a fundamental insight into how nature has been historically constructed as a gendered object.

Both history and nature are extremely complex, complicated, and nonlinear. What would a complex, nonlinear, regendered history with a different plot look like? Would it be as compelling as the linear version, even if that linear version were extremely nuanced and complicated? Val Plumwood suggests that a new relationship with nature will affirm "continuity and kinship for earth others as well as their subjecthood . . . and agency. It will be . . . open to the play of more-than-human forces and attentive to the ancestral voices of place and of earth."[28]

A postmodern ethic and story would posit characteristics other than those identified with modernism, such as many, rather than one authorial voice; a multiplicity of real actors; acausal, nonsequential events; nonessentialized symbols and meanings; dialectical action and process rather than the imposed logos of form; situated and contextualized, rather than universal knowledge. It would be a story of partnership (or a multiplicity of stories and partnerships) that perhaps can only be acted and lived, not written at all.

A NEW STORY

Like others, I yearn for a Recovery from environmental decline—for my own vision of a postpatriarchal, socially just ecotopia for the third millennium. A partnership ethic implies a remything of the Edenic Recovery Narrative or the writing of a new narrative altogether. The new story would not accept the patriarchal sequence of creation, but might instead emphasize simultaneous creation, cooperative male/female evolution, or an emergence out of chaos or the earth. It would not accept the idea of subduing the earth, or even dressing and keeping the garden, since both entail total domestication and control by human beings. Instead each earthly place would be a home, a community, to be shared with other living and nonliving things. The needs of both humans and nonhumans would be dynamically balanced.

In 1990, artist Teresa Fasolino painted the Garden of Eden.[29] A tree bending with ripe apples stands at the center of the garden. Rabbits, peacocks, quail, and swans graze peacefully on a grassy lawn. Rhododendrons, grapes, palms, and ferns give way to oaks and pines as paths recede into distant hills. The human figures in the center are modeled on Albrecht Dürer's images of Adam and Eve—with an important exception. In the new story, both humans hold the apple; the snake is absent. Humans are partners with each other and with nature. Both bear responsibility for their own fate and the fate of nature. This is the story of one possible future for the earth. But if such a story can be written or experienced, it will be the product of many new voices and will have a complex plot and a different ending from that told in Genesis. Women, minorities, other cultures, and the earth, along with men, will be active partners. A new ending, however, will not come about if we simply read and reread the story into which we were born. A new story can be written only through human action.

Fig. 11.1. Teresa Fasolino's 1990 rendition of Albrecht Dürer's *Adam and Eve* shows both partners holding the apple. The snake is absent. Courtesy of Teresa Fasolino

EPILOGUE

I HAD A VERY GOOD NAME FOR THE ESTATE, AND IT WAS MUSICAL AND
PRETTY—GARDEN-OF-EDEN. PRIVATELY, I CONTINUE TO CALL IT THAT,
BUT NOT ANY LONGER PUBLICLY. THE NEW CREATURE SAYS IT IS ALL
WOODS AND ROCKS AND SCENERY, AND THEREFORE HAS NO RESEM-
BLANCE TO A GARDEN. SAYS IT *looks* LIKE A PARK, AND DOES NOT LOOK
LIKE ANYTHING *but* A PARK.
—*Mark Twain, "Extract from Adam's Diary"*

When Mark Twain wrote the *Diaries of Adam and Eve* in the 1890s, he
made no reference to God as creator. Adam and Eve simply find themselves in the garden and set about the business of living. Eve is the scientist who experiments and observes, Adam the more uncertain and obedi-
ent of the two. Eve sets out to name and understand the new world; Adam
escapes her and builds a solitary shelter. After the Fall into the real world,
it is Adam who takes charge and Eve who follows him around just because
he is masculine. In the end, however, Adam realizes that Eve means more
to him than the lost garden and that indeed wherever she is, there is Eden.
The *Diaries* are both a commentary on the realities of life in nineteenth-
century America and a bold vision of its reversal in an Edenic world.
Twain's insight remains refreshing although it is not one of partnership.
My own vision is one in which both women and men are equally intelli-

gent, equally skeptical, and equally accommodating of each other. A partnership relationship goes beyond equality for women and men in the marketplace, beyond equality in the home and school. It involves mutual respect, mutual give and take, and mutual understanding of needs, as well as equal opportunities for education and work.

For Twain's Adam, Eden is a garden to be accepted as a backdrop to life; for Eve, it is a park to be explored, studied, and loved. Adam samples the grapes and melons; Eve gazes at the stars, revels in the flowers, and makes friends with the animals. After the Fall, Adam takes up hunting and fishing, and Eve gives up her experiments with fire, her questions about shooting stars, and her puzzlement over falling water to focus on love and child rearing. Eve's experience of Eden before the Fall comes closest to a partnership between humanity and nature. She is interested in everything about her world, but not in destroying it. She interacts with animals and plants as equals, not as a superior scientist who studies them for their usefulness only. Twain's *Diaries*, however, present nineteenth-century stereotypes of female and male responses to nature. Eve is the one who appreciates the color and majesty of nature in Eden; Adam is interested primarily in its practical value. In a partnership world, both women and men would have equal capacities for understanding nature's use value and an appreciation of its aesthetic value. Both would have equal abilities to use nature's gifts to fulfill vital needs and to respond to nature's need to simply *be*. Both would have equal capacities for love and child rearing.

A partnership ethic is only one part of a new narrative or set of narratives about the human relationship with nature. And new narratives are only one part of what is needed for a sustainable world. The global ecological crisis and the decline of nature need to be reversed by new ways of producing, reproducing, and interpreting life on the planet. Poverty, hunger, and sickness need to be reversed by new forms of economics, politics, and science. Minorities and third world nations need to be full participants in global economics and ecology. Ecological economics, organic farms and gardens, sustainable livelihoods, green politics, wild places, ecological designs, human-scale cities, reverence for nature, chaos and complexity theories, and partnership ethics are among many new ways to achieve a sustainable relationship with nature. Nature's fate and humanity's fate are deeply intertwined. May both survive and fully live.

NOTES

Chapter 1

1. Issues concerning the corporatization of new American downtown strip malls appear in T. J. Sullivan, "Cookie Cutters Shaping U.S. Cities," *Ventura County Star,* Jan. 3, 1999, A1, A8.

2. Rachel Carson, *Silent Spring* (New York: Houghton Mifflin, 1962).

3. Lynn White Jr., "The Historical Roots of Our Ecologic Crisis," *Science* 55 (1967): 1203–7, reprinted in Ian G. Barbour, ed., *Western Man and Environmental Ethics: Attitudes Toward Nature and Technology* (Reading, Mass.: Addison-Wesley, 1973), 18–30; quotations on 25, 29. Lewis Moncrief, "The Cultural Basis of Our Environmental Crisis," in Barbour, ed., *Western Man and Environmental Ethics,* 31–42. See also Carolyn Merchant, The *Death of Nature: Women, Ecology, and the Scientific Revolution* (San Francisco: Harper Collins, 1980).

4. William Cronon, "A Place for Stories: Nature, History, and Narrative," *Journal of American History,* 4, no. 4 (1992): 1347–76, quotation on 1348. Cronon compared the plots of Paul Bonnifeld, *The Dust Bowl: Men, Dirt, and Depression* (Albuquerque: University of New Mexico Press, 1979) and Donald Worster, *Dust Bowl: The Southern Plains in the 1930s* (New York: Oxford University Press, 1979).

5. Donald Worster, "Ecology of Order and Chaos," *Environmental History Review* 14, nos. 1–2 (1990): 14–16; James Gleick, *Chaos: The Making of a New Science* (New York: Viking, 1987); M. Mitchell Waldrop, *Complexity: The Emerging Science at the Edge of Order and Chaos* (New York: Simon and Schuster, 1992).

6. Theodore Steinberg, *Down to Earth: Nature's Role in American History* (New York: Oxford University Press, 2002), 284.

7. On ideas of Eden and the golden age in cultures throughout the world, see Richard Heinberg, *Memories and Visions of Paradise: Exploring the Universal Myth of a Lost Golden Age,* rev. ed. (Wheaton, Ill.: Quest Books, 1995). Heinberg states, "Our search has taken us from Mesopotamia to Iran, Egypt, India, China, Australia, North America, and Africa. Everywhere, we have encountered essentially the same myth—the story of a primordial era when humanity and Nature enjoyed a condition of peace, happiness, and abundance. . . . If a single source did exist, the diffusion from that source must have occurred so long ago that the process of borrowing is now impossible to trace. The myth can just as easily be interpreted as having originated

independently in many locations" (54); and further, "Two of these traditions the Hebraic and the Greek continue to shape Western values and ideals" (49). On tropical Edens, see Richard Grove, *Green Imperialism: Colonial Expansion, Tropical Island Edens, and the Origins of Environmentalism, 1600–1860* (New York: Cambridge University Press, 1995).

8. See Norman Cohn, *Noah's Flood: The Genesis Story in Western Thought* (New Haven, Conn.: Yale University Press, 1996); William B. B. Ryan, *Noah's Flood: The New Scientific Discoveries About the Event that Changed History* (New York: Simon and Schuster, 1998); and T. D. Kendrick, *The Lisbon Earthquake* (London: Methuen, 1956).

CHAPTER 2

1. Roy B. Chamberlain and Herman Feldman, *The Dartmouth Bible: An Abridgment of the King James Version, with Aids to its Understanding As History and Literature, and As a Source of Religious Experience* (Boston, Mass.: Houghton Mifflin,1961); Genesis 1:26–28; introduction, 9–10.

2. Chamberlin and Feldman, *Dartmouth Bible,* introduction, 8–9; Harold Bloom, ed., and David Rosenberg, trans., *The Book of J,* (New York: Vintage, 1990).

3. Chamberlin and Feldman, *Dartmouth Bible,* Genesis 2:7–22; introduction, 8–9. Everett Fox, ed., *The Five Books of Moses* (New York: Schocken, 1995), Genesis 2:23: "She shall be called Woman/Isha, for from Man/Ish she was taken." Adam is named in Genesis 2:19: "God formed every beast of the field, and every fowl of the air; and brought them unto Adam to see what he would call them." "Woman" is created in Genesis 2:21–22, but is not named Eve until after the couple's disobedience and punishment in Genesis 3:20: "And Adam called his wife's name Eve; because she was the mother of all living." The name Eve may have come from the Sumerian name Nin-ti, meaning "lady of the rib" or "lady of Life." See W. Gunther Plaut, ed., *The Torah, A Modern Commentary* (New York: Union of Hebrew Congregations, 1981), 30, n. 21. On the literature pertaining to the Adam and Eve story, see Michael E. Stone, *A History of the Literature of Adam and Eve* (Atlanta: Scholars Press, 1992); Gary A. Anderson and Michael E. Stone, ed., *A Synopsis of the Books of Adam and Eve,* 2d ed., revised (Atlanta: Scholars Press, 1998); Kristen E. Kvam, Linda S. Schearing, and Valarie H. Ziegler, ed., *Eve and Adam: Jewish, Christian, and Muslin Readings on Genesis and Gender* (Bloomington: Indiana University Press, 1999); Gary Anderson, Michael Stone, and Johannes Tromp, ed., *Literature on Adam and Eve: Collected Essays* (Leiden: Brill, 2000); Paul Morris and Deborah Sawyer, ed., *A Walk in the Garden: Biblical, Iconographical, and Literary Images of Eden* (Sheffield, Eng.: Sheffield Academic Press, 1992); John R. Levison, *Texts in Transition: The Greek Life of Adam and Eve* (Atlanta: Society of Biblical Literature, 2000).

4. Theodore Hiebert, *The Yahwist's Landscape: Nature and Religion in Early Israel* (New York: Oxford University Press, 1996), 32–35.

5. Hiebert, *The Yahwist's Landscape,* 53–55, quotations on 55 and 53.

6. Chamberlin and Feldman, *Dartmouth Bible,* Genesis 3:1–7, 22–24; Bill Moyers, *Genesis: A Living Converstaion* (New York: Doubleday, 1996), 67; Hiebert, *The Yahwist's Landscape,* 33–35.

7. Evan Eisenberg, *The Ecology of Eden* (New York: Alfred A. Knopf, 1998), 86–89, quotation on 87.

8. J. Baird Callicott, "Genesis Revisited: Muirian Musings on the Lynn White, Jr. Debate," *Environmental Review* 14, nos. 1–2 (1990): 65–92, esp. 81. Moyers, *Genesis,* 71–76. See Genesis 1:29–30; Genesis 2:9; Genesis 3:18, 19, 23; Hiebert, *The Yahwist's Landscape,* 40–41.

9. J. L. Russell, "Time in Christian Thought," in *The Voices of Time: A Cooperative Survey of Man's Views of Time As Expressed by the Sciences and Humanities,* ed. J. T. Fraser (Amherst: University of Massachusetts Press, 1981), quoted in Max Oelschlaeger, *The Idea of Wilderness: From Prehistory to the Age of Ecology* (New Haven, Conn.: Yale University Press, 1991), 67.

10. Genesis 1:31; Genesis 2:6–7; Genesis 3:1, 14, 18.

11. Victor Rotenberg, "The Lapsarian Moment" (unpublished manuscript, University of

California-Berkeley, 1993); Henry Goldschmidt, "Rupture Tales: Stories and Politics in and Around the Garden of Eden" (unpublished manuscript, University of California, Santa Cruz, 1994), quotations on 8–9; I thank Victor Rotenberg and Henry Goldschmidt for sharing their manuscripts with me. As postmodern philosopher Jacques Derrida puts it, the story is an ontotheology "determining the . . . meaning of being as presence, as parousia, as life without difference"; see Derrida, *Of Grammatology*, trans. Gayatri Chakravorty Spivak (Baltimore: Johns Hopkins University Press, 1976), 71.

12. *Oxford English Dictionary*, compact ed., 2 vols. (Oxford: Oxford University Press, 1971), vol. 1., s.v. "Eden"; vol. 2, s.v. "paradise"; Plaut, *The Torah*, 29, note 8. In the Jewish tradition, Eden is the home of the righteous after death. On time in the Christian tradition, see Oelschlaeger, *The Idea of Wilderness*, 65–66.

13. Jeffrey L. Sheler, "The Christmas Covenant," *U.S. News and World Report*, Dec. 19, 1994, 62–71, esp. 66. Religious sects differ as to forms of millennialism. Premillennialists, such as fundamentalist and evangelical Christians, believe a catastrophe or final battle of Armageddon will initiate the age of Christ on earth. Postmillennialists argue for Christ's return only after a golden age of peace on earth brought about by working within the church. Antimillennialists, who include most Protestants and Roman Catholics, do not accept the one-thousand-year reign of Christ on earth, but instead believe in a period prior to the final resurrection in which Christ works through the church and individual lives.

14. A. L. Moore, *The Parousia in the New Testament* (Leiden: E. J. Brill, 1966), 2, 3, 5, 16, 17, 20, 21, 25–26, 28. Moore notes "The divine intervention in history was the manifestation of the Kingdom of God. . . . [T]his would involve a total transformation of the present situation, hence the picture of world renewal enhanced sometimes by the idea of an entirely supernatural realm" (25–26). Further, "Concerning the central figure in the awaited End-drama there is considerable variation. In some visions the figure of Messiah is entirely absent. In such cases 'the kingdom was always represented as under the immediate sovereignty of God.'" (21)

15. The concept of a recovery from the biblical Fall appears in the seventeenth century. According to the *Oxford English Dictionary*, recover is "[t]he act of recovering oneself from a mishap, mistake, fall, etc."; vol. 2, s.v. "fall." See also Bishop Edward Stillingfleet, *Origines Sacrae* (London, 1662), II, i, sec 1.: "The conditions on which fallen man may expect a recovery"; William Cowper, *Retirement* (1781), 138: "To . . . search the themes, important above all Ourselves, and our recovery from our fall"; and Richard Eden, *The Decades of the Newe Worlde or West India* (1555), 168: "The recoverie of the kyngedome of Granata." The term *recovery* also embraced the idea of regaining a "natural" position after falling and a return to health after sickness. It acquired a legal meaning in the sense of gaining possession of property by a verdict or judgment of the court. In common recovery, an estate was transferred from one party to another. See John Cowell, *The Interpreter* (1607), s.v. "recoverie": "A true recoverie is an actuall or reall recoverie of anything, or the value thereof by Judgement." Another meaning was the restoration of a person or thing to a healthy or normal condition, or a return to a higher or better state, including the reclamation of land. [See anonymous,] *Captives bound in Chains . . . the misery of graceless Sinners, and the hope of their recovery by Christ* (1674); Bishop Joseph Butler, *The Analogy of Religion Natural and Revealed* (1736), 2: 295: "Indeed neither Reason nor Analogy would lead us to think . . . that the Interposition of Christ . . . would be of that Efficacy for Recovery of the World, which Scripture teaches us it was"; Joseph Gilbert, *The Christian Atonement* (1836), 1:24: "A modified system, which shall include the provision of means for recovery from a lapsed state"; James Martineau, *Essays, Reviews, and Addresses* (1890–91), 2:310: "He is fitted to be among the prophets of recovery, who may prepare for us a more wholesome future." John Henry Newman, *Historical Sketches* (1872–73) 2:1:3:121: "The special work of his reign was the recovery of the soil."

16. On the tragic and comic visions of the human, animal, vegetable, mineral and unformed worlds, see Northrup Frye, *Fables of Identity* (New York: Harcourt Brace, 1963), 19–20.

17. Bloom and Rosenberg, *The Book of J*, 62; A. Cohen, ed., *Soncino Chumash, or, Five Books of Moses with Haphtaroth* (Hindland, Surrey, Eng.: Soncino Press, 1947), 11; Plaut, ed., *The Torah* (1981), 30; Aryeh Kaplan, trans., *The Living Torah: The First Five Books of Moses and the Haftarot* (New York: Mazanim, 1981), 9; *Tanakh* (1985), 5; Arthur S. Maxwell, *The Bible Story*, rev. ed. (Hagerston, Md.: Review and Herals Publishing Association, 1994), 47–49. Kaplan, *The Living Torah* says, "Your passion will be to your husband and he will dominate you" (Genesis 3:16). The King James version of the Bible and the 1947 *Soncino Chumash* call both the animals and the woman "help meets"; the 1981 Plaut edition of *The Torah* and the 1985 *Tanakh* refer to them as "fitting helpers;" Kaplan's 1981 *Living Torah* denotes them "compatible helpers," while Everett Fox, ed., *The Five Books of Moses* (New York: Schocken Books, 1995) uses "a helper corresponding to him." *The Book of J*, thought by Harold Bloom to have been written by a woman, calls both the animals and the woman (created to help Adam "tend" and "watch" the Garden of Eden) "partners" (Genesis 2:18, 20). The children's *Bible Story* (1994) calls them "mates," while Eve is Adam's "life companion."

18. Plaut, *The Torah*, 28, 32. Victor Roland Gold, et al, ed., *The New Testament and Psalms: An Inclusive Version* (New York: Oxford University Press, 1995) translates God as Father-Mother. The Lord's Prayer (Matthew 6:9–10) thus reads "Our Father-Mother in heaven, hallowed be your name. Your dominion come."

19. Phyllis Trible, quoted in Plaut, *The Torah*, 33, n. 15. On Eve as the first scientist see Mark Twain, "Eve's Diary," in *The Diaries of Adam and Eve* (replica of the 1904–5 1st ed.), in *The Oxford Mark Twain*, ed. Shelley Fisher Fishkin (New York: Oxford University Press, 1996).

20. Ray Maria McNamara, Graduate Theological Union, Berkeley, personal communication with the author. Reverend William Moore Boyce Jr., Richmond, Virginia, a free translation of Genesis 2:18; Genesis 1:28 and 31 (1998): "Then the Lord God said: 'It is not good for humans to be alone. I will make them helpers, partners, and colleagues to each other'. . . . So God created humankind in God's own image, in the image of God they were created, male and female they were created, and God saw the whole creation and indeed it was very, very good."

21. A. Cohen, *The Soncino Chumash*, 7 note. The King James version of the Bible and the *Soncino Chumash* translate the Genesis 1:28 passage in almost identical terms, using the familiar terms *subdue* and *dominion*: "And God blessed them and God said unto them: 'Be fruitful and multiply and replenish the earth and subdue it; and have dominion over the fish of the sea and over the fowl of the air, and over every living thing that creepeth upon the earth.'" Cohen notes that the Hebrew word for *subdue* could be read as applying only to the singular individual ("subdue thou it") and therefore was "addressed only to man whose function it is to subdue, but not to woman." The New Century version of the *Bible* (1987) reads, "Have many children and grow in number. Fill the earth and be its master. Rule over the fish of the sea. . . ." Here mastery and rule are the message. Plaut's edition of *The Torah* (1981) also replaces the words "subdue it" with "master it," while changing "have dominion over" to "rule." It reads, "God blessed them and God said to them, 'Be fertile and increase, fill the earth and master it; and rule the fish of the sea, the birds of the sky, and all the living things that creep on earth.'" The *Tanakh*, a new translation of the *Torah* rendered in 1985, like the 1981 Plaut version, uses "increase," "master," and "rule." Harsher, however, is the translation in Kaplan *The Living Torah*, which uses "conquer" and "dominate." The passage reads, "God blessed them. God said to them, 'Be fertile and become many. Fill the land and conquer it. Dominate the fish of the sea, the birds of the air, and every beast that walks the land.'" A new translation rendered by David Seidenberg ("Some Texts from the Torah on the Relationship between Humanity and Nature," unpublished manuscript, 1993), employs "conquer" (as does the Kaplan edition), while also translating the land as female: "And Elohim blessed them and said to them, 'bear fruit and increase and fill up the land and conquer/occupy her and prevail over the fish of the sea and over the bird of the skies and over every animal crawling on the land.'" For more information see Jeremy Cohen, *"Be Fertile and Increase, Fill the Earth and Master It:" The Ancient and Medieval Career of a*

Biblical Text. (Ithaca: Cornell University Press, 1989). These comparisons among Genesis 1:28 renderings in the Christian and Judaic traditions seem to confirm the mandate to populate, "subdue," "master," "rule," and "conquer" the (female) land. Encoded into Western culture, such language was used historically to justify spatial expansion, colonial territories, manifest destiny, and the westward conquest of other peoples and lands.

22. Plaut, *The Torah*, 39; Lynn White Jr., "The Historical Roots of our Ecologic Crisis," *Science* 155 (1967): 1203–7, reprinted in Ian Barbour, ed., *Western Man and Environmental Ethics: Attitudes toward Nature and Technology* (Reading, Mass.: Addison Wesley, 1973), 18–30, quotation on 25.

23. René Dubos, "Conservation, Stewardship, and the Human Heart," *Audubon*, September 1972, 21–28, quotation on 27; see also Dubos, "A Theology of the Earth," in Ian G. Barbour, ed., *Western Man and Environmental Ethics*, 43–54; Robin Attfield, *The Ethics of Environmental Concern* (New York: Scribner's, 1974); and Bruce Babbitt, "Stewards of Creation," *Christian Century*, 113, no. 16 (1996), 500–503.

24. Plaut, *The Torah*, 38.

25. Cohen, ed., *Soncino Chumash* (1947), 10; Plaut, ed., *The Torah* (1981), 30; Kaplan, ed. *The Living Torah* (1981), 9; *Tanakh* (1985), 5; Bloom and Rosenberg, *The Book of J*, 62; Seidenberg, *Some Texts from the Torah*, 1. Plaut, *The Torah*, however, changes the wording to "to till it and tend it," introducing into Eden more explicitly the possibility of agriculture. Kaplan's *Living Torah* and Fox's *Schocken Bible* use "to work it and watch it," while the 1985 *Tanakh* (again, like the Plaut 1981 version) employs "to till it and tend it." Rosenberg's 1990 translation of the *Book of J* renders the passage as follows: "Yahweh lifts the man, brings him to rest in the garden of Eden, to tend it and watch." As in his Genesis 1:28 translation, Seidenberg renders the garden as female and translates the verbs as to "work/serve and watch over" her. His translation reads, "And YHVH Elohim took the human and placed him/it in 'ayden garden to work/serve her and to watch over her." Here again the female connection to the land and garden are made explicit, but "man" is instead rendered "human." This language interprets humanity as caretaker of the land. On biocentric ethics, see Paul Taylor, *Respect for Nature: A Theory of Environmental Ethics* (Princeton, N.J.: Princeton University Press, 1986). On ecocentric ethics, see Aldo Leopold, "The Land Ethic," in *A Sand County Almanac* (New York: Oxford University Press, 1949), 201–25; J. Baird Callicott, *In Defense of the Land Ethic: Essays in Environmental Philosophy* (Albany: State University of New York Press, 1989); and Holmes Rolston III, *Philosophy Gone Wild: Essays in Environmental Ethics* (Buffalo, N.Y.: Prometheus Books, 1986).

26. Oelschlaeger, *The Idea of Wilderness*, 11–12, 14, 16, 17–18, 20, 23, quotation on 11–12.

27. Ibid., 24.

28. Ibid., 25, 28.

29. Ibid., 60, 65, 67.

30. Ibid., 31, 39.

31. Ibid., 42, 47–48.

32. Carol Manahan, "The Genesis of Agriculture and the Agriculture of Genesis," unpublished manuscript. On the domestication of crops and the rise of settled agriculture, see David R. Harris and Gordon C. Hillman, ed. *Foraging and Farming: The Evolution of Plant Exploitation* (Boston: Unwin Hyman, 1989); Daniel Zohary and Pinhas Spiegel-Roy, "Beginnings of Fruit-Growing in the Old World," *Science* 187 (1975): 319–27.

33. John Passmore, quoted in Oelschlaeger, *The Idea of Wilderness*, p. 46.

34. Mark S. Smith, *The Early History of God: Yahweh and the Other Deities in Ancient Israel* (San Francisco: Harper Collins, 1990), xix–xxvii, quotation on xxvii.

35. Henri Frankfort, H.A. Frankfort, John A. Wilson, Thorkild Jacobsen, and William A. Irwin, *Before Philosophy: The Intellectual Adventure of Ancient Man* (Baltimore: Penguin, 1949), 241–48, 253, quotations on 241–42.

36. J. Donald Hughes, *Ecology in Ancient Civilizations* (Albuquerque: University of New Mexico Press, 1975), 20–28.

37. Friedrich Engels, "Origins of the Family, Private Property, and the State" in *Selected Works* (New York: International, 1968); Johann Jacob Bachhofen, "Mother Right: An Investigation of the Religious and Juridical Character of Matriarchy in the Ancient World" (1861), in *Myth, Religion, and Mother Right: Selected Writings of J. J. Bachnofen,* trans. Ralph Manheim (Princeton, N.J.: Princeton University Press, 1967), 69–207; August Bebel, *Woman in the Past, Present, and Future* (San Francisco: G. B. Benham, 1897); Robert Briffault, *The Mothers,* (1927; abridged ed. New York: Atheneum, 1977); Jane Ellen Harrison, *Prolegomena to the Study of Greek Religion* (Cambridge: Cambridge University Press, 1922; originally published 1903); Jane Ellen Harrison, *The Religion of Ancient Greece* (London: Archibald Constable, 1905); Jane Ellen Harrison, *Myths of the Social Origins of Greek Religion* (Cambridge: Cambridge University Press, 1912); Jane Ellen Harrison, *Mythology* (1924; reprint New York: Harcourt, Brace and World/Harbinger, 1963); Helen Diner, *Mothers and Amazons: The First Feminine History of Culture* (1929; reprint New York: Anchor Press, Doubleday, 1973); M. Esther Harding, *Women's Mysteries Ancient and Modern* (1955; reprint London: Rider, 1971); Elizabeth Gould Davis, *The First Sex* (Baltimore, Md: Penguin Books, 1972); Merlin Stone, *When God Was a Woman* (New York: Harcourt Brace Jovanovich, 1976); Adrienne Rich, *Of Woman Born* (New York: W. W. Norton, 1976); Françoise d'Eaubonne, *La feminisme ou la mort* (Paris, 1974), Marija Gimbutas, *The Goddesses and Gods of Old Europe, 6500–3500 B.C.* (Berkeley and Los Angeles: University of California Press, 1982); Pamela Berger, *The Goddess Obscured: The Transformation of the Grain Protectress from Goddess to Saint* (Boston: Beacon Press, 1985); Gerda Lerner, *The Creation of Patriarchy* (New York: Oxford, 1986); Monica Shöö and Barbara Mor, *The Great Cosmic Mother: Rediscovering the Religion of the Earth* (San Francisco: Harper Collins, 1987); Riane Eisler, *The Chalice and the Blade* (San Francisco: Harper Collins, 1988); Elinor Gadon, *The Once and Future Goddess* (San Francisco: Harper Collins, 1989); and Rosemary Radford Ruether, *Gaia and God: An Ecofeminist Theology of Earth Healing* (San Francisco: Harper Collins, 1992).

38. Davis, *The First Sex,* 16–17.

39. Stone, *When God Was a Woman,* xii-xiii: "Archaeological, mythological and historical evidence all reveal that the female religion, far from naturally fading away, was the victim of centuries of continual persecution and suppression by the advocates of the newer religions which held male deities as supreme. And from these new religions came the creation myth of Adam and Eve and the tale of the loss of Paradise."

40. See Gimbutas, *The Goddesses and Gods of Old Europe.*

41. Rich, *Of Woman Born,* 56: "A prehistoric civilization [was] centered around the female, both as mother and head of family, and as deity—the Great Goddess who appears throughout early mythology, as Tiamat, Rhea, Isis, Ishtar, Astarte, Cybele, Demeter, Diana of Ephesus, and by many other names: the eternal giver of life and embodiment of the natural order, including death."

42. Lerner, *The Creation of Patriarchy,* 153: "The young god who slays Tiamat in the epic is Marduk, the god worshipped in the city of Babylon. Marduk first emerges during the time of Hammurabi of Babylon, who has made his city-state dominant in the Mesopotamian region."

43. Stone, *When God Was a Woman,* 10–11, 139–44.

44. Lerner, *Creation of Patriarchy,* 154: "The changing position of the Mother-Goddess, her dethroning, takes place in many cultures and at different times, but usually it is associated with the same historical processes. . . . In Egypt, where the male God early predominates, we can also find traces of a still earlier predominance of the Goddess. Isis . . . [was] 'the prototype of the life-giving mother and faithful wife.'"

45. Stone, *When God was a Woman,* 51–53; Shöö and Mor, *The Great Cosmic Mother,* 235–37, According to Shöö and Mor, "The Olympian god . . . is not born from woman, or

earth, or matter, but from his own absolute will. He represents a static perfection, in human form, incapable of transformation or ecstatic change; as a God, he is an intellectual concept" (235).

46. Davis, *The First Sex*, 142–44, quotation on 144.

47. Stone, *When God was a Woman*, 198–223, quotation on 223.

48. Eisler, *The Chalice and the Blade*, xvii, 105, 185–203; Ruether, *Gaia and God*, 2–3; and Rosemary Radford Ruether, "Gender and the Problem of Prehistory," unpublished manuscript, 35.

CHAPTER 3

1. Jared Diamond, *Guns, Germs, and Steel: The Fates of Human Societies* (New York: W. W. Norton, 1997), 87, 167, 135–38.

2. Hesiod, "Works and Days," in *Theogeny and Works and Days* (New York: Oxford University Press, 1988), 40.

3. J. Donald Hughes, *Ecology in Ancient Civilizations* (Albuquerque: University of New Mexico Press, 1975), 68–80; Clarence Glacken, *Traces on the Rhodian Shore: Nature and Culture in Western Thought From Ancient Times to the End of the Eighteenth Century* (Berkeley and Los Angeles: University of California Press, 1967), 1–18.

4. Plato, "Critias," in *The Dialogues of Plato*, (1892) trans. B. Jowett (New York: Random House, 1937), 2: 73–75, quotations on 75.

5. Publius Ovid, *Metamorphoses*, (C.E. 7), trans. Rolfe Humphries (Bloomington: Indiana University Press), 6, lines 100–11.

6. On the meanings of nature and nation and the following interpretation of Virgil, see Kenneth Olwig, *Nature's Ideological Landscape* (London: Allen and Unwin, 1984), 3–9.

7. Ibid., 6; Virgil, *Georgics* 1, lines 151–52, quoted in Olwig, *Nature's Ideological Landscape*, 6.

8. Olwig, *Nature's Ideological Landscape*, 3–9; Virgil, *Georgics* 2, lines 106–7, and *Eclogues* 4:4–34.

9. Lucretius, *Of the Nature of Things*, trans. William Ellery Leonard (New York: E. P. Dutton, 1950), book 5, lines 922–1008, 1135–85.

10. Ibid., book 6, lines 1136–1284; book 5, lines 811–70.

11. Dante Alighieri, *The Divine Comedy*, in *The Portable Dante*, ed. Mark Musa (New York: Penguin, 1984).

12. Robert Pogue Harrison, *Forests: The Shadow of Civilization* (Chicago: University of Chicago Press, 1992), 86.

13. Ibid., 86, 87.

14. Dante, "Inferno," in *The Portable Dante*, canto 1.

15. Ibid., canto 1, lines 2, 5, 7, 29, 64, 132; canto 2, line 63; canto 3, lines 28, 29, 118, 66, 69, 112–13, 115–16, 118.

16. Dante, "Purgatory," in *The Portable Dante*, canto 28, lines 2, 28, 79, 121–22.

17. Ibid., canto 29, lines 24–27; Canto 32, lines 38–39.

18. Ibid., canto 33, lines 143–45.

19. Dante, "Paradise," in *The Portable Dante*, canto 30, lines 62–63, 65–67, 109–10, 117, 122–23; Harrison, *Forests*, 87.

20. Dante, "Paradise," in *The Portable Dante*, canto 23, lines 71–72; canto 32, lines 121–23; "Purgatory," in *The Portable Dante*, canto 29, line 24; canto 33, line 32.

21. On Eve, see Dante, "Purgatory," in *The Portable Dante*, canto 33, line 53. On Beatrice and the science of light, see "Paradise," John Prest, *The Garden of Eden: The Botanic Garden and the Re-Creation of Paradise* (New Haven, Conn.: Yale University Press, 1981), 21–22.

22. Avril Henry, ed., *The Mirour of Mans Saluacioun: A Middle English Translation of Speculum Humanae Salvationis* (Philadelphia: University of Pennsylvania Press, 1987), 43.

23. Ibid., 45, 51, 53.

24. Pamela Berger, *The Goddess Obscured: The Transformation of the Grain Protectress from Goddess to Saint* (Boston: Beacon Press, 1985).

25. Prest, *Garden of Eden*, 21–22.

26. St. Genevieve, patron saint of Paris, was declared a saint when she was seven years old by St. Germain of Auxerre. She is venerated for saving Paris from the ravages of Attila the Hun by encouraging the people in fasting and prayer and assuring them of the protection of God. In apparent response, the Huns turned aside. She lived a life dedicated to charity, austerity, and prayer until her death in 512 C.E.

27. Prest, *Garden of Eden*, 21; Geoffrey Chaucer, "The Merchant's Tale," in *Works*, ed. F. N. Robinson (Boston: Houghton Mifflin, 1957), lines 2044–46, 2143–46.

28. David F. Noble, *The Religion of Technology: The Divinity of Man and the Spirit of Invention* (New York: Alfred A. Knopf, 1997), 22–23; Marjorie Reeves, *Joachim of Fiore and the Prophetic Future* (London: SPCK, 1976), 1–28.

29. Sheler, Jeffrey L. "The Christmas Covenant," *U.S. News and World Report*, December 19, 1994: 62–71.

30. Noble, *Religion of Technology*, 16–17.

31. George Ovitt Jr., *The Restoration of Perfection: Labor and Technology in Medieval Culture* (New Brunswick, N.J.: Rutgers University Press, 1987), 127; Noble, *Religion of Technology*, 19–20.

32. Noble, *Religion of Technology*, 26–27; Charles Webster, *The Great Instauration: Science, Medicine and Reform, 1626–1660* (London: Duckworth, 1975), esp. 1–12, 324–27.

33. Christopher Columbus, letter, October 18, 1498, in Thomas and Carol Christensen, ed. *The Discovery of America and Other Myths* (San Franciso: Chronicle Books, 1992), 7–8.

34. John Prest, *The Garden of Eden: The Botanic Garden and the Re-Creation of Paradise* (New Haven, Conn.: Yale University Press, 1981), 32.

35. Prest, *Garden of Eden*, 35, 37. During the Renaissance, artists illustrated the Garden of Eden story through woodcuts and paintings. The Creation chapter, with Adam and Eve's admission to the Garden of Eden, drew the greatest attention. Perhaps the most famous is Michelangelo's *Creation of Adam*, in which God transmits the spark of life to Adam's outstretched hand; less well-known is his "Creation of Eve" in which God draws Eve out of a sleeping Adam's rib. The woodcut from a 1503 edition of Ludolphus's *Mirror of Man's Salvation* shows God welcoming Adam and Eve lockstep through a portal into an enclosed circular garden containing two trees—the tree of Life and the tree of the knowledge of good and evil—and from which four rivers flowed (see fig. 2.1 in chapter 2). G.B. Andreini, in his *L'Adamo, sacra rapresentatione* (1617), depicted Adam naming the animals outside the entrance to the garden. A second illustration from the same work showed God creating Adam outside the garden with the animals waiting to be named followed by Eve's creation from Adam's rib inside the garden walls. The garden itself was a geometrically laid park, with the tree of the knowledge of good and evil at its center; see Prest, *Garden of Eden*, 10, 12, 13. The Temptation, Fall, and Expulsion chapters of the story likewise received great attention. J. P. Bergomensis in 1510 showed two successive scenes: the left side depicted Eve taking the apple from the serpent, while Adam stood innocently by; the right side showed the couple in hasty retreat from an angel hovering above them, waving a sword. J. J. du Pré's illustration of 1488 showed the serpent tempting Eve in the background, while in the foreground Adam and Eve, covering themselves with fig leaves, are expelled through the garden gate, no longer in lockstep (see fig. 2.2, in chapter 2). Beside them a cherubim brandishes a flaming sword to guard the Tree of Life. See also Prest, *Garden of Eden*, 22, 15.

Perhaps the most well-known depictions of the Temptation are the woodcuts and paintings of Albrecht Dürer and Lucas Cranach. Dürer's *The Fall of Man* (1504) juxtaposes Adam and Eve in a dark forest surrounded by domesticated animals—goats, cattle, cats, rabbits, and mice—with wilderness images of a mountain goat perched precariously on a rocky ledge behind

Eve, while a jungle parrot sits on a branch held by Adam. The snake transfers the apple from its mouth to Eve's hand, while Adam extends his arm in anticipation. Cranach's *Adam and Eve* (1526) (fig. 3.3 in chapter 3) shows Eve offering the apple to Adam after having been enticed by the snake coiled around the tree of the knowledge of good and evil. Here Eve is portrayed as the bold instigator of the experiment, while Adam scratches his head quizzically—a puzzled, uncertain participant in the forbidden venture. (For Cranach, see Max J. Friedländer and Jakob Rosenberg, *The Paintings of Lucas Cranach* (London: Sotheby Parke Bernet, 1978), illustration 191. Animals, in medieval representations of the Garden of Eden, were gentle and tame. They formed a "peaceable kingdom" where the "lion would lie down with the stag," as in Jan Brueghel the elder's (1568–1625) *Garden of Eden*. Here "wild" animals behaved like the domesticated sheep and gentle doves of the pastoral setting; all of nature lived in harmony. (See Prest, *Garden of Eden*, 4–5, 21–22).

36. Ibid., 21–22. The discovery of new plants and animals not mentioned in the Bible presented dilemmas. Potatoes, tomatoes, chocolate, pineapples, tobacco, vanilla, and morning glories did not have biblical names. Nowhere on the Ark were found llamas, alpacas, iguanas, turkeys, bisons, or guinea pigs. It seemed that God had set aside certain parts of his creation to be rediscovered in other parts of the world at a future time. Notes Prest, "If God had revealed an aspect of himself in each plant and animal that he created, the creatures could not be wholly depraved, and with the discovery of America the idea grew up that what had happened at the Fall was not so much that nature had been poisoned, but that it had been scattered. . . . In the Garden of Eden, Adam and Eve had been introduced to the completed picture. When they sinned, God had put some of the pieces away in a cupboard—an American cupboard—to be released when mankind improved, or He saw fit"; Prest, *Garden of Eden*, 21–22.

37. Zygmunt Bauman, "Gamekeepers Turned Gardeners," in *Legislators and Interpreters: On Modernity, Post-modernity, and Intellectuals* (Oxford: Polity Press, 1987), 51–67, esp. 51–53.

38. Ibid., 51–53; Dianne Harris, "Lombardia Illuminata: The Formation of an Enlightenment Landscape in Eighteenth Century Lombardy" (Ph.D. diss., University of California-Berkeley, 1996); Prest, *Garden of Eden*, 1–3.

39. Bauman, "Gamekeepers Turned Gardeners," 52–53.

40. Prest, *Garden of Eden*, 33, 42; quotation on 39.

41. Eustace M. W. Tillyard, *The Elizabethan World Picture* (New York: Vintage, 1959, 42; see also Charles Whitney, *Francis Bacon and Modernity* (New Haven, Conn.: Yale University Press, 1986), 123.

CHAPTER 4

1. Carolyn Merchant, *The Death of Nature: Women, Ecology and the Scientific Revolution* (San Francisco: Harper Collins, 1980), 42–68; H. C. Darby, "The Clearing of the Woodland in Europe," in *Man's Role in Changing the Face of the Earth*, ed. William L. Thomas Jr., 2 vols. (Chicago: University of Chicago Press, 1956), 1: 183–216; Gottfried Pfeifer, "The Quality of Peasant Living in Central Europe," in Thomas, ed., *Man's Role in Changing the Face of the Earth*, 1: 240–77; Michael Williams, "Forests," in B. L. Turner, II, William C. Clark, Robert W. Kates, John F. Richards, Jessica T. Matthews, and William B. Meyer, eds., *The Earth As Transformed by Human Action: Global and Regional Changes in the Biosphere over the Past Three Hundred Years* (New York: Cambridge University Press, 1990), 179–201, esp. 180–81; Clive Ponting, *A Green History of the World: The Environment and the Collapse of Great Civilizations* (New York: St. Martin's Press, 1991), 96–106.

2. Ponting, *A Green History of the World*, 97; William H. Te Brake, "Air Pollution and Fuel Crises in Preindustrial London," *Technology and Culture* 16 (1975): 337–59.

3. John U. Nef, *The Rise of the British Coal Industry*, 2 vols. (Hamden, Conn.: Archon, 1966), 1: 156–64; Eugene F. Rice, *The Foundations of Early Modern Europe, 1450–1559* (New York: W. W. Norton, 1970); John F. Richards, "Land Transformation," in Turner, et al. eds., *The*

Earth as Transformed by Human Action, 163–78, esp. 164, table 10–1, 164; Williams, "Forests," 180–81, esp. table 11-1, 180; Ponting, *A Green History of the World*, 98.

4. On the origin story of capitalism, see Marshall Sahlins, *Culture and Practical Reason* (Chicago: University of Chicago Press, 1976), 53: "The development from a Hobbesian state of nature is the origin myth of western capitalism."

5. *Oxford English Dictionary*, 2nd ed. (Oxford, England: Clarendon Press, 1989), s.v. "wild"; John Stilgoe, *Common Landscape of America, 1580–1845* (New Haven, Conn.: Yale University Press, 1982), 7–12.

6. *Oxford English Dictionary*, s.v. "wild"; vol. 20, 330–35; Stilgoe, *Common Landscape of America*, 7–12.

7. Genesis 2:17–19; Numbers (Annals of the Wilderness); Isaiah 35:1; Roderick Nash, *Wilderness and the American Mind* (New Haven, Conn.: Yale University Press, 1977), 13–17.

8. Merchant, *Death of Nature*, 131.

9. *Oxford English Dictionary*, s.v. "civic," "civilization."

10. Carolyn Merchant, *Ecological Revolutions: Nature, Gender, and Science in New England* (Chapel Hill: University of North Carolina Press, 1989), 39–40.

11. Merchant, *Ecological Revolutions*, 41; Merchant, *Death of Nature*, 131.

12. See Richard Ashcraft, "Leviathan Triumphant: Thomas Hobbes and the Politics of Wild Men," in *The Wild Man Within* (Pittsburgh: University of Pittsburgh Press, 1972), 147, 151. Also Joseph de Acosta, *The Natural and Moral History of the Indies*, (English translation 1604 by Edward Grimston), ed. Clements R. Markham, 2 vols. (London: Hakluyt Society, 1880), 1: 70, and 2: 410, 426–27, 450; Garcilaso de la Vega, *Royal Commentaries of the Incas*, trans. Harold V. Livermore, 2 vols. (Austin: University of Texas Press, 1869), 1: 42.

13. Ashcraft, "Leviathan Triumphant," 151, 152. On the Virginia massacre see Alden T. Vaughan, "English Policy and the Massacre of 1622," *William and Mary Quarterly* 35 (1978): 57–84.

14. See also John Donne, "An Anatomie of the World: The First Anniversary," in *The Poems of John Donne*, ed. Herbert Grierson (London: Oxford University Press, 1957), 208–26. Donne's anniversary poems, written in 1611–12 to commemorate the death of the young Elizabeth Drury, cast the earth as dead and dying, with sickness permeating the entire cosmos. With Drury's death, heaven and earth had decayed, the human lifespan had been shortened, "man's" stature truncated, and its mental powers weakened. Decline in human vigor extended to all of nature and even the heavens themselves. The earth had become a cripple, a wan ghost, an ugly monster, and a dry cinder. At the end of each section, Donne drove home the point with the dirge-like refrain: "Shee is dead, she's dead."

15. Richard Foster Jones, *Ancients and Moderns: A Study of the Rise of the Scientific Movement in Seventeenth Century England* (St. Louis: Washington University Studies, 1961), 22–29; Victor Harris, *All Coherence Gone* (Chicago: University of Chicago Press, 1949), 1–46. For Goodman, the barrenness of nature was a direct consequence of humanity's original sin. The Fall had introduced thorns, briars, and thistles into the environment. The earth had lapsed from producing noble lions, tigers, and unicorns into procreating lowly worms and gnats. The weather was no longer propitious for growing crops, droughts marred spring planting, and fall freezes destroyed harvests. Mountains had eroded, rivers were clogged with muck, and seas inundated the land. The heavens too were mutable and corrupt. Spots blemished the sun, the years were getting shorter, comets streaked across the fixed stars, and the moon's surface was pocked with craters.

16. Henry Vaughan, quoted in Marjorie Hope Nicolson, *Mountain Gloom and Mountain Glory: The Development of the Aesthetics of the Infinite* (1959; reprint Seattle: University of Washington Press, 1997), 83. See Henry Vaughan, "Corruption," in *The Complete Poems*, ed. Alan Rudrum (New Haven, Conn.: Yale University Press, 1976), 197.

17. John Milton, quoted in Nicolson, *Mountain Gloom and Mountain Glory*, 86–87. See also John Milton, *Paradise Lost: A Poem in Ten Books* (London: Peter Parker, 1668), book 9, lines 782, 997.

18. Thomas Burnet, *The Sacred Theory of the Earth*, intro. by Basil Willey (Carbondale: Southern Illinois University Press, 1965), 53, 64, 133–34: "In this smooth earth were the first Scenes of the World, and the first Generations of Mankind; it had the Beauty of Youth and blooming Nature, fresh and fruitful, and not a wrinkle, scar, or fracture in all its body; no Rocks nor Mountains. . . . the Air was calm and serene. . . . 'Twas suited to a golden Age, and to the first innocency of Nature." The entire orginal earth was paradise, "that seat of pleasure which our first Parents lost, and which all their posterity have much ado to find again." Lost in the Fall was the perpetual spring, the longevity of animals, and the "great fertility of the soil." See also Nicolson, *Mountain Gloom and Mountain Glory*, 198–200.

19. Burnet, *The Sacred Theory of the Earth*, 84; Burnet writes that had not Noah built his ark, all mankind would have disappeared and the earth would have been "nothing but a Desert, a great ruine, a dead heap of Rubbish, from the Deluge to the Conflagration." The earth that remained after the waters receded was the earth of the present era and state of nature. See also Nicolson, *Mountain Gloom and Mountain Glory*, 198–200.

20. Burnet, *Sacred Theory of the Earth*, 24.

21. Francis Bacon, "Novum Organum," in *Works*, ed. James Spedding, Robert Leslie Ellis, and Douglas Devon Heath, 14 vols. (London: Longmans Green, 1870), 114–15, 247–48, emphasis added. See also Bacon, "Valerius Terminus," in *Works*, 3: 217, 219. On domination, see William Leiss, *The Domination of Nature* (New York: George Braziller, 1972), 48–52; Charles Whitney, *Francis Bacon and Modernity* (New Haven, Conn.: Yale University Press, 1986), 123.

22. Bacon, "Preparative Towards a Natural and Experimental History," in *Works*, 4: 263, emphasis added.

23. Bacon, "The New Atlantis," in *Works*, 3: 155–65; Merchant, *Death of Nature*, 180–86.

24. René Descartes, "Discourse on Method (1637)," in *Philosophical Works of Descartes*, ed. E. S. Haldane and G. R. T. Ross, eds., 2 vols. (New York: Dover, 1955), 1: 119.

25. Isaac Newton, *Philosophiae Naturalis Principia Mathematica* (1687); trans. by A. Motte as *Mathematical Principles of Natural Philosophy*, (1729), rev. Florian Cajori (Berkeley and Los Angeles: University of California Press, 1934); David Kubrin, "How Sir Isaac Newton Helped Restore Law n' Order to the West," *Liberation*, 16, no. 10 (Mar. 1972): 32–41; Christopher Hill, *The World Turned Upside Down: Radical Ideas during the English Revolution* (New York: Viking Press, 1972).

26. Merchant, *Death of Nature*, 229–30.

27. On premodern property hierarchies in society, see Carol M. Rose, *Property and Persuasion: Essays on the History, Theory, and Rhetoric of Ownership* (Boulder, Colo.: Westview Press, 1994) , 58–59.

28. The state of nature as used in the seventeenth century referred to the condition of humanity before the foundation of organized society, a uncultivated or undomesticated condition, or the moral state natural to man as opposed to the state of grace. See *Oxford English Dictionary*, s.v. "nature," no. 14, "state of nature."

29. Ronald Meek, *Social Science and the Ignoble Savage* (Cambridge: Cambridge University Press, 1976), 14–19, quotation from Grotius on 15; Thomas Hobbes, *Leviathan* (1651), in *English Works*, vol. 3 (Aalen, Germany: Scientia, 1966), book 1, ch. 13.

30. Meek, *Social Science and the Ignoble Savage*, quotations from Pufendorf on 18, 19.

31. John Locke, "The First Treatise," in *Two Treatises of Government* (1689), ed. Peter Laslett (Cambridge: Cambridge University Press, 1967; John Locke, *Second Treatise of Government* (1689), ed. Richard H. Cox (Arlington Heights, Ill.: Harlan Davidson, 1982); Robert Filmer, *Patriarcha: or the Natural Power of Kings* (London: 1680).

32. On Locke's place in the debate between ancients and moderns, see Richard H. Cox, introduction to Locke, *Second Treatise*, 7; see also xxv–xxvi. Contradictory implications existed depending on how people read Locke's text Cox points out (xxv–xxvi). Was the state of nature for Locke bad, as Viscount Bolingbroke argued in 1704, or good, as historian Basil Willey later claimed. For Bolingbroke, Locke's "state of freedom . . . would have been a state of war and violence, of mutual . . . oppression, . . . [such as] Hobbes imagined to have been the state of nature." Henry St. John, Viscount, Bolingbroke, *Political Writings*, ed., Isaac Kramnick (New York: Meredith Corporation, 1970), 12–13. But Willey concluded that "the state of nature is so far from resembling the ill condition described by Hobbes, that it approximates rather to the Eden of the religious tradition, or the golden age of the poets. . . ." Basil Willey, *The Seventeenth Century Background: Studies on the Thought of the Age in Relation to Poetry and Religion* (New York: Columbia University Press, 1952), 266–67. There were two different stories, two different strategies for action, and two different outcomes. If Bolingbroke was right, there was no pathway to improvement. If Willey was right, no reason existed to even attempt improvement. But the two views can be reconciled if they are both seen through the lens of reinventing Eden.

33. Locke, "First Treatise," 178, sec. 27; quotation on 179, sec. 28, lines 12–13, 16. See also Locke, "First Treatise," 176, sec. 25.

34. Locke, "First Treatise," quotations on 177, sec. 27, lines 3–4 and 223, sec. 86, lines 26–28. See also Locke, "First Treatise," 227, sec. 92; 230, sec. 97; 177, sec. 27; 183, sec. 34.

35. On Locke's *Second Treatise* as a property narrative, see Rose, *Property and Persuasion*, 26, 38, 41, which summarizes Locke's narrative as follows: "Although the parts are somewhat scattered, the *Treatise* clearly unfolds a story line, beginning in a plenteous state of nature, carrying through the growing individual appropriation of goods, then proceeding to the development of a trading money economy, and culminating in the creation of government to safeguard property" (26). Further, "[Locke] starts off with a tale of people in a state of nature, acquiring natural products like acorns and apples through the very labor of gathering them; then realizing that wealth could be stored through the collection of durables (like nuts and little pieces of gold); and finally, growing nervous at the 'very unsafe, very unsecure' enjoyment of property in the state of nature and joining with others to establish the civil society that will protect everyone's hard-earned property." (38) My account of the underlying structure of Locke's narrative is inspired by Rose's idea, but elaborates the details differently.

36. Locke, *Second Treatise*, quotation on 33, sec. 56; see also 47, secs. 77–78. Locke, "First Treatise," 179–80, secs. 29, 30. God did not give "any Authority to Adam over Eve, or to Men over their Wives, but only [foretold] what should be the Woman's Lot." (Locke, "First Treatise," 192, sec. 47). Further, "If it be said that *Eve* was subjected to *Adam*, it seems she was not so subjected to him, as to hinder her *Dominion* over the Creatures or *Property* in them. . . ." ("First Treatise," 179, sec. 29). While Filmer had held that the man was "the nobler and Principal Agent in generation," Locke stated that the father and mother had joint dominion over the child and that the mother had an equal if not greater share in generation. He thus took a step away from patriarchal authority and toward the possibility of equality for women. ("First Treatise," 192, sec. 47; 198, sec. 55.)

37. Locke, *Second Treatise*, 35, sec. 59.

38. Locke, *Second Treatise*, 5–9; "For 'tis not every compact that puts an end to the state of nature between men, but only this one of agreeing together mutually to enter into one community, and make one body politic; other promises, and compacts, men may make one with another, and yet still be in the state of nature" (9). "To avoid this state of war . . . is one great reason of men's putting themselves into society, and quitting the state of nature" (Locke, *Second Treatise*, 13).

39. On the joining of dominion with appropriation, see Locke, *Second Treatise*, 22, sec. 35. In refuting Filmer's *Patriarcha*, which had argued for the divine right of kings, Locke denied

that Adam had received any inherited right to rule over the world that could arguably be traced back to Adam. It was absurd, Locke thought, that Adam would be punished by being thrown out of Eden to till the ground and at the same time be given a throne and absolute rule over the world forever after (Locke, "First Treatise," 190, sec. 44). If Filmer was correct, Locke asserted, it would mean that all human beings were slaves to a single monarch and there could be no freedom for any person on earth. "Adam's private dominion and paternal jurisdiction" did not survive the Fall (Locke, *Second Treatise*, 1).

40. Locke, *Second Treatise*, 18, secs. 19; 26–27, sec. 28; 20, sec. 30.

41. Ibid., quotations on 21, sec. 32; 22, sec. 35.

42. Ibid., 28, sec. 4; 29, sec. 46; 31, sec. 50.

43. Ibid., 23, sec. 36.

44. Ibid., 53, sec. 89; 130–31, secs. 211–12; 58, sec. 95. "Those who are united into one body, and have a common established law and judicature to appeal to, with authority to decide controversies between them, and punish offenders, *are in civil society* one with another; but those who have no such common appeal, I mean on earth, are still in the state of nature, each being, where there is no other, judge for himself and executioner; which is, as I have before showed it, the perfect *state of nature*" (*Second Treatise*, 52, sec. 87). This "*puts men* out of a state of nature *into* that of a *commonwealth*" (*Second Treatise*, 53, sec. 89). "For the *end of civil society*, being to avoid and remedy those inconveniences of the state of nature, which necessarily follow from every man's being judge in his own case . . ." (*Second Treatise*, 53, sec. 90). "*No man in civil society can be exempted from the laws of it.* For if any man may do, what he thinks fit, and there be no appeal on earth, for redress or security against any harm he shall do; I ask, whether he be not perfectly still in the state of nature, and so can be *no part or member of that civil society*" (*Second Treatise*, 57, sec. 94). "The *beginning of politic society* depends upon the consent of the individuals to join into and make one society" (*Second Treatise*, 64, sec. 106).

45. Locke, *Second Treatise*, 75, sec. 123; 76–77, secs. 128–29; 77, sec. 131.

46. On the process by which the dominant storyteller makes the new position seem natural, see Rose, *Property and Persuasion*, 39.

47. For Smith's history of civil society, see Andrew Skinner's introduction to Adam Smith, *The Wealth of Nations* (1776), ed. Andrew Skinner (New York: Penguin, 1986), 11–97; quotation from Adam Smith, *Lectures on Jurisprudence*, ed. Edwin Cannan (1896), in Skinner, introduction to Smith, *Wealth of Nations*, 31. Meek, *Social Science and the Ignoble Savage*, 99–130.

48. Meek, *Social Science and the Ignoble Savage*, 16, 127, 99–130. For Smith's quotation on Rousseau's *Discourse on the Origins of Inequality*, reviewed by Smith in 1855, see Meek, 116.

49. On overcoming faulty human nature through morality, see, Adam Smith, *The Theory of Moral Sentiments* (1790), ed. D. D. Raphael and A. L. Macfie, 6th ed. (Oxford: Clarendon Press, 1976), 86. For Smith, the positive side of human nature is a "moral sentiment" to act benevolently (conscience). Additionally, the state that restrains people from harming others and their property (justice) acts as a social check on runaway self-interest. In the moral as well as the economic sphere, all this occurs without knowledge of an overall plan on the part of the individual actors in accordance with an "invisible hand." See Smith, *Theory of Moral Sentiments*, 184–85: "They [the rich] are led by an invisible hand to make nearly the same distribution of the necessaries of life, which would have been made, had the earth been divided into equal portions among all its inhabitants, and thus without intending it, without knowing it, advance the interest of the society and afford means to the multiplication of the species. When Providence divided the earth among a few lordly masters, it neither forgot nor abandoned those who seemed to have been left out in the partition. These last too enjoy their share of all that it produces."

50. Ibid., quotations on 168.

51. Kathryn Sutherland, "Adam Smith's Master Narrative: Women and the *Wealth of Nations*," in *Adam Smith's Wealth of Nations: New Interdisciplinary Essays*, ed. Stephen Copley

and Kathryn Sutherland (Manchester: Manchester University Press, 1995), 96–121, quotations on 112, 118.

52. See Thomas H. Birch, "The Incarceration of Wildness: Wilderness Areas As Prisons," in *The Great New Wilderness Debate*, ed. J. Baird Callicott and Michael P. Nelson (Athens, Ga.: University of Georgia Press, 1998), pp. 443–70.

53. David Lowenthal, "Awareness of Human Impacts: Changing Attitudes and Emphases," in Turner, et al., eds., *The Earth As Transformed by Human Action*, 121–35; John Evelyn, *Fumifugium* (1661; reprint Oxford: Old Ashmolean Reprints, 1930).

54. John Evelyn, *Silva, Or a Discourse on Forest Trees* (York, England, 1776 [1662]); John Crombie Brown, ed. and trans., *The French Forest Ordinance of 1669* (Edinburgh: Oliver and Boyd, 1883); Clarence Glacken, *Traces on the Rhodian Shore: Nature and Culture in Western Thought from Ancient Times to the End of the Eighteenth Century* (Berkeley and Los Angeles: University of California Press, 1967), 484–91; Merchant, *Death of Nature*, 237–240.

55. John Ray, *The Wisdom of God Manifested in the Works of the Creation* (1691), 10th ed. (London: Innys and Manby, 1935) 206, 215; Merchant, *Death of Nature*, 246–252.

56. William Derham, *Physico-Theology: or A Demonstration of the Being and Attributes of God, from His Works of Creation* (1713), 6th ed. (London: Innys, 1728;), 257, 260, 280.

57. Nicolson, *Mountain Gloom and Mountain Glory*, 285, 286, 299.

58. Ibid., 279, 293, 300–301.

59. Edmund Burke, *A Philosophical Enquiry into the Origins of Our Ideas of the Sublime and Beautiful* (1757), 2d ed. (London: R. and J. Dodsley, 1759), part 2, secs. 1, 2; part 3, sec. 26.

60. Immanuel Kant, *Observations on the Feeling of the Beautiful and Sublime* (1761), trans. John T. Goldthwait (Berkeley and Los Angeles: University of California Press, 1960), sec. 2.

CHAPTER 5

1. Hugh Talmage Lefler and Albert Ray Newsome, *North Carolina: The History of a Southern State* (Chapel Hill: University of North Carolina Press, 1954), 4, 5; Thomas Morton, *New English Canaan*, in *Tracts and Other Papers Relating Principally to the Origin, Settlement, and Progress of the Colonies in North America, from the Discovery of the Country to the Year 1776*, 2 vols., ed. Peter Force (Washington, D.C.: Peter Force, 1836–38), 2: 36–37.

2. Thomas Harriot, *A Briefe and True Report of the New Found Land of Virginia, The Complete 1590 Theodor de Bry Edition*, with a new introduction by Paul Hulton (New York: Dover, 1972), 41.

3. Mark Stoll, *Protestantism, Capitalism, and Nature in America* (Albuquerque: University of New Mexico Press, 1997), 56.

4. World Resources Institute, *World Resources, 1998–99* (New York: Oxford University Press, 1998), 293–95; Michael Williams, "Forests," in B. L. Turner II, William C. Clark, Robert W. Kates, John F. Richards, Jessica T. Matthews, and William B. Meyer, eds., *The Earth as Transformed by Human Action: Global and Regional Changes in the Biosphere over the Past Three Hundred Years* (New York: Cambridge University Press, 1980), 179–201; Charles F. Carroll, *The Timber Economy of Puritan New England* (Providence, R.I.: Brown University Press, 1973), 33–37, 123–27.

5. John Winthrop, *Winthrop's Conclusions for the Plantation in New England (1629), Old South Leaflets*, vol. 50 (Boston: Directors of the Old South Work, 1897), 4–5.

6. William Bradford, *Of Plimoth Plantation* (Boston: Wright and Potter, 1901), 95.

7. Vladimir Propp, "Morphology of the Folktale," *International Journal of American Linguistics* 24, no. 4 (1958): 1–114, esp. 46–48; Roland Barthes, "The Struggle with the Angel," in Stephen Heath trans. *Image, Music, Text* (New York: Noonday Press, 1977), 139–41.

8. John Cotton, quoted in Peter N. Carroll, *Puritanism and the Wilderness, 1629–1700* (New York: Columbia University Press, 1969), 13–14.

9. Bradford, *Of Plimoth Plantation*, 95.

10. Morton, *New English Canaan*, 2: 1–152.

11. Thomas Hooker, *Application of Redemption—The Ninth and Tenth Books*, 2 d ed. (Cornhil, England; Peter Cole, 1659), book 9; Roger Williams, quoted in Peter Fritzell, "The Wilderness and the Garden: Metaphors for the American Landscape," *Forest History* 12, no. 1 (1968): 16–23, on 22. Peter Bulkeley, *The Gospel Covenant: Or the Covenant of Grace Opened* (London: Benjamin Allen, 1646), 143. In the eighteenth century, Boston pastor Charles Morton followed both the Genesis origin story and the Baconian ideal when he wrote in 1728 that because of the sin of the first parents, agriculture and husbandry must be used to combat weeds and soil sterility through fencing, tilling, manuring, and draining the land. Almanac maker Nathaniel Ames, in 1754, informed his readers that the divine artificer initially had made the body of man "a machine capable of endless duration," but that after Eve's ingestion of the forbidden apple, the living principle within had fallen into disharmony with the body, disrupting the smooth functioning of its parts. See Charles Morton, *Compendium Physicae, from the 1697 Manuscript Copy*, vol. 33 (Boston: Colonial Society of Massachusetts Publications, 1940), xi, xxix, xxxi; Nathaniel Ames, *Astronomical Diary or Almanac* (Boston: J. Draper, 1758), endpapers.

12. Robert Beverley, *The History and Present State of Virginia* (London: R. Parker, 1705), 246–48.

13. Charles Sellers, *The Market Revolution: Jacksonian America, 1815–1846* (New York: Oxford University Press, 1991), 1–40, 57–59, 72–76.

14. Carolyn Merchant, *Ecological Revolutions: Nature, Gender, and Science in New England* (Chapel Hill: University of North Carolina Press, 1989), 149–97.

15. Sellers, *Market Revolution*, 35–36, 114–17.

16. David W. Noble, *The Eternal Adam and the New World Garden: The Central Myth in the American Novel since 1830* (New York: George Braziller, 1968), 3–24.

17. Ibid., 4.

18. George Bancroft, *History of the United States* (Boston: Little, Brown, 1840), cited in Noble, *The Eternal Adam*, 7.

19. Annette Kolodny, *The Lay of the Land: Metaphor As Experience and History in American Life and Letters* (Chapel Hill: University of North Carolina Press, 1975), 78, 79.

20. George Rogers Taylor, *The Transportation Revolution, 1815–1860* (New York: Reinhart, 1951); Alfred D. Chandler, "Anthracite Coal and the Beginnings of the Industrial Revolution in the United States," *Business History Review* 46, no. 2 (1972): 141–81.

21. Calvin Colton, "Labor and Capital," in *The Junius Tracts* (New York: Greeley and McElrath, 1844), no. 7.

22. Ralph Waldo Emerson, "The Young American," *The Dial* 4, (1844): 484–507; quotations on 489, 491.

23. Leo Marx, *The Machine in the Garden: Technology and the Pastoral Ideal in America* (New York: Oxford University Press, 1964).

24. John James Audubon, *Delineations of American Scenery and Character (1808–1834)* (New York: G. A. Baker, 1926), 4, cited in Kolodny, *The Lay of the Land*, 76.

25. Noble, *The Eternal Adam*, 16–17; Kolodny, *The Lay of the Land*, 92, 102; James Fenimore Cooper, *The Pioneers* (1823), vol. 4 of *The Works of James Fenimore Cooper* (London: George Routledge and Sons, 1895), 247–56, quotation on 256.

26. Matthew Baigell, *Thomas Cole* (New York: Watson Guptill, 1981), plates 7, 16; William Cronon, "Telling Tales on Canvas," in *Discovered Lands, Invented Pasts*, Jules David Prown, Nancy K. Anderson, William Cronon, Brian W. Dippie, Martha Sandweiss, Susan Prendergast Schoelwer, and Howard R. Lamar (New Haven, Conn.: Yale University Press, 1992), 37–87.

27. Henry Adams, "The American Land Inspired Cole's Prescient Visions," *Smithsonian* 25, no. 2 (1994): 99–107; Baigell, *Thomas Cole*, plates 10, 15.

28. Herman Melville, "The Encantadas, or 'Enchanted Isles,'" in *Herman Melville*, ed. R. W. B. Lewis (New York: 1962), 123, 127, 130–4, cited in Donald Worster, *Nature's Economy: A History of Ecological Ideas*, 2d ed. (New York: Cambridge University Press, 1995), 121; Noble, *The Eternal Adam*, 35, 46–7, and quotation from Melville on 42.

29. Thomas Huxley, "Prolegomena (1894)," in *Evolution and Ethics* (London: 1947), 38–44, cited in Worster, *Nature's Economy*, 179. Worster notes that the Victorians "were at least as intent on carrying the crusade against nature to the actual physical surface of the earth, on making the land over to serve as a kind of visible, external evidence of their accession to grace" (178).

30. John Quincy Adams, *Congressional Globe*, 1846, 339–42; Thomas Hart Benton, *Congressional Globe*, 1846, 917–18; Isaiah, 35:1: "And the desert shall rejoice and blossom as the rose."

31. Isaiah, 35:1: "And the desert shall rejoice and blossom as as the rose." Isaiah, 40:3: "Prepare ye the way of the Lord, make straight in the desert a highway for our God. 40:4: "Every Valley shall be exalted, and every mountain and hill shall be made low: and the crooked shall be made straight, and the rough places plain." Reverend Dwinell, quoted in John Todd, *The Sunset Land, or the Great Pacific Slope* (Boston: Lee and Shepard, 1870), 252; Henry Nash Smith, *Virgin Land: The American West As Symbol and Myth* (Cambridge, Mass.: Harvard University Press, 1950); Marx, *The Machine in the Garden*.

32. Frederick Jackson Turner, "The Significance of the Frontier in American History," *Annual Report of the American Historical Association for the Year 1893*, American Historical Association, 1894), 199–227.

33. Todd, *Sunset Land*, 146; G.J. Barker-Benfield, "The Spermatic Economy," *Feminist Studies*, 1, no. 1 (1972): 45–72.

34. Todd, *Sunset Land*, 125, 159, 160; Barker-Benfield, "Spermatic Economy," 51, 52.

35. Todd, *Sunset Land*, 233; Francis Bacon, "The Great Instauration," *Works*, ed. James Spedding, Robert Leslie Ellis, and Douglas Devon Heath, 14 vols. (London: Longmans Green, 1870), 4: 29; Bacon, "Novum Organum" part 2, *Works*, 4: 247. Todd, *Sunset Land*, 251.

36. Todd, *Sunset Land*, 124, 133, 219.

37. Richard White, *The Organic Machine: The Remaking of the Columbia River* (New York: Hill and Wang, 1995), 111–12.

38. Brigham Young and George A. Smith, quoted in Richard V. Francaviglia, *The Mormon Landscape: Existence, Perception, and Creation of a Unique Image in the American West* (New York: AMS Press, 1978), 84, 85. I thank Sarah Trainor for this reference.

39. Mark Fiege, *Irrigated Eden: The Making of an Agricultural Landscape in the American West* (Seattle: University of Washington Press, 1999), 11–19, 49–51, and quotation on 46.

40. Fiege, *Irrigated Eden*, 51, 208; Donald Worster, *Rivers of Empire: Water, Aridity, and the Growth of the American West* (New York: Pantheon, 1985), 308.

41. George Freeman, "Among the Irrigators of Fresno," *Overland Monthly* 9 (1887): 621–27, quotation on 622; John Bennett, "The District Irrigation Movement in California," *Overland Monthly* 29 (1897): 252–57, quotation on 257; *Visalia Delta*, quoted in Worster, *Rivers of Empire*, 104; November 8, 1898; *Los Angeles Times*, August 10, 1905; Worster, *Rivers of Empire*, 308.

42. Worster, *Rivers of Empire*, 324–35.

43. Max Horkheimer, *The Eclipse of Reason* (New York: Oxford University Press, 1947), 109ff.

CHAPTER 6

1. Martin Lunenfeld, *1492: Discovery, Invasion, Encounter* (Lexington, Mass.: D. C. Heath, 1991), 118–19.

2. Lunenfeld, *1492: Discovery, Invasion, Encounter*, 119–21. Europa, dressed in flowing robes and wearing a crown, stares boldly out into the distance. She holds a scepter in her right hand

and reaches down to grasp the cross of Christianity mounted on a spherical orb depicting the world, which she dominates by her power and knowledge. On either side are globes representing knowledge of the celestial and terrestrial spheres, while behind her is a grape arbor and beneath her a frieze of bulls heads symbolizing knowledge of agriculture and husbandry. Asia, partially draped in flowing silk and jeweled headdress and glancing downward, holds a burning urn of spices and incense, while Africa, bare-breasted, wearing only a partial cloth and head scarf and looking sideways, holds a fruited branch.

3. José Rabasa, "Allegories of Atlas," in *The Post-Colonial Studies Reader*, ed. Bill Ashcroft, Gareth Griffiths, and Helen Tiffin (London: Routledge, 1995), 358–64, quotations on 358; Gerhard Mercator, *Atlas; or A Geographicke Description of the World*, (1636), introd. by R. A. Skelton (Amsterdam: Theatrum Orbis Terrarum, 1968), 39–40. Mercator's *Atlas* codified the masculine/feminine oppositions introduced by earlier mapmakers. In his preface, he wrote that the Atlas would "set before your eyes, the whole world" as "in a mirror." Further, "This work then is composed of Geographie (which is a description of the knowne Earth and parts thereof) and Historie, which is (*Oculus Mundi*) the eye of the World." His world map depicted, on a flat surface, spherical projections of the Old World on the right and the New World on the left. In the four corners of the map, outside the circles containing the continents were four men who had set the bounds of the known world: Julius Caesar, Claudius Ptolemais, Gerardus Mercator, and Iudocus Hondius (co-author of the *Atlas*). Next to each, along the border toward the center, were allegorical depictions of the four elements—fire and air on the top; water and earth on the bottom. In the top center appeared the celestial globe, while in the bottom center was the now familiar picture of the four female continents. Europe appeared in the center, fully clothed and crowned, holding a book and scepter, representing knowledge and power over the rest of the world. At her feet presenting her with gifts were Asia on the left offering jewels, while America and Africa, partially clothed appeared on the right.

4. Mercator, *Atlas*, 40.

5. Annette Kolodny, *The Lay of the Land: Metaphor As Experience and History in American Life and Letters* (Chapel Hill: University of North Carolina Press, 1975), 10–12; John Smith, "A Description of New England," in *Tracts and Other Papers Relating Principally to the Origin, Settlement, and Progress of the Colonies in North America, from the Discovery of the Country to the Year 1776*, 2 vols., ed. Peter Force (Washington, D.C.: Peter Force, 1836–38), 2: 9; Thomas Morton, *New English Canaan*, in Force, ed., *Tracts and Other Papers*, 2: 10.

6. Kolodny, *The Lay of the Land*, 14–17, quotations on 14, 17; George Alsop, "Character of the Province of Maryland," in *Narratives of Early Maryland, 1633–1684*, ed. Clayton Colman Hall (New York: Charles Scribner's Sons, 1910), quotations on 343–44; Robert Beverley, *History and Present State of Virginia* (London: R. Parker, 1705), 296–99.

7. Henry Nash Smith, *Virgin Land: The American West As Symbol and Myth* (Cambridge, Mass.: Harvard University Press, 1950), viii; Kolodny, *The Lay of the Land*, preface.

8. Henry Colman, *Address before the Hampshire, Franklin, and Hampden Agricultural Society Delivered in Greenfield, Oct. 23, 1833* (Greenfield, Mass.: Phelps and Ingersoll, 1833), 5–6, 15, 27.

9. Frank Norris, *The Octopus, A Story of California* (1901; reprint New York: Penguin, 1986), 127. I thank David Igler for bringing these passages to my attention.

10. Norris, *Octopus*, 127, 130–31.

11. John Salkin and Laurie Gordon, *Orange Crate Art: The Story of the Labels That Launched a Golden Era* (New York: Warner Books, 1976), 20ff. La Paloma used a seductive Mexican woman set within a cactus-covered desert made fruitful, while Orange Queen displayed a Mexican maiden holding a basketful of oranges in front of a round, ripened orange.

12. Ibid., 20ff. Rainbow oranges, grown and packed by J. J. McIndoo of Tulare County, depicted a rainbow arching over fruit-laden orange groves with snow-covered Sierras in the background and sliced oranges and orange blossoms in the foreground.

13. Mark Fiege, *Irrigated Eden: The Making of an Agricultural Landscape in the American West* (Seattle: University of Washington Press, 1999), 2, jacket illustration, and fig. 19. Mary Hallock Foote painted *The Irrigating Ditch* in 1889, showing a woman holding a young child looking tranquilly over an irrigation channel, while a man in the background labored in the fields planting crops on the land.

14. K. D. Kurutz and Gary F. Kurutz, *California Calls You: The Art of Promoting the Golden State, 1870 to 1940* (Sausalito, Calif.: Windgate Press, 2000), 25, 27, 29, 35. The Michigan Central Railroad advertised trips to California via "the Niagara Falls Route," with a brochure showing a Mexican-style hacienda set in an Edenic landscape of fruit trees and mountains, while the Santa Fe Railroad depicted a train emerging out of snow-covered mountains into arbors of orange laden trees dripping with fruit.

15. Eustace M. W. Tillyard, *The Elizabethan World Picture* (New York: Vintage, 1959), 42.

16. On landscape paintings as narrative moments, see William Cronon, "Telling Tales on Canvas: Landscapes of Frontier Change," in *Discovered Lands, Invented Pasts*, Jules David Prown, Nancy K. Anderson, William Cronon, Brian W. Dippie, Martha Sandweiss, Susan Prendergast Schoelwer, and Howard R. Lamar (New Haven, Conn.: Yale University Press, 1992), 37–87.

17. For representations and interpretations of the three paintings discussed below see, William H. Truettner, ed. *The West as America: Reinterpreting Images of the Frontier, 1820–1920* (Washington, D.C.: National Museum of Art, 1991), 120, 135, 136, 137.

18. Frank Norris, *The Pit, A Story of Chicago* (1903; reprint New York: Grove Press, 1956).

19. William Cronon, *Nature's Metropolis: Chicago and the Great West* (New York: W. W. Norton, 1991). Cronon quotes the passage here from Norris's *The Pit* on the page preceding his "Prologue."

20. Norris, *The Pit*, 62.

21. Ibid., 60–63.

22. On Karl Marx's concept of the endowment of money with organic, living properties and its application among the Indians of the Cauca valley in Colombia, see Michael Taussig, "The Genesis of Capitalism amongst a South American Peasantry: Devil's Labor and the Baptism of Money," *Comparative Studies in Society and History* 19 (1977): 130–53.

23. Norris, *The Pit*, 374.

24. Donald Worster, *Nature's Economy: A History of Ecological Ideas*, 2d ed. (New York: Cambridge University Press, 1995); Carolyn Merchant, *The Death of Nature: Women, Ecology, and the Scientific Revolution* (San Francisco: Harper Collins (1980), ch. 1. The following is drawn from Carolyn Merchant, *Ecological Revolutions: Nature, Gender, and Science in New England* (Chapel Hill: University of North Carolina Press, 1989), 254–57.

25. Worster, *Nature's Economy*; Roderick Nash, *Wilderness and the American Mind*, 3d ed. (New Haven, Conn.: Yale University Press, 1982), 85, 122–25.

26. George Economou, *The Goddess Natura in Medieval Literature* (Cambridge, Mass.: Harvard University Press, 1972); Carolyn Merchant, *The Death of Nature*, 10.

27. Henry David Thoreau, "Thursday" in *A Week on the Concord and Merrimac Rivers* in Carl Bode, ed., *The Portable Thoreau* (New York: Penguin, 1977), 196. John Muir, *The Mountains of California* (Berkeley: Ten Speed Press, 1977), 336.

28. Henri Frankfort, H. A. Frankfort, John A. Wilson, Thorkild Jacobsen, and William A. Irwin, *Before Philosophy: The Intellectual Adventure of Ancient Man* (Baltimore: Penguin, 1949); Calvin Martin, *Keepers of the Game: Indian Animal Relationships and the Fur Trade* (Berkeley and Los Angeles: University of California Press, 1978); William Christie MacLeod, "Conservation among Primitive Hunting Peoples," *Scientific Monthly* 43 (1936): 562–66.

29. Thoreau, "Concord River" in *A Week on the Concord and Merrimac Rivers* in Bode, ed., *Portable Thoreau*, 145; "Thursday," 197; "Friday," 222.

30. Nash, *Wilderness and the American Mind*, ch. 3, 4; Leo Marx, *The Machine in the Garden: Technology and the Pastoral Ideal in America* (New York: Oxford University Press, 1964); Annette

Kolodny, *The Lay of the Land*; Annette Kolodny, "Honing a Habitable Landscape: Women's Images for the New World Frontiers," in *Women and Language in Literature and Society*, ed. Sally McConnell-Ginet, Ruth Borker, and Nelly Furman (New York: Praeger, 1980), 188–204.

31. Thoreau, "A Winter Walk," in Bode, ed. *Portable Thoreau*, 67; "The Maine Woods," 100; "Walking," 621; Muir, *Mountains of California*, 362.

32. Thoreau, "Friday," in *A Week on the Concord and Merrimac Rivers* in Bode, ed., *Portable Thoreau*, 222; "Walking," 590; "A Winter Walk," 60; John Muir, *Our National Parks* (Boston: Houghton Mifflin, 1901), 2.

33. Thoreau, "Friday," in *A Week on the Concord and Merrimac Rivers* in Bode, ed., *Portable Thoreau*, 221. Muir, *Mountains of California*, 84; ed., *Portable Thoreau*, 149; Thoreau, "Saturday," in *A Week on the Concord and Merrimac Rivers* in Bode, "Life Without Principle," 633.

34. Bode, ed., *Portable Thoreau*, 151, 158; Emerson quoted in Nash, *Wilderness and the American Mind*, 126.

35. Thoreau, "Thursday," in *A Week on the Concord and Merrimac Rivers* (1849) in Bode, ed., *Portable Thoreau*, 193–94; Thoreau, "Walking," in Bode, ed., *Portable Thoreau*, 621; Muir, *Mountains of California*, 84–85, 246.

36. Ibid., 361.

37. Thoreau, "The Beanfield," in *Walden* (Boston: Ticknor and Fields, 1854), 168–71.

38. Walter M. Kendrick, "Earth of Flesh, Flesh of Earth: Mother Earth in the Faerie Queen," *Renaissance Quarterly* 27 (1974): 548–53; George Perkins Marsh, *Man and Nature* (Cambridge, Mass.: Belknap Press, 1965 [1864]), 36.

39. Marsh, *Man and Nature*, 35–36, 38.

40. Bernhard Fernow, *Economics of Forestry* (New York: Thomas Y. Crowell, 1902), 2, 17.

41. Gifford Pinchot, *Breaking New Ground* (Washington, D.C.: Island Press, 1947), quotations on 323, 326.

42. Theodore Roosevelt, "Opening Address by the President," in *Proceedings of a Conference of Governors in the White House, May 13–15, 1908*, ed. Newton C. Blanchard (Washington, D. C.: Government Printing Office, 1908), 6.

43. Theodore Roosevelt, *Wilderness Writings*, ed. Paul Schullery (Salt Lake City: Peregrine Smith Books, 1986), 11–27.

44. Cardinal James Gibbons, "Greetings," in *Proceedings of the Second National Conservation Congress at Saint Paul, September 5–8, 1910* (Washington, D.C.: National Conservation Congress, 1911), 3.

45. Mrs. Mathew Scott, "Address," in *Proceedings of the Fourth National Conservation Congress, Indianapolis, October 14, 1912* (Indianapolis: National Conservation Congress: 1912), 250–51.

46. Carolyn Merchant, "Women of the Progressive Conservation Movement, 1900–1916," *Environmental Review* 8, no. 1 (1984): 57–85.

47. Ibid., Vera Norwood, *Made from this Earth: American Women and Nature* (Chapel Hill: University of North Carolina Press, 1993); Polly Welts Kauffman, *National Parks and the Woman's Voice: A History* (Albuquerque: University of New Mexico Press, 1996); Jennifer Price, *Flight Maps: Adventures with Nature in Modern America* (New York: Basic Books, 1999); Glenda Riley, *Women and Nature: Saving the "Wild" West* (Lincoln: University of Nebraska Press, 1999); Isabella Bird, *A Lady's Life in the Rocky Mountains* (Norman: University of Oklahoma Press, 1960; originally published serially in *Leisure Hour*, 1878); Mary Austin, *The Land of Little Rain* (1903; reprint Boston: Houghton Mifflin, 1950); Olive Thorne Miller, *Bird Ways* (Boston: Houghton Mifflin, 1885); Mabel Osgood Wright, *Birdcraft: A Field Book of Two Hundred Song, Game, and Water Birds* (New York: Macmillan, 1895); Sarah Orne Jewett, *A White Heron: A Story of Maine* (New York: Crowell, 1963); Florence Merriam Bailey, *A-Birding on a Bronco* (Boston: Houghton Mifflin, 1896).

48. Mark Stoll, *Protestantism, Capitalism, and Nature in America* (Albuquerque: University of New Mexico Press, 1997), 166–68.

49. J. Horace McFarland, *Proceedings of a Conference of Governors in the White House, Washington, D.C., May 13–15, 1908* (Washington D.C.: Government Printing Office, 1909), 140. See also Augustus Gardner, *Our Children* (Hartford, Conn.: Belknap and Bliss, 1872), 36, on "the mountains and forests of the west" as "vast reservoirs of health and strength" from which "we may annually recruit our exhausted energies at every fresh contact with our worthy mother earth."

50. Roderick Nash, *Wilderness and the American Mind*, 3d ed. (New Haven, Conn.: Yale University Press), 141–42.

51. Paul Santmire, "Historical Dimensions of the American Crisis," in *Western Man and Environmental Ethics*, ed. Ian G. Barbour (Reading, Mass.: Addison-Wesley, 1973), 82–85.

CHAPTER 7

1. Roland Nelson, Penobscot, as recorded by Frank Speck, "Penobscot Tales and Religious Beliefs," *Journal of American Folklore* 48, no. 187 (1935): 1–107, quotation on 75. This corn mother origin story is a variant on a number of eastern United States and Canadian transformative accounts, recorded from oral traditions, that attribute the origins of corn to a mythical corn mother who produces corn from her body, grows old, and then instructs her lover or son how to plant and tend corn. The killing of the corn mother in most of the origin stories may symbolize a transition from gathering/hunting to active corn cultivation. The snake lover may be an influence from the Christian tradition or a more universal symbol of the renewal of life (snakes shed their skins) and/or the male sexual organ. On corn mother origin stories, see John Witthoft, *Green Corn Ceremonialism in the Eastern Woodlands* (Ann Arbor: University of Michigan Press, 1949), 77–85; Joe Nicholas, Malechite, Tobique Point, Canada, August 1910, as recorded by W. H. Mechling, *Malechite Tales* (Ottawa: Government Printing Bureau, 1914), 87–88; for the Passamaquoddy variant, see Mrs. W. Wallace Brown, "The Legend of Indian Corn," *Journal of American Folklore* 3 (1890): 214; for Creek and Natchez variants, see J. R. Swanton, "Myths and Tales of the Southeastern Indians," *Bulletin of the Bureau of American Ethnology* 88 (1929) 9–17; on Iroquois variants, see Jesse Cornplanter, *Legends of the Longhouse* (Philadelphia: J. B. Lippincott, 1938), and Arthur Parker, "Iroquois Use of Maize and Other Food Plants," *New York State Museum Bulletin* no. 144 (1910): 36–39; and "The Corn Mother in America and Indonesia," *Anthropos* 46 (1951): 853–914. Examples of corn mother origin stories from the Southwest include the Pueblo emergence from the dark interior of the earth into the light of the fourth world where corn mother plants Thought Woman's gift of corn. See Ramón Gutiérrez, *When Jesus Came the Corn Mothers Went Away* (Stanford, Calif.: Stanford University Press, 1991). For a discussion of the relationship of the corn mother to Mother Earth, see Sam Gill, *Mother Earth: An American Story* (Chicago: University of Chicago Press, 1987), 4, 125.

2. On Great Plains environmental histories as progressive and declensionist plots, see William Cronon, "A Place for Stories: Nature, History, and Narrative," *Journal of American History* 78, no. 4 (1992): 1347–76. The Indian and European origin stories can be interpreted from a variety of standpoints other than the declensionist and progressive narrative formats I have emphasized here (such as romance and satire). Additionally, the concepts of desert, wilderness, and garden are nuanced and elaborate motifs that change valences over time.

3. Genesis 1, J. Baird Callicott, "Genesis Revisited: Murian Musings on the Lynn White, Jr. Debate," *Environmental Review*, 14, nos. 1–2 (1990): 65–92.

4. Benjamin Franklin, "Remarks Concerning the Savages of North America," in *Franklin's Wit and Folly: The Bagatelles*, ed. Richard E. Amacher (New Brunswick, N.J.: Rutgers University Press, 1953), 89–98. Franklin's story is probably satirical rather than literal.

5. Francis Paul Prucha, *The Indians in American Society: From the Revolutionary War to the Present* (Berkeley and Los Angeles: University of California Press, 1985), 6–8, quotation on 7.

6. Ibid., 7.

7. Ibid., 12, 15.

8. George P. Belden, *Belden, the White Chief; or Twelve Years among the Wild Indians of the Plains* (Cincinnati: C. F. Vent, 1870), 92, 166, 438, cited in Mark David Spence, *Dispossessing the Wilderness: Indian Removal and the Making of the National Parks* (New York: Oxford University Press, 1999), 38.

9. Samuel Bowles, *The Switzerland of America* (Hartford, Conn.: Hartford Publishing, 1869), 145–47, cited in Spence, *Dispossessing the Wilderness*, 27.

10. Prucha, *Indians in America*, 18–22, quotations on 20 and 22.

11. Ibid., 23.

12. Ibid., 53.

13. Chief Luther Standing Bear, *Land of the Spotted Eagle* (Boston: Houghton Mifflin, 1933), xix.

14. Neal Salisbury, "Red Puritans: The 'Praying Indians' of Massachusetts Bay and John Eliot," *William and Mary Quarterly*, 3d sec., 31, no. 1 (1974): 27–54; William Simmons, "Conversion from Indian to Puritan," *New England Quarterly* 52, no. 2 (1979): 197–218.

15. Franklin, "Remarks concerning the Savages of North America," 91.

16. J. Baird Callicott, "The Wilderness Idea Revisited: The Sustainable Development Alternative," *Environmental Professional* 13 (1991): 236–45.

17. William Bradford, *Of Plimoth Plantation* (Boston: Wright and Potter, 1901), 94–95; George Catlin, *North American Indians*, 2 vols. (1844; reprint Philadelphia: Leary, Stuart, 1913); 1:294–95.

18. Spence, *Dispossessing the Wilderness*, 55–70; Robert H. Keller and Michael F. Turek, *American Indians and National Parks* (Tucson: University of Arizona Press, 1998), 22–25. On Indians and tourism in the National Parks, see also Philip Burnham, *Indian Country, God's Country: Native Americans and the National Parks* (Washington, D.C.: Island Press, 2000); on hunting and poaching in Yellowstone, see Karl Jacoby, *Crimes against Nature: Squatters, Poachers, Thieves, and the Hidden History of American Conservation* (Berkeley and Los Angeles: University of California Press, 2001), 81–146.

19. Spence, *Dispossessing the Wilderness*, 71–100, quotations on 78, 87; Keller and Turek, *American Indians and National Parks*, 43–64.

20. Rebecca Solnit, "Up the River of Mercy," *Sierra* , 77, no. 6 (1992): 50–57, 78–84; John Muir, *My First Summer in the Sierra* (New York: Penguin, 1987 [1911]), 58, 226; Spence, "Dispossessing the Wilderness," 101–32, Harris quotation on 109; Keller and Turek, *American Indians and National Parks*, 20–22.

21. Mary Austin, *The Land of Little Rain* (1903; reprint Boston: Houghton Mifflin, 1950) 1, 33, 63. On Austin's view of Indians and the desert see Vera Norwood, "Heroines of Nature: Four Women Respond to the American Landscape," *Environmental Review*, 8, no. 1 (1984): 34–56, esp. 41–44. Another environmentalist sympathetic to Indians was John Wesley Powell, director of the Bureau of Ethnology and author of the *Report on the Lands of the Arid Region of the United States*, ed. Wallace Stegner (Cambridge, Mass.: Harvard University Press, 1962 [1878]).

22. Winthrop Jordan, *White over Black: American Attitudes toward the Negro, 1550–1812* (1968; reprint New York: W. W. Norton, 1977), 23–28.

23. Ibid., 524–25, esp. n. 22.

24. Donald Worster, *The Wealth of Nature: Environmental History and the Ecological Imagination* (New York: Oxford University Press, 1993), 9–10.

25. Edie Yuen, Lisa J. Bunin, and Tim Stroshane, "Multicultural Ecology: An Interview with Carl Anthony," *Capitalism, Nature, Socialism* 8, no. 3 (1997): 41–62, esp. 49.

26. Thomas Jefferson, *Notes on the State of Virginia* (London: J. Stockdale, 1787), quotations from queries 19: 276–77 and 14: 229–34.

27. Robert Bullard, "Environmental Racism and the Environmental Justice Movement," in

Bullard, ed., *Confronting Environmental Racism: Voices from the Grassroots* (Boston: South End Press, 1993), 15–16.

28. Henry David Thoreau, *Walden and Civil Disobedience* with an introduction by Michael Meyer (New York: Penguin, 1983), introduction, 29–36, quotations from "Walden" on 216, from "Civil Disobedience," on 389, 390, 391. On Thoreau's concept of community see Roderick Nash, *The Rights of Nature: A History of Environmental Ethics* (Madison: University of Wisconsin Press, 1989), 37. On Thoreau as an opponent of slavery, see Patricia Nelson Limerick, "Hoping against History," in *Justice and Natural Resources: Concepts, Strategies, and Applications*, ed. Kathryn M. Mutz, Gary C. Bryner, and Douglas S. Kenny (Washington, D.C.: Island Press, 2002), 343.

29. Thomas W. Hanchett, *Sorting out the New South City: Race, Class, and Urban Development in Charlotte, 1875–1975* (Chapel Hill: University of North Carolina Press, 1998), 116–44; Robert Woods, ed., *The City Wilderness: A Settlement Study* (Boston: Houghton Mifflin, 1898), 1–2; Booth Tarkington, *The Turmoil, a Novel* (New York: Harper and Brothers, 1915), 1–5.

30. Jeffrey Romm, "The Coincidental Order of Environmental Injustice," in Mutz, Bryner, and Kenny, eds., *Justice and Natural Resources*, 117–38, quotations on 122–23.

31. Yuen, Bunin, and Stroshane, "Interview with Carl Anthony," 50; Nash, *The Rights of Nature*, 38–39; Stephen Fox, *John Muir and His Legacy: The American Conservation Movement* (Boston: Little, Brown, 1981), 41–43, quotations on 42; John Muir, *A Thousand-Mile Walk to the Gulf* (San Francisco: Sierra Club Books, 1991), quotation on xvi.

32. Muir, *Thousand Mile Walk*, 25.

33. Ibid., 25, 31.

34. Ibid., 30, 60.

35. Zora Neale Hurston, *Their Eyes Were Watching God* (1937; reprint New York: Harper Collins, 1990), 129, 130.

36. Ibid., 25, 161–62, 169.

37. Patricia Nelson Limerick, "Hoping against History," 340–42; Aldo Leopold, "The Land Ethic," in *A Sand County Almanac* (New York: Oxford University Press, 1949), 204.

38. Nash, *The Rights of Nature*, 6–7, 200–213, quotations on 202, 203; Leopold, "The Land Ethic," in 202. Nash points out that "slavery in the United States was not negotiated away. For similar reasons it might be unreasonable to expect that what Aldo Leopold was the first to call 'the enslavement of . . . earth' could be abolished without profound social disruption"; Nash, *The Rights of Nature*, 8. The legacy of slavery as extended to the earth led Leopold to an ethic of cooperation among people and between people and nature. In his "Conservation Ethic" of 1933, Leopold wrote, "Civilization is not . . . the enslavement of a stable and constant earth. It is a state of mutual and interdependent cooperation between human animals, other animals, plants, and soil, which may be disrupted at any moment by the failure of any of them"; see Leopold, "The Conservation Ethic," in *The River of the Mother of God and other Essays by Aldo Leopold*, ed. Susan L. Flader and J. Baird Callicott (Madison: University of Wisconsin Press, 1991), 183.

39. Limerick, "Hoping against History," 344–45.

40. Robert Bullard, *Dumping in Dixie: Race, Class, and Environmental Quality* (Boulder, Colo.: Westview Press, 1990).

41. Gayatri Chakravorty Spivak, "Can the Subaltern Speak?" in *Marxism and the Interpretation of Culture*, ed. Cary Nelson and Lawrence Grossberg (London: Macmillan, 1988), reprinted in *The Post-Colonial Studies Reader*, ed. Bill Ashcroft, Gareth Griffiths, and Helen Tiffin (New York: Routledge, 1995), 24–28.

42. Hawley Truax, "Minorities at Risk," *Environmental Action*, January/February (1990): 20–21; Charles Lee, "Toxic Wastes and Race in the United States: A National Report on the Racial and Socio-Economic Characteristics of Communities with Hazardous Waste Sites" (New York: United Church of Christ Commission for Racial Justice, 1987); Jesus Sanchez, "The Environment: Whose Movement?" *Green Letter* 5, no. 1 (1989): 3–4, 14–16; Philip

Shabecoff, "Environmental Groups Faulted for Racism," *San Francisco Chronicle*, Feb. 1, 1990; Robbin Lee Zeff, Marsha Love, and Karen Stults, *Empowering Ourselves: Women and Toxics Organizing* (Arlington, Va.: Citizen's Clearing House for Hazardous Wastes, n.d.); Andrew Szasz, *Ecopopulism: Toxic Waste and the Movement for Environmental Justice* (Minneapolis: University of Minnesota Press, 1994).

43. J. M. Blaut, *The Colonizer's Model of the World: Geographical Diffusionism and Eurocentric History* (New York: Guilford Press, 1993); see also Ashcroft, Griffith, and Tiffin, *The Post-Colonial Studies Reader*.

CHAPTER 8

1. Richard Keller Simon, "The Formal Garden in the Age of Consumer Culture: A Reading of the Twentieth-Century Shopping Mall," in *Mapping American Culture*, ed. Wayne Franklin and Michael Steiner (Iowa City: University of Iowa Press, 1992), 124–25, 231–50.

2. Margaret Crawford, "The World in a Shopping Mall," in *Variations on a Theme Park*, ed. Michael Sorkin (New York: Hill and Wang, 1992), 3–30.

3. David Guterson, "Enclosed, Encyclopedic, Endured: One Week at the Mall of America," in *A Forest of Voices: Reading and Writing the Environment*, ed. Chris Anderson and Lex Runciman (Mountain View, Calif.: Mayfield, 1995), 124–36; see esp. 126, 128, quotation on 126; Crawford, "The World in a Shopping Mall," 27; Simon, "The Formal Garden in the Age of Consumer Culture," 244.

4. Crawford, "The World in a Shopping Mall," 7; Simon, "The Formal Garden in the Age of Consumer Culture," 238; Guterson, "Enclosed, Encyclopedic, Endured," 132–34.

5. Guterson, "Enclosed, Encyclopedic, Endured," 133–34.

6. Ibid., 132.

7. Crawford, "The World in a Shopping Mall," 9, 28–30; Bruce Horovitz, "Malls are Like, Totally Uncool, Say Hip Teens," *USA Today*, May 1, 1996, 1–2.

8. Philip Elmer-Dewitt, "Fried Gene Tomatoes," *Time*, May 30, 1994, 54–55.

9. Francesca Lyman, "Are We Redesigning Nature in Our Own Image? An Interview with Jeremy Rifkin," *Environmental Action*, April 1983, 20–25; P. J. Regal, "Models of Genetically Engineered Organisms and their Ecological Impact," in *Ecology of Biological Invasions in North America and Hawaii*, ed. Harold Mooney (New York: Springer-Verlag, 1986); Marc Lappé, *Broken Code: The Exploitation of DNA* (San Francisco, Calif.: Sierra Club Books, 1984); Marc Lappé and Britt Bailey, *Against the Grain: Biotechnology and the Corporate Takeover of Your Food* (Monroe, Maine: Common Courage Press, 1998); Jon Beckwith, *Making Genes, Making Waves* (Cambridge, Mass.: Harvard University Press), 2002.

10. Robin Mather, *A Garden of Unearthly Delights: Bioengineering and the Future of Food* (New York: E. P. Dutton, 1995), 25–49; Elmer-Demitt, "Fried Gene Tomatoes," 54, 55.

11. Mather, *Garden of Unearthly Delights*, 27–30, 42; Herb Greenberg, "Calgene's Biotech Bounty Disappears From Grocers' Shelves," *San Francisco Chronicle*, Jan. 17, 1995, B1, B3.

12. Mather, *Garden of Unearthly Delights*, 31–33, 44–46.

13. Michael Pollan, "Genetic Pollution of Corn in Mexico," *New York Times*, Dec. 9, 2001.

14. Mather, *Garden of Unearthly Delights*, 84–94, quotations on 90, 91–92.

15. Ibid., 121–22.

16. Jane Kay, "Frankenfish Spawning Controversy," *San Francisco Chronicle*, April 29, 2002, A4.

17. Mather, *Garden of Unearthly Delights*, 35, 80, 131–33; Claude Gelé, "L'Agriculture manque de robots," *Sciences and Techniques* 26 (1986): 22–29 and cover illustration. Such technology, which delivers perfect fruit, pure milk, and lean meat to the supermarket, masks the labor of the field and processing plant. Much of that labor now comes from Mexico, legally or illegally, via the tomato, chicken, and pork trails. Men and women work on their feet all day grading, packing, and inspecting tomatoes. Men who inject cows, mix feed, and clean milking equipment often labor under bitterly cold or hot, humid conditions. Women who catch and

correct chickens missed by the eviscerating machinery work under cold, moist conditions that may cause illnesses leading to job loss. Yet for industry, the problems are offset by the advantages. (Mather, *Garden of Unearthly Delights*, 43–45. 80–82, 132–33.)

18. Roger Lewin, "In the Beginning was the Genome," *New Scientist* 21, no. 1726 (1990): 34–38; Tom Wilkie, *Perilous Knowledge: The Human Genome Project and Its Implications* (Berkeley and Los Angeles: University of California Press, 1993); Timothy F. Murphy and Marc C. Lappé, eds., *Justice and the Human Genome Project* (Berkeley and Los Angeles: University of California Press, 1994).

19. Lewin, "In the Beginning was the Genome," 34, 35, 38.

20. Jeremy Rifkin, *Algeny* (New York: Penguin, 1984); Jeremy Rifkin, *The Biotech Century: Harnessing the Gene and Remaking the World* (New York: Jeremy P. Tarcher.Putnam, 1998); Marc Lappé and Britt Bailey, eds., *Engineering the Farm: Ethical and Social Aspects of Agricultural Biotechnology* (Washington, D.C.: Island Press, 2002); Joseph S. Alper, Catherine Ard, Adrienne Asch, Peter Conrad, Lisa N. Geller, and Jon Beckwith, eds., *The Double-Edged Helix: Social Implications of Genetics in a Diverse Society* (Baltimore: Johns Hopkins University Press, 2002).

21. Charles Krauthammer, "A Special Report on Cloning," *Time*, March 10, 1997, 60–61, quotation on 60; J. Madeleine Nash, "The Age of Cloning," *Time*, March 10, 1997, 62–65; Sharon Begley, "Little Lamb Who Made Thee?" *Newsweek*, March 10, 1997, 53–57.

22. Nash, "The Age of Cloning," 64–65.

23. Krauthammer, "Special Report," 61; Tim O'Brien, illustration for Nash, "The Age of Cloning," 62–63; Nash, "The Age of Cloning," 65; Jeffrey Kluger, "Will We Follow the Sheep?" *Time*, March 10, 1997, 67–72; Robert Wright, "Can Souls be Xeroxed?" *Time*, March 10, 1997, 73.

24. Kenneth L. Woodward, "Today the Sheep, Tomorrow the Shepherd," *Newsweek*, March 10, 1997, 60; Kluger, "Will We Follow the Sheep?" 70–72.

25. James Shreeve, "Sunset on the Savanna," *Discover*, July, 1996, 116–24, esp. 117.

26. Misia Landau, *Narratives of Human Evolution* (New Haven, Conn.: Yale University Press, 1991), 1–12.

27. Shreeve, "Sunset on the Savanna," 118, 125.

28. Charles Darwin, *The Descent of Man and Selection in Relation to Sex*, 2 vols. (New York: D. Appleton, 1873), vol. 2, ch. 21, 372, 386.

29. Shreeve, "Sunset on the Savanna," 119, 121, 123.

30. Donna Haraway, *Primate Visions* (New York: Routledge, 1989), 27–29, quotations on 26, 29.

31. Haraway, *Primate Visions*, 26–27, 42; Henry Goldschmidt, "Rupture Tales: Stories and Politics in and around the Garden of Eden" (unpublished paper, University of California-Santa Cruz, 1994), 14–18.

32. Haraway, *Primate Visions*, 27.

33. On the innocence of nature and the role of conservation and eugenics in combating capitalist decadence, see Haraway, *Primate Visions*, 54–55.

34. David Perlman, "Gene Study Traces 'Adam' to Africa," *San Francisco Chronicle*, May 26, 1995, A1, A19; John Noble Wilford, "Studies Shed New Light on Father of All Men," *San Francisco Chronicle*, Nov. 23, 1995, A14; Svante Pääbo, *Science*, 268, no. 5214 (May 26, 1995): 1141–2.

35. Michael Pollan, "The Idea of a Garden," in *Second Nature: A Gardener's Education* (New York: Atlantic Monthly Press, 1991), 176–201, quotation on 177.

36. Ibid., quotations on 183, 184, 185, 188, 193; emphasis in the original.

37. Ibid., quotations on 191, 192, 193, 196. On women and gardens see Ann B. Shteir, *Cultivating Women, Cultivating Science: Flora's Daughters and Botany in England, 1760–1860* (Baltimore: Johns Hopkins University Press, 1996); Elizabeth Keeney, *The Botanizers: Amateur Scientists in Nineteenth Century America* (Chapel Hill: University of North Carolina Press, 1992); Londa Schiebinger, *Nature's Body: Gender in the Making of Modern Science* (Boston:

Beacon Press, 1993); Elizabeth Grey Wheelwright, *The Physick Garden: Medicinal Plants and their History* (Boston: Houghton Mifflin, 1935), Norwood, *Made From this Earth*.

38. Ibid., quotations on 189, 197.

39. Ibid., quotation on 199.

CHAPTER 9

1. Rachel Carson, *Silent Spring* (Boston: Houghton Mifflin, 1962), 1–9, quotation on 9.

2. Jeffrey L. Sheler, "The Christmas Covenant," *U.S. News and World Report*, Dec. 19, 1994: 62–71. New Age devotees offer another version of millennarianism. The year 2000 signifies the "dawning" of the age of Aquarius, a period of 2000 years following the age of Pisces, sign of the fish—symbol of Christ. Owing to the precession of the equinoxes (the motion against the background of stars of the point where the celestial equator and ecliptic intersect), the sun at the vernal equinox (March 20–21 of each year) by early in the twenty-first century will be in the zodiacal sign of Aquarius for approximately 2000 years. For some New Agers, a new plane of consciousness, universal peace, and cosmic awareness will be entered. The harmonic convergence, the celestine prophecy, mountaintop powerpoints, crystals, and star-born angels are all manifestations of the coming new level of human consciousness.

3. World Resources Institute, *World Resources, 1998–99* (New York: Oxford University Press, 1998), 244–45, 274–75.

4. Ibid., 293, 295.

5. Paul Ehrlich, *Ecocatastrophe* (San Francisco: City Lights Books, 1969); Donella H. Meadows, Dennis L. Meadows, Jørgen Randers, and William W. Behrens III, *The Limits to Growth* (New York: Signet, 1972); Bill McKibben, *The End of Nature* (New York: Random House, 1989).

6. World Resources Institute, *World Resources*, 170–86.

7. Max Horkheimer and Theodor Adorno, trans. John Cumming, *Dialectic of Enlightenment* (1944; reprint New York: Continuum, 1993), 3, 7, 9.

8. Max Oelschlaeger, *The Idea of Wilderness: From Prehistory to the Age of Ecology* (New Haven, Conn.: Yale University Press, 1991), 9.

9. Ibid., 61.

10. George Sessions, "Ecocentrism and the Anthropocentric Detour," *ReVision* 13, no. 3 (1991): 109–15, quotation on 109; George Sessions, ed., *Deep Ecology for the Twenty-first Century: Readings on the Philosophy and Practice of the New Environmentalism* (Boston: Shambala, 1995).

11. Murray Bookchin, *The Ecology of Freedom: The Emergency and Dissolution of Hierarchy* (Palo Alto, Calif.: Cheshire Books, 1982), 43. See also Joel Koval, "Negating Bookchin," in *Murray Bookchin: Nature's Prophet* (Santa Cruz, Calif.: Capitalism, Nature, Socialism/Center for Political Ecology, 1996), pamphlet 5, p. 8: "The emergence of domination and hierarchy and its dissolution in the ecological society is now a retelling of the legend of the Fall and Redemption, the master mythos of the Judeo-Christian tradition."

12. McKibben, *The End of Nature*, 49–61, quotation on 60.

13. Ibid., 8. On ecological decline, see also Edward F. Renshaw, *The End of Progress: Adjusting to a No-Growth Economy* (North Scituate, Mass.: Duxbury Press, 1976); Ehrlich, *Ecocatastrophe*; Meadows, et al., *Limits to Growth*.

14. Daniel Quinn, *Ishmael: An Adventure of the Mind and Spirit* (New York: Bantam, 1992), 37.

15. Ibid., 181, 222, 229, quotation on 222.

16. Ibid., 89, 147, 166–67, quotations on 89, 167.

17. Ibid., 245, 246, 253.

18. Gretchen C. Daily, Anne H. Ehrlich, and Paul R. Ehrlich, "Optimum Population Size," *ERG News* (Energy and Resources Group, University of California-Berkeley) 4, no. 2 (1994): 1–3.

19. Tadd Gastrin, unpublished comment, written for the Nature Transformed Institute, National Humanities Center, Durham, North Carolina, June 28, 1998.

20. Françoise d'Eaubonne, "The Time for Ecofeminism" (1974), trans. Ruth Hottell," in *Ecology*, ed. Carolyn Merchant (Atlantic Highlands, N.J.: Humanities Press, 1994), 174–97.

21. Merchant, ed., "Introduction," in *Ecology*, 10; d'Eaubonne, 177–78, quotations on 185, 186, 188.

22. Merchant, ed., "Introduction," in *Ecology*, 11; d'Eaubonne, quotations on 193, 194.

23. Chellis Glendinning, *My Name is Chellis and I'm in Recovery from Western Civilization*, (Boston: Shambala, 1994), 3–13, and quotations on 79, 81.

24. Ibid., 213.

25. Examples of feminist critiques include Gerda Lerner, *The Creation of Patriarchy* (New York: Oxford, 1986); Marija Gimbutas, *The Goddesses and Gods of Old Europe, 6500–3500 B.C.* (Berkeley and Los Angeles: University of California Press, 1982); Monica Shöö and Barbara Mor, *The Great Cosmic Mother: Rediscovering the Religion of the Earth* (San Francisco: Harper Collins, 1987); Merlin Stone, *When God Was a Woman* (New York: Harcourt Brace Jovanovich, 1976); Adrienne Rich, *Of Woman Born* (New York: W. W. Norton, 1976); Elizabeth Gould Davis, *The First Sex* (Baltimore: Penguin, 1972).

26. On the history of the question of male and female abilities in science, see Londa Schiebinger, *The Mind Has No Sex? Women in the Origins of Modern Science* (Cambridge, Mass.: Harvard University Press, 1989). On the philosophical and psychological dimensions of the sex/gender question in science see Evelyn Fox Keller, *Reflections on Gender and Science* (New Haven, Conn.: Yale University Press, 1985).

27. Linda J. Nicholson, "Introduction" to *Feminism/Postmodernism*, ed. Linda J. Nicholson (New York: Routldege, 1990), 2, 3.

28. Carolyn Merchant, "Partnership Ethics," in *Earthcare: Women and the Environment* (New York: Routledge, 1996), 209–24; Riane Eisler, *The Chalice and the Blade* (San Francisco: Harper Collins, 1988), xvii, 105, 185–203; Rosemary Radford Ruether, *Gaia and God: An Ecofeminist Theology of Earth Healing* (San Francisco: Harper Collins, 1992).

29. Jacques Derrida, *Of Grammatology*, trans. Gayatri Chakravorty Spivak (Baltimore: Johns Hopkins University Press, 1976).

30. Arran E. Gare, *Postmodernism and the Environmental Crisis* (New York: Routledge, 1995), 3, 139–41.

31. Ibid., 142–43, quotation on 143.

32. Ibid., quotation on 142.

33. Ibid., 152.

34. Ron Zimmerman, unpublished comment, written for the Nature Transformed Institute, National Humanities Center, Durham, North Carolina, June 28, 1998.

CHAPTER 10

Portions of this chapter appeared previously in Carolyn Merchant, *Radical Ecology: The Search for a Livable World* (New York: Routledge, 1992), 93–99.

1. Stuart Kauffman, *At Home in the Universe: The Search for the Laws of Self-Organization and Complexity* (New York: Oxford University Press, 1995), 9–16, quotation on 10.

2. Kauffman, *At Home in the Universe*, 1.

3. Carolyn Merchant, *The Death of Nature: Women, Ecology, and the Scientific Revolution* (San Francisco: Harper Collins, 1980).

4. Kauffman, *At Home in the Universe*; M. Mitchell Waldrop, *Complexity: The Emerging Science at the Edge of Order and Chaos* (New York: Simon and Schuster, 1992).

5. Steven Pyne, quoted in Ed Marston, "Experts Line up on all Sides of the Tree-Grass Debate," *High Country News* 28, no. 7 (1996): 12–13, quotation on 13.

6. David Bohm, *Wholeness and the Implicate Order* (Boston: Routledge and Kegan Paul, 1980), 195; Merchant, *Radical Ecology*, 93–94.

7. Ilya Prigogine, *Order Out of Chaos: Man's New Dialogue with Nature* (New York: Bantam, 1984); Merchant, *Radical Ecology*, 94–96.

8. James Gleick, *Chaos: The Making of a New Science* (New York: Viking, 1987), 9–32. Edward Lorenz, "Predictability: Does the Flap of a Butterfly's Wings in Brazil Set Off a Tornado in Texas?" (paper presented at the annual meeting of the American Association for the Advancement of Science in Washington, D. C., December 29, 1972, reprinted in Carolyn Merchant, ed., *Ecology* (Atlantic Highlands, N.J.: Humanities Press, 1994), 360–62; Merchant, *Radical Ecology*, 96–97.

9. Ilya Prigogine and Isabelle Stengers, *Order Out of Chaos: Man's New Dialogue with Nature* (New York: Bantam, 1984); James Gleick, *Chaos: The Making of a New Science* (New York: Viking, 1987); Edward Lorenz, *The Essence of Chaos* (Seattle: University of Washington Press, 1993); N. Katherine Hayles, *Chaos Bound: Orderly Disorder in Contemporary Literature and Science* (Ithaca, N.Y.: Cornell University Press, 1990); N. Katherine Hayles, ed., *Chaos and Order: Complex Dynamics in Literature and Science* (Chicago, Ill.: University of Chicago Press, 1991); N. Katherine Hayles, "Gender Encoding in Fluid Mechanics: Masculine Channels and Feminine Flows," *differences* 4, no. 2 (1992): 16–44.

10. On the "God trick" of seeing everything from nowhere, see Donna Haraway, "Situated Knowledges," in *Simians, Cyborgs, and Women: The Reinvention of Nature* (New York: Routledge, 1991), 183–201, esp. 189, 191, 193, 195.

11. Murray Gell-Mann, *The Quark and the Jaguar* (New York: W. H. Freeman, 1994), 367–71; George J. Gummerman and Murray Gell-Mann, eds., *Understanding Complexity in the Prehistoric Southwest*, Santa Fe Institute Studies in the Sciences of Complexity, vol. 16 (Reading, Mass.: Addison-Wesley, 1994), 3.

12. Gell-Mann, *The Quark and the Jaguar*, 149–50, 369.

13. Ibid., 367–69, 371, quotation on 369.

14. Gumerman and Gell-Mann, *Understanding Complexity*, 4, 345.

15. Gell-Mann, *The Quark and the Jaguar*, 374–75, quotation on 375.

16. For the diversity-stability hypothesis, see Eugene P. Odum, *Fundamentals of Ecology* (1953); Eugene Odum, "The Strategy of Ecosystem Development," *Science* 164 (1969): 262–70. On shortcomings of equilibrium theories in ecology, see Seth R. Reice, "Nonequilibrium Determinants of Biological Community Structure," *American Scientist* 82, no. (1994): 424–35. On the history and disruption of the balance of nature theory, see Daniel Botkin, *Discordant Harmonies: A New Ecology for the Twenty-First Century* (New York: Oxford University Press, 1990); S. T. A. Pickett and P. S. White, eds., *The Ecology of Natural Disturbance and Patch Dynamics* (Orlando, Fla.: Academic Press, 1985). On the problem of a stable world behind socially constructed representations, see Elizabeth Ann R. Bird, "The Social Construction of Nature: Theoretical Approaches to the History of Environmental Problems," *Environmental Review* 11, no. 4 (1987): 255–64. On the history of chaos theory in ecology, see Donald Worster, "Ecology of Order and Chaos," *Environmental History Review* 14, nos. 1–2 (1990): 4–16.

17. Daniel Botkin, *Discordant Harmonies*, 25.

18. James Lovelock, "Gaia As Seen through the Atmosphere," *Atmospheric Environment* 6 (1972): 579; James Lovelock and Lynn Margulis, "Atmospheric Homeostasis by and for the Biosphere: The Gaia Hypothesis," *Tellus* 26 (1973): 2; Lynn Margulis and James Lovelock, "Biological Modulation of the Earth's Atmosphere," *Icarus* 21 (1974): 471; James Lovelock, *Gaia: A New Look at Life on Earth* (New York: Oxford University Press, 1979); James Lovelock, *The Ages of Gaia: A Biography of Our Living Earth* (New York: W. W. Norton, 1988); Merchant *Radical Ecology*, 98–100.

19. Lovelock, *Gaia: A New Look at Life on Earth*.

20. Glennda Chui, "The Mother Earth Theory," *San Jose Mercury News*, March 8, 1988, 1C–2C; James Kirchner, "The Gaia Hypothesis: Can It Be Tested?" *Reviews of Geophysics*, 27, no. 2 (1989): 223–35.

21. Charlene Spretnak, *Lost Goddesses of Early Greece: A Collection of Pre-Hellenic Mythology* (Ann Arbor, Mich.: Moon books, 1978), 30–31; J. Donald Hughes, "Gaia: Environmental Problems in Chthonic Persepective," *Environmental Review*, 6, no. 2 (1982) 92–104; Charlene Spretnak, "The Concept of the Earth as Bountiful Goddess in Pre-Indo-European Cultures of Old Europe," in *Conference Proceedings, National Audubon Society Expedition Institute, "Is the Earth a Living Organism?"* (Sharon, Conn.: Northeast Audubon Center, 1985), 61–64; Norman Myers, ed., *The Gaia Atlas of Planet Management* (New York: Doubleday Anchor, 1984).

22. William Irwin Thompson, ed., *Gaia: A Way of Knowing* (Great Barrington, Mass.: Lindisfarne Press, 1987; Elisabet Sahtouris, *Gaia: The Human Journey from Chaos to Cosmos* (New York: Simon and Schuster, 1989); Michael Allaby, *A Guide to Gaia: A Survey of the New Science of Our Living Earth* (New York: Dutton, 1989); Joseph Lawrence, *Gaia: The Growth of an Idea* (New York: St. Martin's Press, 1990); Alan Miller, *Gaia Connections: An Introduction to Ecology, Ecoethics, and Economics* (Savage, Md.: Rowman and Littlefield, 1990); Val Plumwood, "Gaia and Greenhouse: How Helpful Is the Use of Feminine Imagery for Nature?" in *Changing Directions: The Proceedings of Ecopolitics IV,* ed. Ken Dyer and John Young, (Adelaide, Australia: Graduate Centre for Environmental Studies, University of Adelaide, 1990), 622–28; Spretnak, "The Concept of the Earth as Bountiful Goddess," 62–64; Carolyn Merchant, "Gaia: Ecofeminism and the Earth," in *Earthcare: Women and the Environment* (New York: Routledge, 1996), 3–5.

CHAPTER 11

This chapter draws on material previously perviously published in Carolyn Merchant, *Earthcare: Women and the Environment* (New York: Routledge, 1996), 209–24.

1. Carolyn Merchant, *Earthcare*, 216–19; Merchant, "Partnership Ethics: Business and the Environment," in *Environmental Challenges to Business*, ed. Patricia Werhane, 1997 Ruffin Lectures, University of Virginia Darden School of Business (Bowling Green, Ohio: Society for Business Ethics, 2000), 7–18; and Merchant, "Partnership with Nature," in "Eco-Revelatory Design: Nature Constructed/Nature Revealed," *Landscape Journal* (1998) special issue: 69–71.

2. On Native American "sacred bundles," see Barbara Leibhardt, "Law, Environment, and Social Change in the Columbia River Basin: The Yakima Indian Nation as a Case Study, 1840–1933" (Ph.D. diss., University of California-Berkeley, 1990).

3. Frederick J. Long and Matthew Arnold, *The Power of Environmental Partnerships* (Fort Worth, Tex.: Dryden Press, 1994); Management Institute for Environment and Business, *Environmental Partnerships: A Business Handbook* (Fort Worth, Tex.: Dryden Press, 1994); Management Institute for Environment and Business, *Environmental Partnerships: A Field Guide for Governmental Agencies* (Fort Worth, Tex.: Dryden Press, 1994); Management Institute for Environment and Business, *Environmental Partnerships: A Field Guide for Nonprofit Organizations and Community Interests* (Fort Worth, Tex.: Dryden Press, 1994); Alan R. Beckenstein, Frederick J. Long, Matthew B. Arnold, and Thomas N. Gladwin, *Stakeholder Negotiations: Exercises in Sustainable Development* (Chicago: Richard D. Irwin, 1995); John K. Gamman, *Overcoming Obstacles in Environmental Policymaking: Creating Partnerships through Mediation* (Albany: State University of New York Press), 1994.

4. Merchant, *Earthcare*, 219; Carolyn Merchant, *Ecology* (Atlantic Highlands, N.J.: Humanities Press, 1994), 372; World Summit on Sustainable Development, "Political Declaration," article 15, adopted Sept. 4, 2002.

5. Merchant, *Earthcare*, 218.

6. Max Horkheimer, *The Eclipse of Reason* (New York: Oxford University Press, 1947), 101, 115.

7. David Abram, *The Spell of the Sensuous: Perception and Language in a More-Than-Human World* (New York: Vintage, 1996), 256, 273, 274.

8. Val Plumwood, "Wilderness Skepticism and Wilderness Dualism," in J. Baird Callicott and Michael P. Nelson, ed., *The Great New Wilderness Debate* (Athens and London: University

of Georgia Press, 1998), 652–90; Roger L. DiSilvestro, *Reclaiming the Last Wild Places: A New Agenda for Biodiversity* (New York: John Wiley, 1993), xiv–xv. I thank Holmes Rolston III for this reference.

9. Michael J. Vandeman, "Why We Should Provide Wildlife Habitat Off-Limits to Humans," unpublished paper; Dave Foreman, "Wilderness Areas for Real," in J. Baird Callicott, ed., *The Great New Wilderness Debate*, (Athens, Ga.: University of Georgia Press, 1998), 405.

10. On chaos theory, see James Gleick, *Chaos: The Making of a New Science* (New York: Viking, 1987); Edward Lorenz, *The Essence of Chaos* (Seattle: University of Washington Press, 1993); N. Katherine Hayles, *Chaos Bound: Orderly Disorder in Contemporary Literature and Science* (Ithaca, N.Y.: Cornell University Press, 1990); N. Katherine Hayles, ed., *Chaos and Order: Complex Dynamics in Literature and Science* (Chicago: University of Chicago Press, 1991); Ralph Abraham, *Chaos, Eros, and Gaia* (San Francisco: Harper and Row, 1994). On the difference between chaos theory and complexity theory, see Mitchell Waldrop, *Complexity: The Emerging Science at the Edge of Order and Chaos* (New York: Simon and Schuster, 1992).

11. George Perkins Marsh, *Man and Nature* (New York: Charles Scribner's Sons, 1864), 35, 36.

12. Herbert Marcuse, "Nature and Revolution," in *Counterrevolution and Revolt* (Boston: Beacon Press, 1972), 65, 69.

13. Aldo Leopold, "The Farmer As a Conservationist," *American Forests* 45 (1939): 294–99, cited in Susan L. Flader and J. Baird Callicott, eds., *The River of the Mother of God and Other Essays by Aldo Leopold* (Madison: University of Wisconsin Press, 1991), 235.

14. Riane Eisler, *The Chalice and the Blade* (San Francisco: Harper Collins, 1988), xvii, 105, 185–203; Eisler, *Sacred Pleasure: Sex, Myth, and the Politics of the Body* (San Francisco: Harper Collins, 1996), 347–401, quotations on 376, 399.

15. Val Plumwood, *Feminism and the Mastery of Nature* (New York: Routledge, 1993), 155, 196.

16. Alison Jaggar, "Globalizing Feminist Ethics," *Hypatia* 13, no. 4 (1998): 7–31, quotations on 17, 22. See also Jaggar, "Multicultural Democracy," *Journal of Political Philosophy* 7, no. 3 (1999): 308–29.

17. Management Institute for Environment and Business, *Environmental Partnerships: A Business Handbook*, 3, Merchant, "Partnership Ethics: Business and the Environment."

18. In constructing this example, I have drawn on a hypothetical case presented in Management Institute for Environment and Business, *Environmental Partnerships: A Business Handbook*, 11–12, but I have added representatives of affected natural entities.

19. Ibid., 11–12, Merchant, "Partnership Ethics."

20. Ibid., 12, Merchant, "Partnership Ethics."

21. Management Institute for Environment and Business, *Environmental Partnerships: A Field Guide for Nonprofit Organizations and Community Interests*, 11.

22. Long and Arnold, *Environmental Partnerships*, 5.

23. Ibid.

24. Management Institute for Environment and Business, *Environmental Partnerships: A Field Guide for Government Agencies*, 32, Merchant, "Partnership Ethics."

25. Ian McHarg, *Design with Nature* (Garden City, N.Y.: Doubleday, 1969), 5; Lewis Mumford, introduction to McHarg, *Design with Nature*, viii.

26. The examples herein are drawn from Carolyn Merchant, "Partnership with Nature," 69–71, used by permission of the University of Wisconsin Press.

27. McHarg, *Design with Nature*, 19.

28. Val Plumwood, *Environmental Culture: The Ecological Crisis of Reason* (London: Routledge, 2002), 229.

29. Teresa Fasolino, cover illustration to Carolyn Merchant, *Earthcare: Women and the Environment* (New York: Routledge, 1996).

BIBLIOGRAPHY

Abram, David. *The Spell of the Sensuous: Perception and Language in a More-Than-Human World.* New York: Vintage, 1996.

Acosta, Joseph de. *The Natural and Moral History of the Indies.* Ed. Clements R. Markham. 2 vols. London: Hakluyt Society, 1880. Reprinted from the English translation by Edward Grimston in 1604.

Adams, Henry. "The American Land Inspired Cole's Prescient Visions." *Smithsonian* 25, no. 2 (1994): 99–107.

Adams, John Quincy. *Congressional Globe* 1846: 339–42.

Alighieri, Dante. *The Portable Dante.* Ed. Mark Musa. New York: Penguin, 1984.

Allaby, Michael. *A Guide to Gaia: A Survey of the New Science of Our Living Earth.* New York: Dutton, 1989.

Alper, Joseph S., Catherine Ard, Adrienne Asch, Peter Conrad, Lisa N. Geller, and Jon Beckwith, eds. *The Double-Edged Helix: Social Implications of Genetics in a Diverse Society.* Baltimore: Johns Hopkins University Press, 2002.

Alsop, George. "Character of the Province of Maryland," in *Narratives of Early Maryland, 1633–1684.* Ed. Clayton Colman Hall. New York: Charles Scribner's Sons, 1910.

Ames, Nathaniel. *Astronomical Diary or Almanac.* Boston: J. Draper, 1758.

Anderson, Gary A. and Michael Stone, eds. *A Synopsis of the Books of Adam and Eve.* 2d ed., revised. Atlanta: Scholars Press, 1998.

Anderson, Gary, Michael Stone, and Johannes Tromp, eds. *Literature on Adam and Eve: Collected Essays.* Leiden: Brill, 2000.

Ashcraft, Richard. "Leviathan Triumphant: Thomas Hobbes and the Politics of Wild Men." In *The Wild Man Within: An Image in Western Thought from the Renaissance to Romanticism,* ed. Edward Dudley and Maximillian E. Novak, Pittsburgh: University of Pittsburgh Press, 1972, 141–81.

Ashcroft, Bill, Gareth Griffiths, and Helen Tiffin, eds. *The Post-Colonial Studies Reader.* New York: Routledge, 1995.

Attfield, Robin. *The Ethics of Environmental Concern.* New York: Scribner's, 1974.

Audubon, John James. *Delineations of American Scenery and Character (1808–1834).* New York: G. A. Baker, 1926.

Austin, Mary. *The Land of Little Rain*. Boston: Houghton Mifflin, 1950; originally published 1903.

Babbitt, Bruce. "Stewards of Creation." *The Christian Century*, 113, no. 16 (1996), 500–503.

Bachofen, Johann Jacob. *Myth, Religion, and Mother Right: Selected Writings of J. J. Bachofen*. Trans. Ralph Manheim. Princeton, N.J.: Princeton University Press, 1967.

Bacon, Francis. *Works*. 14 vols. Ed. James Spedding, Robert Leslie Ellis, and Douglas Devon Heath. London: Longmans Green, 1870.

Baigell, Matthew. *Thomas Cole*. New York: Watson Guptill, 1981.

Bailey, Florence Merriam. *A-Birding on a Bronco*. Boston: Houghton Mifflin, 1896.

Bancroft, George. *History of the United States*. Boston: Little, Brown, 1840.

Barbour, Ian G., ed. *Western Man and Environmental Ethics*. Reading, Mass.: Addison-Wesley, 1973.

Barker-Benfield, G. J. "The Spermatic Economy," *Feminist Studies*, 1 no. 1 (1972): 45–71.

Barthes, Roland. "The Struggle with the Angel." In *Image, Music, Text*. Trans. Stephen Heath. New York: Noonday Press, 1977, 139–41.

Bauman, Zygmunt. "Gamekeepers Turned Gardeners." In *Legislators and Interpreters: On Modernity, Post-modernity, and Intellectuals*. Oxford: Polity Press, 1987, 51–67.

Bebel, August. *Woman in the Past, Present, and Future*. San Francisco: G. B. Benham, 1897.

Beckenstein, Alan R., Frederick J. Long, Matthew B. Arnold, and Thomas N. Gladwin. *Stakeholder Negotiations: Excerises in Sustainable Development*. Chicago: Richard D. Irwin, 1995.

Beckwith, Jon. *Making Genes, Making Waves*. Cambridge, Mass.: Harvard University Press, 2002.

Begley, Sharon. "Little Lamb Who Made Thee?" *Newsweek*, March 10, 1997: 53–57.

Belden, George P. *Belden, the White Chief; or Twelve Years among the Wild Indians of the Plains*. Cincinnati: C. F. Vent, 1870.

Bennett, John. "The District Irrigation Movement in California," *Overland Monthly* 29 (1897): 252–57.

Benton, Thomas Hart. *Congressional Globe* 1846: 917–18.

Berger, Pamela. *The Goddess Obscured: The Transformation of the Grain Protectress from Goddess to Saint*. Boston: Beacon Press, 1985.

Beverley, Robert. *The History and Present State of Virginia*. London: R. Parker, 1705.

Birch, Thomas H. "The Incarceration of Wildness: Wilderness Areas As Prisons." In *The Great New Wilderness Debate*. Ed. J. Baird Callicott and Michael P. Nelson. Athens, Ga.: University of Georgia Press, 1998, 443–70.

Bird, Elizabeth Ann R. "The Social Construction of Nature: Theoretical Approaches to the History of Environmental Problems." *Environmental Review* 11, no. 4 (1987): 255–64.

Bird, Isabella. *A Lady's Life in the Rocky Mountains*. Norman: University of Oklahoma Press, 1960; originally published in *Leisure Hour*, 1878.

Blaut, J. M. *The Colonizer's Model of the World: Geographical Diffusionism and Eurocentric History*. New York: Guilford Press, 1993.

Bloom, Harold, ed. and David Rosenberg, trans. *The Book of J*. Trans. Rosenberg, David. New York: Vintage, 1990.

Bode, Carl, ed. *The Portable Thoreau*. New York: Penguin, 1977.

Bolingbroke, Henry St. John Viscount. *Political Writings*. Ed. Isaac Kramnick, New York: Meredith Corporations, 1970.

Bonnifeld, Paul. *The Dust Bowl: Men, Dirt, and Depression*. Albuquerque: University of New Mexico Press, 1979.

Bookchin, Murray. *The Ecology of Freedom: The Emergency and Dissolution of Hierarchy*. Palo Alto, Calif.: Cheshire Books, 1982.

Botkin, Daniel. *Discordant Harmonies: A New Ecology for the Twenty-First Century*. New York: Oxford University Press, 1990.

Bowles, Samuel. *The Switzerland of America*. Hartford, Conn.: Hartford Publishing, 1869.

Bradford, William. *Of Plimoth Plantation*. Boston: Wright and Potter, 1901.

Briffault, Robert. *The Mothers*. Abridged edition. New York: Atheneum, 1977; originally published 1927.

Brown, John Crombie, ed. and trans. *The French Forest Ordinance of 1669*. Edinburgh: Oliver and Boyd, 1883.

Brown, Mrs. W. Wallace. "The Legend of Indian Corn." *Journal of American Folklore*. 1 (1890): 214.

Bullard, Robert. *Dumping in Dixie: Race, Class, and Environmental Quality*. Boulder, Colo.: Westview Press, 1990.

———, ed. *Confronting Environmental Racism: Voices from the Grassroots*. Boston: South End Press, 1993.

Burke, Edmund. *A Philosophical Enquiry into the Origins of Our Ideas of the Sublime and Beautiful*. 2d ed. London: R. and J. Dodsley, 1759.

Burnham, Philip. *Indian Country, God's Country: Native Americans and the National Parks*. Washington, D.C.: Island Press, 2000.

Burton, Richard F. *The City of the Saints and across the Rocky Mountains to California*, 1863 [1861].

Callicott, J. Baird. "Genesis Revisited: Muirian Musings on the Lynn White, Jr. Debate." *Environmental Review* 14, nos. 1–2 (1990): 65–92.

———. *In Defense of the Land Ethic: Essays in Environmental Philosophy*. Albany: State University of New York Press, 1989.

———. "The Wilderness Idea Revisited: The Sustainable Development Alternative." *Environmental Professional* 13 (1991): 236–45.

———, ed. *The Great New Wilderness Debate: An Expansive Collection of Writings Defining Wilderness from John Muir to Gary Snyder*. Athens, Ga.: University of Georgia Press, 1998.

Carroll, Charles F. *The Timber Economy of Puritan New England*. Providence, R.I.: Brown University Press, 1973.

Carroll, Peter N. *Puritanism and the Wilderness, 1629–1700*. New York: Columbia University Press, 1969.

Carson, Rachel. *Silent Spring*. Boston: Houghton Mifflin, 1962.

Catlin, George. *North American Indians*. Philadelphia: Leary, Stuart, 1913; originally published, 1844.

Chamberlin, Roy B. and Herman Feldman. *The Dartmouth Bible, An Abridgment of the King James Version, with Aids to its Understanding as History and Literature, and as a Source of Religious Experience*. Boston: Houghton Mifflin, 1961.

Chandler, Alfred D. "Anthracite Coal and the Beginnings of the Industrial Revolution in the United States." *Business History Review* 46, no. 2, (1972): 141–81.

Chaucer, Geoffrey. "The Merchant's Tale." In *Works*. Ed. F. N. Robinson. Boston: Houghton Mifflin, 1957.

Christensen, Thomas and Carol, eds. *The Discovery of America and Other Myths*. San Francisco: Chronicle Books, 1992.

Chui, Glennda. "The Mother Earth Theory." *San Jose Mercury News*, March 8, 1988, 1C–2C.

Clarke, Kenneth. *Landscape into Art*. London: Penguin, 1956.

Cohen, A. *The Soncino Chumash*. Hindland, Surrey, UK: The Soncino Press, 1947.

Cohen, Jeremy. *"Be Fertile and Increase, Fill the Earth and Master It:" The Ancient and Medieval Career of a Biblical Test*. Ithaca: Cornell University Press, 1989.

Cohn, Norman. *Noah's Flood: The Genesis Story in Western Thought*. New Haven, Conn.: Yale University Press, 1996.

Colman, Henry. "Address Before the Hampshire, Franklin, and Hampden Agricultural Society Delivered in Greenfield, Oct. 23, 1833." Greenfield, Mass.: Phelps and Ingersoll, 1833.

Colton, Calvin. "Labor and Capital." In *The Junius Tracts*. New York: Greeley and McElrath, 1844.

Cooper, James Fenimore. *The Pioneers*. (1823) Vol. 4 of The Works of James Fenimore Cooper. 25 vols. London: George Routledge and Sons, 1895.

Cornplanter, Jesse. *Legends of the Longhouse*. Philadelphia: J. B. Lippincott, 1938.

Crawford, Margaret. "The World in a Shopping Mall." *Variations on a Theme Park*. Ed. Michael Sorkin. New York: Hill and Wang, 1992, 3–30.

Crèvecoeur, J. Hector St. John de. "What Is an American?" In *Letters from an American Farmer*. New York: E. P. Dutton, 1957 [1782].

Cronon, William. *Nature's Metropolis: Chicago and the Great West*. New York: W. W. Norton, 1991.

———. "A Place for Stories: Nature, History, and Narrative." *Journal of American History* 78, no. 4, (1992): 1347–76.

———. "Telling Tales on Canvas: Landscapes of Frontier Change." In Jules David Prown, Nancy K. Anderson, William Cronon, Brian W. Dippie, Martha Sandweiss, Susan Prendergast Schoelwer, and Howard R. Lamar, *Discovered Lands, Invented Pasts*. New Haven, Conn.: Yale University Press, 1992, 37–87.

Daily, Gretchen C., Anne H. Ehrlich, and Paul R. Ehrlich, "Optimum Population Size," *ERG News* (Energy and Resources Group, University of California-Berkeley) 4, no. 2 (1994): 1–3.

Darby, H. C. "The Clearing of the Woodland in Europe," in *Man's Role in Changing the Face of the Earth*. Ed. William L. Thomas Jr. 2 vols. Chicago: University of Chicago Press, 1956.

Darwin, Charles. *The Descent of Man and Selection in Relation to Sex*. 2 vols. New York: D. Appleton, 1873.

Davis, Elizabeth Gould. *The First Sex*. Baltimore: Penguin Books, 1972.

d'Eaubonne, Françoise. "The Time for Ecofeminism," trans. Ruth Hottell. In *Ecology*. Ed. Carolyn Merchant. Atlantic Highlands, N.J.: Humanities Press, 1994 [1974], 174–97.

Derham, William. *Physico-Theology: or A Demonstration of the Being and Attributes of God, from His Works of Creation*. 6th ed. London: Innys, 1728; originally published 1713.

Diner, Helen. *Mothers and Amazons: The First Feminine History of Culture*. New York: Anchor Press, Doubleday, 1973; originally published 1929.

Derrida, Jacques. *Of Grammatology*. Trans. Gayatri Chakravorty Spivak. Baltimore: Johns Hopkins University Press, 1976.

Diamond, Jared. *Guns, Germs, and Steel: The Fates of Human Societies*. New York: Norton, 1997.

DiSilvestro, Roger L. *Reclaiming the Last Wild Places: A New Agenda for Biodiversity*. New York: John Wiley, 1993.

Donne, John. *The Poems of John Donne*. Ed. Herbert Grierson. London: Oxford University Press, 1957.

Dubos, René. "Conservation, Stewardship, and the Human Heart." *Audubon* September 1972, 21–28.

———. "A Theology of the Earth." In *Western Man and Environmental Ethics: Attitudes toward Nature and Technology*. Ed. Ian Barbour. Reading, Mass.: Addison-Wesley, 1973, 43–54.

Economou, George. *The Goddess Natura in Medieval Literature*. Cambridge, Mass.: Harvard University Press, 1972.

Ehrlich, Paul. *Ecocatastrophe*, San Francisco: City Lights Books. 1969.

Eisenberg, Evan. *The Ecology of Eden*. New York: Alfred Knopf, 1998.

Eisler, Riane. *The Chalice and the Blade*. San Francisco: Harper Collins, 1988.

———. *Sacred Pleasure: Sex, Myth, and the Politics of the Body*. San Francisco: Harper Collins, 1996.

Elmer-Dewitt, Philip. "Fried Gene Tomatoes." *Time*, May 30 1994: 54–55.

Emerson, Ralph Waldo. "English Traits." In *The Complete Works of Ralph Waldo Emerson*, with a biographical introduction and notes by Edward Waldo Emerson Vol. 5. Boston: Houghton Mifflin, 1903–4.

————. "The Young American." *The Dial* 4 (1844): 484–507.

Engels, Friedrich. *Origins of the Family, Private Property, and the State* in *Selected Works*. New York: International Publishers, 1968.

Evelyn, John. *Fumifugium*. Oxford: Old Ashmolean Reprints, 1930 [1661].

————. *Silva, Or a Discourse on Forest Trees*. York, England: 1776 [1662].

Fernow, Bernhard. *Economics of Forestry*. New York: Thomas Y. Crowell, 1902.

Fiege, Mark. *Irrigated Eden: The Making of an Agricultural Landscape in the American West*. Seattle: University of Washington Press, 1999.

Filmer, Robert. *Patriarcha: Or the Natural Power of Kings*. London: Printed for R. Chiswell, 1680.

Flader, Susan L. and J. Baird Callicott, eds., *The River of the Mother of God and other Essays by Aldo Leopold*. Madison: University of Wisconsin Press, 1991.

Fox, Everett, ed. *The Five Books of Moses*. New York: Schocken, 1995.

Francaviglia, Richard V. *The Mormon Landscape: Existence, Perception, and Creation of a Unique Image in the American West*. New York: AMS Press, 1978.

Frankfort, Henri, H. A. Frankfort, John A. Wilson, Thorkild Jacobsen, and William A. Irwin. *Before Philosophy: The Intellectual Adventure of Ancient Man*. Baltimore, Md: Penguin Books, 1949 [1946].

Franklin, Benjamin. "Remarks concerning the Savages of North America." *Franklin's Wit and Folly: The Bagatelles*. Ed. Richard E. Amacher. New Brunswick, N.J.: Rutgers University Press, 1953.

Freeman, George. "Among the Irrigators of Fresno." *Overland Monthly* 9 (1887): 621–27.

Friedländer, Max J. and Jakob Rosenberg. *The Paintings of Lucas Cranach*. London: Sotheby Parke Bernet, 1978.

Fritzell, Peter. "The Wilderness and the Garden: Metaphors for the American Landscape." *Forest History* 12, no. 1 (1968): 16–23.

Frye, Northrup. *Fables of Identity*. New York: Harcourt Brace, 1963.

Gadon, Elinor. *The Once and Future Goddess*. San Francisco: Harper Collins, 1989.

Gamman, John K. *Overcoming Obstacles in Environmental Policymaking: Creating Partnerships through Mediation*. Albany: State University of New York Press, 1994.

Gardner, Augustus. *Our Children*. Hartford, Conn.: Belknap and Bliss, 1872.

Gare, Arran E. *Postmodernism and the Environmental Crisis*. New York: Routledge, 1995.

Gelé, Claude. "L'Agriculture manque de robots." *Sciences and Techniques* 26 (1986): 22–29.

Gell-Mann, Murray. *The Quark and the Jaguar*. New York: W. H. Freeman, 1994.

Gibbons, Cardinal James. "Greetings." *Proceedings of the Second National Conservation Congress at Saint Paul, September 5–8, 1910*. Vol. 2. Washington, D.C.: National Conservation Congress, 1911.

Gill, Sam. *Mother Earth: An American Story*. Chicago: University of Chicago Press, 1987.

Gimbutas, Marija. *The Goddesses and Gods of Old Europe, 6500–3500 B.C.* Berkeley and Los Angeles.: University of California Press, 1982.

Glacken, Clarence. *Traces on the Rhodian Shore: Nature and Culture in Western Thought From Ancient Times to the End of the Eighteenth Century*. Berkeley: University of California Press, 1967.

Gleick, James. *Chaos: The Making of a New Science*. New York: Viking, 1987.

Glendinning, Chellis. *My Name is Chellis and I'm in Recovery from Western Civilization*. Boston: Shambala, 1994.

Gold, Victor Roland, et al, ed. *The New Testament and Psalms: An Inclusive Version*. New York: Oxford University Press.

Goldschmidt, Henry. "Rupture Tales: Stories and Politics in and around the Garden of Eden." Unpublished paper. University of California-Santa Cruz, 1994.

Greenberg, Herb, "Calgene's Biotech Bounty Disappears from Grocers' Shelves." *San Francisco Chronicle*, Jan. 17, 1995, B1, B3.

Griffin, Susan. *Woman and Nature: The Roaring Inside Her*. New York: Harper Collins, 1978.

Grove, Richard. *Green Imperialism: Colonial Expansion, Tropical Island Edens, and the Origins of Environmentalism, 1600–1860*. New York: Cambridge University Press, 1995.

Gummerman, George J., and Murray Gell-Mann, eds. *Understanding Complexity in the Prehistoric Southwest*. Reading, Mass.: Addison-Wesley, 1994.

Guterson, David. "Enclosed, Encyclopedic, Endured: One Week at the Mall of America." In *A Forest of Voices: Reading and Writing the Environment*. Ed. Chris Anderson and Lex Runciman. Mountain View, Calif.: Mayfield, 1995, 124–36.

Gutiérrez, Ramón. *When Jesus Came the Corn Mothers Went Away*. Stanford, Calif.: Stanford University Press, 1991.

Hanchett, Thomas W. *Sorting Out the New South City: Race, Class, and Urban Development in Charlotte, 1875–1975*. Chapel Hill: University of North Carolina Press, 1998.

Haraway, Donna. *Primate Visions*. New York: Routledge, 1989.

———. "Situated Knowledges." In *Simians, Cyborgs, and Women: The Reinvention of Nature*. New York: Routledge, 1991, 183–201.

Harding, M. Esther. *Women's Mysteries Ancient and Modern*. London: Rider, 1971; originally published 1955.

Harriot, Thomas. *A Briefe and True Report of the New Found Land of Virginia*. The Complete 1590 Theodor de Bry edition, with a new introduction by Paul Hulton. New York: Dover, 1972.

Harris, Dianne. "Lombardia Illuminata: The Formation of an Enlightenment Landscape in Eighteenth Century Lombardy." Ph.D. dissertation, University of California-Berkeley, 1996.

Harris, Neil. *The Artist in American Society: The Formative Years, 1790–1860*. New York: George Braziller, 1966.

Harris, Victor. *All Coherence Gone*. Chicago: University of Chicago Press, 1949.

———. *Myths of the Social Origins of Greek Religion*. Cambridge: Cambridge University Press, 1912.

———. *Prolegomena to the Study of Greek Religion*. Cambridge: Cambridge University Press, 1922; originally published 1903.

———. *The Religion of Ancient Greece*. London: Archibald Constable, 1905.

Harrison, Jane Ellen. *Mythology*. New York: Harcourt, Brace and World, 1963; originally published 1924.

Harrison, Robert Pogue. *Forests: The Shadow of Civilization*. Chicago: University of Chicago Press, 1992.

Hatt, Gudmund. "The Corn Mother in America and Indonesia." *Anthropos* 46 (1951): 853–914.

Hayles, N. Katherine. *Chaos Bound: Orderly Disorder in Contemporary Literature and Science*. Ithaca, N.Y.: Cornell University Press, 1990.

———. "Gender Encoding in Fluid Mechanics: Masculine Channels and Feminine Flows." *differences* 4.2 (1992): 16–44.

———, ed. *Chaos and Order: Complex Dynamics in Literature and Science*. Chicago: University of Chicago Press, 1991.

Hazard, Paul. *European Thought in the Eighteenth Century: From Montesquieu to Lessing*. Cleveland: Meridian, 1965 [1946].

Heinberg, Richard. *Memories and Visions of Paradise: Exploring the Universal Myth of a Lost Golden Age*. Rev. ed. Wheaton, Ill.: Quest Books, 1995.

Henry, Avril, ed. *The Mirour of Mans Saluacioun: A Middle English Translation of Speculum Humanae Salvationis*. Philadelphia: University of Pennsylvania Press, 1987.

Hesiod. "Works and Days." In *Theogeny and Works and Days*. Trans. M. L. West. New York: Oxford University Press, 1988.

Hiebert, Theodore. *The Yahwist's Landscape: Nature and Religion in Early Israel.* New York: Oxford University Press, 1996.

Hobbes, Thomas. *Leviathan.* Vol. 3. Aalen, Germany: Scientia, 1966 [1651].

Hodgen, Margaret T. *Early Anthropology in the Sixteenth and Seventeenth Centuries.* Philadelphia: University of Pennsylvania Press, 1964.

Holy Bible, New Century Version. Dallas: Word Publishing, 1987.

Horkheimer, Max. *The Eclipse of Reason.* New York: Oxford University Press, 1947.

Horkheimer, Max and Theodor Adorno. Trans. John Cummings. *Dialectic of Enlightenment.* New York: Continuum, 1993 [1944].

Horovitz, Bruce. "Malls Are Like, Totally Uncool, Say Hip Teens." *USA Today* May 1, 1996: 1–2.

Hughes, J. Donald. *Ecology in Ancient Civilizations.* Albuquerque: University of New Mexico Press, 1975.

———. "Gaia: Environmental Problems in Chthonic Perspective." *Environmental Review* 6, no. 2 (1982): 92–104.

Hurston, Zora Neale. *Their Eyes Were Watching God.* New York: Harper Collins, 1990; originally published 1937.

Huxley, Thomas. "Prolegomena (1894)." In *Evolution and Ethics.* London, 1947.

Jacoby, Karl. *Crimes against Nature: Squatters, Poachers, Thieves, and the Hidden History of American Conservation.* Berkeley and Los Angeles: University of California Press, 2001.

Jaggar, Alison. "Globalizing Feminist Ethics." *Hypatia* 13, no. 4 (1998): 7–31.

———. "Multicultural Democracy." *Journal of Political Philosophy* 7, no. 3 (1999): 308–29.

Jewett, Sarah Orne. *A White Heron: A Story of Maine.* New York: Crowell, 1963.

Jones, Richard Foster. *Ancients and Moderns: A Study of the Rise of the Scientific Movement in Seventeenth Century England.* St. Louis: Washington University Studies, 1961.

Jordan, Winthrop. *White over Black: American Attitudes Toward the Negro, 1550–1812.* New York: W. W. Norton, 1977 [1968].

Kant, Immanuel. *Observations on the Feeling of the Beautiful and Sublime.* Trans. John T. Goldthwait. Berkeley and Los Angeles: University of California Press, 1960.

Kaplan, Aryeh, trans. *The Living Torah: The First Five Books of Moses and the Haftarot.* New York: Mazanim, 1981.

Kauffman, Polly Welts. *National Parks and the Woman's Voice: A History.* Albuquerque: University of New Mexico Press, 1996.

Kauffman, Stuart. *At Home in the Universe: The Search for the Laws of Self-Organization and Complexity.* New York: Oxford University Press, 1995.

Kay, Jane. "Frankenfish Spawning Controversy." *San Francisco Chronicle,* April 29, 2002, A4.

Keeney, Elizabeth. *The Botanizers: Amateur Scientists in Nineteenth Century America.* Chapel Hill: University of North Carolina Press, 1992.

Keller, Evelyn Fox. *Reflections on Gender and Science.* New Haven, Conn.: Yale University Press, 1985.

Keller, Robert H. and Michael F. Turek. *American Indians and National Parks.* Tucson: University of Arizona Press, 1998.

Kendrick, T. D. *The Lisbon Earthquake.* London: Methuen, 1956.

Kendrick, Walter M. "Earth of Flesh, Flesh of Earth: Mother Earth in the Faerie Queen." *Renaissance Quarterly* 27 (1974): 548–53.

Kirchner, James. "The Gaia Hypothesis: Can It Be Tested?" *Reviews of Geophysics,* 27, no. 2 (1989): 223–35.

Kluger, Jeffrey. "Will We Follow the Sheep?" *Time,* March 10, 1997: 67–72.

Kolodny, Annette. "Honing a Habitable Landscape: Women's Images for the New World Frontiers." *Women and Language in Literature and Society.* Ed. Sally McConnell-Ginet, Ruth Borker and Nelly Furman. New York: Praeger, 1980, 188–204.

————. *The Lay of the Land: Metaphor As Experience and History in American Life and Letters.* Chapel Hill: University of North Carolina Press, 1975.

Koval, Joel. "Negating Bookchin." In *Murray Bookchin: Nature's Prophet.* Santa Cruz, Calif.: Capitalism, Nature, Socialism/Center for Political Ecology, 1996.

Krauthammer, Charles. "A Special Report on Cloning." *Time*, March 10, 1997: 60–61.

Kubrin, David. "How Sir Isaac Newton Helped Restore Law n' Order to the West," *Liberation* 16, no. 10 (March 1972): 32–41.

Kurutz, K.D. and Gary F. Kurutz. *California Calls You: The Art of Promoting the Golden States, 1870–1940.* Sausalito, Calif.: Windgate Press. 2000.

Kvam, Kristen, Linda S. Schearing, and Valarie H. Ziegler, eds. *Eve and Adam: Jewish, Christian, and Muslim Readings on Genesis and Gender.* Bloomington: Indiana University Press, 1999.

Landau, Misia. *Narratives of Human Evolution.* New Haven, Conn.: Yale University Press, 1991.

Lappé, Marc. *Broken Code: The Exploitation of DNA.* San Francisco, Calif.: Sierra Club Books, 1984.

Lappé, Marc and Britt Bailey. *Against the Grain: Biotechnology and the Corporate Takeover of Your Food.* Monroe, Me.: Common Courage Press, 1998.

Lappé, Marc and Britt Bailey, eds. *Engineering the Farm: Ethical and Social Aspects of Agricultural Biotechnology.* Washington, D.C.: Island Press, 2000.

Lasch, Christopher. *The New Radicalism in America, 1889–1963.* New York: W. W. Norton, 1965.

Lawrence, Joseph. *Gaia: The Growth of an Idea.* New York: St. Martin's Press, 1990.

Lee, Charles. "Toxic Wastes and Race in the United States: A National Report on the Racial and Socio-Economic Characteristics of Communities with Hazardous Waste Sites." New York: United Church of Christ Commission for Racial Justice, 1987.

Lefler, Hugh Talmadge and Albert Ray Newsome, *North Carolina: The History of a Southern State.* Chapel Hill: University of North Carolina Press, 1954.

Leibhardt, Barbara. "Law, Environment, and Social Change in the Columbia River Basin: The Yakima Indian Nation As a Case Study, 1840–1933." Ph.D. Dissertation. University of California-Berkeley, 1990.

Leiss, William. *The Domination of Nature.* New York: George Braziller, 1972.

Leopold, Aldo. "The Farmer As a Conservationist," *American Forests* 45 (1939): 294–99.

————. *A Sand County Almanac.* New York: Oxford University Press, 1949.

Lerner, Gerda. *The Creation of Patriarchy.* New York: Oxford, 1986.

Levison, John R. *Texts in Transition: The Greek Life of Adam and Eve.* Atlanta: Society of Biblical Literature, 2000.

Lewin, Roger. "In the Beginning Was the Genome." *New Scientist* 21, no. 1726 (1990): 34–38.

Locke, John. "The First Treatise." In *Two Treatises of Government.* Ed. Peter Laslett. 2d ed. Cambridge: Cambridge University Press, 1967 [1689].

————. *Second Treatise of Government.* Ed. Richard H. Cox. Arlington Heights, Ill.: Harlan Davidson, 1982 [1689].

Long, Frederick J. and Matthew Arnold. *The Power of Environmental Partnerships.* Fort Worth, Tex.: Dryden Press, 1994.

Lorenz, Edward. *The Essence of Chaos.* Seattle: University of Washington Press, 1993.

Lovelock, James. *The Ages of Gaia: A Biography of Our Living Earth.* New York: W. W. Norton, 1988.

————. *Gaia: A New Look at Life on Earth.* New York: Oxford University Press, 1979.

————. "Gaia As Seen through the Atmosphere," *Atmospheric Environment* 6 (1972): 579.

Lovelock, James and Lynn Margulis. "Atmospheric Homeostasis by and for the Biosphere: The Gaia Hypothesis." *Tellus* 26 (1973): 2.

Lowenthal, David. "Awareness of Human Impacts: Changing Attitudes and Emphases." In *The Earth As Transformed by Human Action: Global and Regional Changes in the Biosphere over the Past Three Hundred Years*. Ed. B. L. Turner, II, William Clark, Robert W. Kates, John F. Richards, Jessica T. Matthews, and William B. Meyer. New York: Cambridge University Press, 1980, 121–35.

Lucretius. *Of the Nature of Things*. Trans. William Ellery Leonard. New York: E. P. Dutton, 1950.

Lund, Mrs. Haviland. "Conservation of Land and Man." *Proceedings of the Fourth National Conservation Congress, Indianapolis, October 14, 1912*. Indianapolis: National Conservation Congress, 1912.

Lunenfeld, Martin. *1492: Discovery, Invasion, Encounter*. Lexington, Mass.: D. C. Heath, 1991.

Lyman, Francesca. "Are We Redesigning Nature in Our Own Image? An Interview with Jeremy Rifkin." *Environmental Action*, April (1983), 20–25.

MacLeod, William Christie. "Conservation among Primitive Hunting Peoples." *Scientific Monthly* 43 (1936): 562–66.

Management Institute for Environment and Business. *Environmental Partnerships: A Business Handbook*. Fort Worth, Tex.: Dryden Press, 1994.

———. *Environmental Partnerships: A Field Guide for Government Agencies*. Fort Worth, Tex.: Dryden Press, 1994.

———. *Environmental Partnerships: A Field Guide for Nonprofit Organizations and Community Interests*. Fort Worth, Tex.: Dryden Press, 1994.

Margulis, Lynn and James Lovelock. "Biological Modulation of the Earth's Atmosphere." *Icarus* 21 (1974): 471.

Marsh, George Perkins. *Man and Nature*. Cambridge, Mass.: Belknap Press, 1965 [1864].

Marston, Ed. "Experts Line Up on all Sides of the Tree-Grass Debate." *High Country News* 28, no. 7 (1996): 12–13.

Martin, Calvin. *Keepers of the Game: Indian Animal Relationships and the Fur Trade*. Berkeley and Los Angeles: University of California Press, 1978.

Marx, Leo. *The Machine in the Garden: Technology and the Pastoral Ideal in America*. New York: Oxford University Press, 1964.

Mather, Robin. *A Garden of Unearthly Delights: Bioengineering and the Future of Food*. New York: Dutton, 1995.

Maxwell, Arthur S. *The Bible Story*. Revised ed. Hagerston, Md.: Review and Herald Publishing Association, 1994.

McHarg, Ian. *Design with Nature*. Garden City, N.Y.: Doubleday, 1969.

McKibben, Bill. *The End of Nature*. New York: Random House, 1989.

Meadows, Donella H., Dennis L. Meadows, Jørgen Randers, and William W. Behrens III. *The Limits to Growth*. New York: Signet, 1972.

Mechling, W. H. *Malechite Tales*. Ottawa: Government Printing Bureau, 1914.

Meek, Ronald. *Social Science and the Ignoble Savage*. Cambridge: Cambridge University Press, 1976.

Melville, Herman. "The Encantadas, or 'Enchanted Isles.'" In *Herman Melville*. Ed. R. W. B. Lewis. New York, 1962.

Mercator, Gerhard. *Atlas; or A Geographicke Description of the World*, 1636. Introduction by R. A. Skelton. Amsterdam: Theatrum Orbis Terrarum, 1968.

Merchant, Carolyn. *The Death of Nature: Women, Ecology, and the Scientific Revolution*. San Francisco: Harper Collins, 1980.

———, ed. *Ecology*. Atlantic Highlands, N.J.: Humanities Press.

———. *Earthcare: Women and the Environment*. New York: Routledge, 1996.

———. *Ecological Revolutions: Nature, Gender, and Science in New England*. Chapel Hill: University of North Carolina Press, 1989.

————. "Partnership Ethics: Business and the Environment." In *Environmental Challenges to Business*. Ed. Patricia Werhane. 1997 Ruffin Lectures, University of Virginia Darden School of Business. Bowling Green, Ohio: Society for Business Ethics, 2000, 7–18.

————. "Partnership with Nature." "Eco-Revelatory Design: Nature Constructed/Nature Revealed." *Landscape Journal* (1998): special issue, 69–71.

————. *Radical Ecology: The Search for a Livable World*. New York: Routledge, 1992.

————. "Women of the Progressive Conservation Movement, 1900–1916." *Environmental Review* 8, no. 1 (1984): 57–85.

Myers, Norman, ed. *The Gaia Atlas of Planet Management*. New York: Doubleday Anchor, 1984.

Mill, John Stuart. *Essays on Politics and Culture*. Ed. Gertrude Himmelfarb. Garden City, N.Y.: Doubleday, 1962.

Miller, Alan. *Gaia Connections: An Introduction to Ecology, Ecoethics, and Economics*. Savage, Md.: Rowman and Littlefield, 1990.

Miller, Joaquin. *My Own Story*. Chicago: Belford Clarke, 1890.

Miller, Olive Thorne. *Bird Ways*. Boston: Houghton Mifflin, 1885.

Mitchell, John. *The Earth Spirit*. New York: Avon, 1975.

Moncrief, Lewis. "The Cultural Basis of Our Environmental Crisis,"in *Western Man and Environmental Ethics*. Ed. Ian G. Barbour. Reading, Mass.: Addison-Wesley, 1973.

Moore, A. L. *The Parousia in the New Testament*. Leiden: E. J. Brill, 1966.

Morris, Paul and Deborah Sawyer, eds. *A Walk in the Garden: Biblical, Iconographical, and Literary Images of Eden*. Sheffield, Eng.: Sheffield Academic Press, 1992.

Morton, Charles. *Compendium Physicae, from the 1697 Manuscript Copy*. Vol. 33. Boston: Colonial Society of Massachusetts Publications, 1940.

Morton, Thomas. *New English Canaan*. In *Tracts and Other Papers Relating Principally to the Origin, Settlement, and Progress of the Colonies in North America, from the Discovery of the Country to the Year 1776*. Ed. Peter Force. Vol. 2. Washington, D.C., 1838.

Moyers, Bill. *Genesis: A Living Conversation*. New York: Doubleday, 1996.

Muir, John. *The Mountains of California*. Berkeley: Ten Speed Press, 1977.

————. *Our National Parks*. Boston: Houghton Mifflin, 1901.

————. *My First Summer in the Sierra*. New York: Penguin, 1987 [1911].

————. *A Thousand-Mile Walk to the Gulf*. San Francisco: Sierra Club Books, 1991.

Murphy, Timothy F., and Marc C. Lappé, eds. *Justice and the Human Genome Project*. Berkeley and Los Angeles: University of California Press, 1994.

Mutz, Kathryn M., Gary C. Bryner, and Douglas S. Kenny, eds. *Justice and Natural Resources: Concepts, Strategies, and Applications*. Washington, D.C.: Island Press, 2002.

Nash, J. Madeleine. "The Age of Cloning." *Time*, March 10 1997, 62–65.

Nash, Roderick. *The Rights of Nature: A History of Environmental Ethics*. Madison: University of Wisconsin Press, 1989.

————. *Wilderness and the American Mind*. 3d ed. New Haven, Conn.: Yale University Press, 1982.

Nef, John U. *The Rise of the British Coal Industry*. 2 vols. Hamden, Conn.: Archon, 1966.

Newton, Isaac. *Mathematical Principles of Natural Philosophy*, trans. A. Motte, 1729, revised Florian Cajori. Berkeley and Los Angeles: University of California Press, 1934.

Nicholson, Linda J. "Introduction" to *Feminism/Postmodernism*. Ed. Linda J. Nicholson. New York: Routldege, 1990.

Nicolson, Marjorie Hope. *Mountain Gloom and Mountain Glory: The Development of the Aesthetics of the Infinite*. Seattle: University of Washington Press, 1997; originally published 1959.

Noble, David F. *The Religion of Technology: The Divinity of Man and the Spirit of Invention*. New York: Knopf, 1975.

Noble, David W. *The Eternal Adam and the New World Garden: The Central Myth in the American Novel Since 1830*. New York: George Braziller, 1968.

Norris, Frank. *The Octopus, A Story of California*. New York: Penguin Books, 1986 [1901].
———. *The Pit, A Story of Chicago*. New York: Grove Press, 1956 [1903].
Norwood, Vera. "Heroines of Nature: Four Women Respond to the American Landscape." *Environmental Review* 8, no. 1 (1984): 34–56.
———. *Made from this Earth: American Women and Nature*. Chapel Hill: University of North Carolina Press, 1993.
Odum, Eugene P. *Fundamentals of Ecology*. Philadelphia: Saunders, 1953.
———. "The Strategy of Ecosystem Development." *Science* 164 (1969): 262–70.
Oelschlaeger, Max. *The Idea of Wilderness: From Prehistory to the Age of Ecology*. New Haven, Conn.: Yale University Press, 1991.
Olwig, Kenneth. *Nature's Ideological Landscape*. London: Allen and Unwin, 1984.
Ovid, Publius. *Metamorphoses*. Trans. Rolfe Humphries. Bloomington: Indiana University Press, 1955 [written A.D. 7].
Ovitt, George, Jr. *The Restoration of Perfection: Labor and Technology in Medieval Culture*. New Brunswick, N.J.: Rutgers University Press, 1987.
Oxford English Dictionary. Compact edition. 2 vols. Oxford: Oxford University Press, 1971.
Pääbo, Svante. "The Y Chromosome and the Origin of All of Us (Men)," *Science* May 26 (1995): 1141–2.
Parker, Arthur. "Iroquois Use of Maize and Other Food Plants." *New York State Museum Bulletin* (1910).
Perlman, David. "Gene Study Traces 'Adam' to Africa." *San Francisco Chronicle*, May 26, 1995, A1, A19.
Pfeifer, Gottfried. "The Quality of Peasant Living in Central Europe." In *Man's Role in Changing the Face of the Earth*. 2 vols. Ed. William L. Thomas, Jr. Chicago: University of Chicago Press, 1956, vol. I, 240–77.
Pickett, S. T. A. and P. S. White, eds. *The Ecology of Natural Disturbance and Patch Dynamics*. Orlando, Fla.: Academic Press, 1985.
Pinchot, Gifford. *Breaking New Ground*. Washington, D.C.: Island Press, 1947.
Plato. *The Dialogues of Plato*. Trans. B. Jowett. New York: Random House, 1937 [1892].
Plaut, W. Gunther, ed. *The Torah: A Modern Commentary*. New York: Union of Hebrew Congregations, 1981.
Plumwood, Val. *Environmental Culture: The Ecological Crisis of Reason*. London: Routledge, 2002.
———. *Feminism and the Mastery of Nature*. New York: Routledge, 1993.
———. "Gaia and Greenhouse: How Helpful is the Use of Feminine Imagery for Nature?" In *Changing Directions: The Proceedings of Ecopolitics IV*. Ed. Ken Dyer and John Young. Adelaide, Australia: Graduate Centre for Environmental Studies, University of Adelaide, 1990. 622–28.
———. "Wilderness Skepticism and Wilderness Dualism." In J. Baird Callicott and Michael P. Nelson eds. *The Great New Wilderness Debate*. Athens and London: University of Georgia Press, 1998, 652–90.
Pollan, Michael. "Genetic Pollution of Corn in Mexico," *New York Times*. Dec. 9, 2001.
———. *Second Nature: A Gardener's Edcuation*. New York: Dell, 1991.
Ponting, Clive. *A Green History of the World: The Environment and the Collapse of Great Civilizations*. New York: St. Martin's Press, 1991.
Powell, John Wesley. *Report on the Lands of the Arid Region of the United States*. Ed. Wallace Stegner. Cambridge, Mass.: Harvard University Press, 1962 [1878].
Prest, John. *The Garden of Eden: The Botanic Garden and the Re-Creation of Paradise*. New Haven, Conn.: Yale University Press, 1981.
Price, Jennifer. *Flight Maps: Adventures with Nature in Modern America*. New York: Basic Books, 1999.

Prigogine, Ilya, and Isabelle Stengers. *Order Out of Chaos: Man's New Dialogue With Nature.* New York: Bantam, 1984.

Proceedings of a Conference of Governors in the White House, Washington, D. C., May 13–15, 1908. Washington, D. C. Government Printing Office, 1909.

Propp, Vladimir. "Morphology of the Folktale." *International Journal of American Linguistics* 24, no. 4 October (1958): 1–114.

Prown, Jules David, et al. *Discovered Lands, Invented Pasts.* New Haven, Conn.: Yale University Press, 1992.

Prucha, Francis Paul. *The Indians in American Society: From the Revolutionary War to the Present.* Berkeley and Los Angeles: University of California Press, 1985.

Quinn, Daniel. *Ishmael: An Adventure of the Mind and Spirit.* New York: Bantam, 1992.

Rabasa, José. "Allegories of Atlas." In *The Post-Colonial Studies Reader.* Ed. Bill Ashcroft, Gareth Griffiths, and Helen Tiffin. London: Routledge, 1995.

Ray, John. *The Wisdom of God Manifested in the Works of the Creation.* 10th ed. London: Innys and Manby, 1935; originally published 1691.

Reeves, Marjorie. *Joachim of Fiore and the Prophetic Future.* London: SPCK, 1976.

Regal, P. J. "Models of Genetically Engineered Organisms and their Ecological Impact." *Ecology of Biological Invasions in North American and Hawaii.* Ed. Harold Mooney. New York: Springer-Verlag, 1986.

Reice, Seth R. "Nonequilibrium Determinants of Biological Community Structure." *American Scientist* 82 (1994): 424–35.

Renshaw, Edward F. *The End of Progress: Adjusting to a No-Growth Economy.* North Scituate, Mass.: Duxbury Press, 1976.

Rice, Eugene F. *The Foundations of Early Modern Europe, 1450–1559.* New York: Norton, 1970.

Rich, Adrienne. *Of Woman Born.* New York: Bantam, 1976.

Richards, John F. "Land Transformation." In *The Earth As Transformed by Human Action: Global and Regional Changes in the Biosphere over the Past 300 Years.* Ed. B. L. Turner, II, et al. New York: Cambridge University Press, 1980, 163–78.

Rifkin, Jeremy. *Algeny.* New York: Penguin, 1984.

———. *The Biotech Century: Harnessing the Gene and Remaking the World.* New York: Jeremy P. Tarcher/Putnam, 1998.

Riley, Glenda. *Women and Nature: Saving the "Wild" West.* Lincoln: University of Nebraska Press, 1999.

Rolston, Holmes III. *Philosophy Gone Wild: Essays in Environmental Ethics.* Buffalo N.Y.: Prometheus Books, 1986.

Roosevelt, Theodore. "Opening Address by the President." *Proceedings of a Conference of Governors in the White House, May 13–15, 1908.* Ed. Newton C. Blanchard. Washington, D.C.: Government Printing Office, 1908.

———. *Wilderness Writings.* Ed. Paul Schullery. Salt Lake City: Peregrine Smith Books, 1986.

Rose, Carol M. *Property and Persuasion: Essays on the History, Theory, and Rhetoric of Ownership.* Boulder, Colo.: Westview Press, 1994.

Rotenberg, Victor. "The Lapsarian Moment." Unpublished Manuscript, 1993.

Ruether, Rosemary Radford. *Gaia and God: An Ecofeminist Theology of Earth Healing.* San Francisco: Harper Collins, 1992.

Russell, J. L. "Time in Christian Thought." *The Voices of Time: A Cooperative Survey of Man's Views of Time As Expressed by the Sciences and Humanities.* Ed. J. T. Fraser. 2d ed. Amherst: University of Massachusetts Press, 1981.

Ryan, William B. B. *Noah's Flood: The New Scientific Discoveries About the Event that Changed History.* New York: Simon and Schuster, 1998.

Sahlins, Marshall. *Culture and Practical Reason.* Chicago: University of Chicago Press, 1976.

Sahtouris, Elisabet. *Gaia: The Human Journey from Chaos to Cosmos*. New York: Simon and Schuster, 1989.

Salisbury, Neal. "Red Puritans: The 'Praying Indians' of Massachusetts Bay and John Eliot." *William and Mary Quarterly* 3rd ser., 31 no. 1 (1974): 27–54.

Salkin, John and Laurie Gordon. *Orange Crate Art: The Story of the Labels that Launched a Golden Era*. New York: Warner Books, 1976.

Sanchez, Jesus. "The Environment: Whose Movement?" *Green Letter* 5, no. 1 (1989): 3–4, 14–16.

Santmire, Paul. "Historical Dimensions of the American Crisis." In *Western Man and Environmental Ethics*. Ed. Ian G. Barbour. Reading, Mass.: Addison Wesley, 1973, 82–85.

Schiebinger, Londa. *The Mind Has No Sex? Women in the Origins of Modern Science*. Cambridge, Mass.: Harvard University Press, 1989.

———. *Nature's Body: Gender in the Making of Modern Science*. Boston: Beacon Press, 1993.

Scott, Mrs. Mathew. "Address." *Proceedings of the Fourth National Conservation Congress, Indianapolis, October 14, 1912*. Indianapolis: National Conservation Congress, 1912.

Seidenberg, David. "Some Texts from the Torah on the Relationship between Humanity and Nature." Unpublished manuscript, 1993.

Sellers, Charles. *The Market Revolution: Jacksonian America, 1815–1846*. New York: Oxford University Press, 1991.

Sessions, George. "Ecocentrism and the Anthropocentric Detour." *ReVision*, 13, no. 3 (1991): 109–15.

Sessions, George, ed. *Deep Ecology for the Twenty-first Century: Readings on the Philosophy and Practice of the New Environmentalism*. Boston: Shambala, 1995.

Shabecoff, Philip. "Environmental Groups Faulted for Racism." *San Francisco Chronicle*, February 1, 1990.

Sheler, Jeffrey L. "The Christmas Covenant." *U.S. News and World Report*, Dec. 19, 1994: 62–71.

Shreeve, James. "Sunset on the Savanna." *Discover*, July 1996, 116–24.

Shteir, Ann B. *Cultivating Women, Cultivating Science: Flora's Daughters and Botany in England, 1760–1860*. Baltimore: Johns Hopkins University Press, 1996.

Simmons, William. "Conversion From Indian to Puritan." *New England Quarterly* 52, no. 2 (1979): 197–218.

Simon, Richard Keller. "The Formal Garden in the Age of Consumer Culture: A Reading of the Twentieth-Century Shopping Mall." In *Mapping American Culture*. Ed. Wayne Franklin and Michael Steiner. Iowa City: University of Iowa Press, 1992, 231–50.

Sjöö, Monica, and Barbara Mor. *The Great Cosmic Mother: Rediscovering the Religion of the Earth*. San Francisco: Harper and Row, 1987.

Slotkin, Richard. *Gunfighter Nation: The Myth of the Frontier in Twentieth-Century America*. New York: Atheneum, 1992.

———. *Regeneration through Violence: The Mythology of the Frontier*. Middletown, Conn.: Wesleyan University Press, 1973.

Smith, Adam. *An Inquiry into the Nature and Causes of the Wealth of Nations*. Ed. Edwin Cannan. New York: Modern Library, 1937.

———. *Essays on Philosophical Subjects*. Ed. Joseph Black and James Hutton. Edinburgh, 1795.

———. *The Theory of Moral Sentiments*. Ed. D. D. Raphael and A. L. Macfie. 6th ed. Oxford: Clarendon Press, 1976 [1790].

———. *The Wealth of Nations*. Ed. Andrew Skinner. New York: Penguin, 1986 [1776].

Smith, Henry Nash. *Virgin Land: The American West As Symbol and Myth*. Cambridge, Mass.: Harvard University Press, 1950.

Smith, Mark S. *The Early History of God: Yahweh and the Other Deities in Ancient Israel*. San Francisco: Harper Collins, 1990.

Solnit, Rebecca. "Up the River of Mercy." *Sierra* 77, no. 6 1992, 50–57, 78–84.

Speck, Frank. "Penobscot Tales and Religious Beliefs." *Journal of American Folklore* 48, no. 187 (1935): 1–107.

Spence, Mark David. *Dispossessing the Wilderness: Indian Removal, and the Making of the National Parks.* New York: Oxford University Press, 1999.

Spivak, Gayatri Chakravorty. "Can the Subaltern Speak?" In *Marxism and the Interpretation of Culture.* Ed. Cary Nelson and Lawrence Grossberg. London, Eng.: Macmillan, 1988.

Spretnak, Charlene. "The Concept of the Earth As Bountiful Goddess in Pre-Indo-European Cultures of Old Europe," *Conference Proceedings, National Audubon Society Expedition Institute, "Is the Earth a Living Organism?"* (Sharon, Conn.: Northeast Audubon Center, 1985), 61–64.

———. *Lost Goddesses of Early Greece: A Collection of Pre-Hellenic Mythology.* Ann Arbor, Mich.: Moon Books, 1978.

Standing Bear, Chief Luther. *Land of the Spotted Eagle.* Boston: Houghton Mifflin, 1933.

Steinberg, Theodore. *Down to Earth: Nature's Role in American History.* New York: Oxford University Press, 2002.

Stilgoe, John. *Common Landscape of America, 1580–1845.* New Haven, Conn.: Yale University Press, 1982.

Stoll, Mark. *Protestantism, Capitalism, and Nature in America.* Albuquerque: University of New Mexico Press, 1997.

Stone, Merlin. *When God Was a Woman.* New York: Harcourt Brace Jovanovich, 1976.

Stone, Michael E. *A History of the Literature of Adam and Eve.* Atlanta: Scholars Press, 1992.

Sullivan, T. J. "Cookie Cutters Shaping U.S. Cities." *Ventura County Star,* January 3, 1999.

Sutherland, Kathryn. "Adam Smith's Master Narrative: Women and the *Wealth of Nations.*" In *Adam Smith's Wealth of Nations: New Interdisciplinary Essays.* Ed. Stephen Copley and Kathryn Sutherland. Manchester: Manchester University Press, 1995, 96–121.

Swanton, J. R. "Myths and Tales of the Southeastern Indians," *Bulletin of the Bureau of American Ethnology* 88 (1929): 9–17.

Szasz, Andrew. *Ecopopulism: Toxic Waste and the Movement for Environmental Justice.* Minneapolis: University of Minnesota Press, 1994.

Tanakh, A New Translation of the Holy Scriptures, According to the Traditional Hebrew Text. Philadelphia: Jewish Publication Society, 1985.

Tarkington, Booth. *The Turmoil, a Novel.* New York: Harper and Brothers, 1915.

Taussig, Michael. "The Genesis of Capitalism amongst a South American Peasantry: Devil's Labor and the Baptism of Money," *Comparative Studies in Society and History* 19 (1977): 130–53.

Taylor, George Rogers. *The Transportation Revolution, 1815–1860.* New York: Reinhart, 1951.

Te Brake, William H. "Air Pollution and Fuel Crises in Preindustrial London," *Technology and Culture* 16 (1975): 337–59.

Thomas, William L. ed. *Man's Role in Changing the Face of the Earth.* 2 vols. Chicago: University of Chicago Press, 1956.

Thompson, William Irwin, ed. *Gaia: A Way of Knowing.* Great Barrington, Mass.: Lindisfarne Press, 1987.

Thoreau, Henry David. *Walden and Civil Disobedience.* New York: Penguin, 1983.

Tillyard, Eustace M. W. *The Elizabethan World Picture.* New York: Vintage, 1959.

Todd, John. *The Sunset Land, or the Great Pacific Slope.* Boston: Lee and Shephard, 1870.

Truax, Hawley. "Minorities at Risk," *Environmental Action,* January–February 1990, 20–21.

Truettner, William H., ed. *The West As America: Reinterpreting Images of the Frontier, 1820–1920.* Washington, D.C.: National Museum of Art, 1991.

Turner, B. L. II, William Clark, Robert W. Kates, John F. Richards, Jessica T. Matthews, and William B. Meyer. *The Earth as Transformed by Human Action: Global and Regional Changes in the Biosphere over the Past Three-Hundred Years*. New York: Cambridge University Press, 1990.

Turner, Frederick Jackson. "The Significance of the Frontier in American History." *Annual Report of the American Historical Association for the Year 1893*. Washington, D. C.: American Historical Association, 1894: 199–227.

Twain, Mark. *The Diaries of Adam and Eve*. Replica of the 1904–1905 1st ed. *The Oxford Mark Twain*. Ed. Shelley Fisher Fishkin. Vol. 26. New York: Oxford University Press, 1996.

Vaughan, Alden T. "English Policy and the Massacre of 1622," *William and Mary Quarterly* 35 (1978): 57–84.

Vaughan, Henry. *The Complete Poems*. Ed. Alan Rudrum. New Haven, Conn.: Yale University Press, 1976.

Vega, Garcilaso de la. *Royal Commentaries of the Incas*. Trans. Harold V. Livermore. 2 vols. Austin: University of Texas Press, 1869.

Waldrop, M. Mitchell. *Complexity: The Emerging Science at the Edge of Order and Chaos*. New York: Simon and Schuster, 1992.

"Walt Whitman." *Scribner's Monthly* 21, no. 1, (1880): 47–64.

Webster, Charles. *The Great Instauration: Science, Medicine, and Reform, 1626–1660*. London: Duckworth, 1975.

Wheelwright, Elizabeth Grey. *The Physick Garden: Medicinal Plants and their History*. Boston: Houghton Mifflin 1935.

White, Lynn, Jr. "The Historical Roots of Our Ecologic Crisis," *Science* 55 (1967): 1203–7.

White, Richard. *The Organic Machine: The Remaking of the Columbia River*. New York: Hill and Wang, 1995.

Whitney, Charles. *Francis Bacon and Modernity*. New Haven, Conn.: Yale University Press, 1986.

Wilford, John Noble. "Studies Shed New Light on Father of All Men." *San Francisco Chronicle*, November 23, 1995, A14.

Wilkie, Tom. *Perilous Knowledge: The Human Genome Project and Its Implications*. Berkeley and Los Angeles: University of California Press, 1993.

Willey, Basil. *The Seventeenth Century Background: Studies on the Thought of the Age in Relation to Poetry and Religion*. New York: Columbia University Press, 1952.

Williams, Michael. "Forests." In *The Earth As Transformed by Human Action: Global and Regional Changes in the Biosphere over the Past 300 Years*. Ed. B. L. Turner II, et al. New York: Cambridge University Press, 1980, 179–201.

Winthrop, John. *Winthrop's Conclusions for the Plantation in New England*. (1629) Vol. 50. Boston: Directors of the Old South Work, 1897.

Witthoft, John. *Green Corn Ceremonialism in the Eastern Woodlands*. Ann Arbor, Mich.: University of Michigan Press, 1949.

Wright, Mabel Osgood. *Birdcraft: A Field Book of Two Hundred Song, Game, and Water Birds*. New York: Macmillan, 1895.

Woloch, Nancy. *Women and the American Experience*. New York: E. P. Dutton, 1984.

Woods, Robert, ed. *The City Wilderness: A Settlement Study*. Boston: Houghton Mifflin, 1898.

Woodward, Kenneth L. "Today the Sheep, Tomorrow the Shepherd." *Newsweek*, March 10, 1997, 60.

World Resources Institute. *World Resources, 1998–99*. New York: Oxford University Press, 1998.

Worster, Donald. *Dust Bowl: The Southern Plains in the 1930s*. New York: Oxford University Press, 1979.

———. "Ecology of Order and Chaos." *Environmental History Review*, 14, nos. 1–2 (1990): 14–16.

———. *Nature's Economy: A History of Ecological Ideas*. 2d ed. New York: Cambridge University Press, 1995.

————. *Rivers of Empire: Water, Aridity, and the Growth of the American West*. New York: Pantheon, 1985.

————. *The Wealth of Nature: Environmental History and the Ecological Imagination*. New York: Oxford University Press, 1993.

Wright, Robert. "Can Souls be Xeroxed?" *Time*, March 10, 1997, 73.

Yeats, John. *Natural History of Commerce*. London, 1870.

Yuen, Edie, Lisa J. Bunin, and Tim Stroshane. "Multicultural Ecology: An Interview with Carl Anthony." *Capitalism, Nature, Socialism* 8, no. 3 (1997): 41–62.

Zeff, Robbin Lee, Marsha Love, and Karen Stults. *Empowering Ourselves: Women and Toxics Organizing*. Arlington, Va.: Citizen's Clearing House for Hazardous Wastes, n.d.

INDEX

Abram, David, 227

Accumulation, 81–82

Acid rain, 190–191

Acosta, Joseph de, *Natural and Moral History of the Indies*, 70

Adam: fallen, 17, 22; Hebrew root word (feminine) meaning arable land, 13, 16; Natty Bumppo (character) as American Adam, 106–107; as the New World hero, 84, 97–99, 103, 104; original, 22; as patriarch, 22–23, 50, 104; as redeemed in Dante, 50–51; representing mastery or reason, 47, 80

Adama, arable land, 13

Adam and Eve, **51, 52**, 59; Biblical creation of, 12–14, **15**, 254_255n.35; as leavers and takers, 194; in the New World Eden, 95; post–Edenic, 51

Adams, John Quincy, 110

Addison, Joseph, *Pleasures of the Imagination*, 87

Aenid (Virgil), 44

Africa, 93; African Savannah as Eden, 177–181

African Americans, post-Civil War struggles for advancement, 158–159

African Eve, 180–181

African Hall, 179–180

Agrarian ideal, colonial farming as, 102–103

Agriculture, 44; effects of early large–scale, 27, 42–43; farming as a stage in property development, 81; the Fertile Crescent, 40–41; invention of the plow, 66–67; origin areas ("crop cradles"), 172–173; sustainable agriculture, 172; three field system, 66–67; transition to, 28

Agriculture origin story (Penobscot Indians), 146–147

Akeley, Carl, 179–180

Alighieri, Dante. *See* Dante Alighieri

Alsop, George, "Character of the Province of Maryland", 123

America: the American dream, 4, 101; as a virgin or voluptuous maiden, 119–120, **120**, 122, 123; Protestantism in, 96; subsistence farming culture in, 101–102. *See also* Consumer mall

American Geophysical Union, conference on the Gaia hypothesis, 218–219

American Indians: agroecological system of polycultures, 146, 147, 148; decimation of and legitimating narrative(s), 145–146, 147–151; disappearance of noted, 106; efforts to Christianize, 150–152, 155; Indians removed from, 152–154; nomadic Plains Indians, 148;

origin stories as progressive narratives, 146–147; rejecting European conceptions of the land, 150–151; as "savages" of the New World, 69–70. *See also* Indian policy

American Museum of Natural History, African Hall, 179–180

American Recovery Narrative, 115–116; colonial farming as the agrarian ideal, 102–103; the heroic narrative, 97–99, 104; irrigation to recreate idyllic landscapes, 114–115; in literature and visual art, 106–110, **107, 108**; Morton's new Canaan, 99, 112; transforming the American West, 110–111, 113

American West: the desert transformed to a garden, 123–124; Far West, 110–111; Great Plains, 110–111, 113; reclamation of arid lands, 110–111, 114–115, 126

Amerigo Vespucci, 119–120, **129**

Amodo Indians, 234–235

Anat, 33, 35. *See also* Eve

Anat, mother of Yahweh, 33, 35

Animals: domestication of, 40–41, 107, 110; species extinctions, 152

Anthony, Carl, 159–160

Appalachian Mountain Club, 140

Arid lands reclamation, 110–111, 114–115, 126

Army Corps of Engineers, U.S., 237

Artemis, 33

Asherah, 28

Athene, 33

Atmosphere, earth's, 218

Atomic theories, 17th. c. revival of, 76–77

Audubon, John James, 105–106

Augustine, St., 18, 46

Austin, Mary, *The Land of Little Rain*, 140–141, 154

Bachofen, Johann J., 30

Bacon, Francis, 74–75, 110; fallen nature in, 56

Bacon, Roger, 57

Balance of nature: chaos and complexity theory challenging, 6; discordant harmonies, 216–217

Bancroft, George, 103

Bannock Indians, 152

Bargmann, Julie and Stacy Levy, 239

Barlowe, Arthur, 94

Bauman, Zygmunt, 60–61

Beatrice (Dante's): prefiguring science, 51; as redeemed Eve and idealized woman, 47, 50

Beauvais, Vincent de, 57

Being as indivisible (Parmenides), 41–42

Benton, Thomas Hart, manifest destiny doctrine, 110

Berger, Pamela, *Goddess Obscured*, 54

Berkeley, George, 128

Berkshire Mountains restoration project, 181–182

Beverley, Robert, 100, 123

Bible: King James Version, 97; order of creation in, 77; as privileged text, 200. *See also* New Testament; Old Testament; and *by Book*

Binary narratives, 200–201

Binary thinking, 200; linear and oppositional thinking, 4, 29

Biocentrism, 26

Biodiversity, 203, 215, 216, 238; genetically engineered organisms a potential threat to, 172–173; progress achieved at the cost of, 3–4, 40, 163–164, 191; sacrificed to progress, 3–4

Bioengineering. *See* Biotechnology

Biophysical existence, 201–202

Biosphere, 217

Biotechnology, 170–174; cloning of mammals, 175, 177; DNA, 171, 174–175; genomes, 174–175, 176(8.1), 177; perfecting the products of fallen nature, 172–173; potential unintended consequences of, 172–173, 174–175

Bird, Isabella, 140

Blackfeet Indians, 153

Bladensburg, Maryland, river restoration project, 237

Blake, Edward, Jr., 237

Bohm, David, 209–210

Book of J., 13

Book of Revelation, 56

Boone, Daniel, 123

Borges, Jorge Luis, 214

Botanical gardens, 59, 60, 61

Bovine growth hormone, 173

Boyce, William Jr., 24

Brackenridge, Hugh, *Modern Chivalry*, 155

Bradford, William, *Of Plimouth Plantation*, 98–99, 111, 127, 152

Bubonic plague, 67

Bulkeley, Peter, 100

Bullard, Robert, 157

Bunnell, Lafayette, 153

Bureau of Reclamation, U.S., 114, 115

Burke, Edmund, *Philosophical Enquiry into the Origins of Our Ideas of the Sublime*, 87, 88

Burnet, Thomas, *Sacred Theory of Earth*, 72, **73**

Butterfly effect, 212, 214

Byrd, William, 123

Calgene Co., 171–172

California: Central Valley, 113, 115; development of, 115; as an Edenic garden, 125–126; State Water Project, 115

Capitalism: capitalist origin and Recovery story, 68, 80–81, 173–174, 256n.4; commerce, 81, 104, 112; global resource extraction, 240; growth orientation, 217, 239–240; the market revolution, 105–116; rise of mercantile capitalism, 67–68, 76, 77, 80–81, 93. *See also* Commodification; Private property

Carson, Kit, 123

Carson, Rachel, *Silent Spring*, 4–5, 187–188

Cartesian dualism, 76, 86–87

Cathedral Pines restoration project, 181–182, 184

Cave paintings, 26

Central Valley, California, 113, 115

Chance, 215

Chaos: chaos theory, 6, 209, 213; nature as chaotic and unpredictable, 6, 8, 29, 62–63, 69, 70, 121, 182, 213, 237–239; order out of chaos, 205, 210–211

Chaucer, Geoffrey, *Merchant's Tale*, 54

Cherokee Indians, 160

Chesapeake Bay, Jamestown settlement, 70, 100

Chlorofluorocarbons (CFCs), 235

Christ: in Dante, 51; Redemption in, 13

Christianity: domination of nature theme in, 5, 77, 141; Parousia (end of the world)

in, 20; stewardship ethic in, 85, 96, 141. *See also* Bible

Christianization efforts, 150–152, 155

Christian Recovery Narrative. *See* Recovery of Eden—the Christian narrative

Chromosomes, 171

Cities: the city in the garden, 44, 131, 133; the city wilderness, 158; of Europe, 67; garden cities, 3

Civilization: civil society, 45, 69, 82; emerging from nature through property and natural rights (Locke), 78–82, 100, 126; European culture, 70; four stages of society (Smith), 82–84, 148; justice, 45; as nature transformed, 2, 33, 78, 127–129, **128**, **129**, 130; stages of (Virgil), 43–45. *See also* Cities; Government

Civil Rights Act, 162

Clemens, Samuel. *See* Twain, Mark

Clinton, William Jefferson, 162

Cloning: ethical considerations, 177; of mammals, 175, 177; reproduction and, 175, 177. *See also* Biotechnology

Club of Rome, *Limits to Growth*, 190

Coal extraction, 238–239

Colbert, Jean–Baptiste, 85

Cole, Thomas, declensionist narrative in, 107–109, **107**, **108**

Collective memory, 240

Colman, Henry, 124

Colonial ecological complex, 147

Colonialism. *See* European colonization

Colton, Calvin, 105

Columbia River Basin salmon run, 235

Columbus, Christopher, 57–58

Commerce, 81, 104, 112. *See also* Capitalism

Commodification: commodified images of Eve, 125; commodities, 81. *See also* Capitalism; Consumer mall

Complexity theory, 6, 206, 209, 213; chance, 215; complex adaptive systems, 214, 215

Conservation and preservation, 158–159; movements splitting over Hetch-Hetchy dam, 141–142; redemptive themes in, 3. *See also* Conservationism; Preservationism

——— early precedents for: 19th. century artists and scientists noting environmental decline, 105–106; concern over air

pollution (17th. c.), 84–85; forest conser-
vation proposals (17th. c.), 85; French
Forest Ordinance of 1669, 85. *See also*
Romanticism
Conservationism: forestry movement, 138; as
the recovery of nature through good
management, 136–137; utilitarian
approach in, 138–140
Consumer capitalism. *See* Capitalism
Consumer mall: as a new Garden of Eden,
1–2, 167–170, 184; mall culture,
169–170
Cooper, Anthony Ashley, 87
Cooper, James Fenimore, *The Pioneers*,
106–107
Corn mothers, 146–147
Corporations: corporate interests and envi-
ronmental concerns, 240; corporate
self–regulation, 235
Cotton boom, Southern, 147, 156
Cotton Gin, 156
Cotton, John, 98
Counternarratives: of indigenous peoples,
2–3, 146, 150–151; on racial injustice
and colonization, 145, 158–159,
164–165. *See also* Environmental declen-
sionist narrative; Feminist declensionist
narrative; Feminist Recovery Narrative(s)
Cranach, Lucas, *Adam and Eve*, **52**, 53
Crèvecoeur, J. Hector St. John de, *Letters*,
102–103
Cronon, William, 5–6
Crop cradles, 172–173
Crop rotation: long fallow system, 101, 102;
short fallow system, 102; the three field
system, 66–67
Crow Indians, 152
Cultural diversity: multiculturalism, 163,
232–233; partnership programs including, 238–239; progress achieved at cost
of, 3–4, 40, 163–164, 191
Cycles and change in nature, 41, 45–46, 72,
73

Dairy management, 173
Dante Aligheri, *Divine Comedy*, 39, 48–49;
Fall and Recovery Narrative in, 47–48,
49, 51; merging Greco-Roman and
Christian narratives, 47–48; Virgil as

guide in, 47, 48. *See also* Beatrice
(Dante's)
Dark Ages, 46
Darwin, Charles, *Descent of Man*, 179
Darwinism, 110, 206;
David, 27
Davis, Elizabeth Gould, 35, 30
Dawes Act, 150
Dawn of the Dead (film), 168
DDT, 4, 187–188
Death of wilderness, 192–193
D'Eaubonne, Françoise, *Feminism or Death*,
195–196, 30
De Bry, Theodore, 94, **95**
"Decay" of nature, 65–66, 70–72, **73**
Declensionist narratives. *See*
Counternarratives; Environmental
declensionist narrative; Fall from Eden;
Feminist declensionist narrative
Deconstruction, 200, 201
Deep ecologists, 191
Deforestation, 190; of New World forests,
96–97, 101, 163; of old world forests,
66–68, 84. *See also* Forests
Demeter, 33, 35, 54
Democracy and the good state, 101, 106;
free land a component of, 102, 112
Democritus, 76
Dennis, John, 87
Derham, William, *Physico-Theology*, 85–86
Derrida, Jacques, 200, 201
Descartes, René, 76, 86; Cartesian dualism,
76, 86–87
Descartes, René, *Discourse on Method*, 76
Desert: arid lands reclamation, 110–111,
114–115, 126; as Indian lands (Austin),
154; as infertile, 18; outside Eden, 14,
55, 107, **107**; transformed to garden,
123–124; as the wilderness, 69, 70
Diamond, Jared, 40–41
Diner, Helen, 30
Discordant harmonies, 216–217
Disenchantment of the world, 191, 206–207
Di Silvestro, Roger L., 230
Divine Comedy. See Dante Aligheri, *Divine
Comedy*
Divine forest (Dante), 48–50
Divine right of kings, 78–80
DNA, 171, 174–175, **176**, 210

Doering, Rich, 169
Dolly, cloning of, 175, 177
Domestication of animals, 40–41, 107, 110
Domestic partners, 224
Domination of nature: as an aspect of the
    Enlightenment, 75, 89; control of unpre-
    dictability requiring, 62–63; expressed in
    Genesis 1:28, 13, 24, 47, 80, 81, 96, 97,
    250_251n.21; gender domination and,
    232; gendered nature a justification for,
    56, 62–63, 124; images of sexual assault,
    112–113; mechanistic science and world-
    view enabling, 5, 66, 75–77, 205–206,
    225; romantic themes opposing, 134;
    theme in *Isaiah 40:3–4*, 111
Dorians, 33
Dubos, René, 25
DuPont Chemical Cos., 234–235
Dürer, Albrecht, 242, **243**, 254_255n.35
Dust Bowl, declensionist vs. progressive nar-
    ratives of, 5–6

Eades, Joseph Kevin, 237
Earth as a self regulating system, 217–218
Earthly Eden, 50; botanical gardens and
    zoos, 59; created through technology, 5,
    20, 56–57, 61–63; the New World as,
    57–59, **58**, 66. *See also* New World Eden
Earth, Mother. *See* Mother Earth/Mother
    Nature
Earthquakes, 8
Earth Summit (1992), 224
East Bay Conservation Corps, 235
Ecocentric ethic, 25
Ecofeminism, 195–196
Ecological crisis. *See* Environmental crisis
Ecological revolution, 196
Ecologues (Virgil), 44
Ecology, 216–217; and chaos theory, 6; issue
    of balance of nature in, 216–217; ecolog-
    ical processes, 175
Ecology-Feminism Center, 195
Economics: new economic forms needed,
    240. *See also* Capitalism; Natural
    resources; Private property
Eden: as a divine forest in Dante, 48–50;
    Biblical, 1, 2, 13–14; as bountiful and
    fruitful, 28, 94; colonized (*See also* New
    World), 2, 3, 163; depictions of, 54–56,

55; as an enclosed garden or park, 18, 47;
    the Fertile Crescent and, 41; as irrigated
    by rivers or spring fed, 14, **15**; nature as
    the idealized garden, 12, 18–19, 35, **55**.
    See also American Eden; Earthly Eden;
    Gardens; New World Eden
Eden commodified. *See* Commodification
Edenic myth. *See* Adam and Eve; Eden; Fall
    from Eden ; Recovery of Eden—the
    Christian narrative
Egocentric ethics, 229, 233
Egypt, 31
Ehrlich, Paul, 190, 194–195
Eisenberg, Evan, *Ecology of Eden*, 16
Eisler, Riane: *Chalice and the Blade*, 35, 232,
    30; *Sacred Pleasure*, 232
Emancipation Proclamation, 162
Emerson, Ralph Waldo: progressivism in, 105;
    transcendentalism in, 118, 133, 135–136
Endangered Species Act (ESA), 163
Enfoldment, 210
Engels, Friedrich, 30, 191, 252n.37
Enlightenment: reason, 80, 198; the
    Scientific Revolution, 20, 65, 66, 89; sec-
    ular Recovery Narrative of, 65, 83,
    88–89, 110; theme of domination or
    penetration in, 53, 56, 75. *See also* Bacon,
    Francis; Domination of nature;
    Science—and technology
——— as a false narrative, 188, 191,
    198–199
Environmental contamination, 4, 187–188
Environmental crisis, 4–5, 38, 189–191, 201,
    225
Environmental declensionist narrative, 5–7,
    188; apocalyptic scenarios, 189–191; as
    evidence-based, 37; loss of primordial
    unity with nature (Oelschlaeger), 26–29,
    32; progress achieved at cost of cultural
    and biotic diversity, 3–4, 40, 163–164,
    191; in visual art (Cole), 107–109, **107**,
    108
Environmental decline: 19th. century artists
    and scientists noting, 105–106; in
    ancient times (noted in Plato), 42–43;
    human activity perceived as related to
    (19th. c.), 5–7, 105–106, 116; nature's
    fallen status as the reason for (17th c.),
    65–66, 70–72, 105–106

Environmental history, 5
Environmental justice, 3, 157, 162, 164–165
Environmental Recovery Narrative(s),
    118–119, 189
Epicurus, 76
Erigena, John Scotus, 56–57
Essences/essentialism, 23, 143, 241
Europe: cities of, 67; growth of population in
    late medieval, 66–67; managing resources
    of colonized territories, 93; Old Europe,
    30–31
European colonization, 2, 3, 163
European culture, 70
European heroes, 120
Eve: as a modern women (Locke), 80, 89; as
    Anat (mother of Yahweh), 33, 35; as
    black (See also African Eve), 155; com-
    modified images of, 125; as created from
    Adam's rib, 13, 35; as the first scientist,
    23, 53, 198; as mother or maternal, 35,
    104, 118, 213; the name of, 248n.2; orig-
    inal sin of, 48, 49–50, 51–52, 52; as vir-
    gin (See also Eden), 117–119, 213; as
    willful woman, 53
———— as fallen nature, 18–19, 22, 75, 88,
    117–118, 135–136, 213; in Bacon, 56;
    decay of nature related to Eve's fall,
    65–66, 70–72, 73; mainstream narrative
    connections to, 125, 127. See also
    Nature—as female; Sexual imagery of
    gendered nature
Evelyn, John, 84–85, 86
African Savannah as Eden, 177–181
Executive Order 12898, 162
Exodus, 99
Explicate order, 209
Expulsion from the Garden of Eden (Cole),
    107, 107
Extraction, 81

Fall from Eden: as disenchantment of the
    world, 191, 206–207; Eve's original sin
    the cause of, 48, 49–50, 51–52, 52;
    expulsion of Adam and Eve from the
    Garden (Gen. 3), 12, 16–18, 107, 107;
    fallen nature, 22, 75, 88, 118, 135–136;
    human labor resulting from, 17, 28, 51,
    66; mainstream narrative based in, 3,
    11–12, 206; post-Edenic landscape,

16–17, 18; the temptation (See also
    Serpent), 12, 14, 16, 17. See also Eden;
    Eve
Farming: the agrarian ideal, 102–103; as a
    stage in property development, 81;
    inland farming, 101–102 the plow,
    66–67; subsistence farming culture
    (American), 101–102. See also Crop rota-
    tion
Fasolino, Teresa, depiction of the Garden of
    Eden, 242
Female symbolism: civilization as female
    nature transformed, 2, 33, 78, 127–129,
    128, 129, 130; continents as female, 120,
    121, 121; corn mothers as transformers
    (Penobscot Indian), 146–147; earth as
    female, 43, 104, 121, 140, 188, 193; fem-
    inine space, 84, 104; liberty or the course
    of empire depicted in female form,
    127–129, 129; Neolithic mother god-
    desses, 29–33, 32, 34, 35–36; New World
    depicted as a virgin or voluptuous
    maiden, 119–120, 120, 122, 123; Plato's
    (female) soul of the world, 127, 131, 134.
    See also Eve; Nature—as female; Virgin
    Mary
Feminist declensionist narrative, 2–3, 196; as
    evidence-based, 37; female deities
    replaced by patriarchal gods, 29–33, 32,
    34, 35–36, 197–198; reversing the
    Biblical narrative, 33, 35
Feminist postmodern critique, 198
Feminist Recovery Narrative(s), 189,
    195–198; antecedents of partnership
    ethic in, 35–36, 231–232
Feminist science, 198
Fernow, Bernhard, Economics of Forestry,
    138–139
Fertile Crescent, 40–41
Feudalism, 46; gamekeeper cultures, 60
Fiege, Mark, Irrigated Eden, 114–115
Food and Drug Administration, U.S., 172
Foraging and hunting, 28, 197
Foreman, Dave, 230
Forest Reserve Act, 158
Forestry movement, 138
Forests: as common resources, 46; Eden-like
    or "virgin", 48–50, 59, 103–104; human
    evolution as emergence from, 178–179;

old world forests, 66–68; as symbolic of dark forces (medieval), 46, 48, 68. *See also* Deforestation

Formal garden, 61, **62**

Fox, Stephen, 159

"Frankenfish", 173. *See also* Genetically engineered organisms

Frankfort school, 191

Franklin, Benjamin: progressive narrative of, 101; satirical remarks on colonial efforts to "civilize" Indians, 147, 151–152

Freeman, George, 115

French Forest Ordinance of 1669, 85

Fuegians, Darwin's description of, 179

Gaia hypothesis, 217–219

Game hunting, 179–180

Gamekeeper gardeners, 60–61

Gardener, as male, 181, 183

Garden ethic (Pollan), 181–184

Garden of Eden. *See* Eden

Gardens, 26; as a metaphor for Eden, 59; botanical gardens, 59, 60, 61; enclosed gardens, 18, 25, 47, 163; enclosed gardens—medieval, 54–56, **55**, 168; garden in the forest (the recovered garden), 103–104, 108; gardens of forking paths (Borges), 214; modern formal garden, 61, **62**, 88; wilderness transformed into a garden (Recovery Narrative), 2, 62–63, 153, 154, 163

Gare, Arran E, *Postmodernism and the Environmental Crisis*, 201–202

Gast, John, *American Progress*, 127, **128**

Gell-Mann, Murray, *The Quark and the Jaguar*, 214

Gendered nature: as a problematic notion, 119, 181, 184, 236. *See also* Nature—as female

Gender symbolism. *See* Female symbolism; Male symbolism; Sexual imagery of gendered nature

Gene, 171

Genesis 1: gender equality inferred in, 13, 23; textual origins of, 13; theme of dominion over nature in (*Gen. 1:28*), 13, 24, 47, 80, 81, 96, 97

Genesis 2: creation of Eve from Adam in, 13, 248n.3, 254_255n.35; Garden of Eden

in, 13–14, 94; stewardship theme in (*Gen. 2:15*), 24–25, 96; textual origins of, 13

Genesis 3: expulsion from Eden, 12, 16–18; humans condemned to labor in, 17, 28; temptation of Eve, 12, 14, 16, **17**

Genesis 7, Noah's flood, 8, 29, **73**

Genetically engineered organisms: corn, 172–173; fast ripening fruits, 170, 171–172; transgenic animals in the wild, 173; transgenic plant pollution, 172–173

Genetic code: as the Bible of nature, 171. *See also* Biotechnology

Genomes, 174–175, 176(8.1), 177

Georgics (Virgil), 44

Gibbons, James, 140

Gimbutas, Marija, *Goddesses and Gods of Old Europe*, 30, 31

Glacier National Park, 153

Glendinning, Chellis, "In Recovery from Western Civilization", 196–197

Glenn W. Daniel King Estate Park, 238

Global population, 189–190, 194–195

Global warming, 190

God: chaos theory challenging creator role of, 213; scientific revolution diminishing the role of, 206–207

Goddesses: Anat (*See also* Eve), 33, 35; Athene, 33; mother goddesses (Neolithic), 29–33, **32**, **34**, 35–36

Gods: father gods, 31, 33, 36, 44, 107, 213; Neolithic son gods, 32, 33, 54. *See also* Christ; Monotheism; Yahweh

God's eye view, 198

"God word", 199–200

Golden age, Greco-Roman, 39–40, 42, 43

Goldschmidt, Henry, 18

Goodenough, Ursula, 175, 177

Government: democracy and the good state, 101, 102, 106, 112; receiving mandate from nature, 78, 79–80; social contract theory of, 45, 78

Great Basin, 113

Great Mother (Paleolithic), 252n.37; original unity with lost, 26–29, **32**, 37, 197–198; roused by capitalism (Norris), 133. *See also* Mother Earth/Mother Nature; Neolithic mother goddesses

Great Plains, 110–111, 113

Greco-Roman golden age, 39–40, 42, 43;

Greek mythology, 74; Virgil's second golden age, 44–45

Greco-Roman world: classical atomic theory, 76; the fall of Rome, 46; Greek civilization, 33, 39, 41, 42–43, 46; narratives of decline, 42–43; Roman progressive narratives, 43–45; view of nature, 41, 45–46; Virgil symbolizing classical learning in the *Divine Comedy*, 48

Greenhouse effect, 190

Green justice. *See* Environmental justice

Grinnell, George Bird, 153

Grotius, Hugh, 78

Hamilton, Alexander, 101

Harriot, Thomas, *Brief and True Report the Newfoundland of Virginia*, 94, **95**

Harrison, Jane Ellen, 30

Harrison, Robert Pogue, 47–48, 50

Hearnshaw, F. J. C., 49

Heaven, as recovered Eden, 18, 19, 20

Hebrews, town-based cultures of, 27–28. *See also* Asherah; Pentateuch; Torah; Yahweh

Heisenberg, W.K., uncertainty principle, 212, 214

Heraclitus, 41

Hercules, pillars of, **74**

Heroic narratives: Adam as the New World hero, 84, 97–99, 103, 104; components of, 97–99; human evolution as a hero narrative, 177–181

Hesiod, 42

Hetch Hetchy Valley, controversy over damming of, 141–142, 143

Hiebert, Theodore, 14, 16

Hierarchy, 31, 77, 257n.27. *See also* Domination of nature

Hobbes, Thomas, 45; *Leviathan*, 78

Hogue, Alexander "Erosion No. 2", **188**

Holomovement, 209–210

Homesteaders, early American, 25

Homestead ideal, 150

Homocentric ethics, 217, 229

Hooker, Richard, 62

Hooker, Thomas, 99–100

Horkheimer, Max, 116, 227

Horkheimer, Max and Theodor Adorno, *Dialectic of Enlightenment*, 191

Horus, 54

Hudson River School, 107

Huet, P.D., *la situation du paradis terreste*, 59

Hughes, J. Donald, "Gaia: An Ancient View of our Planet", 219

Hugh of St. Victor, 57

Human evolution as a hero narrative, 177–181

Human Genome Program, 174

Human-nature relationship: as a partnership, 199; as deeply personal, 134–135, 136; as disrupted in early human times, 26–29, 191–192, 196–197; human appropriation of nature, 79, 80–82; of impersonal management, 173; an irreconcilable gulf between (Augustinian), 18, 46; as one of equal and active agents, 228–231, 236–237; primordial unity posited, 26–27, 191, 196. *See also* Female symbolism; Male symbolism; Nature—as female; Partnership ethic

Hunting and gathering, 28, 197

Hurricanes, 8

Hurston, Zora Neale, *Their Eyes Were Watching God*, 145, 160–161

Huxley, Thomas, 110

Hydraulic technology, 113, 114

Idealist philosophy, 37

Iltis, David, "The Lesson", 221–222

Implicate order, 209–210

Imported species, 114–115

Inanna, 35

Indian policy, 148–151; removal of native inhabitants from national parks, 152–154; reservation system, 148, **151**, 160, 164

Indians. *See* American Indians

Indigenous peoples: as based in nature, 196–197, 199–200; "civilizing" of, 2; as New World "savages", 69–70, 179; oral cultures, 200, 227; sacrificed to progress, 3–4. *See also* American Indians

Indigenous peoples' counternarratives: of Fall and Recovery, 2–3, 146; of the land not as a wilderness, 150–151. *See also* African Americans; American Indians; Indian policy; Racial injustice and colonization

Iron Age, 28

Irrigation, 113–114, 126, 190. *See also* River restoration project; Water runoff project
Isaiah 40:3–4, 111
Ishtar, 32–33, 35, 54
Isis, 33, **34**, 35, 54
Israelites. *See* Hebrews

Jackson, Andrew, 102, 103, 148–149
Jadwin, Curtis, 132–133
Jaggar, Alison, 232–233
Jamestown settlement, 70, 100
Jefferson, Thomas, 156
Jehovah. *See* Yahweh
Jewett, Sarah Orne, 141
Joachim of Fiore, recovery of Eden narrative, 56, 57
Jove/Zeus, 33, 44
Judge Temple (fictional character), 106

Kant, Immanuel, *Observations on the Feeling of the Beautiful and Sublime*, 87–88
Kauffman, Stuart, 206
Kings, divine right of, 78–80
Kirchner, James, 219
Knowles, Joe, *Alone with Nature*, 142
Kolodny, Annette, *The Lay of the Land*, 104, 124
Kovacic, David, simulation models of wildfires, 238
Kyoto protocol, 190

Labor: of humans as a result of the Fall, 17, 28, **51**, 66; male labor as heroic (*See also* Adam), 84
Land, arable land (*adama*), 13, 16, 18, 66
Landau, Misia, 178
Landscape, re-creational qualities of, 114–115
Landscape architecture, 236–238
LaPlace, Pierre Simon, 213
Lapsarian moment, 18
Leatherstocking tales (Cooper), 106–107
Leavers and takers, 194
Leopold, Aldo, conservation ethic, 161–162, 231
Leutze, Emanuel, *Westward the Course of Empire*, 127–129, **129**
Liberty, 128, **130**
Limerick, Patricia Nelson, 158, 161, 162

Lincoln, Abraham, 158, 162
Locke, John, *Two Treatises on Government*: on the creation and the Fall, 78, 79–80; Eve as a modern women in, 80, 89; progressive Recovery Narrative in, 80–82, 100, 126, 258ns.32, 35_38 , 258_259n.39, 259.n44
Logos, 199, 200
Long, Frederick J. and Matthew Arnold, 274n 3
Lorenz, Edward, on the butterfly effect, 212, 214
Lost Edens: golden age (Greco-Roman), 39–40, 42, 43; matriarchal era overthrown (feminist), 29–33, **32**, **34**, 35–36; oneness of nature mother and humankind (Oelschlaeger), 26–29, **32**, 37. *See also* Fall from Eden
Lovelock, James, 217; and Lynn Margulis, 217–218
Lucifer, 53. *See also* Serpent
Lucretius, *De Reum Natura*, 45, 76
Ludolphos of Saxony, *Mirror of Man's Salvation*, 51, **51**, 53
Luther Standing Bear, 150–151

MacGregor tomato, 171–172
Madison, James, 101
Magna Carta, 162
Magna Mater, in Oelschlaeger, 26–29, **32**, 37. *See also* Great Mother (Paleolithic)
Mainstream Recovery Narrative, 184, 240–241; in art and fiction, 105, 106–110, **107**, **108**, 132–133; Biblical roots of, 11, 13, 18–19, 39; Christian narrative segueing into, 11–12, 77, 127, 205; classical science central to (*See also* Enlightenment), 207; an earthly Eden created through technology, 5, 20, 56–57, 61–63, 65, 75; legitimating colonial domination, 145–146, 147–151; linear and oppositional qualities of, 4, 29; moving from wild nature to civilization, 126–127; nature as fallen Eve in, 56, 83, 110, 184; philosophical progressive narratives presaging, 126–127. *See also* American Recovery Narrative; Earthly Eden; Progressive narratives; Science—and technology

Male symbolism: Adam as the New World hero, 84, 97–99, 103, 104; chaotic natural forces as male, 160–161; imperial power as male, 119–120, **129**; masculine encounter with nature valorized, 139–140, 142; science as male, 22. *See also* Adam; Gods

Mall. *See* Consumer mall

Mall culture, 169–170

Mall of America, 169

Manifest destiny doctrine, 110, 112

Maplewood, Minnesota, water runoff project, 236–237

Marcuse, Herbert, 231

Market revolution, 105–116

Marsh, George Perkins, *Man and Nature*, 137–138, 231

Marxism, 29–30

Marx, Karl, 191, 196

Maryland, 123

Mary, Virgin. *See* Virgin Mary

Masculinity. *See* Male symbolism

Massachusetts Bay colony, 99–100

Material reality, 201–202, 213

Mathematical method, 76–77

Mather, Robin, 173

Matriarchal theory, 196

Matthew 25:14, 85

Maynard, George Willowby, 129, **131**

McHarg, Ian, 239; *Design With Nature*, 236; landscape architecture of, 236–238

McKenney, Thomas L., 148

McKibben, Bill, *The End of Nature*, 190, 193

McNamara, Ray Maria, 24

Meadows, Donella H., et al, *The Limits to Growth*, 190

Mechanism, 230; enabling the domination of nature, 5, 66, 75–77, 205–206, 225; nature as a machine, 76–77, 113. *See also* Enlightenment

Medieval enclosed gardens, 54–56, **55**, 168

Medieval era. *See* Middle Ages

Megamalls, 168. *See also* Consumer mall

Mercantile capitalism, 67–68, 76, 77, 80–81. *See also* Capitalism

Mercator, Gerhard, *Atlas*, 122, 263n.3

Merchant, Carolyn, 167, 255n.1, 272n.28, 275n.26

Mersenne, Marin, 76

Mesopatamia, 31, 32; the Fertile Crescent, 40–41; Old World Eden in, **58**, 59, **60**

Middle Ages, forests symbolic of dark forces during, 46, 48, 68

Millar, Norman, 239

Millenarianism, , 56, 271n.2

Miller, Olive Thorne, 141

Mitochondria, 181

Modernity: Frankurt school critique of, 191; modern formal garden, 61, **62**; modernism as a master narrative, 241; postmodern critique of. *See* Postmodernism

Modern narrative. *See* Mainstream Recovery Narrative

Moncrief, Lewis, 5

Monotheism, 28–29, 197

Monsanto Chemicals, 172–173

Moore, A. L, *Parousia*, 20

Moral consideration of nature, 223, 244

Mormons, 114

Morton, Thomas, *New English Canaan*, 99, 112

Mosaic Decalogue, 161. *See also* Old Testament

Mother Earth/Mother Nature, 43, 104, 121, 140, **188**, 193. *See also Magna Mater*; Nature—as female

Mother goddesses: Neolithic, 29–33, **32**, **34**, 35–36; patriarchal gods replacing, 31, 33, 35

Mozingo, Louise, 238

Muir, John: avoiding Civil War service, 159; imagery of nature in, 118, 133–134, 135, 136; racial attitudes of criticized, 150–160, 153; theocentric ethic in, 141; "Thousand-Mile Walk to the Gulf", 159–160

Mulholland, William, 115

Multiculturalism, 163, 232–233

Mumford, Lewis, 236

Mycenaeans, 33

Myths, 2, 200. *See also* Narratives

Narratives: binary narratives, 200–201; formative powers of, 3; grand narrative, 201–202; idealist philosophy inherent to, 37; interacting with reality, 201; internalized as ideology, 241; master narratives, 202, 240; homological narratives, 202; as

no deterministic, 37–38; nonlinear, 208, 215; polyphonic or multiple narratives, 202–203, 241; privileged texts of master narratives, 199–200
—— of decline. *See* Environmental declensionist narrative; Fall from Eden ; Feminist declensionist narrative
—— of progress. *See* Progressive narratives
Nash, Roderick, 157, 159, 162, 268n.38
Nassauer, Joan Iverson, 236
National Audubon Society, Gaia symposium, 219
National Conservation Congress, 140
National parks: creation of, 141; Indians removed from, 152–154
National Park Service Act, 142
National People of Color Environmental Leadership Summit, 224
Natty Bumppo (fictional character), 106–107
Natural resources: forests as common, 46; global extraction of, 240; the New World as the site of, 93, 96, 105; sacrificed to progress, 3–4; uneven access to, 163
Natural rights, 79, 162
Natural selection. *See also* Evolution
Nature: aesthetic appreciation of, 191, 227–228; as a machine (*See also* Mechanism), 76–77, 113; apprehension of the sublime in, 86–88, 89; as a socially constructed concept, 143; as an autonomous actor, 220, 226–227, 229–230; as bountiful/fruitful, 28, 42; as chaotic/unpredictable/violent, 6, 8, 29, 62–63, 69, 70, 121, 182, 213, 237–239; cycles and change in, 41, 45–46, 72, **73**; having unchanging laws, 76; moral order associated with, 18, 83; as *natura naturans* (active) and *natural naturata* (ordered), 127; as a subject (not personified), 218, 219, 221–222. *See also* Genetic code; Human-nature relationship; "State of nature"
—— and Eden myth: as Eve, 22, 75, 88, 117–118; as fallen, 22, 75, 88, 118, 135–136; as the idealized garden (*See also* Eden), 12, 18–19, 35, **55**; post-Edenic landscape, 16–17, 18. *See also* Eve

—— as female, 2, 23, 104, **120**, 121, 182; as a socially constructed notion, 143; as bountiful/fruitful, 28, 42; environmentalism incorporating imagery of, 3, 118; as the original deity (*See also* Magna Mater), 31, 43; as a problematic notion, 119, 181, 184, 236; sexual imagery of the enclosed garden, 53, 54–56, 75; as a virgin, 103–104, 118–119, 129. *See also* Female symbolism; Sexual imagery of gendered nature
—— as wilderness. *See* Wilderness
Nature-God relationship: God as clockmaker, 76; God as transcendent (Yahweh), 29; nature as God's plan, 83, 85–86; nature as sacred (*Magna Mater*), 26–27
Nature writing, 191, 227–228
Near East, 27–28
Neolithic era, 26–27, 30, **32**
Neolithic mother goddesses, 29–33, **32, 34**, 35–36
New Testament, 20; *Book of Revelation*, 56; *Matthew 25:14*, 85; *Romans 8:22*, 17–18
Newtonian physics, 77, 110; contemporary theories limiting application of, 205, 209, 210, 213
Newton, Isaac, *Mathematical Principles of Natural Philosophy*, 77

New World Eden: Adam as the New World hero, 84, 97–99, 103, 104; Adam and Eve depicted in, 94, **95**; as a virgin land, 119–120, **120, 121**, 122, 124; invoked with Biblical imagery, 57–59, 61–62, 96–97, 99–100, 107, **107**; Mormons bringing a religious mandate to create, 113–114. *See also* American Recovery Narrative
New World environment: decimation of animals, 97; forests and deforestation, 96–97, 101, 163; native plants replaced by European weeds and crops, 97; "savages" of, 69–70, 179; asthe site of natural resources, 93, 96, 105; soil erosion, 96–97; the wilderness in, 69–70, 107
New York City
Central Park, garbage problem

Nicholson, Linda J., 198
Nicolson, Marjorie Hope, 86–87
1960s, 5–6
Noah's flood (*Gen. 7*), 8, 29, **73**
Noble, David W, *The Eternal Adam and the New World Garden*, 103
Nonlinear narratives, 208, 215
Nonlinear relationships, 211
Norris, Frank, *The Octopus*, 124–125, 130, 132, 133
Noumenal world, 213
Novum Organum frontispiece, **74**

Oakland, California, restoration of oak groves, 238
Oelschlaeger, Max, *Idea of Wilderness*, 26–29, 191–192
Old Europe, 30–31
Old Testament, 13, 161; *Exodus*, 99; *Isaiah 40:3–4*, 111; *Song of Solomon*, 54. *See also by Book*
Open systems, vs. closed systems, 210–211, 228
Oral cultures, 200, 227
Order out of chaos, 205, 210–211
Origin stories: Biblical creation (*See also Genesis 1*; *Genesis 2*), 12–14, **15**, 177; capitalist origin story, 68, 80–81; of Penobscot Indians, 146. *See also Evolution*
Ortelius, Abraham, *Theatrum Orbis Terrarum*, 120, **121**, 122
Osiris, 33
Other (the), 201, 202
Ovid, *Metamorphoses*, 43, 138
Oxbow (Cole), 108–109, **108**
Ozone depletion, 190

Paleolithic era, 26–27, 199; culture of, 26–27, 30, **32**. *See also* Great Mother (Paleolithic)
Paleolithic mind (Oelschaeger), 199–200
Paradise: as recovered Eden, 18, 19, 20. *See also* Eden
Parks, 3, 230, 238
Parminides, 41–42
Parousia (end of the world), 20, 249n.14
Partnership ethic: Biblical precedents for, 23–24, **51**; consensus and negotiation

process, 228–229, 233–235; defined, 26, 38, 223, 224, 225; difficulties in implementing, 239–240; environmental partnerships, 223–225, 233–237; the Fall as loss of partnership with the land, 18; gender partnership and, 35–36, 80, 89, 231–232, 242; historical roots of, 231–233; involving stakeholders, 228–229, 234, 235; nonhuman entities represented, 235; personal relation with nature (of romantics) compatible with, 134–135, 136–137. *See also* Sustainability
Pastoralism, 16–17; domestication of animals, 40–41, 107, 110
Pasture land, 66–67, 68
Patriarchy: emergence of capitalism within, 77, 84; feminist critique of, 195–196, 198–199; as the overthrow of female divinity, 31, 33, 36, 252n.40 and n.42; postpatriachal society, 242; property ownership system and, 101. *See also* Domination of nature; Gods
Paul, St., on nature as fallen, 17–18
Pennsylvania, reforestation project in, 238–239
Penobscot Indians, origin story of, 146
Pentateuch, 13
Persephone, 33
Pesticides, 4, 187–188
Pinchot, Gifford, 139
Pioneers, 128–129
Plants: native plant communities, 237; origin areas ("crop cradles"), 172–173; transgenetic pollution in, 173
Plato: on myth, 200; pure forms vs. appearances in, 37, 41; soul the world in, 127, 131, 133, 134
——— works: *Critias*, 42–43; *Timaeus*, 134
Plessy v. Ferguson, 159
Plow, 66–67, 124–125. *See also* Agriculture
Plumwood, Val, 230, 241; *Feminism and the Mastery of Nature*, 232
Pollan, Michael, the garden ethic, 181–184
Pollution, 67–68, 164
Population: growth of global, 189–190, 194–195; growth of late medieval European, 66–67
Posilac, 173

Postmodernism: critique of modernism, 191; feminist postmodern critique, 198; privileged texts of modernity questioned, 199, 200

Poverty, 163, 217

Power, formal garden displaying, **62**

Preservationism: preserving wild nature as goal of, 137, 143, 208, 229; women in the preservation movement, 140–141. *See also* Muir, John

Prigogine, Ilya, 210–211

"Primitive man", 142

Private property, 65–66, 101; gridlines, 116; as the key to civil society, 77–78, 89; Locke's three stages of, 81–82; residing in natural rights, 79. *See also* Property rights movement

Privilege and marginalization, 200

Process physics, 109–110

Production, 38

Progress, acheived at cost of cultural and biotic diversity, 3–4, 40, 163–164, 191. *See also* Capitalism

Progressive narratives: Bradford on the American Eden, 97–99; capitalist recovery story, 68, 80–81; the "decay" of nature justifying, 65–66; democracy and the good state, 101, 102, 106, 112; the Enlightenment's secular narrative of Recovery, 65, 88–89; European colonization based in, 2, 3; in literature and fiction, 105, 106–107, 132–133; mechanistic science enabling progress, 5, 75–77; realities providing a challenge to, 163–164; stages of development, 80–84, 100, 148, 163; Turner's heroic narrative of the frontier, 111–112; in the visual arts, 107–110, **107**, **108**. *See also* Domination of nature; Science—and technology

Prometheus, 74

Property ownership. *See* Private property

Property rights movement, 163, 240

Propp, Vladimir, on the heroic narrative, 98–99, 111

Protestantism, in America, 96

Pufendorf, Samuel, 78

Puritanism, 99–100, 104–105

Pyne, Stephen, *Fire in America*, 207–208

Quantum mechanics, 206, 212

Quarks, 214

Quinn, Daniel, *Ishmael*, 193–194

Race: and environmental justice, 3, 157, 162, 164; racial views of early conservationists evaluated, 157–158, 159–160, 161–162; white/black skin-color dichotomy, 129, 154–155

Racial injustice and colonization, 145, 158–159, 164–165

Racial segregation, 159

Radiation effects, 4–5

Railroads, 112, 126

Raker Act, 141–142, 143

Raleigh, Walter, *History of the World*, 58, 59

Ray, John, *Wisdom of God Manifested in the Works of the Creation*, 85

Reality: material reality, 201–202, 213; narrative interacting with, 201

Reason, 80, 110, 198. *See also* Enlightenment

Recovery Narratives: need for a new (*See also* Sustainability), 207–208, 241, 242; Platonic components of, 37, 41–42; political philosophy and, 45. *See also* Feminist Recovery Narrative; Mainstream Recovery Narrative

Recovery of Eden—the Christian narrative: Biblical basis of, 11, 13, 18–19, 39, 249n.15; in Dante's *Divine Comedy*, 50–51; as a darkness-into-light story, 46, 129; Eden on earth (*See* Earthly Eden); as a faith based narrative, 36, 37; Joachim of Fiore narrative of, 56; Platonism assimilated into, 42

Redemption, 13

Reforestation, 238–239

Relationship, 232

Relativity theory, 206, 212

Religion and nature, 197–198. *See also* Christianity

Renaissance, 42

Reproduction, 38; cloning and, 175, 177

Reservoirs, 113, 115

Restoration, 181–182, 184; landscape restoration, 184; restoration ecology, 28

Resurrection, 13, 20

Revolt of nature (Horkheimer), 116. *See also* Environmental crisis

Rio Declaration on Environment and
Development, 124
River restoration project, 237
Robots, 174
Roman progressive narratives, 43–45; con-
verging with Christian narrative, 46. *See
also* Greco-Roman golden age; Greco-
Roman world
Romans 8:22, 17–18
Romanticism: a deeply personal relation with
nature expressed in, 134–135, 136;
images of "fallen" nature in, 135–136;
nature imaged as an revered mother in,
3, 118, 133–134
Romm, Jeffrey, on racism and early conser-
vationism, 158–159
Roosevelt, Theodore, 139–140; *Wilderness
Writings*, 139–140
Ruether, Rosemary Radford: *Gaia and God*,
35–36; "Gender and the Problems of
Prehistory", 36

Salomon's House, 75
Sanderson, Bill
illustrations of the genome as knowledge,
176(8.1 and 8.2)
"Savages"of the New World, 69–70, 179; the
"savage mind", 199–200. *See also*
Indigenous peoples
Schurz, Carl, 150
Science
——— classical science and the mainstream
narrative, 206, 207. *See also*
Enlightenment; Scientific Revolution
——— new theoretical approaches: challenging classical science, 206–208, 230;
chaos theory, 6, 209, 213; complexity
theory, 6, 206, 209, 213–215; ecology,
216–217; feminist science, 198; postmodern or postclassical science, 220, 230;
process physics, 109–110; relativity theory, 206, 212; thermodynamics of open
systems, 210–211
——— and technology: attaining worldly
Eden through, 56–57, 61–63, 65, 75;
hydraulic technology, 113–114; the
machine in the garden, 105; the "organic
machine", 113; railroad construction,
112. *See also* Mechanism

Scientific Revolution, 20, 65, 66, 89; dimin-
ishing the role of God (Kaufman),
206–207. *See also* Enlightenment
Scot, Michael, 57
Secular narrative of Recovery through
Enlightenment, 65, 88–89
Secular Recovery Narrative. *See* Progressive
narratives
Sensuous experience, 227
Serpent: associated with female deities of
Mesopotamia, 35; DNA spiral as
(knowledge), 174–175, 176(8.1); in the
Garden of Eden, 11, 18; Jove inducing
venom in, 44
Sexual imagery of gendered nature: civilized
(sexually suppressed) female as moral
model, 142; the enclosed garden, 54–55,
55; metaphors of sexual assault, 112–113;
penetration metaphors, 53, 56; seduction
metaphors, 124–125; submission
required, 62–63; the Virgin Mary's
womb, 53, 75
Shepard, Paul, 191
Shoshone Indians, 152, 154
Sierra Club, 140, 158–140159
Silver Mountains, 203
Simulation models, 238
Slavery, 93, 147, 155–156, 268n.38;
Emancipation Proclamation, 162; resist-
ance to, 157–158
Smith, Adam: on the four stages of society,
82–84, 148; on overcoming fallen nature
through morality, 259n.49; *Wealth of
Nations*, 83
Smith, George A., 114
Smith, Henry Nash, *Virgin Land*, 123–124
Smith, John, 123
Smith, Mark S., 28
Snake. *See* Serpent
Social class (access to recovered Edens lim-
ited by), 3
Social constructions: of nature, 143; of God,
36
Social ecology, 208
Soil depletion, 17, 96–97, 156, 190, 191
Southwest, 113
Spencer, Edmund, *The Fairie Queen*, 138
Spretnak, Charlene, *Lost Goddesses of Early
Greece*, 219

Squanto, 99

"State of nature", 80, 83, 88; as anarchy (opposite of civil society), 45, 69

Stein, Achva Benzinberg, 239

Steinberg, Theodore, 6

Stewardship ethic: in the 18th. c. (Derham), 85–86; in conservationism, 140; expressed in *Genesis. 2:15*, 24–25, 96; in *Matthew 25:14*, 85. *See also* Conservationism

St. Francis Dam, 115

St. Genevieve with her Flock, 54–55, **55**

Stoll, Mark, 141

Stone Age culture. *See* Paleolithic era

Stone Age culture, 26–27, 30, **32**

Stone, Merlin, 35

Straet, Jan van der, *America*, 119–120, 120

Sublimity in nature, 86–88, 89; the terrifying sublime (Kant), 88

Subsistence farming culture, 101–102

Surrogate mothers, 177

Sustainability, 38, 194–195, 208; sustainable agriculture, 172; sustainable development, 208, 224–225. *See also* Partnership ethic

Sutherland, Kathryn, 83–84

Symbolism, contextualized, 241

Tammuz, 32, 54

Tarkington, Booth, *The Turmoil*, 158

Technology. *See* Science—and technology

Teton Dam Reservoir, 115

Thermodynamics of open systems, 210–211

Thoreau, Henry David: expressing a relationship with nature, 118, 133–136; protesting slavery, 157–158

Tiamat, 33, 35

Tierra del Fuego, 179

Tillyard, Eustace M. W., *Elizabethan World Picture*, 62

Til, Salomon van, *Terra Eden*, **60**

Tobacco plantations, 100, 156

Todd, John, *The Sunset Land*, 112–113

Tojetti, Domenico, *Progress of America*, 128–129, **130**

Torah, 24, 250n.21, 251n.25

Toxic waste, and race, 164

Transcendentalism, 118

Transgenic organisms: animals, 173; plants, 170, 171–173; transgenes, 172–173. *See also* Biotechnology

Transgenic pollution, 172–173, 174–175

Tree of Knowledge, 1, 13, **15**, 17, 52; association with sexual consciousness, 35; in the *Divine Comedy*, 50

Tree of Life, 1, **15**, **17**

Tribble, Phyllis, 23

Turner, Frederick Jackson, heroic narrative of the frontier, 111–112

Twain, Mark: "Adam's Diary", 117; "Eve's Diary", 65, 205

Uncertainty principle, 212, 214

Unfoldment, 210

United Church of Christ, "Toxic Waste and Race in the United States", 164

Urbanization, 67

Vega, Garcilaso de la, 70

Versailles gardens, 6

Vespucci, Amerigo, 119–120, **129**

View from Mt. Holyoke (Cole), **108**

Virgil: as Dante's guide in the *Divine Comedy*, 47, 48; on developmental stages and cyclical return, 43–45, 130

Virgin: Eve as (in Eden), 117–119, 213; forests as, 48–50, 59, 103–104; goddess Athene, 33, 35; nature as, 103–104, 118–119, 129

Virginia, 94, **95**, 100; Massacre of 1622, 70

Virgin land (the New World as), 119–120, **120**, **121**, 122, 124

Virgin Mary, 50, 53; as a garden, 54–56; images of nature invoking, 135; resemblance to mother goddesses, 54; womb of, 53, 75

Volcanoes, 8

Water runoff project, 236–237

West

Far West, 110–111

West Edmonton Mall, 167–169

Western culture

Fall and Recovery Narrative as central to, 22

White, John, 94

White, Lynn, Jr., "The Historical Roots of Our Ecologic Crisis", 5

White, Richard, *The Organic Machine*, 113

Wilderness: as the absence of human occupation, 147–148, 152–153; as a retreat, 68; death of the idea of, 191–192; depletion of, 106, 190; as desert or forest, 69; the negative wild, 55–56, 68, 86, 89, 129; the New World wilderness, 69–70; representing animality of a fallen world (medieval), 48; as the villain in the American heroic narrative, 98–99; wilderness terror, 88, 97–98, 100. *See also* Desert; Forests

Wilderness Act, 154, 162

Wilderness into civilization, 65, 68–71, 108, 127–129; transformed into a garden (the Recovery Narrative), 2, 62–63, 153, 154, 163

Wilderness preservation, 137, 143, 208, 229

Wildfire, 237–238

Wildlife Habitat Enhancement Council, 234–235

Wild men, 70

Williams, Roger, 100

Wilmut, Ian, 175

Winter, Paul
Missa Gaia, 219

Witch trials, 70

Witches, 46, 68

Wolves, 46, 48

Women's labor, invisibility of, 84

Woods, Robert, "The City Wilderness", 158

Words, 199, 200, 201

World Summit on Sustainable Development, 224–225

Worster, Donald, 116, 155–156

Wright, Mabel Osgood, 141

Yahweh, 13, 27, 28–29; as son of Anat (feminist), 33, 35

Yellowstone National Park: removal of Indians from, 152–153; wildfire in, 237–238

Yosemite Indians, 153

Young, Brigham, 114

Zeus/Jove, 33, 44

Zimmerman, Ron, 203

Zoos and game preserves, 59–61

Zuarza, Alonxo da, Eden-like descriptions of the New World, 58–59